By:

JULIE and PETER MAXTED

First published 1990
by
Work & Travel International
P.O. Box 172
Manchester M60 3TJ

Printed in Great Britain by BPCC Wheatons Ltd, Exeter

Contents

Chapter 1

Introduction

Ever since Ug the caveman first hitched a lift on a passing coracle and went off to work picking berries for Monsieur Og, the lure of work and travel overseas has exerted its powerful pull. Some people know they're going to travel very early in their lives, for others the decision creeps up on them and suddenly they're on the Chinese border thinking "How did I get here?"

Whatever the rationale behind the decision to go, travelling and living and working in different countries rarely brings anything but great benefit to whoever does it. "Travel broadens the mind," goes the saying and living and working overseas does still more. It can also have very tangible benefits when you return. Many enlightened employers today will be impressed if their new staff have lived or worked abroad – they know that they will be better and more flexible people as a result.

People have made their fortune overseas, have met their life partner or found their vocation and many have discovered more about themselves. Others have learnt lessons just as valuable – what they don't want to do for example or that their travelling companion has a totally incompatible personality. Most however just enjoy themselves for a few months or years and come home refreshed and with an enhanced sense of the great variety and richness of the world.

Most people decide to travel in their late teens or early twenties. This is when plenty of time is often available although money is often short. At the other end of the spectrum are those who may have plenty of money from a steady job, but then time is often limited, allowing only a frantic two weeks on the Costa Del Yobbo each year. Still, there is no reason why you cannot travel at any age. People have crossed the Andes in their 60's, taken young children round India by train, taken a year off from their jobs to work in and see the United States or Europe. If the mood takes you, just get up and go!

Chapter 2

Ready .....

Deciding to go

Taking the decision to go is often a spur of the moment thing and boredom is frequently cited as one of the main reasons many working travellers decide to try their luck abroad. The boredom may be with a town, a job or a whole lifestyle but it seems to be one of the greatest of travellers' stimuli.

Other reasons include unemployment which, of course, goes hand in hand with boredom, the break up of a relationship or, quite often, the need that most young people feel at some time to leave home and become fully independent.

Most of the reasons given so far are to a greater or lesser extent, negative. There are more positive ones. "I've always wanted to travel" say Thursday's children. A desire, even a need, to see foreign lands and experience different cultures can simmer for years and then suddenly come to the boil. Maybe a book or magazine article is the catalyst; perhaps a TV programme, which inspires you to have a look at the rainforest before it is all destroyed, makes up your mind.

The most common stimulus is the personal experience of another traveller. You are sitting in the same old pub on a Friday night with the same old people when in comes Joe (or Steve or Sue) who's been working in Australia and then travelling in India. You and your friends try to sound uninterested in how he or she crewed on a boat from Freemantle to Sri Lanka, try to pretend that its been much more interesting and exciting in Neasthorpe or Cheltifax, but the seed has been sown. Pretty soon you're weighing up the cost and weight of different types of sleeping bags and reading books like this one. You're nearly on your way.

There is however, a big step between wanting to do something and actually doing it. The world is full of dreamers, armchair travellers, some of whom can tell you how to get across Cairo (they've read the travel books) but could never describe that special smell of spice, diesel and donkey that lingers in the nostrils once you've actually been there.

The best way to take that big step is to go out and spend a proportion of your hard-saved cash. Buy a ticket. It doesn't matter if it's a coach ticket to London, a ferry ticket to Calais or (best of all) a plane ticket to anywhere beyond this sceptred isle. You've made the commitment, you've stepped onto the diving board. Now it's much easier to dive into the pool than climb, crestfallen, back down the ladder.

Travelling Companions

There are a number of things that you'll need to take with you (and a lot more to leave behind) and we'll discuss most of these in the next chapter. One of the biggest decisions concerns travelling companions. There are three ways to go. The first is in a group. Unless you are thinking of an overland adventure, through Africa or South America for example, then group travel is for wimps. Wait until you're in your sixties before you start looking at more exotic parts of the world through tinted windows of an air-conditioned tour bus.

The second way is with a partner. If you have already decided jointly to travel - either with a close friend or boyfriend/girlfriend or spouse - then there is nothing further to think about. Although

2

many relationships have foundered on the rocks of travelling and working overseas, many more have been strengthened. Once you have nursed someone through a bout of dysentery in a bus station in Bogota, you'll cope with anything.

If you haven't made a joint decision then solo versus partnership travel needs to be looked at in terms of advantages versus disadvantages.

Travelling alone gives you total freedom. You don't have arguments over what to do, where to eat or if you can afford to buy something. You go exactly where you want to go and when you want to. You also meet far more people when you are travelling alone. Other travellers and local people will be much more responsive and many useful contacts and even friendships can be made. You also learn a good deal about yourself when travelling alone. You are thrown on your own resources, make your own decisions and take the consequences of your own actions. You'll learn more about yourself on a three month trip through Europe than in thirty years of psycho-analysis!

The two main problems that you will encounter when travelling alone are loneliness and a lack of help if there are problems. Whether you are lonely or not will largely depend on your own personality but do be prepared for times, however extrovert and gregarious you are, when you will be lonely. The second problem is more serious. If you get into trouble or especially if you fall sick, than the lack of a travelling companion can be really upsetting. It's bad enough getting lonely or depressed when you are well, it's ten times worse when you are sick.

Travelling with a partner does have significant advantages to compensate for the disadvantages of squabbling over destination/venues or lack of independence. There is always someone to share in the good experiences and help overcome the bad ones. Time can be saved too; for example one of you can get train tickets while the other buys food. Finally, travelling with a friend is often cheaper – half a double room always costs less than a single room, food can often be bought more cheaply, costs can be shared.

There is one thing you should always remember. Choose a travelling companion with great care. That mildly amusing habit they have at home may turn you into a screaming lunatic when it's late and you're stuck in a Yugoslav bus station with no food. If you like sun-bathing but your friend wants to visit the sights then there are going to be major arguments. Above all, don't go with a member of the opposite sex hoping that the trip will be the start of a relationship. It's more likely to be a total disaster.

The best way to decide between travelling alone or with a partner is to take an honest look at yourself. Are you perfectly happy on your own for long periods and able to cope with most situations? Or are you happiest with people and when you can share experiences? The answer to these questions will help you choose.

Finally, you can always test the water. Take a short trip in the U.K. with your prospective travelling companion or on your own – even a long weekend will do. It will tell you much of what you need to know.

Planning your route

If you are aiming to travel for some time and work eventually at a fixed destination, or if you are just going travelling and maybe doing some casual work on the way, then you should plan your route fairly carefully. If it is important that you spend as little money as possible then hitching overland, when possible, is the cheapest mode of transport. But if this is likely to involve the overnight stays, twenty meals, a couple of bus trips across towns and a new pair of boots at the end then perhaps a £50 train ticket might be better. Take factors like this into account when planning your route.

Invest in a good map and study routes carefully. If you are going a long way, through many countries, take a look at the Times Atlas of the World in your local library. That way you'll realise that the direct route from Delhi to Peking is not really very practical.

Take the climate into account. Do you visualise New York as being hot or cold - or neither? In the winter it can be snowed in and the temperature sink well below freezing. In the summer you can fry an egg on the pavements. Don't make the mistake of heading for an exotic beach in the Philippines after you've worked in Japan or Australia and then finding you've hit the rainy season and all you can see is a choppy grey sea viewed through a curtain of falling water. Finally remember that in the Southern Hemisphere the seasons are reversed. It can be just as cold in Santiago in July as it is in Seville in January.

Personal preparation

To get yourself mentally ready for travelling and working abroad just immerse yourself in information about your destination(s). Read, talk and think about it all the time. That way culture shock will be lessened, especially if you are going to the Third World, and eventual assimilation quickened.

If you are planning a trip to escape from a problem or because you are depressed then a word of warning. The only thing that you have to take with you is you. If you are miserable about something in Sydenham, will it look any better in Sydney? The answer is almost certainly no, and you are thousands of miles from home.

Physically you need to be reasonably fit but that's all. If you are planning something particularly strenuous - mountain biking up Kilimanjaro for example, then no doubt you've already been up and down Snowdon four times in one day. Otherwise if you can walk a few miles without major discomfort then you'll be fine.

Finding a job abroad from here

Finding a job abroad before you leave is perfectly possible and can give your trip a focus and yourself a certain amount of security. Chapter 5 is full of useful addresses and specific countries are covered in Chapter 6. If you write to an address overseas, inquiring about a job or indeed anything else, then enclose an International Reply Coupon (IRC) available from main Post Offices.

Jobs abroad are advertised in the UK in several publications. The Directory of Summer Jobs Abroad (for the summer holiday period) is available from Vacation Work International. A selection of year-round jobs is printed in Jobsearch Worldwide, published monthly.

You could advertise yourself, although this is an expensive and somewhat chancy option. A number of newspapers are included in Chapter 6.

Vacation Work International, 9 Park End Street, Oxford OX1 1HJ.
Tel: 0865 241978

Jobsearch Worldwide, BroadLanes, Mylor Downs, Falmouth, Cornwall, TR11 5UL.
Tel: 0872 865232

Making contacts

There are a number of organisations you can join before you leave that will give you useful contacts and addresses overseas. These vary from the academic, through the voluntary and pen friend sector to the numerous adventure clubs.

The Central Bureau offers a wide range of educational visits and exchanges including schemes for teachers in most disciplines, language assistants, students and school students.

The Experiment in International Living offers opportunities for travellers to stay with host families in many different parts of the world either as individuals, couples or, occasionally, in groups. The length of stay varies.

Servas offers the opportunity for serious travellers to stay with host families in 111 countries. You can stay for up to two nights, sometimes with shared meals.

The Globetrotters Club exists for people to share experiences and advice and to pass on useful information. The club has members worldwide.

The Central Bureau, Seymour Mews, London W1H 9PE.
The Experiment in International Living, Otesaga, Upper Wyche, Malvern, Worcs., WR14 4EN.
Servas, 47 Edgely Road, Clapham, SW4 6ES.
The Globetrotters Club, BCM/Roving, London WC1N 3XX.

Chapter 3

Steady....

Things to take

The sign of an inexperienced traveller is the vast mountain of luggage that he or she hauls around. You see them struggling up stairs, jammed in the doors of restaurants or sitting sadly by the roadside waiting to hitch a lift from a ten ton truck – as that's the only thing that will accommodate all their possessions. Those who have worked or travelled abroad for some time are conspicuous by the single small bag that contains all their worldly goods. A few clothes, money and documents and some essential medicines are all that are really necessary. Travel light.

Luggage

In the bag versus rucksack debate, we are firmly on the side of the former. A rucksack only really comes into its own if you are carrying a fair amount over some distance. If, therefore, part of your trip is likely to involve some serious walking or trekking then a rucksack is useful. If you do take one then may we plead with you to forego the brilliant dayglo orange or pink ones that mar so many of the world's beauty spots these days. Stick to green or grey.

The light canvas or nylon holdalls that are on sale almost everywhere are ideal for a long trip. Buy a reasonably sturdy one (not the very cheapest which fall apart at embarrassing moments like customs searches) and make sure it has a good shoulder strap. Ideally it should be small enough to qualify as hand luggage on a plane which will save you the long delays at airports that plague those who have to wait for their luggage to appear from the hold. It will also give you an easy way to judge how much, or rather how little, to take with you.

The only other item you'll need to carry will be something for money and important documents. The three choices are a handbag or small shoulder bag, a belt pouch or a money belt. Which you choose depends on personal taste – the money belt is the most secure but also the most uncomfortable, the handbag the most comfortable and flexible but the least secure. Try out your choice before you go.

Sleeping bags

Whether you take one or not depends on where you'll be staying – which in turn usually depends on your budget. However a sleeping bag is generally a good idea and can double as a cushion or beach mat or even bed. Pick a lightweight one that can be carried in or clipped on to your travel bag.

Documentation

There are a few essential documents that you must take with you and a number of others that are very useful. The only one that you will not be able to do without is your passport. This is also the one you must not lose. Gone are the days when unscrupulous travellers used to sell British or American passports in Morocco or Nepal and then get another one from the nearest Embassy. Today if you claim to have lost your passport then you are likely to be given the third degree and maybe put on the next flight home – at your own expense.

It is much better to have the full British passport when you travel. This lasts for 10 years and is available from a number of passport offices in London, Liverpool, Newport, Peterborough,

6

Glasgow and Belfast. You will have to write to them well in advance as the backlog of work from the recent strike is causing long delays; leave at least three months and don't bother to try and ring as you will only get a recorded message. The cost of a passport is currently £15 for 10 years or £30 for the larger 94 page passport; if you plan to travel through many countries then it is worth getting the larger one.

There is a cheaper passport available called the British Visitors passport which can be used in Western Europe, Tunisia, Yugoslavia and Iceland. It costs £7.50 and is only valid for a year. Sometimes it is quicker to obtain this than a full passport and this is the only advantage that we can think of for getting one.

Passport Office, Hampton House, 47-53 High Street, Belfast BT1 2QS.
Passport Office, 3 Northgate, 96 Milton Street, Cowcaddens, Glasgow G4 0BT.
Passport Office, India Buildings, Water Street, Liverpool L2 0QZ.
Passport Office, Clive House, 70 Petty France, London SW1H 9HD.
Passport Office, Olympia House, Upper Dock Street, Newport NP9 1XA.
Passport Office, Aragon Court, Northminster Road, Peterborough PE1 1QG.

Student Cards

Student Cards (International Student Identity Card or ISIC) are a boon, a godsend, a truly wonderful invention. You can get cheap travel You can get discounts on equipment and entry fees to various sites. Sometimes they will even smooth your way into a country (you are obviously not going to stay forever if you are a student and have a course to return to). So if, by hook or by crook you can get hold of a card then do so. Out of date cards are still quite acceptable in many places. It is also possible to obtain a forged student card in many parts of the world – though we are not recommending this you understand. Athens is one of the best places for this.

To get an ISIC legally in this country you need a passport-sized photo, proof of full time student status and £5.00. Either take these to your student union office or send them to the address below.
Travel Cuts, 295a Regent Street, London W1R 7YA.

YHA cards

It is well worth joining the Youth Hostel Association before you leave Britain. The YHA card will open many doors – particularly those to cheap accommodation.

To be a member of the Youth Hostel Association is particularly worthwhile in Britain and Western Europe where the official hostels (some 2,000) will only let you in if you have a card. In most other parts of the world the regulations are less strict but a card will still come in handy. The YHA card currently costs £4.00 if you are under 20 and £7.60 if you are 21 plus. You can also get life membership for £80.00.

YHA, Trevelyan House, 8 St Stephens Hill, St Albans, Herts AL1 2TD. Tel: 0727 55215

Other documents

A full driving license is always useful as is an International License. Take copies of any qualifications you may have and of course any letters of introduction that may come in useful. Don't forget to take your travel and health insurance certificates with you and a copy of the numbers on your travellers cheques.

Health

The classic attitude of prospective travellers who hear about the health dangers that can be encountered overseas is, 'Ah, but it won't happen to me'. We've got news for you – it can happen to anyone. Perhaps the label on the tank marked 'boiled water' is not telling the truth, maybe the waiter in the five star restaurant hasn't washed his hands, perhaps the American style fast food joint in downtown Manila doesn't have the same attitude to cleanliness that it might if situated in downtown Manhattan. Nobody can be completely sure that they won't get sick abroad (or in this country for that matter as Edwina Currie will tell you).

However there are a number of sensible precautions that you can take to minimise the risk and thus ensure that your travels are considerably easier. Most of these are common sense but quite often that only becomes apparent after the worst has happened. If any traveller was asked to choose between losing his or her possessions or health then the choice would not be hard.

There are several useful leaflets that anyone who is thinking of going abroad should obtain. 'Before You Go' and 'While You're Away' are essential reading. Both can be obtained from your local Department of Health or, if they are out of stock, by writing to the overseas section in Newcastle or by telephoning 0800 555777 (free).

Food and drink
Be careful when eating certain foods and drinking water when you don't know the source. The foods to avoid are shellfish, unwashed fruit and vegetables and any food that has been left for some time or has been reheated. A good rule is - if you haven't seen it being cooked then don't eat it. Make sure that the water you drink is safe and that the ice in your drinks is too. Some travellers have got hepatitis from drinking boiled water with contaminated ice in it. If you need to sterilise water yourself then boil it for at least ten minutes (just bringing it to the boil is not enough) or use sterilising tablets. Boil milk too unless it has been pasteurised and don't forget to purify the water that you use to clean your teeth.

Most restaurants and cafes will have no objection to you looking in the kitchen. If it has an open sewer running through it then it is time to try somewhere else. Likewise if the food has obviously been sitting around all day. Of course this means that your choice of meal in many Greek and Turkish restaurants - where they often cook all the food at lunchtime for the whole day - is going to be a bit limited.

A good rule is to eat at restaurants which have a high turnover so the food is likely to be freshly cooked. For this reason station (bus or train) restaurants are often a good bet as are the much-maligned roadside stalls where the food - especially in the Far East - is likely to be hot, healthy and cheap.

One reason why many travellers get sick is because of a poor diet. Often this is because they are trying to stretch their budget in order to stay somewhere longer or go further. However when you meet travellers in India who have lived on vegetables and rice and suffer from protein deficiency, you will soon realise that this is a false economy. A good idea is to take a bottle of vitamin tablets with you to supplement your diet.

Medicine and medical help
Here are some essentials: Adhesive plasters and some form of anti-septic cream or liquid, water sterilisation tablets, insect repellent and some 'tummy tabs' - Milk of magnesia, Kaolin & morphine or similar. That really is about all you'll need if you are sensible.

If you do get sick then keep to a really simple diet for a day or so (that's if you can bear to eat at all) and let the illness take its course. Most problems clear up fairly quickly. If symptoms persist then visit a local doctor. This will vary in price depending on where in the world you are, so good insurance is essential.

There are three different types of country as far as health requirements are concerned.
1. The 'E111' countries. These include all the countries of the European Community. You can get emergency medical treatment free if you have a form E111. Get one from your local Department of Health before you go. It does not cover all medical expenses and will not pay for an emergency return to the UK. You will still need insurance. If you don't take the form with you then ask the doctor or health authority in the country you are visiting to send to England for one.

2. The 'reciprocal' countries. Some places have arrangements so that British visitors can get treatment free or at a reduced cost and their nationals have a reciprocal arrangement when they visit the UK. Not all treatment is free however so make sure you ask, if possible before any treatment has been given. Once again, a decent insurance policy is advised. The following countries have reciprocal arrangements with us: Australia, Austria, Bulgaria, Czechoslovakia, Finland, East Germany, Hungary, Iceland, Malta, New Zealand, Norway, Poland, Rumania, Sweden, USSR, Yugoslavia and all remaining British colonies and dependent territories such as Hong Kong or the Falklands.

3. Others. All other countries will charge you for all medical treatment so comprehensive insurance cover is absolutely essential.

Insects and animals

It is, of course, virtually impossible to avoid being bitten by insects while overseas but most bites are relatively harmless. The exception is that of the malarial mosquito which is prevalent throughout the tropics. Take anti-malaria tablets (either daily or weekly) and make sure that you start them before you go and continue them after you return for the required length of time. One thing to be careful of is if you have a stopover in a malaria zone even if you are only staying a few hours (a friend caught malaria after a six hour stopover in Kuala Lumpa, Malaysia on his way from London to Sidney). If you become sick on your return to Britain then be sure to tell the doctor if you've recently been in a malaria-rife country. The symptoms of malaria are all too often mistaken for those of flu and the disease not diagnosed until its too late.

The main danger from animals when travelling abroad is not some savage mauling from a lion or becoming breakfast for a crocodile but catching a disease. The most dangerous disease you are likely to catch from an animal bite or scratch is rabies. Don't touch strange animals, especially carnivorous ones like dogs. If you are bitten then wash the wound and get medical attention quickly. You may need an injection for rabies and should also, if not immunised, get one for tetanus. Contact the nearest consulate or embassy for help.

AIDS and VD

Some areas of the world like New York, Haiti and parts of East Africa now have a virtual epidemic of AIDS. Contrary to popular press mythology this cannot be caught from towels, toothbrushes, swimming pools or talking to someone who is gay. It can be caught by having sex with someone who is infected or from contaminated blood, for example on a syringe needle. Take the obvious precautions and you won't get HIV (the AIDS virus).

Other forms of sexually transmitted disease can be just as dangerous and men in particular should be wary of the fleshpots of South East Asia like Bangkok and Manila. Condoms are some protection, take reliable ones with you.

Department of Health, Overseas Branch, Newcastle NE98 1YX.

Insurance

In those countries which do not have a reciprocal health agreement with Britain (see above) it is important to have insurance. Apart from health there is also the risk of possesions being lost or stolen, of travel cancellations or situations where you may be liable for someone else's injury. All these eventualities should be catered for with a decent insurance policy.

There are a large number of companies offering travel and health insurance, and most travel agencies have lists of the largest. Few are interested in travellers who intend to be abroad for a long time however and their premiums are often high. A typical travel insurance policy from one of the big companies over one year might cost as much as £500 for example. Those companies which are interested in long stay insurance include Endsleigh (though you must be a student) and the Travellers Insurance Association (part of Commercial Union). The latter offer a policy which covers you whilst you are working abroad (which most travel insurance policies don't) and is available through Jobsearch Publications.

For another view on insurance and a useful tip if you're going to the States, see "The Wild Frontier" in Chapter 8.

Endsleigh Insurance, Ambrose Street, Cheltenham, Glos. GL50 3NR
Jobsearch Publications, Broads Lane, Mylor Downs, Cornwall TR11 5UL.

Money

There really needn't be much debate over the two questions of how much to take and how to take it. You should take as much as you need to live in reasonable comfort for the intended duration of your trip. Suggesting exact figures is ridiculous. If you are travelling around India you will only need one tenth of the amount you'd need for a trip of the same duration in Scandinavia. Any reasonably up-to-date travel guide will give you approximate prices for accommodation and travel in a given country and you can then calculate accordingly.

By far the best method of taking money abroad is in the form of travellers cheques. The most widely accepted are American Express followed by Citibank, Thomas Cook and First National Bank. However in most countries all the types issued in the UK are acceptable. Which currency to take them in (eg sterling, US dollars, Swiss francs) depends on the present state of a particular currency and whether it is rising or falling. Check carefully before you decide as it is quite easy to lose large chunks of your hard-earned cash as you travel if the currency you have chosen then falls steadily. In the US take your travellers cheques in US dollars as anything else is barely acceptable and will cause you long delays.

Don't take much cash – change cheques as you need them but it is worth having an emergency stash, say $50 in a separate place to the rest of your money and documents. This is of course for emergencies.

Credit cards are accepted in most countries and are very useful – though do make sure that you have a regular amount paid in to the cc account. In Europe, Eurocheques are just as good as travellers cheques and may involve you paying less commission, depending on which bank you use.

Always leave some money at home with a friend or relative who can be contacted in an emergency and get money out to you quickly.

We do not recommend "losing" your travellers cheques by selling them or cashing them under another name and then trying to claim new ones, Travellers cheque companies are getting very wary of this and you will have to put up with a lot of questioning and a considerable wait – often of days or even weeks. Sometimes they simply refuse to replace them.

This scam, which in fact of course is simple fraud, also means that genuine claimants who are often desperate, have to put up with the same cross-examination and delay. It is the ones who cheat who cause problems for the others. The travellers cheque companies don't lose – like big stores building shoplifting costs into their profit mark ups, they simply increase the premiums and the rest of us pay.

Chapter 4

How to get there

Air

Travelling by air has, of course, the advantage of getting you to your destination quickly though you may miss much of the excitement and adventure of other forms of slower transport. If money is not much of a problem or you have limited time, then there are many companies that offer cheap air fares to virtually any part of the world. It is worth booking through a reputable firm and checking the small print for such clauses as cancellations etc. In our experience the cheapest airlines can be somewhat frustrating though the savings made do compensate. An overnight stop in Bucharest on your way to Pakistan, for example, with one of the cheapest airlines, Tarom (Rumanian Airlines), might sound like a romantic/interesting way to get there but be prepared for problems with overnight accommodation which might have been overlooked by the travel agent, or having to spend rather more for a meal than you had planned.

In general the cheapest airlines are the Eastern European ones as well as some of those in the Middle East such as Iraq and Syria. This is often because the routing is awkward and involves a lot of backtracking. This invariably means that several hours are added to the flight but paradoxically that you save a considerable amount of money.

Discount travel agencies or 'bucket shops' as they are more widely known are an excellent way to get cheap flights to nearly every destination in the world, though you may find that the amazing low fare you saw advertised is only available on Tuesday and leaves at a totally unrealistic time! 'Poundsavers' claims to offer the cheapest fares to anywhere, an around-the-world trip for only £799 for example, from London to Bangkok to Hong Kong to Taipei to Tokyo to San Francisco to New York to London, or £110 return to Munich, Rome, Madrid, or Vienna. Soliman Travel specialises in fares to Spanish-speaking countries (Spain, Latin America, Puerto Rico) but also offers cheap flights to the Middle East (£100-150 to Tel Aviv). Pan Pacific is London's specialist to Australia and New Zealand. Another 'cheapie' is Jupiter Travel with a flight to Bangkok of £373 advertised recently.

Tickets bought from 'bucket shops' have the advantage in that they can be booked in advance, but if you have already planned to go abroad and don't mind where exactly or when you want to go, then stand-by flights on scheduled airlines are a very cheap way to fly. By constantly phoning airlines it is possible to get to your destination at a discount of as much as 50% The same is true of tour operators who need to fill up charter flights at the last minute and by ringing up or going to the airport on the day of departure you can buy a ticket at a drastically reduced price. In America there are actually "distress merchandise" companies which specialise in selling unsold seats and provide their subscribers with recorded listings of last-minute discounts on imminent travel departures. Bangkok in Thailand and Athens, Greece are two cities where 'bucket shops' abound and so are worth including in your itinerary.

In Britain and the US small travel agencies come and go with alarming rapidity and therefore long-established firms like STA Travel Ltd or Trailfinders are probably the safest way to travel by air as they offer back-up service and advice facilities.

STA Travel publishes The Student Travel Handbook (not just for students!) which details most of their services and they offer low cost flights worldwide, European weekend breaks and trains and their own specialist travel insurance as well as a complete range of guide books. They have a network of 100 offices worldwide and provide a service called the International Help Desk. This means that wherever any of their passengers are in the world, they can phone (reversing the charges if necessary) with any problems that may arise from ticket changes or losses, problems arising through robbery, injury, sickness, lost travelling companions etc. This service is worth its weight in scheduled airline tickets.

Trailfinders also provide a wide range of services such as library and information centre, map and book shop and a medical advice and immunisation centre. They offer some of the lowest air fares and their own insurance policy that gives cover for up to 12 months and is available for one-way travel and to residents outside the UK. When you book with Trailfinders you will be given a special Travel Pass entitling you to exclusive discounts of up to 55% on accommodation, car hire and local tours worldwide. They publish a free Trailfinder Magazine three times a year (March, July and December) which they send to libraries and universities. The States will feature in the March edition and New Zealand in the July edition.

Becoming an Air Courier is another way of travelling cheaply by air. A courier travels on behalf of a courier company, accompanying documents which are contained in the hold of the plane. Only one courier is required for each flight, but sometimes a second person might be able to travel on the next flight. Alternatively another person can book a full return ticket with the relevant airline and travel on the same flight as the courier. Ideally the courier company likes to fill the schedules 2-3 months in advance. However due to seasonal variations in demand, shorter notice seats are frequently available. Most flights operate on fixed schedules of 1-3 week durations.

If you cancel at the last minute or miss your flight, you will probably lose the full amount as you are not actually buying a ticket, you are being charged an administration fee, so it is advisable to take out adequate travel insurance. Polo Express offer a 3 week return fare to Adelaide for £525, Barbados 2 week return for £250, Nairobi one way for £185; CPJ have an open dated ticket to Cairo for £200 or 13 nights in Rio de Janeiro for £300; CTS offer a one way ticket to Sydney for £350 or £625 return, an open return to Lisbon for £80. So although most courier companies have a maximum length of stay, some do offer the opportunity to travel without this restriction.

Courier companies operate in other parts of the world so if you want to fly then it is worth checking under "Air Courier Services" in the equivalent Yellow Pages of the country you are in. Courier companies operate from major US cities like Los Angeles, San Francisco, New York, Chicago, Miami and San Juan, flying overseas to Rio de Janeiro, Tokyo, Hong Kong, London, Brussels, Amsterdam, Geneva, Milan, Madrid, Sydney and Auckland. From America, the least expensive flights seem to be those to Europe in the winter months and generally the return date is left open to Frankfurt, Amsterdam and Brussels.

Do be wary of acting as a courier for companies or individuals in parts of South America and the Far East. If the price is especially cheap or they offer to pay you, the chances are that the goods are something best not carried across international borders.

STA Travel Ltd, 74 and 86 Old Brompton Road, 117 Euston Road, London
Tel: 01 937 9962 (Intercontinental), 01 937 9971 (North America)
01 937 9921 (Europe)

Trailfinders, 42-48 Earls Court Road, Kensington, London W8 6EJ
Tel: 01 938 3366 (Long haul flights), 01 937 5400 (European & transatlantic)

Poundsavers, 254 Earls Court Road, London, Tel: 01 373 6465

Soliman Travel, 233 Earls Court Road, London, Tel: 01 370 6446

Pan Pacific, 16A Soho Square, London, Tel: 01 734 3094

Jupiter Travel, 50 New Oxford Street, London, Tel: 01 436 2711

London Student Travel Agency, 52 Grosvenor Gardens, Tel: 01 730 3402

Student Travel Centre, 18 Rupert Street, London, Tel: 01 434 1306

Student Travel, 234 Earls Court Road, London, Tel: 01 373 0495

Worldwide Student Travel, 37 Store Street, London, Tel: 01 581 8233

Wexas, 45 Brompton Road, Knightsbridge, London, Tel: 01 589 3315

Encounter Overland, 267 Old Brompton Road, London, Tel: 01 370 6845

Exodus Expeditions, 9 Weir Road, London, Tel: 01 675 5550

Explore Worldwide Ltd, 7 High Street, Aldershot, Hants, Tel: 0252 319448

Top Deck Travel, 133 – 135 Earls Court Road, London, Tel: 01 370 4555

Twickers World, 22 Church Street, Twickenham, Tel: 01 892 7606/8164

Sherpa Expeditions, 131a Heston Road, Hounslow, Middx, Tel: 01 577 2717

Bales Tours Ltd, Bales House, Barrington Road, Dorking, Surrey,
Tel: 0306 885991

Access International Inc, 250 West 57th Street, New York, NY 10107
Tel: 212/333 7280

Apex Travel Inc, 46-46 Vernon Boulevard, Long Island City, New York 11101
Tel: 718/784 1111

Getaway Travel Inc, 1105 Ponce de Leon Blvd, Coral Gables, Florida 33134
Tel: 305/446 7855

Maharajah Travels, 518 Fifth Ave, New York, NY 10036
Tel: 212/391 0122

Pan Express Travel Inc, 25 West 39th Street, Suite 705, New York, NY 10018
Tel: 212/719 9292

The Vacation Outlet (in Filene's basement), Washington St, Boston, MA 02108
Tel: 617/267 8100

Euro-Asia Inc, 4203 East Indian School Rd, Phoenix, AZ 85018
Tel: 602/955 2742

All Unique Travel, 1030 Georgia St, Vallejo, CA 94590
Tel: 707/648 0237

Community Travel Service, 5237 College Ave, Oakland, CA 94618
Tel: 415/653 0990

Express Discount Travel, 5945 Mission Gorge Road, San Diego, CA 92120
Tel: 619/283 6324

Sunline Express Holidays, 210 Post St, San Francisco, CA 94108 Tel: 415/398 2111

Travel Team, 4518 University Way NE, Seattle, WA 98105 Tel: 206/632 0520

Courier Companies

Courier Travel Services, Unit 2, London House, 243/253 Lower Mortlake Rd, Richmond, Surrey
TW9 2LL
Tel: 01 940 3334 - London
317 3193 - Sydney
(3) 718 1332 - Hong Kong
568 3381 - Los Angeles

CPJ Travel, Orbital Park, 178-188 Great South West Road, Hounslow, Middx
TW4 6JS, Tel: 01 890 9393 Ext 3407

Polo Express, 208 Epsom Square, London Heathrow Airport, Hounslow, Middx
TW6 2BL, Tel: 01 759 5383

TNT Skypak, 400 Post Ave, Westbury, New York, NY 11590
Tel: NY 516/338 7760

World Courier, 137-42 Guy R Brewer Blvd, Jamaica, New York, NY 11434

A-1 International Courier, 6930 NW 12th St, Miami, Florida 33126
Tel: 305/594-1184

Rush Couriers Inc, 481 49th St, Brooklyn, New York, NY 11220
Tel: 718/439-8181

Air Facilities, 3100 NW 72nd Ave, Suite 111, Miami, Florida 33122
Tel: 305/477-8300

Graf Airfreight, 5811 Willoughby Ave, Hollywood, California 90038
Tel: 213/461 1547

Bicycle

There can be few better ways of actually "seeing" the country you are travelling in than cycling.
It is cheap (comparatively) to maintain a bike, costs nothing to run and you have the freedom to
go exactly where you please. You can get to places that public transport doesn't, and that would
be a daunting prospect if you had to walk. If you intend to spend some time in a place working,
then cycling has the advantage of your being able to move from one part to another easily, either
looking for work or travelling to work.

The Cyclists' Touring Club has an excellent range of services for those intending to take a bicycle
abroad and for only £18.50 a year it is well worth becoming a member. The services they offer
include: free legal aid, free third party insurance, free bimonthly magazine which advertises
cycling companions in their classified section, shop and mail order facilities, free technical
advice from types of equipment to maintenance problems, and many more. The Touring
Department publish various information sheets offering advice on subjects such as cycle-camping
and travelling with a cycle by air.

Country information sheets give general information for more than 60 different countries,
including passport/visa requirements, cycling conditions, climate, touring areas/terrain,
accommodation, taking bikes on trains, recommended maps and books and a list of useful
contacts for further information. Details of Tours/Routes gives suggestions for both 'fixed
centre' and 'moving on' tours and routes within and between many of these countries. 'Long
Distance Touring Notes' gives general advice for long-distance cycle tourers and 'Notes by Round
the World Cyclists' gives general advice from those who have done it plus details of a Round the
World Cyclists' Register. The CTC organises and has information about various cycling events at
home and abroad including organised cycling holidays.

For those who prefer motorbikes, the Harley Owners Group (HOG) based in America offers club membership to Harley-Davidson owners. As a member you will receive information about club benefits, services, events and travel packages.

They publish a Touring Handbook containing maps of all of the United States and Canada and a listing of motorcycle laws in all the states and provinces and a page of special touring tips. One of the special features of the HOG is the Fly & Ride Service which offers the rental of Harley-Davidson motorcycles for touring. As a member, you are able to rent a Harley-Davidson in Orlando and Miami, Florida; Honolulu, Hawaii; Frankfurt, Germany; Reno, Nevada; Phoenix, Arizona; Los Angeles, California; Boston, Massachusetts; Ft Collins, Colorado; and Vancouver, British Columbia. A 20% discount is allowed on a rental of four weeks or more.

Cyclists' Touring Club (CTC), Cotterell House, 69 Meadrow, Godalming, Surrey GU7 3HS. Tel: (04868) 7217

Harley Owners Group, PO Box 453, Milwaukee, WI 5320, Tel: (414) 342-4680

Bus/Coach

The standards of bus travel have improved dramatically in recent years (in Europe at least!) Although it is a relatively slow way to travel, it is often the cheapest way to get about and in some parts of the world, Nepal and Northern Pakistan and other mountainous regions for example, it is the only way. Thomas Cook produce an Overseas Timetable which is essential for any bus/coach traveller, and a Continental Timetable for Europe. Topdeck Travel specialises in double-decker tours of Europe and Asia; advertisements for other bus companies can be found in local papers and magazines such as City Limits etc.

In America and Canada, Greyhound, Trailways and other bus companies offer an excellent and relatively inexpensive means of travelling. Cheap passes offering unlimited travel for 7, 15 and 30 days are available and these can be purchased in advance if you wish. Green Tortoise offers trips throughout the United States, Mexico and Canada. Plus scheduled service New York to Los Angeles with sleeping facilities. The buses drive mainly at night and during the day passengers can go river rafting on the Colorado, explore major national parks and other sites of interest.

In Australia, Railways of Australia and Greyhound Australia have joined forces to provide a 28 day "Road 'n Rail" pass which offers unrestricted rail and coach travel throughout mainland Australia for less than AUD $27 a day.

Greyhound International Travel, 14-16 Cockspur Street, London WC2H OJR, Tel: 01 839 5591 (U.S.A., Canada, Australia)

Topdeck Travel, 131 Earls Court Road, London, Tel: 01 373 8406

Green Tortoise, PO Box 24459, San Francisco, CA 94124, Tel: 415/821 0803

Car

If you intend to travel and work your way round Europe, going by car is a possible means of doing that. It is an expensive option though, as maintenance costs are high and petrol is expensive. However, if you have the resources and are mechanically minded then sharing the costs and driving with fellow passengers might make this way of travelling more viable. Alternatively you might be able to buy an old "banger" for next to nothing in the country you're going to (this is a popular and cheap way of travelling round Australia). Make sure though that you buy or take with you a make of car that has international outlets so that if you need spares you won't be hanging around for weeks while they are being delivered. It is advisable to join the AA or RAC before you take a car abroad – not only do they provide very comprehensive insurance facilities, they also offer a wide range of advice.

In America and Canada, Auto-Driveaway is the term given to the delivery of cars from one point to another and is very common. You cannot make arrangements in advance to deliver a car because the companies do not know what they will be getting from one week to the next so you will need to be on the spot. Once you are in the States and wish to travel you can locate the nearest driveaway company by checking the Yellow Pages under 'Automobile and Truck Transporters' or 'Driveaway Companies'. The larger cities obviously handle a larger volume of business than the offices in the smaller towns. You have to pay petrol costs (the vehicle has a full tank initially) so generally the smaller the car the better is the fuel consumption, although if you are travelling a long way a larger car may be more comfortable. You are allowed to take two passengers (but not to pick up hitch-hikers) provided they sign the agreement form. You may be offered a RV (Recreational Vehicle – camper) which is heavy on petrol but you have the advantage of free accommodation. It may be cheaper, however, to take a smaller car and camp. You have to deliver the car in the same condition you picked it up so check it thoroughly before you set off for damage which has to be noted on the agreement form. Minor repairs en route are your responsibility (refundable on delivery). Whilst this system has its limitations it is an ideal way to travel, especially if you have a destination in mind anyway and with other people to share the costs the journey can work out quite cheap.

AA, Fanum House, Basingstoke, Hants RG21 2EA

RAC, Lansdowne Rd, Croydon, Surrey CR9 2JA

Auto Driveaway Co, 310 South Michigan Ave, Chicago, Illinois 60604

AAACON, 230 West 41st Street, New York, NY 10037

Dependable Car Travel Service, 130 West 42nd Street, New York, NY 10036

Nationwide Auto Transporters Inc, 2175 Lemoine Ave, Fort Lee, New Jersey 07024

Hitch-hiking

Hitch-hiking is often given a fleeting mention in guide and travel books but is either dismissed out of hand or described in such a manner that it is obvious the writer has never tried it and doesn't trust those who do it. Like many things it is not possible to write about hitching unless you have a good few miles under your belt yourself.

It is undoubtedly the cheapest way of travelling though it is also one of the slowest. Everyone has their own favourite story of the friend who made it from Calais to Istanbul in one ride but these are the (very rare) exception rather than the rule. If you are planning to hitch, allow yourself plenty of time and if you are going a long way expect to spend the odd uncomfortable night by the roadside.

There are a number of general rules that will increase your safety, comfort and speed if you are planing to travel by this method.

1. Appearance. Sadly, there are still some people who judge others by what they look like. If you look reasonably presentable (and this doesn't mean a suit, tie and Gucci luggage) then you are going to get more drivers prepared to stop. If your designer ripped jeans, aged biker jacket or allergy to washing is more important to you than the chances of getting a ride then fair enough. But don't say we didn't warn you.

2. Signs. Generally these are a good idea. Make them clear, large and use waterproof ink. If it's not too much trouble make them before you leave rather than from scraps of cardboard debris from the roadside. Try not to be too obscure in your destination eg 'Athens' rather than 'John's House Sintagma Square' and don't try and be too clever. A sign saying 'Sydney' on the M2 is likely to cause confusion rather than amusement and the offer of an immediate ride to the sparkling wit bearing it. Having said that, we once met a German who travelled all through France with a sign which simply said 'Pourquois pas?'

3. Position. How many times have you been in a car and seen hitch-hikers who it was impossible to pick up because either you saw them too late or because there was nowhere to stop without causing a multiple pile up? Better to spend a few minutes walking up (or even back down) the road to an accessible spot rather than three frustrating hours on a sharp bend or beside a 70 mph stretch of freeway. Make sure that you can be seen in good time, that your sign,if you have one, can be read and that it is easy for the driver to pull over and stop. The ideal spot is at the beginning of a layby or bus stop and just past a junction or similar so the traffic isn't moving too fast.

Unless you are so cold and tired that a night in gaol seems like a good idea, don't hitch on motorways, freeways, autobahns and the like. The laws of each country are different as regards the legality and acceptability of hitching. In Ireland or Israel it is almost the accepted mode of travel. In Japan you are likely to be picked up or mown down.

4. Safety. It is usually much easier to get lifts when you are travelling alone than in company. Two women or a man and woman together will also usually do OK. Two or more blokes together must be prepared for long delays. A woman travelling alone is taking a pretty big risk anywhere and a couple of women are not always safe especially in countries where native women would never be seen hitching. Use your common sense and you will rarely have problems.

Just as some drivers are reluctant to pick up hitch-hikers, so you should be wary of certain types of driver. If they are obviously drunk or in any way suspicious then politely refuse the proferred lift. Try also to keep your temper with the ones who think it's clever to stop up ahead, wait until you are almost at the vehicle and then roar off in a cloud of exhaust or spray of dirty water. They will almost certainly end up in a ditch further up the road.

5. Opportunities. Apart from the obvious advantage of free travel, there are many other opportunities that can arise from hitch-hiking. Often a meal is offered at some point and sometimes a bed for the night. Drivers who give lifts tend to belong to the nicer half of the human race and can be extremely pleasant companions. Often they will have ideas and information about work opportunities in their own town or country and will always be a useful source of advice on where to stay, eat or go to ask for whatever you need next, be it a job or a flight home.

Just as useful as the drivers are the other hitch-hikers you will meet by the roadside. There is a camaraderie amongst them that means much useful information is regularly shared. On many occasions you will pick up some advice on where and how to get work and sometimes you'll even pick up a travelling companion.

One final hint. If you get stopped or questioned by the local police, be courteous and friendly. Even if you don't feel like it. Especially if you don't feel like it. Have your passport handy; foreigners often get off with a warning or even some friendly advice where locals might be booked.

Sea

These days it is much harder to obtain positions at sea with a commercial shipping company unless you are qualified and have the necessary "papers". here is no point in writing to such companies as Cunard, P & O etc if you don't have the necessary qualifications. By far the best bet is crewing for privately owned craft. Advertisements for crews can be found in yachting magazines and Yacht Clubs generally have a notice board for crewing positions or you could try advertising yourself on a Yacht Club notice board. Most people, however, find that the quickest and most reliable method of getting afloat is to go directly to an international yacht harbour and canvass for crew openings. Because there is a regular turnover among crew members, new positions are always opening up.

Most small craft heading west to the Caribbean from UK and European ports leave around October/November. Try looking for a passage shortly before this, or if you are already abroad, at any Mediterranean port from Greece to Gibraltar and the Canary Islands – the last victualling stop before the main crossing.

In America freighter travel may not offer much in the way of savings over cheap air fares, but it has the advantage over flying of allowing you to visit exotic, untouristed ports. Generally the daily cost ranges from US$60 to US$90 and voyages last for 30 days, 45 days, even 70 and 90 days. Waiting lists are normally six weeks long and can be as long as four or five months. An example of a trip on a freighter is a periodic departure from Charleston, sailing to New Orleans, then to Houston, through the Panama Canal to Sydney, Melbourne and Brisbane, from there to three ports in New Zealand, back to the Panama Canal and finishing at Philadelphia (70 days at sea).

Spur-of-the-Moment Cruises Inc specialises in selling sharply discounted cabin berths two or three weeks before departure and savings can be as much as 50% Seven days in the Caribbean, including air fare from the West Coast cost US$ 729, a seven-day cruise of Alaskan waters US$699 (1989 prices).

Crewit Services deliver a lot of boats worldwide as well as organising crew for private boat owners and delivery companies. They cater for novices as well as experienced sailors and have often been able to find people full time employment. Prospective crew and boat owners put their names on the register and Crewit try to match them up. The enrolment fee is £25 for prospective crew and this covers them for a year's sailing. In addition to crew, they also register pursers, engineers, nurses, stewards and doctors for luxury yachts mainly in the Caribbean. They deliver yachts to Germany and other European centres and are negotiating to deliver boats from Australia to the UK as well as to the West Indies and Sweden.

The Cruising Association operate a Crewing Service which is designed simply to put potential crew in touch with skippers. They cannot guarantee that crew will find a berth and suggest that professional agencies are contacted for paid work. If you are not a member of the Cruising Association, the fee is £10 for the year for which you receive details of skippers seeking crew that have applied in the previous two months as well as those that have still not found crew from previous lists. The details you provide them with are also published at various times during the year and they also provide a leaflet giving practical advice to skippers and crew of what to expect and how to avoid possible problems.

Companies which specialise in sailing holidays are also worth contacting, though you have to be prepared to commit yourself to a season. You can find their addresses from brochures at a travel agent and write to the personnel department. One such company is 'Sunsail' (formerly known as the Yacht Cruising Association and Island Sailing) which operate Flotilla sailing holidays in Greece, Turkey, Yugoslavia, Sardinia and Corsica. They require skippers in charge of all sailing matters and mechanic bosuns with previous diesel experience to service and maintain the engines on the thirteen flotilla yachts. The crew live aboard their own pilot yacht and are paid from £80 per week as well as being provided with flights to and from the UK.

Dragon Yachts operate luxury charter yachts in the Carribean, Mediterranean, East Africa, Seychelles and UK. Young people are required for many different types of work from basic crew through to specialist instructors in parakiting, tennis, and many watersports. The "yachts" are more like small cruise liners and the owners are specifically looking for people with a sense of adventure.

Crewit, Cobbs Quay, Hamworthy, Poole, Dorset BH15 4EL. Tel: 0202 678847

Cruising Association, Ivory House, St Katherine Dock, London E1 9AT. Tel: 01 481 0881

Sunsail, The Port House, Port Solent, Portsmouth, Hants PO6 4TH.
Tel: 0705 219847

Dragon Yachts (Worldwide) Ltd., 788 Bath Road, Cranford Middx. TW5 9UL Tel: 01 897 9995

Marine Data Services, PO Box 2394, Woodland, California 95695

Freighter World Cruises Inc, 180 S Lake Ave, Suite 335, Pasadena, CA 91101, Tel: 818/449 3106

Trav L Tips, 163-07 Depot Rd, PO Box 188, Flushing, NY 11358

Freighter Travel Club of America, PO Box 12693, Salem, OR 97309

Pearl's Travel Tips, 175 Great Neck Road, Great Neck, NY 11201, Tel: 516/487 8351

Spur-of-the-Moment Cruises Inc, 10780 Jefferson Boulevard, Culver City, CA 90230, Tel: 213/838 9329

Train

Travelling by train still has a romantic feel to it and a long train journey from, say, Paris to Hong Kong or Alexandria to Cape Town (with a couple of breaks) can be immensely satisfying. It is also an excellent way to meet other travellers and exchange information and advice.

In Europe if you are eligible for a student discount or rail pass then travelling by train can be as cheap as bus/coach travel. Eurotrain offer reduced rail tickets, valid for 2 months, if you are under 26 for journeys throughout Europe and Morocco. Within individual countries, however, unless you have a rail card, students and young people generally have to pay the full fare.

In Asia train travel is definitely the cheapest way of getting about (cycling and hitch-hiking excepted!) though not necessarily the most comfortable as they are always crowded to bursting point. Trains in Thailand are an exception to this as they are very clean, spacious and comfortable. In China, in theory, you can travel 'hard seat', 'hard sleeper' or 'soft seat' (3rd, 2nd and 1st class), but in practice this means you have to travel 2nd class or preferably 1st class as Chinese hospitality prevents a 'guest' in their country from being uncomfortable! In America long distance trains are very expensive, though Amtrak offer rail passes which compete with cheap air fares.

Thomas Cook publishes the Overseas Timetable for countries outside Europe and the Continental Timetable for Europe and these are extremely valuable for anyone wishing to travel extensively by train. You could also contact the National Railways of individual European countries which are represented in the UK for information on rail passes, student discounts etc.

One immensely useful benefit of train travel is that you can use it as cheap accommodation if you go overnight (either by sleeper or just stretched out on a couple of seats). You arrive refreshed at your destination and save both time and money.

Eurotrain, 52 Grosvenor Gardens, London SW1, Tel: 01 730 8518

National Railways represented in the UK:
Belgium: 01 734 1491
France: 01 409 1224
Netherlands: 01 630 1735
Switzerland: 01 734 1921
Italy: 01 434 3844
West Germany (Tourist Office): 01 734 2600
Austria (Tourist Office): 01 629 0461
Luxembourg (Tourist Office): 01 434 2800

Overland Expeditions

'Overlanders' are increasing in popularity as adventurous people are looking for alternatives to run-of-the-mill- holidays. The variety of trips is as varied as the people taking them. But, they can be expensive. For example, a 21-week London-Nairobi truck trip through the Sahara can cost almost £3000 – trucks can generally carry up to 20 passengers, Land Rovers can bulge with as many as eight – it's cramped.

Of course, some trips can be more 'testing' than others, whether it be overland from London to

Australia, Trans African tours, or South American sojourns. If you want to take such a trip, and can afford it, then you have a great choice. Tours can range from 3 weeks to many months, and from budget to expensive. Group members typically contribute to the food kitty, share chores and sleep on camp cots under the stars. The convenience comes from someone else planning and organising the trip. Tours are perfect for anyone lacking lead time, a suitable vehicle and mechanical skills to keep it running, and the larger funds needed for independent travel.

For those who wish to plan their own expedition, safari, overlander or simply a trans-wherever trek, there are many considerations and it is not a matter to be taken lightly. Much is, of course, common sense, but it is advisable to take the following considerations into account:

1. Purpose of trip: Set down your objectives. This will give you a good
starting point for discussion and planning. Is the purpose and basis of your trip simply to get from A to B (eg London to Melbourne), is it for a holiday, sight-seeing (eg a South American 'circle' tour), for excitement and adventure (such as a Saharan overland), treasure hunting, prospecting (searching for lost gold in the Andes), or what? Deciding the exact purpose of your trip taking into account all factors and interest of all participants is vital.

2. Vehicle: Most expeditions involve the use of a motor vehicle, although within this category comes travel by horse, mule, bicycle, motorbike, boat, canoe, etc. An 'expedition' describes the type of trip, not necessarily the means. However, for the purpose of this section we will presume that you intend using a motorised vehicle. You will need to take into account the capacity (number of people, amount of baggage, whether towing a trailer, degree of comfort required, etc) which will relate to the size of vehicle, engine, etc and the countries you will be travelling through. A critical point to bear in mind is the availability of spares and/or service. For example, the first vehicle that will come to most people's minds is the good old Land Rover – but you can't get spares or service for it in a number of countries – Canada for instance. (Land Rover haven't been exported there since 1974). On the other hand, if you're going on a Saharan overland they are the best vehicle since mechanics in the smallest oases usually have the knowledge and parts to repair them. We heard of a couple who crossed the Sahara in a new American 4-wheel drive vehicle – they had to make most of the trip in reverse gear as the automatic transmission developed a fault and neither they nor any local mechanic could fix it! In general the Land Rover is a good all-round choice and the company is extremely helpful in providing information to anyone writing to them.

3. Spare parts: The type of trip, duration, countries of travel and terrain will dictate what spares and ancillary equipment you need – maybe special tyres, winch, oil cooler, double-skin roof, roof racks, towing cables, sand ladders, jerricans or additional fuel tank, etc. It goes without saying that you need a full set of tools and workshop manual. It is also advisable to have back-up at home so that if you do break down and are unable to get parts where you are, you can have them flown out to you (yes, it is expensive, but so is abandoning your vehicle).

4. Crew: Amongst the 'crew' must be a mechanic who can do just about anything with the vehicle to keep it running. If you intend keeping to well-travelled routes there is of course more chance of finding a 'garage' where you can carry out repairs, but some degree of mechanical aptitude is essential. As there will be a number of people travelling and living in a confined space there must be no obvious personality clashes and someone must be in overall command to make decisions when problems do arise.

5. Equipment: Make a careful list of everything you will need. Fit out the vehicle so that this gear can be readily and easily stowed and retrieved. Make sure that you have an adequate first aid kit and everyone knows how to use it. You may need a water storage and purification system, emergency rations etc. Much will depend on where you are going and when.

6. Route planning: This is a very important aspect of any trip and one often not given enough attention. Get the best maps, regardless of cost, and remember that even the most recent maps can be out-of-date to a degree. Take into account when you will be travelling as many roads can be washed-out or blocked by snow at certain times of the year. Due consideration for border

crossings is important in these troubled times so it is essential to get the latest information from the respective embassies.

7. Documentation: Unless your trip is relatively straightforward you are likely to need a mountain of documents. You will need to write to each embassy for details of the requirements (the addresses are listed in the booklet sent with your passport) and obtain an International Driver's Licence from the AA or RAC. Insurance cover is essential, though it may not be available for certain types of expedition and for certain countries, or the premium could be so high as to be unacceptable. For some countries you will need a vehicle 'passport' – carnet de passage en douane, in others it may be necessary to post a bond. Two friends who took a Land Rover overland from the UK to Kenya a few years ago spent more time waiting at borders than they spent actually driving!

8. Costing: Every conceivable consideration and contingency must be taken into account when costing your trip. All too often people leave in an inadequate vehicle with insufficient funds to cover breakdowns etc, and end up abandoning their vehicle and having to hitch-hike.

With the increasing number of tour operators organising overland expeditions you may well be able to get a job as a driver/mechanic or even leader. You need to have an HGV or PSV driving licence and be aged between about 25 and 30. You have be competent in (or be able to learn quickly) a number of skills including driving, mechanics, keeping basic accounts, dealing with local officials, being a guide to historical sites and so on. Vacancies are advertised quite often but it's certainly worth writing (sending a CV) to the various tour companies, addresses of which can be found in travel agents' brochures.

If you have particular skills or expertise for example as a doctor, scientist or specialist mechanic then you may be eligible for a place on an expedition organised by an expedition society. The World Expeditionary Association (WEXAS) publish 'The Traveller's Handbook' which contains advertisements and announcements of forthcoming expeditions and in which you may place your own advertisements, and they also make awards to worthwhile expeditions. The Brathay Exploration Group recruits expedition leaders and the Royal Geographical Society encourages and helps many British expeditions and keeps a register of personnel. As a member of Earthwatch (an American organisation) you have the opportunity to participate in any of over 100 different expeditions worldwide. You merely fill in a 'member profile' card which gives a list of interests (Agriculture, Astronomy, Ethnomusicology, Ornithology etc) and a list of regions (Africa, Arctic, Central America, Pacific Islands, etc) which you tick off and they keep you abreast of openings and assignments on projects around the world. As a member you also receive their magazine 'Earthwatch' which contains information on projects for example, Ishango, Zaire, Volunteers this season will camp and work at a site within the Virunga National Park surrounded by tall grass, scattered trees, and open woodland. This is a rare opportunity to work on one of the oldest archaeological sites yet discovered, and volunteers may see hippos, lions, baboons, impala and elephants.....Share of Costs $1,675 (usually approx 2 weeks).

WEXAS International, 45 Brompton Road, Knightsbridge, London SW3 1DE
Tel: 01 589 3315

Brathay Exploration Group, Brathay Hall, Ambleside, Cumbria LA22 0HP

The Royal Georgraphical Society, 1 Kensington Gore, London SW7

Earthwatch, 680 Mt Auburn Street, Box 403, Watertown, Massachusetts 02272
Tel: (617) 926 8200

Earthwatch, c/o Louise Henson, 29 Coniston Ave, Headington, Oxford OX3 OAN

Dragoman, 10 Riverside, Framlingham, Suffolk 1P13 9AG, Tel: 0728 724184

Exodus Travels Ltd, 9 Weir Road, Balham, London SW12 0LT, Tel: 01 675 7996

Chapter 5

Work Opportunities Abroad

This chapter will take you on a guided tour of the type of work most commonly available overseas. Don't read it word by word, dip into it at the points where it's most useful to you. At the end of each section is a list of useful contact addresses for further information and, in some cases, even specific jobs.

Casual work overseas is generally of a menial nature. It is available therefore, only in countries where there is a high standard of living, as the poorer and third world countries have an abundance of local cheap labour. When you need to supplement your travel funds you should concentrate on the more affluent countries so that you can use this money to travel around the poorer countries where it will go a lot further.

There are numerous ways in which you will be able to find jobs while travelling. You may pick up leads whilst hitch-hiking, from local papers, hostels, bulletin boards or other travellers, or simply by looking around to see what needs to be done. If you see crops ready for harvesting then ask at the nearest farmhouse if any work is available. Other things you may notice that need to be done are car washing, painting, grass cutting, yard clearing, gardening, window cleaning, labouring etc.

Most opportunities arise during the summer months but in autumn there may be leaf sweeping, firewood cutting, clearing-up at resorts and summer camps after the season. In winter there's snow clearing. Bars, restaurants and hotels, where there is always a high turnover of staff, are prime targets at any time. Take any job, anywhere, even if it's for only a couple of hours. You never know where it might lead.

Agriculture

Farmers in many countries depend on casual labour at harvest time to pick fruit as they have to get the crop in quickly before it perishes. If you plan your route carefully there is no reason why you shouldn't be able to work your way round the world picking fruit in country after country. The standard route across Europe, starting in early summer, is picking raspberries in Scotland (May-June), pears in northern France (June-July) or fruit in the Peloponnese of Greece (July-August), harvesting grapes for wine in southwest France, mainly near Bordeaux (late September early October), grapes for cognac in France (mid-late October), olives in Crete (November to March), oranges in Israel (February to May).

The hours are long and you need to be reasonably fit as the work is hard, although you get fit pretty quickly picking fruit. The accommodation is usually basic and you are not paid if you don't work because of bad weather, but you can generally save enough money for your travels as there is nothing to spend it on and you get to meet both locals and other travellers who are a good source of information. Grape picking in France also includes the perk of almost unlimited wine in the evenings.

Apart from the ways of finding a job as already mentioned, government employment agencies in many countries deal with agricultural vacancies of a seasonal nature that local residents won't consider. In France you can sign up for grape picking in the season of the 'vendage' (harvest) at local branches of the Agence National pour l'Emploi (ANPE) in Bordeaux, Reims,

Macon, Beaune, Dijon or Colmar. In West Germany the Arbeitsamters fulfil the same role as the (ANPE).

In Britain, non British travellers can obtain work permits to pick fruit at international farm camps which are recognised by the Home Office. As travellers from all parts of the world can work at these camps they are an excellent source of contacts. The accommodation is usually very basic and the work hard but all fruit picking is at least out of doors and usually in the company of a good bunch of people.

For the more serious agriculturals amongst you there are two organisations, both run from the National Agricultural Centre, that operate exchange study tours in Agriculture: the International Agricultural Exchange Association (IAEA), and the International Farm Experience Programme (IFEP). For both you will need to have had some farming or agricultural experience, but not a great deal.

Applicants for the IAEA should be over nineteen years of age and have at least one year's experience in agriculture. They can choose the type of farming they wish to work in and are placed with selected host families where they will work and live as a member of that family.

There are four trainee categories:

1) Agricultural trainee: male or female trainee with good experience in general agriculture who is prepared and used to participating in all general farm operations;

2) Agri-mix trainee: a trainee who does not have adequate experience to accept responsible work with general agriculture, but with some practical experience, required to take more training outside. Because of limited experience, this trainee will be prepared to assist in the home; the ratio would be 50% as a Home Management Trainee, and 50% of the time as an Agricultural trainee;

3) Horticultural trainee: a trainee specialising in working on fruit orchards, vegetable farms, greenhouses, landscaping, etc.;

4) Home Management trainee: trainees with good general knowledge of how to look after normal household duties, but at the same time prepared to look after children and help in the garden. Farming experience for this job should not be necessary.

The main objectives of the IAEA are (a) to provide rural youth with an opportunity to study agricultural methods in other parts of the world; (b) to develop an understanding of ways of life and cultural patterns in other countries; and (c) to strengthen and improve mutual understanding between the countries involved through the experience and personal contacts established between the trainee and the host family.

The trainees are paid realistic wages, eg in Canada the minimum wage for a male trainee is approximately £100 per week gross. With deductions from this for income tax, board and lodging, the take home pay amounts to approximately £80 per week. Soon after starting work on the host farm the trainee will be visited by an IAEA Supervisor, who has to make sure the trainees and the host family are satisfied with the arrangements. If there are any problems then the Supervisor will try to sort them out, and in a few cases, where necessary, may move unhappy trainees to another placement.

The IAEA make the travel arrangements on a group basis and is responsible for obtaining work permits where required and also employment on approved farms for periods of seven to fourteen months. Orientation courses are arranged for the participants on their arrival in their host country. These usually last five days and are carried out at Agricultural Colleges where resident and IAEA staff instruct trainees on the main differences in agricultural methods and equipment, social conditions, farm safety, etc.

Each participant has to pay the cost of transportation and the IAEA administration fee, which includes obtaining work permits, finding suitable host families and organising orientation seminars and supervision.

The countries where these exchanges operate have Direct One Host Country programmes which last from 6-8 months and are as follows:

United States: The programmes last for 7 months, and include a three weeks unpaid holiday. Trainees depart late March/early April and return early November. Placements are made in California, Montana, North Dakota, Minnesota and Texas. Most trainee categories are available although participants with dairy/cropping experience are preferred.

Canada: These programmes also run for 7 months with 3 weeks unpaid holiday, departing early/mid April, returning mid November. Placements are mainly in British Columbia, Alberta, Saskatchewan, Manitoba and Ontario. All trainee categories are available.

Australia: There are 4 different programmes from 7-9 months duration and include a 2 day stopover on the outward route. The programmes vary from dairy placements, cropping, beef farming and horticulture so all categories of trainees are catered for.

New Zealand: There are 2 programmes, one 6 1/2 months duration and one 8 months duration. Placement areas include most of the regions in both the North and South Island. All trainee categories are available but dairy trainees are particularly encouraged.

Japan: There are 2 programmes, one lasting 8 months and one lasting 12 months. They are open to both male and female trainees but trainees must be in full time agriculture or horticulture. Agricultural placements are near Maebashi in dairy, beef and hogs.

Around the World Programmes, which last thirteen months are also offered and these combine work in Australia and Canada, Australia and the United States, New Zealand and Canada and New Zealand and the United States. All run from October to November.

For more information on any of these exchanges write to IAEA Study Tours.

Those who have had two years' experience in agriculture or horticulture (one of which may be at college), are aged between 18 and 26, have satisfactory references and intend to make a career in agriculture or horticulture could qualify for a place on the International Farm Experience Programme.

The IFEP organises a range of work experience exchange for young farmers and horticulturists in many countries including Canada, the United States and much of Europe. The programmes last from between 3 and 12 months (this can be extended to 21 months in the United States) and participants can leave, in most cases, at the time of their choice.

The work is paid and although fortunes won't be made, participants should be able to cover all their costs. The programme is based on the belief that the experience of working and living in another country provides young people with the chance to broaden their knowledge of the industry, learn new skills and techniques, make new friends and expand their personal horizons.

Not all of the exchanges are solely for work experience. Through CEJA, the European Council of Young Farmers, the Programme is able to offer a combined work experience and language course. Two of the programmes in the United States include a university course, when participants would be able to study an aspect of the industry in detail. On one of these, the MAST Program at the University of Minnesota, a participant would be part of a group of 100 from eleven different countries.

If a person has found a placement abroad on their own but needs assistance with work permits, etc then IFEP will help. They are not able to offer a placement overseas for every applicant, as each programme has a numerical limit and applications may have to be deferred till the following year or changed to another country. Participants in the programme are asked, if possible, to find an employer able to host an incoming trainee though applications are not dependent on finding an employer. The only way IFEP can increase the number of young British people they can place abroad, especially in non-EEC countries, is by finding host employers willing to accept an overseas trainee on their farm or nursery.

Programmes in Europe

Denmark, Germany and Holland provide practical training to suit most needs. (Germany and Holland also provide horticultural placements). Participants can go at any time to suit their employer and themselves and the training lasts from 3-12 months. Most host families speak excellent English. Placements are matched as closely as possible to the participant's requirements and Denmark and Germany will also accept girls for work in the house. The pay is £30 per week plus board and lodging. Participants have to pay their own travel costs plus a registration fee and insurance.

Finland, Norway, Sweden, Switzerland, Poland and Hungary provide practical work on farms and nurseries. All these countries except Finland provide horticultural placements as well. Almost all placements are for the Spring and Summer and last from 3-12 months. Pay is also £30 per week plus board and lodging and travel costs, registration fee and insurance are paid by the participant.

CEJA organise a five week course of French or German held in France, followed by 4 1/2 months of practical training in any of the EEC countries. The programme lasts 6 months in total and courses begin in February and July. Participants receive pocket money and board during the course. During the training wages and free board and lodging are provided. Participants have to pay a registration fee and 75% of their travel costs are refunded.

CEJA also run a 3 month short training course beginning in June, which provides practical training in any of the EEC countries. Participants have to attend meetings in Brussels at the beginning and end of the course. Wages and free board and lodging are given during the practical training.

Additional programmes run by CEJA include 2-8 week courses on Computer Business, landscape gardening, tourism, butter and cheese, forestry and others.

Programmes to North America

In Ontario, Canada there is a 6-12 month practical training programme on dairy farms. If a person already has a job in Ontario IFEP are able to help them obtain a work permit. Ontario is currently the only province in Canada where IFEP can organise work permits as they have no coordinators in the other provinces and therefore have no authority to arrange for work permits elsewhere. Wages are Can $ 900 per month less board and lodging. Participants have to pay a registration fee, travel, medical and personal insurance.

In America, Ohio State University run Scheme A and B . Scheme A is a 12 month programme in horticulture, beginning in March and June. Participants will be working in Ohio while attending the University part-time and studying courses of their choice. Pay is a minimum of US$ 3.35 per hour, and board and lodging may be deducted by some employers. Participants have to pay a registration fee, travel costs, medical and personal insurance.

Scheme B consists of 12 months of practical work in horticulture and agriculture anywhere in the United States. All trainees begin with an orientation course at the University. Pay is also US$ 3.35 per hour with possible deductions on a monthly basis for board and lodging. The registration fee, travel costs, medical and personal insurance have to be paid by the trainee.

The University of Minnesota run a PART Scheme similar to the Ohio Scheme B which involves 5-8 months of practical training on farms. Pay and costs are the same as Ohio.

Ohio State University have a combining scheme which involves six months on one of the large combining crews. Participants have to work long hours, working from Texas to Canada while winter months are spent on arable holdings. Pay and costs are the same as on other programmes. As there are only a limited number of places trainees must apply well in advance of the April starting date.

The University of Minnesota runs the MAST Scheme which consists of a 8-12 month programme of work experience and University tuition for agriculture and horticulture. At least 2 years of practical experience, plus a completed vocational course at college is required before enrolment is possible on the scheme. Programmes start in March, July and November. Pay and costs are the same as previously mentioned with the addition of a tuition fee which is deducted monthly from wages.

Participants on any of these programmes have to apply at least four months before they want to travel. For information on these programmes write to International Farm Experience Programme.

Working Weekends on Organic Farms (WWOOF) offer the chance of first-hand experience of organic gardening and farming both in Britain and in other parts of the world. In return for your help with the workload (full time and quite hard) you will receive good wholesome meals and somewhere to sleep. It's an ideal opportunity to make new friends and partake in such activities as working with horses, cows, goats, sheep, pigs, various fowl; cutting turf, preserving fruit and vegetables; making varied cheeses and yoghurt; stonewalling, hedging, renovating etc. It is also an ideal way to 'get started' in a particular country and learn a little about both the culture and the work opportunities without having to deplete your travel funds. Membership of "WWOOF" costs £3 (UK and Eire), £4 (rest of Europe) and £5 (others) and when you join you will receive the current List of Holdings (ranging from 2 to 60 acres) together with a short description of each one, plus other relevant details. When applying it is important to send a 9 x 6 sae/2 International Postal Reply Coupons.

"WWOOF" is based on a Fix-it-Yourself system whereby Wwoofers get in touch with their prospective host to make arrangements. Length of stay can be a weekend, week, month or longer by mutual agreement between host and Wwoofer.

IAEA Study Tours, IAEA, YFC Centre, National Agricultural Centre, Kenilworth, Warwickshire CV8 2LG, Tel: 02033 696578

IAEA Servicing Offices:
Australia: 50 Oxford Street, Paddington, NSW 2021
Canada: 206, 1501-17th Avenue SW, Calgary, Alberta T2T OE2
Europe: Aaboulevard 56, DK-2200 Copenhagen N, Denmark
New Zealand: Armstrong House, 3/31 Quay Street, PO Box 328, Whakatane
USA: 817 2nd Street South, Great Falls, Montana 59405

International Farm Experience Programme, YFC Centre, National Agricultural Centre, Kenilworth, Warwickshire CV8 2LG, Tel: 0203 696584

WWOOF, Annie Sampson, Crowhill, Newgrove, Tulla, Clare, Eire

Au Pair Posts/Domestic
Working as an au pair is another economic way of spending some time getting to know a country, its language and customs. In many European countries the minimum length of stay is six months and in the United States it's twelve months. In return for board lodging and pocket money (approx £20 per week) you will be expected to help with light household tasks such as ironing, bedmaking, dusting, vacuuming, sewing, washing up, handwashing, preparing simple meals and taking the children to and from school, plus general child care duties. A typical working day is of 5-6 hours, with 3 or 4 evenings babysitting in a 6 day week. The remainder of the evenings, 1 full day and 3 afternoons per week are usually free.

If you fix up a job through an agency there's usually an agency service charge of up to £46 and applicants are responsible for their travel and insurance costs as well as obtaining necessary visas or entry requirements. Countries open to applications from UK nationals include: Austria, Belgium, Denmark, France, the Federal Republic of Germany, Greece, Israel, Italy, Luxembourg, Morocco, Netherlands, Portugal, Spain, Switzerland, Tunisia and the United States. Some agencies also have associate agencies in Canada and Australia.

Whilst most au pair jobs are traditionally filled by women there is no reason why men should not apply too. The au pair programme in the United States is equally open to males as well as females aged between 18 and 25 years. To be eligible you must be a citizen of a western European country with at least a fair degree of fluency in English. Character references and a medical certificate are required, and you will also need to have some child-care experience and preferably be able to drive. You will work a 9 hour day, for 5.5 days a week with 1 weekend free each month. The day is made up of 6 hours of active duties including feeding and playing with the children, and 3 hours of passive supervision including babysitting. The positions last 1 year, starting in June, September or January. The return flight London-New York plus single fare from New York to the family, is provided plus approximately $100 per week pocket money and 2 weeks' holiday.

Posts in Britain are open only to unmarried women aged 17-27 who wish to learn English while living as a member of an English-speaking family. Only nationals of western European countries, including Cyprus, Malta, Turkey and Yugoslavia are eligible, and are permitted to spend no more than a total of 2 years as an au pair. On arrival in Britain as an au pair you must be able to provide the Immigration Officer with a letter of invitation from the host family, giving precise details of the arrangements, including the amount of pocket money, accommodation, free time, details of the host family, house and household, and the exact nature of the work expected. Au pairs may also be required to produce a return ticket or evidence of sufficient funds to pay for return travel. As a general rule you can expect to work up to 5 hours per day with 1 fixed day per week free. You should have your own room and receive approx £22 per week pocket money. EC nationals wishing to stay for longer than 6 months must obtain a residence permit.

In addition to Au Pairs, many agencies also have positions for mothers helps, nannies, housekeepers, cook/housekeepers, butlers, chauffeurs, ladies companions, general domestics, married couples etc and there may be posts in schools, nursing/old people's homes etc. The Lady magazine carries advertisements for many of these jobs and you could always place an advertisement in the magazine yourself.

Once you are in the country you could look in English language papers or visit an au pair agency. Be careful of taking au pair jobs in the Middle East although these often pay very well. We recommend that in this area you always apply through a reputable agency.

Always make sure that you have sufficient funds for a return trip home in case of emergency. If you take a job in advance take with you details of all the work you will be expected to do and the pocket money you will receive.

BUNAC operate KAMP (Kitchen and Maintenance Programme) in the utility areas of childrens' summer camps in the USA. This normally involves work in the kitchens, but work in the laundry and outside, on general maintenance, is also possible. All applicants must be current members of BUNAC (membership fee £3); be full-time students at a British educational institution studying at HND or degree level; be available to work at camp as early as possible in June until the last week in August; attend a KAMP/BUNAC orientation; and not have been to North America before on either KAMP or Work America as both schemes share the same visa programme. Foreign students studying in Britain who can be sure that they will have no problem being issued with a visa by the American Embassy can also apply for KAMP.

The registration fee is £58 for which you get free food and accommodation at the camp, a minimum salary of $490 (net total), access to the recreational facilities of the camp, and up to 6 weeks' travel time after camp. The camp pays your air fare, and your transport from New York to the camp.

The Au Pair International Handbook, Vacation Work, 9 Park End St, Oxford
OX1 1HJ, Tel: Oxford 241978

The Au Pair & Nanny's Guide to Working Abroad, Vacation Work, 9 Park End St,
Oxford OX1 1HJ, Tel: Oxford 241978

Helping Hands Au Pair and Domestic Agency, 10 Hertford Road, Newbury Park,
Ilford, Essex 1G2 7HQ, Tel: 01 597 3138

Anglia Agency, 15 Eastern Avenue, Southend-on-Sea, Essex SS2 5QX
Tel: 0702 613888

Universal Care, Chester House, 9 Windsor End, Beaconsfield, Bucks HP9 2JJ
Tel: 0494 678811

Au Pairs-Italy, 46 The Rise, Sevenoaks, Kent TN13 1RJ, Tel: 0732 451522

Students Abroad, Elm House, 21b The Avenue, Hatch End, Middx HA5 4EN,
Tel: 01 428 5823

EIL Au Pair (for USA), Otesaga, Upper Wyche, Malvern, Worcs WR14 4EN
Tel: 0684 562577

KAMP, BUNAC, 16 Bowling Green Lane, London EC1R 0BD, Tel: 01 251 3472

Working with Children

There are many orgnisations who specialise in adventure holidays for children providing activities
ranging from canoeing, sailing, windsurfing, waterskiing, snorkelling, surfing, rafting, archery,
rifle shooting, abseiling, climbing, assault courses, walking, orienteering etc.

Quest Adventure provides a range of special activity courses for schools and young people. The
organisation has centres in the Lake District, North Devon, the South of France, the Ardeche and
the French Alps. It employs instructors, both qualified and unqualified (they provide training)
for watersports and rifle shooting etc. and group leaders as well as entertainments officers to
co-ordinate evening programmes.

Thomson Holidays recruit children's representatives who should be aged between 18 and 28 years,
single and should have child care or nursing qualifications. Employment is based overseas on a
seasonal basis, usually April to October and there are occasionally possibilities for winter work.
The work involves organising daytime activities, arranging and supervising early dinners, reading
stories, babysitting etc. The salary is paid monthly and basic accommodation is provided in the
hotel. After 9 months service generous holiday concessions are available.

'Sunsail' operate watersports centres in Greece and Turkey and recruit nannies who are paid from
£50 per week. Accommodation is provided as well as half board and flight to and from the UK.

Canvas Holidays employ children's couriers who are responsible for looking after customers'
children and organising activities for them twice a day. Previous experience in teaching, nursery
nursing or playgroup leading is necessary but you don't need to be fluent in a foreign language.
They have also introduced a 'nanny' service to look after children under 4 with a maximum of 5
children under the responsibility of each nanny.

Eurocamp also employ children's couriers on selected campsites from mid-May to mid-September.
They are responsible for organising several hours of activities per day for customers' children and
previous experience of working with children is usually required.

BUNAC organise a camp counsellor programme in the United States which is open to both students and non-students. Traditionally American parents send their children to summer camps – mostly permanent wood-hutted sites where the children can spend from 1 to 8 weeks. The programme is open to anyone between the ages of 19.5 and 35 who positively likes working with children, who is free for at least 9 weeks between mid-June and the end of August, who does not object to hard work and long hours and who can offer some skill or experience in one or more activites such as sports, watersports, music, arts and crafts, science, secretarial, pioneering, entertainments (for shows), dance, first-aid etc. At the end of the counselling programme you have time off up to early October for a holiday and travelling around.

For a registration fee of £48 BUNAC organise your placement as a counsellor at an approved camp, plus orientation and training; organise your work papers and obtain your J-1 special work visa; pay for your flight to and from North America (which is recouped from your salary at camp); provide a night in a hotel/hostel upon arrival in the USA plus your transport to the camp; provide 8-9 weeks free food and accommodation whilst counselling at camp; pay a total net salary of $360 or $420. Your only other expenses are your own travel to and from the interview and orientation and your medical/accident/baggage insurance (£70). You are also required by the visa to take at least £200 for your holiday time before and after camp (BUNAC recommend that you take at least £200 more).

Interviews start in November and continue until the end of May so it's worth applying early and requesting the earliest possible interview date. Membership of BUNAC costs £3.

Quest Adventure, Grosvenor Hall Leisure, Bolnore Rd, Haywards Heath, West Sussex RH16 4BX, Tel: 0444 441300

Thomson Holidays, Greater London House, Hampstead Rd, London NW1 7SD
Tel: 01 387 9321

Canvas Holidays Ltd, Bull Plain, Hertford, Herts, SG14 1DY, Tel: 0992 553535

Eurocamp Travel Ltd, Edmundson House, Tatton St, Knutsford, Cheshire WA16 6BG
Tel: 0565 50022

Adventure Holidays, Vacation Work International, 9 Park End Street, Oxford OX1 1HJ

BUNACAMP, 16 Bowling Green Lane, London ECIR OBD, Tel: 01 251 3472

Teaching
Teaching English as a Foreign Language
There are few places in the world that do not use English either as a spoken medium or as a necessary part of business transaction and communication. Unfortunately, whereas as few years ago, anybody who spoke English could pick up a teaching job fairly easily especially in much of Europe and the Far East, nowadays the competition is so fierce that unless you have a TEFL (Teaching English as a Foreign Language) qualification or experience, it is difficult to find work. There are, of course, the seedy language centres that specialise in 'conversation' but jobs in these are usually very poorly paid. Without qualifications you might be lucky and pick up some private tuition through the local paper or personal contacts particularly if you have been in the country for a while. It is still possible for unqualified teachers to find work in parts of Spain and in Greece. The other factor to bear in mind is that usually you must be prepared to commit yourself to the minimum of a term as it is unfair on students to be left high and dry in the middle of a course. In addition, countries where English language teachers are sought after, such as Japan, Korea, Taiwan and Hong Kong, tend to be very expensive places to live and in our experience you need to work for a long time in order to pay the rent before you can save enough to subsidise your further travels. Finally, as with any skilled job, language teaching is only rewarding if you know what you are doing. Floundering away in front of a bunch of students who either look blank or repeat "no understan'" quickly palls.

Having said all this, teaching English is an excellent way both of meeting the indigenous population and financing your trip, and if you intend to travel extensively and on an open-ended basis, it is well worthwhile obtaining a qualification before you leave. You can obtain a list of centres offering the most widely accepted Royal Society of Arts Preparatory Certificate from the RSA Publications Department by sending them an s.a.e. There is generally a long waiting list for a place on the course which involves 100 hours of exacting training with a practical emphasis.

International House is part of English International, an educational charity trust which specialises in the teaching of English as a foreign language and in teacher training courses in TEFL. They organise a four week course in London and Hastings which costs £616.20 (1989), and you have to find your own accommodation. There are currently some 70 schools in 17 countries (Barcelona, Madrid, Lisbon, Rome, Cairo and Rio, for example) affiliated to the central organisation which is responsible for recruiting and training teachers for these schools, centres so you could always enrol on one of their courses on your travels. They also have schools in the UK. Working in Britain at a school for overseas students is a useful way of practising your skills and building up contacts before going abroad.

Once you are qualified there are many possibilities for working abroad and if you would rather fix up something before you go there are many organisations which can help. The best schools to work in (in terms of pay, organisation and facilities) are those recognised by the British Council. The Association of Recognised English Language Schools (ARELS) produces an annual guide listing all the private schools in the UK which have been recognised by the British Council for TEFL, and who are members of the Association. There is also a monthly bulletin to all members in which qualified TEFL teachers can place an advertisement for a minimal fee. The Central Bureau recruits teachers for one year appointments in TEFL in Bulgaria, Denmark and Hungary and Christians Abroad recruits TEFL teachers for Turkey. Gabbitas-Thring have a few vacancies for EFL teachers in South America, the Middle and Far East and Africa. The British Council Overseas Educational Appointments Department recruits TEFL teachers mainly for its own Direct Teaching Operations overseas. Applicants must have an RSA Preparatory Certificate in TEFL (at the very least), though they prefer the RSA Diploma in TEFL, together with at least one or two years' relevant experience and if you have a Post-graduate Certificate in Education with a substantial TEFL content so much the better.

ERASMUS (European Community Action Scheme for the Mobility of University Students) regularly organise programmes for staff to teach at a university in another member state. Priority is granted to reciprocal programmes in which teachers are exchanged for substantial periods (at least one month) and they provide financial support in respect of travel and accommodation expenses.

Once you are in a country the equivalent to the British Yellow Pages is a useful source of addresses of Language Schools or Business Schools, as are notices in Youth Hostels and the Consulate. English language newspapers also carry advertisements for teachers and it is advisable to start looking before the start of term. The British Council have schools in many parts of the world; as mentioned above, their standards are high.

In some countries, notably Japan and other affluent parts of the Far East, it is possible to find work teaching English to executives in large companies. Surprisingly there is often scope for unqualified people to obtain this type of teaching which is often highly lucrative. You will have to have the confidence to walk into the offices of a large corporation and find the right person to contact (usually the personnel or training officer) and, most importantly, you will need to look very presentable.

RSA Publications Department, Murray Road, Orpington, Kent

International House, 106 Piccadilly, London W1V 9FL, Tel: 01 491 2598

Pilgrims Training Courses, 8 Vernon Place, Canterbury, Kent CT1 3HG, Tel: 0227 455486

Association of Recognised English Language Schools, 125 High Holborn, London WC1V 6QD, Tel: 01 242 3136

Central Bureau for Educational Visits and Exchanges, Seymour Mews House, Seymour Mews, London W1H 9PE

Gabbitas-Thring Services Ltd, 6-8 Sackville Street, Piccadilly, London W1X 2BR
Tel: 01 439 2071/01 734 0161

The British Council Overseas Educational Appointments Dept, 65 Davis Street, London W1Y 2AA, Tel: 01 499 8011

Teaching Other Subjects

If you are a qualified teacher of any subject, especially technical, maths and science subjects, there are a number of organisations which recruit or advertise for staff to work overseas. The Association of Commonwealth Universities' Appointments service provides member universities and certain other institutions with facilities for announcing vacancies and assessing candidates in the UK and elsewhere. These facilities are used most frequently by the universities in Australia, New Zealand, Hong Kong, Malaya, Zimbabwe, Papua New Guinea, Botswana, Lesotho, Swaziland, the South Pacific and the West Indies. The Catholic Institute for International Relations (CIIR) recruits professionally qualified and technically skilled people to take development work in the Third World. Teachers of General Science, English Language, Maths, Agricultural/rural science, Technical Drawing, Metalwork, Woodwork and Building are recruited to work in Zimbabwe's rural secondary schools. Applicants should have a degree in a relevant subject or a full City and Guilds training with a minimum of two years teaching experience or practice. CIIR provides a two year contract, a salary adequate for a single person, a return flight, various allowances and pre-departure briefings.

The Central Bureau administers a scheme for the interchange of qualified, experienced teachers of Modern Languages and related subjects for 3 weeks, 6 weeks, one term or one year with Austria, Belgium, France, The Federal Republic of Germany, Spain, Switzerland, the Soviet Union and also with Denmark. It also organises the UK/US Teachers Exchange Scheme in collaboration with the US Information Agency and the Fulbright Commission. Academic year and half-year exchanges are available for qualified British teachers with at least four years' experience.

Christians Abroad recruits graduate teachers for service abroad in church related schools and colleges and in independent and state controlled institutions, particularly in Africa, the Caribbean and Pacific Islands.

The European Council of International Schools (ECIS) assists international English-medium schools (pupils 3-19 years) throughout the world with staff recruitments. It operates a year-round placement service for teachers/administrators with a minimum of 2 years' teaching experience who register with the Council as individual members, and it organises an annual two-day Recruitment Centre held in London, attended by 60-70 school representatives and 300 candidates.

Gabbitas-Thring Service Ltd recruits well-qualified and experienced staff at all levels for English-medium schools overseas. The League for the Exchange of Commonwealth organises one year post-to-post exchanges for qualified teachers at all levels in Australia, Bahamas, Barbados, Bermuda, Canada, India, Jamaica, Kenya, New Zealand, Sierra Leone, Trinidad and Zimbabwe. Applicants should be British subjects between the ages of 25 and 45 years with at least five years' experience and are expected to arrange accommodation for their exchange partners.

Professional and Executive Recruitment place teachers in posts in Britain and overseas. The Committee for International Cooperation in Higher Education assists in the recruitment of academic, technical, library and administrative staff to universities and colleges in Botswana, Ethiopia, Fiji, Ghana, Guyana, Hong Kong, Kenya, Lesotho, Liberia, Malawi, Malaysia, Malta, Mauritius, Nigeria, Papua New Guinea, Sierra Leone, Singapore, Sudan, Swaziland, Tanzania, Uganda, West Indies and Zambia.

Voluntary Services Overseas (VSO) recruits over 250 teachers each year to assist in the development of education in Third World countries. The range of posts filled cover secondary, primary teacher training, tertiary and special education. For primary, middle and secondary posts in all service children's schools overseas, apply to Service Children's Education at the Ministry of Defence.

The British Council recruits assistant teachers in the infant, junior and senior departments of British-type and international schools in Latin America, Africa, the Middle East and Southern Europe. For the majority of posts at least two years' experience is required, with, for some, specialist knowledge of modern methods of maths and science teaching or in EFL. Occasionally, a Postgraduate Certificate in Education or a qualification in EFL is acceptable without experience.

Association of Commonwealth Universities, 36 Gordon Square, London WC1H OPF, Tel: 01 387 8572

Catholic Institute for International Relations, 22 Coleman Fields, London N1 7AF, Tel: 01 354 0883

Central Bureau for Educational Visits and Exchanges, Seymour Mews House, Seymour Mews, London W1H 9PE, Tel: 01 486 5101

Christians Abroad, Livingstone House, 11 Carteret Street, London SW1H 9DL, Tel: 01 222 2165

European Council of International Schools, 21b Lavant Street, Petersfield, Hants GU32, 3EL, Tel: 0730 68244

Gabbitas-Thring Service Ltd, 6-8 Sackville Street, Piccadilly, London W1X 2BR, Tel: 01 439 2071/01 734 0161

League for the Exchange of Commonwealth Teachers, Seymour Mews House, 2nd floor suite, 26-37 Seymour Mews, London W1H 9PE, Tel: 01 486 2849

Professional and Executive Recruitment, 4th floor, Rex House, 4-12 Lower Regent Street, London SW1Y 4PP, Tel: 01 930 6573/7 (Overseas Posts)

The British Council Overseas Educational Appointments Dept, 65 Davies Street, London W1Y 2AA, Tel: 01 499 8011

Committee for International Cooperation in Higher Education, Higher Education Division, 10 Spring Gardens, London SW1A 2BN, Tel: 01 930 8466

Service Children's Education, Authority 2a, Directorate of Army Education, Ministry of Defence, Court Road, Eltham, London SE9 5NR, Tel: 01 954 2242, ext 4206/4224

Tourism

The tourist industry provides an enormous source of temporary, unskilled jobs throughout the world, perfect for the traveller. In the high season, work permit regulations are often ignored. Hotels, campsites, winter resorts all offer a wide range of jobs during the season and short term work can be found in other months as well – the autumn in Paris (the time of congresses and trade shows), Oktoberfest in Munich (late September to mid-October), Christmas in Rome and Florence (entire month of December), spring in Greece (March).

Hotels and Catering
Hotel work is really confined to Europe, North America, Australia and New Zealand. Third World countries have more than enough local people to do the kind of unskilled hotel work

generally available to the traveller but if you have specialist skills in, say cooking or hotel management, then you will be able to find work in large hotels anywhere.

Unless you speak the language of the country you are in the chances are that you will have to be content with the most menial jobs, such as washing dishes, making beds, cleaning etc. The work is tedious but generally you have the afternoons free. If you have a good knowledge of the language then it is possible to get work as a waiter; receptionists and hotel bar staff require fluent languages and usually these jobs are given to nationals of the country.

If you want to find a job for yourself before you go, Alpotels publish a booklet, costing £5, which gives guidance on how to set about it. It gives advice on how to approach the job once it has been offered, and how to hold on to it. It does not list any actual jobs but does list 90 resorts in Switzerland, 30 in Austria, 30 in France, 5 areas in Germany and 6 in Italy which have seasonal hotels. It describes briefly the character of each resort, what languages are spoken and whether it is primarily a winter or summer resort. They also publish lists (50p a list) of the main hotels in these resorts, to which you can write or which you can visit in search of work.

You could also get a list of hotels from the Tourist Office of the country/ies you intend to visit. The Directory of Summer Jobs Abroad (Vacation Work) has an extensive list of hotel addresses in Europe. You could apply to British tour operators direct for vacancies in their own hotels in France. These hotels are run by an entirely British team for entirely British guests; the standards are lower than in national hotels and the atmosphere more informal. In the mountain resorts there is more time to ski in the afternoon but you get only one free day per week and are paid only 1/3 of the minimum legal wage in France. The advantage of these hotels is that you don't need to speak French. Visit your local travel agency and pick up an assortment of ski brochures. You should write to named hotels' personnel department before the end of the summer, as positions are filled well in advance.

Quest Adventure provide a range of special activity courses for schools and young people in the UK and South of France, the Ardeche, and the French Alps. The centres accommodate from 60 to 500 guests and jobs available include chefs (£85-150 pw), assistant cooks (£55-75 pw), bar staff (£50-100 pw) and domestic staff (£30 pw). Board and lodging, as in nearly all hotel work, is included.

Sunsail operate watersports centres in Greece and Turkey and require bar staff, cooks and catering assistants.

Alpotels (London), PO Box 388, London SW1X 8LX (send sae 8in x 5in)

Quest Adventure, Grosvenor Hall Leisure, Bolnore Road, Haywards Heath, West Sussex RH16 4BX, Tel: 0444 441300

Sunsail, The Port House, Port Solent, Portsmouth, Hants PO6 4TH, Tel: 0705 219847

Anglia Agency (Hotel & Catering), 15 Eastern Avenue, Southend-on-Sea, Essex SS2 5QX, Tel: 0702 613888

Pubs

In many English-speaking parts of the world, Hong Kong and the Caribbean for example, or in places like Majorca and the Costa del Sol, there are a great many English-style pubs where it is possible to find work. Most countries also have bars which, although usually staffed by native residents, will sometimes offer casual work to Western travellers. Bars and pubs are also important meeting places and thus useful for finding out about work of any kind in the area.

Women who look for bar work should be careful though that the pub or bar is just that and not, as is often the case in Hong Kong or parts of London or New York for example, a club with 'hostess' facilities!

Winter resorts

In the larger resorts which cater for thousands of holidaymakers, there are many types of job from chalet maids to snow groomers, lift attendants to instructors, shop assistants to cooks.

The ski season generally spans mid-December to early May in Europe, mid-late November to April in North America, and June to October in Australia and New Zealand.

'Jobs in the Alps' is an agency which places British workers in mountain resorts in Switzerland for the whole winter season as well as the summer. You must be prepared for hard work though as in the national hotels the standards are very high. Most winter jobs start early to mid-December and last until mid-April; there may be a few jobs starting in January when replacements may be needed. Most summer jobs are for three months, from mid/end June to mid/end September. Some by the lakeside are from Easter to October, and very few just July and August. You will be on probation for two weeks and if you wish to leave or the employer is not satisfied you will be replaced. If you wish to remain you must undertake to stay the whole season so you should not apply unless you fully accept the drawbacks and intend to stick it out for the entire period.

French and/or German is usually needed in Switzerland; French always in France; English only is acceptable in Germany.

The jobs available may include waiters, kitchen work (preparing food, washing up), hall porters/night porters, chambermaid and swimming pool cleaners. There are jobs, especially for women, in cafes taking orders, serving food and drink; good language skills are essential for these. Mountain restaurants may need staff to serve, clear away or clean. It is hard and often dull work but you are in contact with the skiers and on the spot to ski if you get time off. You get one and a half free days per week and are given a mid-day meal, in some cases all meals. Accommodation is usually provided which may be up the mountain and you may be given a lift pass. Salaries for most jobs will be in the region of £400 net per month.

All employees get full board and lodging. In Switzerland they are entitled to cheap lift passes and cheap travel. You will work approximately 48 hours a week with two free days; these may have to be missed in high season but will be given later or paid in lieu.

In France hotels pay like the Swiss but days off are limited and may be cancelled or postponed in high season as French hotels employ minimum staff; French is essential. In Germany long term (summer) jobs pay less but you can take two days off per week and, as most Germans speak English, German is not necessary. Jobs in the Alps does not send workers to France or Germany but the British are entitled to work on exactly the same terms as those nationals according to EEC regulations.

Many ski tour operators offer accommodation for their customers in chalets and need to employ chalet maids to cook, clean and generally look after the chalets. The work is hard but usually afternoons are free and accommodation is provided as well as ski passes etc. Contact ski holiday companies through brochures in your local travel agent.

In EEC countries it is worth visiting the local Tourist Offices and Job Centres.

Jobs in the Alps, PO Box 388, London SW1X 8LX, Tel: 01 235 8205

Working in Ski Resorts, Vacation Work International, 9 Park End Street, Oxford OX1 1HJ

Couriers/Reps

Although competition is fairly tough for courier jobs it is an excellent way of combining work with travel. A good knowledge of languages is essential
as the work involves taking groups on tours in Europe or dealing with hotels, making transport arrangements etc.

EF Educational Tours recruit Tour Directors to lead groups of visiting American and Canadian school students on tours of Europe, ranging from 9 to 35 days in length. Most of these visitors choose a 9 – 11 day programme and travel during the Easter holidays. Others choose to travel during the summer and often opt for longer tours. Groups usually consist of 30-50 school children from different parts of the US and Canada, accompanied by their teachers and other adults. They travel mainly by coach, with bed, breakfast and dinner pre-booked. Local guides lead group sightseeing tours in major cities. The Tour Director handles hotel check-ins, reconfirms bookings, gives group briefings, liaises with the teachers accompanying the group, provides interesting commentaries during bus transfers etc. You need to be at least 20 years of age, available to work over Easter and June/July, have a working knowledge of major European cities, be fluent in English and have a knowledge of a second language or two. Although they recruit from central and southern England they also consider applicants who live in the immediate vicinity of Paris, Rome, Madrid and Heidelberg.

Thomson Holidays employ representatives whose job it is to meet clients at the airport, transfer them by coach to their hotel and give them assistance and advice. Fluency in English plus at least one other language (Spanish, Italian, German, Greek, Portuguese, Serbo-Croat or Russian) is essential and representatives are normally placed in a country where the native language is their main foreign language. Basic accommodation which may have to be shared is provided. Salary is paid monthly and a commission is paid on excursion sales. After 9 months service (cumulative) holiday concessions are available. Applicants should be aged between 21 and 30 and should be single.

Apart from the various holiday companies (the addresses of which you will be able to find from travel agents' brochures), World Wine Tours employ couriers for tours in the wine regions of Spain, France, Germany, Italy and Portugal. A knowledge of the wine regions is necessary as well as the ability to speak French and a knowledge of Italian, Spanish or Portuguese is an advantage.
They need staff from March to October and provide accommodation.

Write to the personnel department of large holiday companies for jobs as a courier. They often provide intensive training courses.

EF Educational Tours, EF House, 1 Farman Street, Hove, Brighton BN3 1AL,
Tel: 0273 723651

Contiki, Bromley, Kent. Tel: 01 290 6977

Thomson Holidays Ltd, Greater London House, Hampstead Road, London NW1 7SD,
Tel: 01 387 9321

World Wine Tours Ltd, 4 Dorchester Road, Drayton St Leonard, Oxon OX9 8BH,
Tel: 0865 891919

Campsite Couriers

Campsites require a different type of courier to work on sites where customers stay in large tents or mobile homes and where all the necessary equipment is provided from beds and chairs to knives and forks. The work is physically demanding and requires some practical skills: tents have to be cleaned to a high standard, broken equipment has to be repaired or replaced, tents have to be maintained. In addition the courier has to welcome new arrivals, keep accounts, fill in inventories, organise activities for customers (football, barbecues etc) and generally see to the smooth running of their part of the campsite. A reasonable knowledge of French, Italian, Spanish or German is usually required, though for montage/demontage (setting up and dismantling of tents) no language skills are needed.

Eurocamp employ some couriers for the whole season (April until late September) and others for only half a season, on sites in France, Belgium, Luxembourg, Germany, Switzerland, Austria, Italy, Yugoslavia and Spain. Interviews start in December and continue into the early part of the following year and early application is advised. They require couriers who are employed for at least one half season; senior couriers for the full season; site supervisors for the largest sites; warehouse assistants/drivers for stock control and deliveries of equipment; montage/demontage assistants for the beginning/end of the season only and children's couriers from mid-May to mid-September. They welcome applications from couples and as long as you are over 18 they are fairly flexible about age. Pay is from £70+ a week plus a bonus for each week worked on completion of the contract. Accommodation and travelling expenses (including a return ferry ticket) are provided.

Club Cantabrica organises camping holidays in Italy, Spain and France and require couriers and maintenance staff for the summer season from mid-May until early October. Wages are from £40 per week, plus a bonus at the end of the season. People with experience are preferred and the minimum age is 21 years. Self catering accommodation is provided and they pay travel costs from Watford and insurance.

Canvas Holidays employ some 360 couriers for sites in France, Germany, Switzerland, Austria, Spain, Yugoslavia, Italy and Corsica. They lay great emphasis on the personal touch and expect their couriers to spend time after work visiting customers and arranging get togethers. They need resident campsite couriers, children's couriers and watersports couriers responsible for teaching customers in the use of windsurfers, dinghies or canoes. From mid-April to mid-June they employ a team for montage. Pay is from £75 per week, plus an extra £10 per week for every week worked on completion of the contract. Return travel to Europe, accommodation and medical and property insurance is provided as well as pedal cycle or moped on site.

Eurocamp, Edmundson House, Tatton St, Knutsford, Cheshire WA16 6BG

Club Cantabrica, Holiday House, 146-148 London Rd, St Albans, Herts AL1 1PQ
Tel: 0727 33141/66177

Canvas Holidays Ltd, Bull Plain, Hertford, Herts SG14 1DY, Tel: 0992 553535

Sport Instructors
Many campsites and adventure centres employ sports instructors to teach a variety of water sports and other outdoor activities at their centres abroad. PGL employ a large number of young people at their holiday centres in Britain and Europe as do Quest Adventure. Sunsail require Dinghy sailing/windsurfing instructors and cruising instructors for their watersports centres in Greece and Turkey. Experienced grooms and stable staff are needed for equestrian centres around the world and The Sporting Life and Horse and Hound carry advertisements for these jobs. The Agency 'Outdoors Unlimited' keep a register of instructors so it's worth applying to get your name on the list.

PGL, 874 Station Street, Ross-on-Wye, Herefordshire HR9 7AH, Tel: 0989 764211

Quest Adventure, Grosvenor Hall Leisure, Bolnore Rd, Haywards Heath, West Sussex RH16 4BX, Tel: 0444 441300

Sunsail, The Port House, Port Solent, Portsmouth, Hants PO6 4TH, Tel: 0705 219847

Canvas Holidays Ltd, Bull Plain, Hertford, Herts SG14 1DY, Tel: 0992 553535

Wildlife Parks/Game Reserves/National Forests
In many areas tourism jobs can be combined with conservation work which is becoming more and more important as a combination of an expanding population and shrinking natural resources has made it necessary for us to manage and regulate the use of these resources. Whatever the field you wish to work in, initially you will find that the job involves hard physical work and affords only modest pay. 'Apprenticeship' is essential before a person can assume full responsibilities. The

conservationist must learn how to perform not only technical work but also much of the common routine work of labourer's, mechanics and artisans. The objectives are to improve efficiency, safety and overall performance. A conservationist might have a job as a government forester, but when called upon, must be prepared to perform emergency services in fire fighting, rescue work or first aid or to lead expeditions into remote areas.

Virtually every country in the world is now paying attention to conservation. There are thousands of wildlife refuges, national forests, parks, seashores and the like. In order to obtain formal employment you will usually need to be a permanent resident of that country but once you are 'on location' you stand a good chance of finding work.

If you are interested in finding out more about paid work in the field of conservation, you might find it useful to contact the following environment headquarters in overseas countries listed below:

Afghanistan: Minister of the Interior, Kabul
Argentina: Servicio Agrario Internacional, Secretaria de Estado de Agricultura y Ganaderia, Avda Paseo Colon 974, 1305 Buenos Aires
Australia: Department of Home Affairs and Environment, Wales Ctr, Canberra City, ACT 2601
Austria: Federal Minister for Health and the Environment, Stubenring 1, Vienna A1010
Bahamas, The: Ministry of Agriculture, Fisheries and Local Govt, PO Box N3028 Nassau
Bangladesh: Ministry of Agriculture and Forests, Government of the People's Republic of Bangladesh, Dacca
Barbados: Parks and Beaches Commission, West Wing, Public Bldgs, Bridgetown. Barbados National Trust, 48 Blue Waters, Christ Church
Belgium: Secretary of State for Public Health and Environment, Rijksadministratief Centrum, Cite Administrative, Esplanade B-1010, Brussels
Benin: Minister of Rural Development and Cooperative Action, Porto Novo
Bolivia: Minister of Agriculture and Rural Affairs, Avenida Camacho 1471, La Paz
Botswana: Director of Wildlife and Tourism, PO Box 131, Gaborone
Brazil: Secretaria Especial do Meio Ambiente, Ministero do Interior, Esplanada dos Ministerios, Brasilia, DF 70,000, Brazil
Bulgaria: Ministry of Forestry and Environment, 17 Antim 1 Street, Sofia 4000
Burundi: Ministre de l'Agriculture, de l'Elevage et du Developpement Rural, Bujumbura
Cameroon: Ministry of Agriculture, Yaounde
Canada: Minister of the Environment, Ottawa, Ontario K1A 0H3
Central African Republic: Minister in charge of Water, Forests, Hunting, Fishing and Tourism
Chad: Ministre du Developpement Agricole et Pastoral et des Calamites Naturelles, Ndjamena
Chile: Ministry of National Resources, Av Libertador O'Higgins, 280/Santiago,
China: National Wildlife Protection Association of the Republic of China, 3rd floor, 180 Roosevelt Rd, Sec 5, Taipai, Taiwan, Republic of China
Colombia: Director, INDERENA, Calle 26 No 13B-47, Bogota, DE, Colombia
Costa Rica: Parques Nacionales, Ministerio de Agricultura y Ganaderia, Apartado Postal 10094, San Jose. Departamento de Conservacion y Reforestacion, Instituto Costarricense de Electricidad, Apartado Postal 10032, San Jose. Asociacion Costarricense para la Conservacion de la Naturaleza (ASCONA), Apartado Postal 3099, San Jose
Czechoslovakia: Ministry of Technology and Investment, Division of Environmental Protection, Slezska 9, 120 2g, Praha, 2-Vinohrady. Association for the Protection of Nature, Nerudova 31, 110 00 Praha 1 – Mala strana
Denmark: Minister of the Environment, Slotsholmsgade 12 DK-1216, Copenhagen K
Ecuador: Ministro Ministerio de Recursos Naturales y Energeticos, Sanata Prisca 223 y Manuel Larrea, 239-11 Quito
El Salvador: Ministerio del Interior, Palacio Nacional, San Salvador. Direccion General de Recursos Naturales Renovables, Ministerio de Agricultura y Ganaderia, Blvd Los Heroes y 21 Calle Poniente, San Salvador. Asociacion Amigos de la Tierra (Friends of the Earth), Edificio Comercial Apt 616, San Salvador.
Ethiopia: Wild Life Conservation Dept, PO Box 386, Ras Desta Damtew Ave, Addis Ababa

Fiji: Ministry of Urban Development, Housing and Social Welfare, Govt Bldgs, Suva

Finland: Ministry of Interior, Division of Environmental Protection, Hakaniemenkatu 2, 00530, Helsinki 53

France: Minister for the Environment and Human Ecology, 3 rue de Valas, 75042 Paris, CEDEX 01 Valois, Paris 1er

Germany, Federal Republic: Federal Ministry of Food, Agriculture and Forestry, 5300 Bonn

German Democratic Republic: Minister for Environment and Water Resources, DDR-102 Berlin, Hans Beimler Str 70/72

Ghana: Ministry of Lands and Natural Resources, Dept of Game and Wildlife, Accra

Great Britain: Secretary of State for the Environment, 2 Marsham St, London SW1P 3EB

Guatemala: Direccion Tecnica de Recursos Naturales Renovables, Ministerio de Agricultura, Ganaderia y Alimentacion, 7a Avenida 12-90, Zona 13, Guatemala City 31-02-01

Guyana: Minister of Health and Public Welfare, Upper Brickdam, Georgetown

Haiti: Minister of Agriculture, Natural Resources and Rural Development, Damien

Honduras: Ministry of Natural Resources, Tegucigalpa, DC

Iceland: Ministry of Culture and Education, Minister Hverfisgata 4-6, Reykjavik

India: Ministry of Agriculture, Division of Forestry/Indian Forest Service, New Delhi 110001

Indonesia: Directorate of Nature Conservation and Wildlife Management, Jalan Ir H Juanda No 9, Bogor, West Java

Iran: Department of Environmental Protection, PO Box 1430, North Villa Street Tehran

Ireland: The Secretary, Dept of Agriculture, Kildare St, Dublin 2. The Secretary, Custom House, Dept of the Environment, Dublin 1.

Israel: Environmental Protection Service, Hakirya Building III, Jerusalem. Nature Reserves Authority, Hanatziv 16, Tel Aviv

Italy: Minister of Culture and Environment, Rome

Ivory Coast: Ministre des Eaux et Forets, BP v 94, Abidjan

Jamaica: Minister for Agriculture, c/o The House of Parliament, Duke St, Kingston

Japan: Director General of Environment Agency, 3-1-1 Kasumigaseki, Chiyoda-ku, Tokyo

Jordan: Minister of Municipal and Rural Affairs and the Environment, PO Box 1799, Amman. Royal Society for the Conservation of Wildlife, Jebel Amman, Fifth Circle, Amman

Kenya: Ministry of Tourism and Wildlife, 30027 Nairobi Ministry of Natural Resources, 30126 Nairobi

Korea: Office of Forestry, Conservation Division, Seoul

Kuwait: Minister of Commerce and Industry, PO Box 2944, Kuwait

Lebanon: Minister of Public Health, Agriculture, Cooperatives and Housing, Beirut

Lesotho: Ministry of Agriculture, PO Box MS 24, Maseru

Liberia: Ministry of Agriculture and Forestry, Sinkor, Monrovia

Libya: Minister of State for Agricultural Development, Tripoli

Luxembourg: Minister of Environment, 57-90 blvd de la Petrusse, Luxembourg-Ville, GD

Madagascar: Ministre de la Production Animale et des Eaux et Forets, Antananarivo

Malawi: The Secretary for Forestry and Natural Resources, P/B 350, Lilongwe 3

Malaysia: Ministry of Science, Technology and Environment, Oriental Plaza, Jalan Parry, Kuala Lumpur

Mali: Services of Waters and Forests, rue Testard, Bamako

Malta: Minister of Health and Environment, 15 Merchants Street, Valletta

Mauritania: Minister of Rural Development, PO Box 366, Nouakaott

Mauritius: Ministry of Agriculture, Natural Resources and Environment, Port Louis

Mexico: Secretariat for Health and Welfare, Av Chapultepec No 284-140 piso, Delegacion Cuauhtemoc , 06700 Mexico

Morocco: Minister of Housing, Urban Development and Environment, Rabat

Nepal: National Parks and Wildlife Conservation Office, Banejnor, Kathmandu

Netherlands: Director of Conservation of Nature and Open Air Recreation, PO Box 5406, 2280 HK Rijswijk ZH, The Netherlands

New Zealand: Commission for the Environment, PO Box 10241, Wellington. Environmental Council, PO Box 10382, Wellington. National Parks Authority, c/o Dept of Lands & Survey, PO Box 1200, Wellington. Nature Conservation Council, c/o Dept of Lands & Survey, PO Box 1200, Wellington.

Nigeria: Commissioner for Agriculture and Rural Development, 34036 Ikoyi Rd, Lagos

Norway: Ministry of the Environment, PO Box 8013 dep, Oslo 1. Norges Naturvernforbund (Norwegian Wildlife Organisation), Akersgt 63, Oslo 1

Oman: Adviser for Conservation and Development of the Environment, PO Box 246 Muscat

Pakistan: Ministry of Food, Agriculture and Rural Development, National Council for Conservation of Wildlife, Bungalow No 7-G, St No 51, F-6/4, Islamabad

Panama: Ministerio de Desarrollo Agropecuario, Apartado 5390, Panama 5, Republica de Panama

Paraguay: Minister of Agriculture and Husbandry, Pte Franco y 14 de Mayo, Asuncion

Peru: National Office of Evaluation of Natural Resources (ONERN), Office of the Prime Minister, Lima

Philippines: Ministry of Natural Resources, Diliman, Quezon City. Philippines Parks and Wildlife Commission, Quezon Memorial Park, Quezon City

Poland: Institute of Environmental Protection, 02-078 Warsaw UI,

Portugal: Secretario de Estado do Ordenamento Fisico e do Ambiente, Rua Castilho 50, 1200 Lisboa

Qater: Minister of Industry and Agriculture, PO Box 1966, Doha, Arabian Gulf, Qater

Romania: National Council for Science and Technology, Str Roma No 3234, Bucharest

Rwanda: Office Rwandais du Tourisme et des Parcs Nationaux, BP 905, Kigali

Saudi Arabia: Minister of Agriculture and Water, Riyadh

Senegal: Ministry of Rural Development, Dakar

Sierra Leone: Chief Conservator of Forests, Ministry of Agriculture and Forestry, Tower Hill, Freetown

Singapore: Minister for Environment, Princess House, Alexandra Rd, Singapore 0315

Somalia: Ministry of Tourism, Mogadisho

South Africa: Department of Water Affairs, Forestry and Environmental Conservation, Private Bag X313, Pretoria 0001

Spain: Instituto Nacional para la Conservacion de la Naturaleza (ICONA), Ministerio de Agricultura, P de la Infanta Isabel 1, Madrid 7

Sri Lanka: Director, Wild Life Conservation, c/o National Zoological Gardens of Sri Lanka, Anagarika Dharmapala Mawatha, Dehiwala

Sudan: Ministry of Health, Khartoum

Swaziland: Ministry of Agriculture, PO Box 162, Mbabane, Swaziland. Manager, Mlilwane Game Sanctuary, PO Box 33, Mbabane, Swaziland

Sweden: National Board for Environmental Protection, Box 1302, S-171 25 Solna 1, Sweden

Switzerland: Swiss Federal Office for Environmental Protection, Hallwylstr 4, 3003 Berne. Swiss Federal Forestry Inspectorate, Division of Nature and Scenic Conservation, Laupenstrasse 20, 3001 Berne

Syria: Minister of Agriculture and Agrarian Reform, Damascus

Tanzania: Ministry of Natural Resources and Tourism, Clock Tower Branch Bldg, Ind. Ave, Box 9372, Dar Es Salaam

Thailand: National Research Council, 196 Phaholyothin Rd, Bangkok 9

Togo: Minister of Rural Development

Trinidad and Tobago: Conservator of Forests and Wildlife, Ministry of Agriculture, Forestry Division, Port-of-Spain, Trinidad

Turkey: Office of the Undersecretary for Environmental Affaris, Prime Ministry, Ankara

Uganda: Ministry of Land and Survey, PO Box 7096, Kampala Ministry of Agriculture and Forestry Resources, PO Box 102, Entebbe

USSR: State Committee on Science and Technology, 11 Gorky St, Moscow

United Arab Emirates: Minister of the Interior, Abu Dhabi

Upper Volta: Minister of Environment and Tourism, Ouagadougou

Uruguay: Ministerio de Industria y Energio, Rincon 747, Montevideo

Venezuela: Ministry of Agriculture, Direccion de Recursos Naturales Renovables, Torre Norte, Centro Simon Bolivar, Caracas. Ministry of Environment and Natural Resources, Torre Sur, Centro Simon Bolivar, Caracas

Yugoslavia: Federal Committee for Agriculture, Bulevar Avnoja No 104, 11070 Novi Beograd, Yugoslavia

Zaire: Commissaire d'Etat a l'Environment, Kinshassha

Zambia: Ministry of Water and Natural Resources, Department of National Parks and Wildlife Service, PO Box Private Bag 1, Chilanga

Voluntary Work

There are a great many opportunities for voluntary work all over the world and it is an excellent way of seeing the country you are visiting as well as doing something worthwhile. It is also a good way of learning a language, of perhaps acquiring new skills and making contacts both with local people and fellow travellers who can offer you travel advice and information. It's also a very useful way of acclimatising to a different country or culture without depleting your hard-earned resources.

Agencies who organise voluntary work will ask volunteers about their background, competence, views and intentions so it as well to be quite clear in your own mind why exactly you are offering your services. Are you escaping from unemployment, a boring job or personal problems? Will voluntary service give you experience that will improve your employment prospects? Are you politically motivated? Have you been called by God? Whatever the reason you must be aware that all voluntary work involves commitment whether it be in agriculture, teaching, building, mechanics or nursing.

There are several agencies that provide opportunities for voluntary work.

International Voluntary Service (IVS) organise three schemes:
1. Long-Term volunteering: This is for professionally trained volunteers to work in Southern Africa for a minimum of two years.
2. International Workcamp Programme: Workcamps are organised in Britain, Europe and the USA.
3. Development Education and Exchange Programme: This exchange takes place with some countries in Africa and Asia.

GAP Activity Projects offers school-leavers the chance to spend some time in another country, living and working with its people during a 'gap' year before Higher Education. GAP students are expected to undertake full-time work for a minimum of six months and in return for their services, they are provided with board, accommodation and limited pocket-money. In 1989 over 300 British GAP volunteers worked in Australia, Canada, Falklands, France, India, Israel, Mexico, Nepal, New Zealand, Pakistan and West Germany and GAP is currently exploring opportunities to extend its work to include exchange schemes with the United States, Eastern Europe, Japan and China. A wide variety of work is on offer – teaching or doing general duties in schools, assisting with community projects, caring for the sick and the handicapped, farming help with conservation, office work in banks and businesses. All GAP volunteers pay their own air fares and must take out the necessary insurance. A GAP fee (ranging from £200 to £300) is payable at least a month before departure which is either in the early autumn for those who can leave straightaway or in January/February for those who need to raise money for their 'gap'.

Tear Fund organise a Graduate Apprenticeship Programme (GAP) designed to give field experience to graduates with technical skills who would like, eventually to serve God overseas. You must have a skill and a training appropriate to development work overseas, eg health care, agriculture, forestry, engineering, administration, theological education or trade skills. GAP personnel are attached to a project for approximately one year. Accommodation is provided by the project but the trainee is expected to pay a reasonable contribution. Tear Fund will make an award of not less than £1000 to each trainee and will cover international travel costs and the trainee is expected to raise additional finances equivalent to the amount awarded. Trainees also receive an equipment allowance which covers the cost of personal and medical insurance arranged by Tear Fund.

The ATD Fourth World Movement includes people of all backgrounds and cultures who form a partnership to enable the poorest and most excluded to participate in their communities and change their destiny. The backbone of the movement is a corps of 350 full-time volunteers in 18 countries (Europe, North America, Asia, Latin America and Africa) both single and married men and women of all ages and diverse backgrounds. They organise weekend workcamps in London and summer workcamps near Paris where people who are interested in discovering the Movement's work and possibilities of making their own commitments are welcome to participate.

The Shaftesbury Society is a charity that promotes Christianity in a variety of ways and needs volunteers in the United Kingdom. They establish and operate Christian community centres and churches in urban priority areas; provide education for handicapped young people; provide accommodation, care and support for handicapped adults and old people; provide holidays for the elderly, for handicapped adults and young people; and provide practical help for the urban poor.

Voluntary Service Overseas (VSO) recruits 600 men and women each year to work in Third World countries. Posts with VSO are for a minimum of two years though many people choose to serve for more. Most posts are filled in September, but a significant number of posts are filled each January. Accommodation and payment (based on local rates) are provided by the community, organisation or government making the request. VSO pays for recruiting and training volunteers, their air fares, national insurance, medical insurance and equipment grants. They also pay a mid-tour grant after one year of service. Volunteers should be aged between 20 and 65 and have no dependents though there are certain jobs overseas for which they do accept dependents (ask for their leaflet "VSO and Dependents"). Applicants must have skills and experience in fields such as Natural Resources and Agriculture (crop production, fisheries, forestry etc) Business and Social Development (accountants, lawyers, managers, computer programmers, social workers etc) working with the disabled, education (English teaching, librarians, maths/science teaching etc) health (pharmacists, doctors, midwives, nutritionists etc) or trades, crafts and engineering (bricklayers, plumbers, land surveyors etc).

VSO also recruits and sponsors volunteers to work through the United Nations multi-national programme, the United Nations Volunteers, UNV. British nationals may be asked to work in any developing country alongside volunteers from many other nations. The work is much the same as VSO work, though it is often more specialised and needs a more focused experience. The allowances are larger and unlike VSOs, UNVs may be posted with a dependent spouse and up to two children.

The countries in which VSO works are: Antigua, Bangladesh, Belize, Bhutan, China, Dominica, Egypt, Fiji, The Gambia, Ghana, Grenada, Guinea-Bissau, Indonesia, Kenya, Kiribati, Liberia, Malawi, Malaysia, Maldives, Montserrat, Nepal, Nigeria, Pakistan, Papua New Guinea, Philippines, Sao Tome, St Kitts/Nevis, St Lucia, St Vincent, Sierra Leone, Solomon Islands, Sri Lanka, Sudan, Tanzania, Thailand, Tonga, Tuvalu, Uganda, Vanuatu, Zambia and Zimbabwe.

IVS, 162 Upper New Walk, Leicester LE1 7QA, Tel: 0533 549430

GAP Activity Projects (GAP) Ltd, 7 King's Road, Reading RG1 3AA, Tel: 0734 594914

Tear Fund, 100 Church Road, Teddington, Middx TW11 8QE, Tel: 01 977 9144

ATD Fourth World Movement, 48 Addington Square, London SE5 7LB, Tel: 01 703 3231

The Shaftesbury Society, 2A Amity Grove, Raynes Park, London SW20 0LH, Tel: 01 946 6635

VSO, Enquiries Unit, 317 Putney Bridge Road, London SW15 2PN, Tel: 01 780 1331

Work Camps

Work camps provide volunteers with the opportunity of short-term voluntary work and enable them to live and work together on a common project providing a constructive service to the community. The camps run for periods of 2-4 weeks, April-October and at Christmas and Easter, and the work is usually for 7-8 hours per day, 5-6 days per week. The camps are mainly intended for those aged 16-18+ and the work can include building, gardening and decorating, providing roads and water supplies to rural villages or constructing adventure playgrounds. Accommodation is usually provided, often in schools, community centres, hostels or camping.

Food is generally provided on a self-catering basis with volunteers taking it in turns to prepare and cook meals. Volunteers pay a registration fee and arrange and pay for their own travel and may be expected to contribute towards the cost of board and lodging. Most international workcamps consist of 10-30 volunteers from several countries and English is often the lingua franca, though for community work a knowledge of the country's language is essential. French is the other most widely used language.

It is essential to include a large stamped addressed envelope or at least 2 International Reply Coupons (IRCs) available from the post office when applying to a workcamp organisation.

There are several organisations that operate work camps throughout the world.

The Christian Movement for Peace (CMP) is an international movement open to all who share a common concern for lasting peace and justice in the world and is therefore open to non-Christians as well.

CMP has branches in Belgium, Britain, France, Portugal, Germany, Holland, Malta, Italy and Switzerland. They also exchange volunteers with organisations in Turkey, Morocco, Spain, USA, Poland, Denmark, Canada and Czechoslovakia, and have a few places available on camps in Yugoslavia and Hungary. For workcamps in Eastern Europe it is essential to apply as early as possible.
The work is usually 30-35 hours per week, in exchange for free food and accommodation. Volunteers do not receive pocket money and they are expected to be committed to the success of the project. The work is very varied and includes playschemes, construction, fruit picking, ecology and assisting with community development. The groups of volunteers are mixed and there are usually 10 to 20 people working on any one project. It is often possible to place two or more volunteers together on the same project though CMP usually place most applicants as individuals.

The application fee per project is £15 for those in Britain and £24 for projects abroad. If you have problems paying the fee the office may be able to help if you contact them before applying. Volunteers in Britain (and usually overseas) are insured against third party risks and accidents but volunteers are advised to insure themselves against illness and loss of or damage to personal belongings. Volunteers must pay their own travel costs and make their own arrangements to and from the projects. The minimum age limit is 18 (17 for projects in Britain) and work permits are not required.

Volunteers should try to give a choice of four projects and although some projects are full by the beginning of June, it is often possible to accept volunteers after this date.

Medium term volunteers are funded by the EEC young workers exchange programme and work for six months in community projects in return for basic board, lodging and pocket money.

Some other examples of projects in 1989 were:
"Belgium, supporting an ecological project which informs the public about recycling methods of organic waste into compost and using its products. The centre has contact with projects in Africa and South America, supporting returned volunteers. Work at the demonstration centre will be manual."

"France, Rigney. Restoration work at an old castle and mill, fixing floor boards, and laying a path, with benches, leading to the castle. Accommodation on site."

"Palestine, Jaffa. The league of Arabs in Jaffa tries hard to maintain the Arabic/Palestinian community in Jaffa. They are working on improving the conditions there in the fields of social security, education and housing. Work consists of clearing the street and public places, working in a public garden and reconstruction work."

"Canada, Grindstone Island Coop, Ontario. This is an education centre and runs camps for children aged 7-12 years and 13-25. A wide variety of activities are offered including swimming, arts and crafts, drama, dance and cooperative games. Volunteer cabin counsellors are required to live in with the campers and work with a small group in the late evening and during free time. There is also a maintenance work camp which involves building projects, painting and maintenance. There is also plenty of time for swimming, canoeing etc."

"USA, Pennsylvania. Work on a farm which is a non profit educational centre offering farming, gardening, crafts and music. Volunteers will live in this community and help with cheese making, the animals, gardening, wood gathering and the art exhibition."

The World Council of Churches sponsors workcamps through its Ecumenical Youth Council in Europe (EYCE) programme in several regions of the world, including Europe, the Caribbean and the Middle East and particularly in Africa and Asia. These take place in the spring and summer. The age limit for their work camps is 18 to 30 years and volunteers have to make their own travel arrangements and pay their own travel expenses. They are also expected to make a contribution of about $3 a day towards the general living expenses of the camp.

Examples of workcamps in 1989 were:

"Britain, Isle of Mull. Work included, vegetable gardening, cooking, digging peat, repairing dikes and ditches. Cost: £50 (per week)."

"Poland. This workcamp involved 5 days of working in a Publishing House for approximately 12 hours per day. The remainder of the time was free for excursions, hiking and discussions. Cost: Travel + minimum exchange of 15 DM per day + 5.000 zl."

"Egypt, Sweif City. Participants experienced community living in an old Monastery/Conference Centre, helped to renovate, paint and do carpentry work in the building, as well as assisting in local agricultural projects. It was an opportunity to learn about the history and everyday life of Egypt, share youth concerns and reflect on their economic, social and spiritual life."

"Cuba, Havana. Field work which gave the opportunity for involvement in agricultural projects. Also a Biblical-Theological Reflection Camp. Accommodation in Church properties and family homes. Spanish an advantage.
Cost: Travel + donation."

In Africa workcamps are organised in Kenya, Sierra Leone, Togo and Uganda and work involves tree planting, harvesting, agriculture, and construction. Volunteers are also required for workcamps in India, Malaysia and Pakistan where they will help with construction of roads and dams and bring sanitation and hygiene up to date.

International Voluntary Service (IVS) organise workcamps in Britain, Europe and the USA. The camps last 2-4 weeks, and are held mainly in the summer with a few camps in the winter and spring. Particular skills are not required though you should have previous workcamp or similar experience if you wish to go abroad, especially if you want to go to Eastern Europe. Details of winter workcamps are available in November, spring camps in February and summer camps in April. Details for Eastern Europe are available in March. Membership of IVS is £6 (unwaged), £8 (student), £12 (ordinary). Camps in Britain cost £10, and those abroad £20 in exchange for free food and accommodation. IVS workcamps can be children's holiday schemes; manual work; activities for people with physical or mental disabilities; "solidarity" in support of people in other countries; conservation or ecology work; anti-racist or anti-facist work; women's camps. Anyone over 18 can go on a workcamp and people with disabilities are welcome on many camps.

IVS also organise the Development Education and Exchange Programme which takes place with some countries in Africa and Asia, mostly in the period June to September. Preparation of volunteers begins earlier, with a series of weekend activities in England.

Quaker International Social Projects (a department of the Religious Society of Friends) has two functions, a home and an international operation. The home function is to run 15 short term projects in Britain and Northern Ireland each year. The projects are set up to do work for a local community that could not otherwise be done. The work is done by volunteers, half of whom come from abroad.

The international function is to set up an exchange for volunteers to and from Britain. QISP has agreements with organisations in most of the countries of Europe who run similar projects as well as the Soviet Union, Turkey and North Africa. People wishing to go abroad should have some experience of working on a project in Britain so that they have gained some idea of what it is like to live and work as part of a multicultural group.

As on projects in Britain, volunteers pay for their own travel and any necessary visas and receive free board and lodging at the workcamp. The accommodation is usually provided only for the fixed term of the project although some countries offer holidays afterwards as part of the project. The work is generally not arduous, usually 30 hours a week. There is a wide choice of projects: manual work on environmental or ecological schemes, building playgrounds, working with children and people in disadvantaged areas.
The registration fee for projects abroad is currently £20.

The Tear Fund has links with a wide variety of projects in approximately 80 countries in the developing world. Applicants need to be committed Christians in good health, aged 20 and over. From time to time the Overseas Personnel Department is asked by projects to send a Task Force Team made up of between two and ten people. The skills required vary, depending on the assignment to be undertaken. Practical experience in some field such as engineering, plumbing or building is an advantage although sometimes a general handyman is what is needed. However those without appropriate skills are also considered and often accepted. The type of work ranges from basic repair work to construction of buildings, provision of piped water and specialised installation or repair of equipment. Task Force Teams attend an orientation course during the few days immediately prior to departure from Britain. Assignments for 1990 will operate between July and early September and will last for 7 weeks. There is the possibility of teams being sent at other times of the year as well, depending on the matching of projects with applicants' availability. Potential team members should be able to raise £650 towards costs and Tear Fund arranges all international travel and covers board and lodging costs.

CMP, Bethnal Green URC, Pott Street, London E2 OEF, Tel: 01 729 1877

EYCE Secretariat, 217 Holywood Road, Belfast BT4 2DH, N. Ireland, Tel: 0232 651134/5

IVS, 162 Upper New Walk, Leicester LE1 7QA, Tel: 0533 549430

QISP, Religious Society of Friends, Friends House, Euston Road, London NW1 2BJ
Tel: 01 387 3601

Task Force Team Coordinator, Tear Fund, 100 Church Road, Teddington,
Middx Tw11 8QE, Tel: 01 977 9144 Ext 272

Conservation
Conservation is crucial if our planet is to be saved and our environment safeguarded and relies heavily on volunteers to clean rivers and ponds, protect rare plants and animals, work in national parks and mountain areas, restore canals and railways, restore churches, castles or agricultural buildings, maintain footpaths and bridleways etc.

It is a good idea to get some experience in your own country before setting out on your travels.

In Great Britain the National Trust have a programme of Acorn Projects, Camps and Special Working Holidays on countryside in the care of the National Trust throughout England, Wales and Northern Ireland. Tasks range from dry stone walling in the Peak District to vegetation mapping in Surrey. Both job satisfaction and enjoyment are high priorities on all the Projects, achieving work which is necessary to the Trust, but which could not be afforded without voluntary help.

All you need is to be reasonably fit and happy to accept the friendly atmosphere that a close-knit community offers. Volunteers are encouraged to attend independently but the Trust does accept two people coming on a project together. Facilities can be fairly basic although accommodation is always in buildings such as volunteer hostels, farm houses or village halls.

Most Acorn Projects consist of about 14 volunteers ranging in age from about 18 to the mid 20's and have a leader who, together with the Warden, will show you how and what to do. You do not need to be a member of the National Trust and enthusiasm, rather than experience, is the important requirement for most projects. The normal working day will be from 9.00 am to about 5.00 pm. Evenings are free and there is one free half day in the week. All volunteers are expected to help with the cooking and domestic chores on a rota basis.

A sleeping bag and/or blanket are essential and you will need an air-mattress or Karrimat to sleep on unless bunks or beds are specified. The Trust also requires participants to have an Anti-Tetanus injection before starting work on a project. You will need tough windproof workclothes, rainwear, protective gloves, strong working boots and/or wellingtons. Travel to the Project is at your own expense, though arrivals will be met at the nearest rail or coach station at times specified on the joining instructions.

The Trust also organises 21 Plus Projects for people between the ages of 21 and about 35. Accommodation is based in comfortable Volunteer Hostels having both bunk beds and showers. Obviously these 'wrinklies' need more cosseted surroundings.

If the dates of the 21 Plus Project are not convenient, volunteers are welcome on any Acorn project.

In 1989 the National Trust started to organise week long Construction Projects in the south and west of England. These projects involve rebuilding specialist dry stone walls or old farm buildings under careful instruction with about eleven other volunteers. An interest in building work and a keenness to learn new skills count more than ability or experience although experience is useful.

In addition the Trust recruits volunteers to undertake Biological Surveying in week long residential projects which survey, record and map the flora of botanically important countryside in the care of the National Trust. Volunteers need to have a little knowledge of British flora and be familiar with the use of botanical keys. Each project will include a full day's training about the site and its vegetation, and volunteers are asked to bring a field guide (eg Francis Rose) and a x10 hand lens.

The cost of most Acorn Projects is £19.

International Camps have also been established recently. There are 12 vacancies on each camp and young people aged between 18 and 35 attend from all over Europe. These camps carry out special conservation work in Yorkshire and are an excellent way to make contacts before you go abroad. The charge for the International Camps is £22 per week.

If you are not able to commit yourself to a full week but would like to get some experience of conservation work before you start your travels the National Trust organise Weekend Camps in Yorkshire. The camps run from Friday evenings to Sunday afternoon and the price of £10 includes accommodation and food which you cook yourself.

The British Trust for Conservation Volunteers (BTCV) run a programme of Natural Break conservation working holidays throughout England, Wales and Northern Ireland. Costs start at £27 per week. Some of the projects undertaken by them include tree planting and woodland management, repairing drystone walls, clearing polluted ponds and choked canals and improving access to the countryside.

In addition they organise International Conservation working holidays in which UK volunteers are invited to join members of local European communities in a network of cultural and ecological conservation projects lasting between two and three weeks. Assignments have ranged from rebuilding a 17th century Portuguese bridge to erecting a bird-hide in the Evros Forest in Greece. Experience in practical conservation skills is not necessary and as the project leader or assistant will be bilingual a knowledge of the language is not essential. Prices start around £40 per week and include accommodation, food, transport from the pre-arranged pick-up point and holiday insurance. You need to make your own travel arrangements and inoculation against tetanus is essential. Accommodation is basic and varies from camping to dormitory facilities. Everyone is expected to help with the cooking and cleaning.

Examples of BCTV's camps in 1989 were: "Greece, in the Evros Forest near the Turkish border. The area is a favourite habitat for birds of prey. The Evros Delta nearby is a wetland of international importance. Working with local people to construct steps and a footpath leading to a bird hide. Accommodation is camping out in a village school. Leisure interests include Greek dancing and birdwatching. Cost: £100."

"Greece and Corfu. Restoration of monastery, drystone walling and forest management. Accommodation camping or dormitory. Cost: £100 approx."

"Denmark, the Forest of Gribskov on the edge of Lake Esrum. Working with Senior Scouts and the Forestry Department on canal clearance, revetments and tree work. Cost: £75."

"Italy, Maremma Regional Park on the Mediterranean coast. Habitat management. Dormitory accommodation. Leisure activities: watching the deer, wild boar and crested porcupine resident in the area. Cost: £110."

"Iceland, Porsmork, S. Iceland, or Jokulsarglufur National Park: Path construction etc. Accommodation in a hut owned by the Icelandic Touring Club or camping. Cost: Your own food and travel."

"France, Berck near le Touquet. A chance to work with a group of French volunteers on a coastal access project for the disabled. Camping with cooking and washing facilities. Leisure activities include swimming, windsurfing and sightseeing. Cost £70."

"Turkey, Aide on the Black Sea. Conversion of derelict land to park area by a mixed group from all over Europe. Accommodation in a local hotel. Cost: £50."

"Portugal, Pedrogoa Grande, 145 miles from Lisbon. Working with Portuguese volunteers undertaking revetments and bridge construction."

As with many other voluntary projects, this work can be a useful way of acclimatising and can be followed by a period of travel or paid employment.

'Cathedral Camps' hold camps at Cathedrals, Abbeys and sometimes major Parish Churches throughout Britain. Their aim is the preservation, conservation, restoration and repair of Cathedrals and Christian buildings of the highest architectural significance. Volunteers can expect both spectacular and routine work, such as maintenance work, cleaning roof voids, spiral staircases, wall memorials, traceried woodwork and painting iron railings etc under the guidance of craftsmen. Camps are held at different Cathedrals for one week from mid July to early September. Volunteers work a 36 hour week, 8.30 to 5.00 pm each day, with Saturday afternoon, Sunday and evenings free. Food and self-catering accommodation is provided, usually in the Cathedral hall or similar building. A letter of recommendation is required from anyone attending a Camp for the first time. Volunteers are asked to pay £25 for each Camp. Many Local Education Authorities have awarded grants to Cathedral Camp volunteers towards the cost of the Camp and travelling expenses so it's worth applying to your Local Education Authority. A certain number of bursaries are available for volunteers who are able to show they cannot afford to join a Camp and for volunteers who are unemployed, and British Rail offers a young people's concessionary rate if you are under 24.

The rather grandly titled Commission of the European Communities Directorate-General of

Environment, Nuclear Safety and Civil Protection has limited funds at its disposal in the environmental training field, which it uses to support demonstration projects.

The main source of funding for training projects concerned with environmental protection is the European Social Fund (ESF). If you have a project that you think is of a demonstration nature, you can apply for funding from the ESF by contacting your local authority which may submit an application to the Commission through the appropriate national authorities.

Each county of the UK has its own Nature Conservation or Wildlife Trust organisation who run many different voluntary projects. A complete list of these groups is kept by the Royal Trust for Nature Conservation.

You could also try contacting the various environmental organisations such as Greenpeace, or the local equivalent of Friends of the Earth in different European countries to see if they know of any projects that need conservation volunteers. Most European countries have active Green parties who will also be glad to give advice.

The National Trust, Volunteer Unit, PO Box 12, Westbury, Wilts BA13 4NA, Tel: 0373 826302

BTCV, 36 St Mary's Street, Wallingford, Oxon OX10 0EU, Tel: 0491 39766

Cathedral Camps, Manor House, High Birstwith, Harrogate, North Yorks HG3 2LG, Tel: 0423 770385

Toc H Projects, 1 Forest Close, Wendover, Bucks HP22 6BT (Short-term residential opportunities, including conservation)

The Waterway Recovery Group, Neil Edward, 24a Avenue Road, Witham, Essex CM8 2DT (Conservation, building and demolition projects on canals in England and Wales)

Earthwatch, 680 Mt Auburn St, Box 403, Watertown, Mass 02272, USA. Tel: (617) 926 8200

Greenpeace, 30-31 Islington Green, London N1 8XE. Tel: 01 354 5100

Royal Society for Nature Conservation, The Green, Nettleham, Lincs LNZ 2NR Tel: 0522 752526

Friends of the Earth, 26-28 Underwood Street, London N1 7JQ. Tel: 01 490 1555

Archaeology

'Archaeology Abroad' is an organisation that provides information about opportunities for archaeological fieldwork and excavation outside Britain. They publish an annual bulletin in March and two news sheets in the Spring and Autumn which include details of projects overseas for which volunteers or staff are requested.

Most directors of digs prefer to recruit volunteers and staff who have had experience in excavation techniques and the Council for British Archaeology recommend that inexperienced diggers work on at least one or two British excavations before applying for work abroad. The Council publishes 'British Archaeological News' which lists training excavations and volunteer places in the UK. The majority of digs occur during the summer months and there is an official minimum age limit of 16 years though for many digs the minimum age is 18.

The Archaeological Institute of America publishes the 'Archaeological Fieldwork Opportunities Bulletin' which gives details of digs in most parts of the world (US, Canada, Caribbean, Central America and South America, UK, Europe, Eastern Mediterranean and Near East, Africa and Asia). The digs vary from the very expensive, needing expertise and experience to those providing all expenses with no experience necessary.

Two examples are: "Belize, St George Caye Bay (Sept 10 1798). The objective of the programme is to find and uncover the Spanish Little Armada ships which were sunk in the Bay of St George's Caye by the HMS Merlin and the valiant Belizeans on September 10th 1798. This battle resulted in Great Britain establishing the colony of British Honduras and is an important event in the history of Belize. The tuition for the field school is $4000; lodging, meals, and insurance are included. Transportation to the site is up to the participant. Volunteers are welcome with a minimum stay of one week, but a two week stay is preferred. Experience is required and divers should be certified. The cost for volunteers, with a minimum age of 18, is $1120 which includes accommodation, meals and insurance. Travel to the site, visits to the Maya ruins, Blue Hole and other scenic places in Central America, are not included."

"Brassempouy, France, Grotte du Pape (Upper Paeleolithic). Participants in the field school, museum interns or volunteers should be at least 18 and plan to stay for more than fifteen days in July and August. No experience is necessary and all expenses, excluding travel to the site are paid by the Trustees of the excavations. Training will be in prehistory at the cave where the occupation was during the Upper Paleolithic era. The art of wall painting and artifacts will be studied."

The Institute also provide the following useful information about going on archaeological digs much of which is also applicable to any work overseas.

"Before you leave: Many countries require permission and clearance for foreign workers through antiquities services and government agencies. Unless the option is clearly stated, appearing at a site unannounced would be personally irresponsible and might place the expedition in an uncomfortable situation. Once advance contact has been established with a representative of the expedition team, find out what equipment is necessary, what clothes are the most sensible for work and leisure time, what will be the general schedule of operations, and what amount of sight-seeing will be available.

Read about the local culture and climate and plan your packing accordingly. Pack as lightly as possible, since space is often limited and transportation may be less than efficient... The regular 'Passport' column in Archaeology magazine is an excellent source of expert advice on expedition travel.

Bring a small medicine kit with the usual bandages, disinfectants and ointment. Additional items which are on the worker/traveller's list are an alarm clock, a good flashlight with extra batteries, sunglasses, headscarf or hat, sunscreen, regional guide book, reading material, notebook, pens and pencils, measuring tape marked in inches and centimetres, a canteen and a good pocket-knife.

At the site: ....If you have never worked on an excavation before, do some homework and keep a flexible and cooperative attitude. The former will ensure that you will have some familiarity with professional archaeology, the material which is under investigation, the local culture and climate. The latter will certainly make you a better worker and a more pleasant person to live with under what can be less than ideal conditions...

The director and supervisors will appreciate your questions and your attention to detail and procedure and there are a number of 'dig-life' lessons to learn by word of mouth from other who have had experience. You may be able to avoid learning the lessons the hard way: by trial and error. If you find that you have time on your hands and wish to make the most of the season, staff are usually more than willing to give informal instruction in the different skills required by an expedition (drafting, recording etc).

Try to set up a personal schedule outside of work hours. You will have a better chance of maintaining a comfortable working/sleeping/leisure schedule and a stock of clean clothes...

In closing: Keep your eyes and ears open. Archaeological fieldwork is not the romantic treasure-hunt of Hollywood movies. On the contrary, archaeology is a blend of scientific disciplines and requires, therefore, methodical attention to procedure and detail. The processes of archaeological investigation change constantly and most expeditions staff individuals with a variety of specialised skills over an extended period of time. You can learn a great deal from the experienced excavators and specialists...."

The Institute also advises that applicants on a dig should keep in mind age requirements, responsibilities at the site, working and living conditions. If you have missed a deadline, you should not give up on an excavation which you find particularly interesting. Write immediately to the contact person expressing your enthusiasm. The opportunity may be available for the following season, and there is always the chance that the volunteer or staffing needs have not yet been met.

Earthwatch Expeditions Inc sponsor scientific research expeditions and members share both the costs and labours of field work. They publish a monthly magazine which gives information on archaeological digs as well as expeditions on architecture, marine ecology, ornithology etc. Examples are:

"Hillfort of Portugal (1000 to 200 BC). To discover more about this area's Iron Age, the archaeologist Francisco Queiroga needs volunteers for a third season of Earthwatch support to investigate the Castro de Penices to find out when the fort was built, who built it and how they lived. Share of costs: $1,290."

"Origins of Korean Agriculture, Seoul, Yangyang, Kyongju and Pusan, South Korea. Sarah Nelson is taking a broad-based approach to understanding how the earliest Korean farmers learned and plied their trade... Volunteers will not only scrutinise ancient artifacts but will record and photograph both current and potential prehistoric land use by walking transects over rolling terrain for two-hour stints. Staying in traditional yogwans, or inns, recruits will alternate restaurant food with team-cooked fare. Share of costs: $1,395".

In Great Britain the National Trust has a team of archaeologists which carry out excavations on sites of historic interest on National Trust property, for example at Hadrian's Wall and Corfe Castle. They need volunteers to help with this work and applicants do not need to be National Trust members. Costs are generally £19 for a week and include board and lodging.

British Archaeological News, Council for British Archaeology, 112 Kennington Rd, London SE11 6RE, Tel: 01 582 0494

Archaeology Abroad, 31-34 Gordon Square, London WC1H 0PY

Belgium: Jeugd en Jultureel Erfgoed-Vlaanderen, Slangbeckweg 3, B-3520 Zonhoven

Germany: Internationale Jugendgemeinshaftdienste, Geschaftsstelle Nord, Katharinenstrasse 13, D-3200 Hildesheim

Holland: Nederlandse Jeugdbond Voor Geschiedenis, Bureau NJBG, Prins Willem-Alexanderhof 5, 2595 BE DEN HAAG

Italy: Gruppo Archaeologico D'Italia, Via Tacito 41, 00193 Roma

Spain: Societad Catalan d'arquelogia, Bailen 125, e-08009 Barcelona

USA: The Archaeological Institute of America, 675 Commonwealth Ave, Boston, MA 02215, Tel: (617) 353 9361

Earthwatch Expeditions Inc, 680 Mount Auburn Street, PO Box 403, Watertown, MA 02272, Tel: (617) 926 8200

The National Trust, Volunteer Unit, PO Box 12, Westbury, Wiltshire BA13 4NA, Tel: 0373 826302

Chapter 6

Working Overseas

AUSTRALIA
Main language: English
Currency: Australian dollar
Capital: Canberra
Exports: Wool, Cereals, Metals, Meat
Climate: Spring – Sept-Nov
Summer – Dec-Feb (North 27°C +, humid with rain; South warm)
Autumn – March-May
Winter – June-Aug (North 13°C +, South cool)

Entry Requirements
Australian High Commission, Australia House, Strand, London WC2B 4LA
Australian Consulate, Hobart House, 80 Hanover Street, Edinburgh EH2 2DL
Australian Consulate, Chatsworth House, Lever Street, Manchester M1 2DL
Australian Embassy, Fitzwilton House, Wilton Terrace, Dublin 2
Australian Tourist Commission, 1st Floor, Gemini House, 10-18 Putney Hill,
London SW15. Tel: 01 780 1424

Visas
All travellers, except Australian and New Zealand passport holders, must have a valid visa to enter Australia. (There is no fee for visitor's visa.) These visas can be obtained in person or by mail from one of the visa offices listed above. You should not pay for your tickets until you know that you have a visa. Visitor's visas are available to applicants who intend genuine visits to Australia as tourists, for business purposes (discussions or negotiations), to see relatives, and in certain circumstances for prearranged medical treatment. Visitors admitted to Australia for any reason are NOT permitted to undertake employment or studies. Except for very limited categories, they are not eligible to apply for permanent residence while in Australia.

Working Holiday Visas
The objective of the working holiday scheme is essentially to provide young people with opportunities for cultural exchange. As part of this cultural exchange you may undertake work as an incidental part of your holiday. Full-time employment of more than three months with the same employer would be contrary to the spirit of the scheme. For the most part the work undertaken should be part-time or of a casual nature. The period of temporary stay allowed will be up to 12 months though you might be able to extend this once in Australia (if you have already had a working holiday visa you will NOT be eligible to apply for a second one in this country).

Only single persons or childless married couples who wish to travel extensively around Australia with the option of taking casual work to supplement their holiday funds are eligible. Applicants must be aged between 18 and 25, though in exceptional cases, persons aged up to 30 years may be considered. You should hold a valid UK, Irish, Canadian or Dutch passport and have enough money for return fares and normal maintenance for a substantial part of your planned holiday (usually £1,500 for 6 months, or £2,000 for 12 months). Employment in Australia must not be prearranged except on a private basis and on the applicant's own initiative and you should have reasonable prospects of obtaining temporary employment. Your application should not be submitted without: 3 passport-sized photographs signed by yourself; evidence of funds eg bank or building society statements; your valid passport; a stamped self-addressed envelope for the return of your passport.

Permanent Residence
Australia's migration programme has three major components: Family Migration, Economic Migration, and Special Eligibility Migration.

Family Migration: (a) Preferential Family Migration – This category reunites close family members and fiances of Australian citizens and permanent residents. You must have a relative in Australia who is able to sponsor you. Your sponsor must be able to provide you with accommodation and financial support and have resided lawfully and permanently in Australia for at least 2 years. This residential requirement does not apply if you are sponsored as a spouse minor child or fiance. You may apply in this category if you are related to your sponsor in Australia as a: spouse, fiance, unmarried child under 18 years of age, parent who has more children lawfully and permanently resident in Australia than in any other single country, or the last remaining brother or
sister or non dependent child, outside Australia.

(b) Concessional Family Migration – This category reunites other close relatives of Australian citizens and permanent residents but applicants must also pass the Points Test. You may apply in this category if you are related to your sponsor in Australia as a: non-dependent child, parent who does not meet the Balance of Family test for consideration in the preferential family category, brother or sister or niece or nephew.

Economic Migration: This component covers people who are needed in Australia to meet specific shortages in the labour market or to promote business enterprise. There are four categories:

(1) Tripartite Negotiated Arrangements – for skilled people who have been nominated by an employer within the framework of an industry wide agreement and who are under 55 years of age.

(2) Employer Nomination Scheme – for skilled people who have been nominated by an employer in Australia and are under 55 years of age.

(3) Business Migration Programme – for people with a successful business background who intend to set up a substantial business and with assets amounting to at least $500,000 available for transfer to Australia.

(4) Independent – for young, mature, skilled people from a wide range of employment backgrounds, who are able to pass the Points Test. Special Eligibility Migration: This component covers people who would represent a demonstrable gain to Australia or who have a close association with Australia. They do not need to pass the Points Test. Included are:

(a) Dependent Family Members of New Zealand citizens, spouses and dependent children under 18 years of age.

(b) Former Citizens or Permanent Residents who in certain circumstances, lost their Australian citizenship (eg through marriage) or have spent the greater part of their formative years (up to age 18) in Australia, and have maintained, or now have, stronger ties with Australia.

Travel
Probably the cheapest and most interesting way to get to Australia is with one of the low cost worldwide flights with stopovers in several places en route.

Trailfinders have several routes to Australia: London-Singapore-Sydney or Melbourne-Bali-Bangkok-London (£829); a one-way trip from UK-Amsterdam-Toronto or Vancouver-Honolulu-Fiji-Sydney (£448). (The normal return fare with Trailfinders to Sydney is from £715 to £910 depending on the time of year).

Being an air courier is also a fairly cheap way of flying to Australia though you are usually limited by the amount of time you can stay there. CTS Courier Club however do a one way fare to Sydney for £350 and a return for £625.

Once you are in Australia there are many ways to get around and see the country. Standby fares save 20% on regular economy air fare; you buy your ticket at the airport on the day of departure and you fly when a seat becomes available. Many Australian Airlines offer a 25% reduction on internal flights to visiting adult overseas passengers in conjunction with journeys commenced outside Australia on international round-trip excursions. Tickets may be purchased through your travel agent. The Budget Austrailpass allows unlimited economy travel for all rail travel and should be purchased through your travel agent before your departure to Australia. The pass also entitles you to a 20% discount on Hertz car rental. A 14 day pass costs $A 385, a 90 day pass $A990, and a 7 day extension on any pass costs $A200. Travelling by coach is an economical way to travel around Australia and has the advantage of being extremely flexible. There are many bargain bus passes available which must be purchased before you arrive in Australia. These passes offer unlimited coach travel; a 7 day pass costs approx $A197. The Kangaroo "Road 'n Rail" Pass offers unlimited rail and coach travel through mainland Australia and is valid for 28 days ($A750 economy class).

Camping Tours and Safaris are another way of seeing places off the beaten track, especially the outback. There are usually no age restrictions and all camping gear is carried on board and sleeping bags and mattresses are provided. Some UK representatives for these trips are Sprint, Top Deck Travel and AAT Kings.

Driving yourself is probably the best way to get the most out of your trip to Australia. You could buy a secondhand camper van or 4 wheel drive and get to places that public transport doesn't get to. It would also make job finding, especially in the outback, a lot easier. A camper van has the advantage of inbuilt accommodation. Make sure you buy a model that is common so that spare parts will be easy to find and make sure you or your travelling companion/s are mechanically minded – distances are vast! Members of the AA or RAC can make good use of similar motoring clubs in Australia which provide touring information, maps and publications and breakdown assistance. It is worth remembering to take your membership card with you.

'Australia, A Traveller's Guide' is available free from:
The Australian Tourist Commission, 4th floor, Heathcote House, 20 Savile Row, London W1X 1AE
Trailfinders, 194 Kensington High St, London W8 7RG. Tel: 01 938 3939
STA Travel, 74 & 86 Old Brompton Rd, London SW7. Tel: 01 937 9962
Contiki Holidays, Bromley BR1 1UW, Kent. Tel: 01 290 6777
CTS Ltd, Unit 2, London House, 243/253 Lower Mortlake Rd, Richmond, Surrey TW9 2LL. Tel: 01 940 3334
Exchange Travel, Exchange House, 66/70 Parker Road, Hastings, East Sussex. Tel: 0424 423 571
Southern Cross Travel, 2 The Square, Riverhead, Sevenoaks, Kent TN13 2AA. Tel: 0732 740421
Greyhound International Travel, 14-16 Cockspur Street, London WC2H OJR. Tel: 01 839 5591
Compass, 9 Grosvenor Gardens, London SW1W OBH. Tel: 01 828 4111 (Railway Rep)
Sprint, Suites 313-319 Walmar House, 296 Regent Street, London WIR 5HD. Tel: 01 631 4447
Top Deck Travel, 131-133 Earls Court Rd, Kensington, London W8 6EJ. Tel: 01 938 3366
AAT Kings Tours, 2nd Floor, William House, 14 Worple Rd, Wimbledon, London SW19 4DD. Tel: 01 879 7322
SSA/STA (Student Travel Bureau), 220 Faraday St, Carlton, Melbourne, Victoria 3053. Tel: (03) 347 6911
STA, 1a Lee St, Sydney, NSW 2000. Tel: (02) 212 1255

Accommodation
Hostels are probably the cheapest places to stay. Fees vary from $A4-$14 per night. For admission to Youth Hostels and their affiliates in Australia you need to have a current International Youth Hostel card before you arrive in Australia, though some hostels can arrange membership when you arrive. In addition to those operated by the YHA there are privately run hostels throughout Australia. Full details of these, and suggestions for travelling around on a budget are contained in "Australia, A Travel Survival Kit" (Lonely Planet).

To experience the real Australian lifestyle, you can stay as a paying guest with Australian families in private home accommodation or on a working farm property. Home accommodation is available throughout Australia and ranges from budget to luxurious, from guest rooms to cottages or units. You can book these on arrival in Australia but it is recommended that you get details well in advance.

Youth Hostels Services Ltd, 14 Southampton St, Covent Garden, London WC2E 7HY. Tel: 01 836 8541
YHA, 60 Mary St, Surry Hills, NSW 2010. Tel: (02) 212 1512/1511
Bed and Breakfast Australia, Home From Home Int, Hill Farm, Hittisleigh, Exeter, Devon. Tel: 064 724 613
Australian Farmhost and Farm Holidays, Sprint, Suites 313-9, Walmar House, 296 Regent St, London W1. Tel: 01 631 4447

Working Holidays

Agriculture
The UK Sponsoring Authority for the International Exchange of Young Agriculturists arranges a three month programme to Australia leaving in August or November for a five month programme. This can be combined with a 12 month 'Around the World' programme enabling trainees to work in Australia for 6 months followed by 6 months in Western Canada. Regular farm hours are worked and local standard rates of pay apply. Only applicants intending to make a career in agriculture or horticulture can apply. Participants must be between the ages of 18 and 25 and have at least two year's practical experience.

The IAEA also have an exchange programme similar to that mentioned above. The largest intake of trainees occurs in September with trainees arriving for the summer months. At this time of year trainees are placed on farms in Queensland, New South Wales, Victoria, Tasmania, South Australia and Western Australia to help with cropping, sheep, dairy, vineyards etc. Trainees are paid realistic wages with deductions for income tax, board and lodging and it is possible to cover your costs as there is little to spend your money on.
Each participant has to pay the cost of transportation and the IAEA administration fee, which includes the obtaining of work permits, suitable host families and the carrying out of orientation seminars and supervision.
Applicants should be over 19 years of age and have at least one year's experience of agriculture.

GAP Activity Projects arrange working holidays on farms (sheep, cattle, wheat) for up to 6 months for school leavers who have some time to spare before going on to university or starting a job. The applicant must pay their own air fares and take out the necessary insurance. A GAP fee (ranging from £200 to £300 is payable at least a month before departure which covers administrative costs for organising visas, group-travel arrangements etc. In return they are provided with board, accommodation and limited pocket money.

International Exchange of Young Agriculturists, Agriculture House, Knightsbridge, London SW1X 7NJ
IAEA, NFYFC Centre, National Agricultural Centre, Stoneleigh, Kenilworth, Warwickshire, CV8 2LG
GAP Activity Projects (GAP) Ltd, 7 King's Rd, Reading RG1 3AA. Tel: 0734 594914

Fruit Picking
You can usually find work through the offices of the Commonwealth Employment Service (CES) who have many offices throughout Australia. Their general attitude is usually quite helpful and they have available a booklet giving locations and dates of fruit harvests in all areas. Work can also be obtained by visiting individual orchards and looking at notice boards in various communities. Working hours are generally from 6.00 am to 6.00 pm with 2-3 hours off during the peak of the day.

Rates of pay vary greatly depending on the area, the type of fruit, the condition of the harvest, and your ability as a picker. It is quite possible to pick fruit all year in Australia by following the harvest, although there are, naturally, better months.

South Australia: A wide variety of fruit crops are grown in South Australia. The main crops are oranges, peaches and apricots (the Upper Murray), and apples and pears (Adelaide Hills and Barossa Valley). Cherries, plums and almonds are also grown. Approximately 45% of Australia's vineyard area is located in South Australia where the bulk of grapes are used for winemaking.
The grape harvest is from February to April. Opportunities for grape harvesting and work at wineries are good in the towns of Springton, Eden Valley, Angaston, Nurlootpa, Murananga, Seppeltsfield, Tanunda, Lyndoch, and Rowland Flat.

New South Wales: A large proportion of fruit growing is carried out on inland irrigation areas as well as the Tablelands and coastal area. Tropical fruits are found on the northern coast only. There is a good demand in this area for reliable seasonal labour for harvesting which is carried on pretty well throughout the entire year. Fruits grown are strawberries, cherries, peaches, plums, nectarines, apples, pears, apricots, oranges, grapefruit and lemons.

Western Australia: The main fruits grown are apples, pears, various stone fruits and citrus. Bananas also grow north of Perth. Orchards surround the towns of Chittering, Mundaring, Bickley, Pickering Brook, Karragullen, Roleystone, Dwellingup, Pinjarra and Harvey in the Hills and coastal region near Perth. In the Southwest the major towns where fruit is grown are Bunbury, Donnybrook, Busselton, Margaret River, Bridetown and Pemberton. In the Lower Great Southern region, the districts of Albany, Denmark and Mount Barker grow a limited amount of fruit.

Other Work
Tobacco harvesting in northern Queensland takes places between October and December, and in Victoria from January to March – a total work period of six months if you want to work on the tobacco harvest.

Jobs in the Outback on sheep stations or cereal farms are not so easily come by unless you have some experience, but they are still available. The best places to find such work are by making your interest known in the local pubs of the region, or simply by asking around at stores etc. In such areas everyone knows everyone else and news get around pretty quickly. Some of the farms and 'stations' are vast and it is physically impossible to visit them (unless you have your own transport) so you must make yourself known in the 'service towns'.

Some fishing opportunities are generally available on vessels out of Darwin, Cairns and Townsville. It is helpful if you have some experience, but if you hang around the waterfront long enough you should get lucky.

Bar work and hotel work is available in all the big cities and also along the coast of Queensland in the holiday resorts especially those that serve the Great Barrier Reef.

Au Pair
As Australian agencies are prohibited by law from sending prior information on families' requirement to agencies in Britain, it is worthwhile just turning up at an Au Pair Agency once you are in Australia, armed with references, medical certificates and 3/4 (smiling) passport sized photographs.

Some agencies, however, do have agents in various parts of Australia and can put prospective applicants in touch with them. Provided you are between the age of 17 and 27 you should be able to obtain a working holiday visa from any of the Australian High Commissions listed above. Under the normal conditions of your visa you will be unable to have a position arranged for you in Australia prior to leaving this country. Once you are in Australia you will be able to take up temporary positions provided that these are considered as part of your working holiday.

If you can send Universal Care details before you go (ie, medical clearance from your doctor, 2 references, 4 passport size photos, and a letter to your future employers telling them about yourself) as well as a completed application form, they can send your details to the relevant agent in Australia which you can then contact when you arrive.

Anglia Agency offer a similar service for mother's helps, nannies and positions similar to an au pair, where less responsibility is required. Anglia send full files of prospective applicants and then wait for news as to whether a candidate is deemed suitable. There is no guarantee of work at this end however. It is up to you to present yourself at the associate agency's office in Australia.

Wages in Australia are approximately as follows: Nannies (NNEB) – $250-$300 pw; Mothers' helps – $200-$225 pw; Nannies – $200-$225 pw; Trainees – $80 pw.

Universal Care Ltd, Chester House, 9 Windsor End, Beaconsfield, Bucks HP9 2JJ.
Tel: 0494 678811
Anglia Agency, 15 Eastern Avenue, Southend-on-Sea, Essex SS2 5QX.
Tel: 0702 613888

Teaching

The League for the Exchange of Commonwealth Teachers operate teacher exchanges mostly on a post-to-post basis for twelve months but a few exchanges are arranged for one or two terms (see section on Teaching Ch 5).

The League for the Exchange of Commonwealth Teachers, Commonwealth House, 7 Lion Yard, Tremadoc Road, Clapham, London SW4 7NF. Tel: 01 498 1101

Voluntary Work

Workcamps

Christian workcamps usually run for 3-4 weeks straight after Christmas each year with 15-20 people on each camp. The work is often on building or renovation projects, so building skills or practical skills are very handy but not necessary. There is usually one camp in central Australia on the aboriginal community and another camp either in New South Wales or in Arnhem Land. The workcamps are a great opportunity to live and work with aborigines. Accommodation and food is provided and transport to and from the camps is in private 4WD's and cars. The cost is approximately $150.

Ross Piper, 37 Chapman Avenue, Beecroft 2119, Sydney, Australia.

Conservation

Earthwatch Magazine contains information on projects in Australia. In 1989 for example volunteers were needed to investigate fossilised ancestors of the rainforests in North Queensland and to study the behaviour of the echidna in Adelaide.

The Australian Trust for Conservation Volunteers needs volunteers for practical environmental projects throughout Australia. Food, accommodation and travel whilst working are provided.

Earthwatch, 680 Mount Auburn Street, PO Box 403, Watertown, MA 02272, U.S.A.
Australian Trust for Conservation Volunteers, National Director, PO Box 423, Ballarat 3350, Victoria

AUSTRIA
Main language: German
Currency: Austrian Schilling
Capital: Vienna

Exports: Machinery, iron and steel, textiles, sawn wood
Climate: Winter: Cold (close to or below freezing) Summer: Hot, rainy, cooler in Alpine regions
(15°C-20°C)

Entry requirements
Austrian Embassy, 18 Belgrave Mews West, London SW1X 8HU. Tel: 01 235 3731

National Tourist Office, 30 St George Street, London W1R 9FA

Austrian Institute, 28 Rutland Gate, London SW7

Visas
Holders of British passports do not require a visa for a period not exceeding 6 months and are
allowed to take up employment within that period is they have a work permit.

Work Permits
Work permits are required for ALL types of employment, including Au Pair positions and these
are only issued where there is no national available to do the job for which the permit is sought.
The permit can only be applied for by the future employer in Austria and must be obtained prior
to the intended departure from Great Britain. For any type of employment (except for Au-Pair
positions) a sound knowledge of German is a basic requirement. Finding a job in Austria can be
difficult. The cost of living is high and rented accommodation is difficult to find. Those going
to Austria to look for work should make sure that they have ample funds available. Holders of
British passports do not require a visa for a period of less than 6 months and are allowed to take
up employment within that period, providing they have a work permit.

It is advised that you apply directly to one of the employment offices in Austria by typing a
letter in German including the following details: name and address, date of birth, education,
profession, type of present employment, knowledge of foreign languages, length of intended
stay and type of job required in Austria. You can also get advice from any local office of
the Department of Employment in Great Britain regarding the "Scheme for the International
Clearing of Vacancies and Applications for Employment."

Employment Offices in Austria
Landesarbeitsamt fur das Burgenland, Permayerstrasse 10, 7001 Eisenstadt
Landesarbeitsamt fur Karnten, Kumpfgasse 25, 9010 Klaganfurt
Landesarbeitsamt fur Niederosterreich, Hohenstauffengasse 2, 1013 Wien
Landesarbeitsamt fur Oberosterreich, Gruberstrasse 63, 4010 Linz
Landesarbeitsamt fur Salzburg, Schiesstattstrasse 4, 5021 Salzburg
Landesarbeitsamt fur Steiermark, Bebenbergerstrasse 33, 8021 Graz
Landesarbeitsamt fur Tirol, Schopfstrasse 5, 6010 Innsbruck
Landesarbeitsamt fur Vorarlberg, Rheinstrasse 32, 6901 Bregenz
Landesarbeitsamt fur Wien, Weihburggasse 30, 1011 Wein

Permanent Residence
The applicant has to provide satisfactory proof that he/she has sufficient means of support
in Austria and that a home will be available. Ownership of property in Austria does not
predetermine the permission for immigration. Material independence can be proved by Bank
statements and/or confirmation of receipt of a pension by the Department of Health and Social
Security and/or by a former employer, and/or a Private Pension Scheme. In cases where an
Austrian immigration visa is sought for the purpose of family reunion the application should
contain the name, nationality and exact address of, as well as the relationship to the family
member already resident in Austria. Two sets of the Immigration form (typed in German or in
block letters) should be completed by the applicant and submitted to the Embassy.

Travel

Many discount travel companies offer flights to Austria (see Chapter 4). Eurotrain offer discounts to persons under 26 and tickets are valid for 2 months. YHA Travel issue many special offers for train journeys to Austria: An Austria Ticket Junior which is valid for persons under 26 and allows unlimited 2nd class travel for 9 days; an Austria Ticket for persons over 26 which is valid for 1 month's unmlimited travel; and an Inter Rail Pass for persons up to 26 which is valid for 1 month.

Eurotrain, 52 Grosvenor Gardens, London SW1. Tel: 01 730 3402
YHA Travel, 14 Southampton St, London WC2E 7HY
Victoria Coach Station, 164 Buckingham Palace Rd, London SW1. Tel: 01 730 0202
Euroways Express Coaches Ltd, 52 Grosvenor Gardens, London SW1W.
Tel: 01 730 3643

Accommodation

The Anglo-Austrian Society can provide you with information on accommodation in youth hostels and hotel accommodation in Vienna, and other main cities in Austria. The BfSt (Student Travel Bureau) and OKISTA (Austrian Committe for International Educational Exchange) also has information on accommodation in hostels, pensions and hotels throughout Austria.

Anglo-Austrian Society, 46 Queen Anne's Gate, London SW1H 9AU. Tel: 01 222 0366
BfSt, Schreyvogelgasse 3, A-1010 Vienna, Austria. Tel: (0222) 533 35 89
OKISTA, Turkenstrasse 4, A-1090 Vienna. Tel: (0222) 3475260

Working Holidays

Job Advertising

International Graphic Press, 6 Welbeck Street, London W1M 7PB represents the Austrian paper 'Kurier'

Publicitas Ltd, 525 Fulham Road, London SW6 1HF represents 'Die Presse'

Students who are looking for short-time or holiday employment should contact the Central Bureau for Educational Visits and Exchanges or the Austrian Committee for the International Exchange of Students (OKISTA).

Central Bureau for Educational Visits and Exchanges, Seymour Mews House, Seymour, Mews, London W1H 9PE
Austrian Committee for the International Exchange of Students (OKISTA), Turkenstrasse 4, A-1090 Vienna, Austria

Agriculture

The United Kingdom Sponsoring Authority for the International Exchange of Young Agriculturists arranges work on farms and nurseries for a minimum of three months and a maximum of 12 months, starting at any time of the year. Applicants must have at least 2 years' practical experience.

International Exchange of Young Agriculturists, Agriculture House, Knightsbridge, London SW1X 7NJ

Au Pair

Work permits must be obtained by the future host prior to arrival. There is a minimum age of 18 years and a knowledge of German is usually required. A return ticket is needed or an undertaking to leave Austria at the end of the work period. The following agencies can assist in arranging positions for Au pairs and/or mother's helps:

Universal Care, Chester House, 9 Windsor End, Beaconsfield, Bucks HP9 2JJ.
Tel: 0494 678811
Helping Hands Au Pair and Domestic Agency, 10 Hertford Road, Newbury Park,
Ilford, Essex 1G2 7HQ. Tel: 01 597 3138

En Famille arrange holidays whereby you stay as a paying guest with a family in Austria. Visits can be arranged for any time of the year for any length of stay from one week to one year.

En Famille Overseas, The Old Stables, 60b Maltravers Street, Arundel,
West Sussex BN18 9BG. Tel: 0903 883266

Winter Resorts
Work is available at ski resorts – Badgastein, Brand, Alpbach, Lermoos, Lech, Kitzbuhel, Soll, St Johann, but it is not always easy to pick up work on the spot because of the restrictions.

Ski Europe requires part-time ski instructors for winter sports centres in the Tyrol and Salzburg but applicants with BASI or ASSI will be preferred (especially with foreign languages). Free board, accommodation and ski pass is provided together with a small wage of about £25 a week.

A list of 30 ski resorts in Austria is published in Alpotels and describes the character of each resort. Also available are lists of the main hotels in these resorts to which you can write or which you can visit in search of work. Standards are generally very high and German is essential.

Ski Europe, 6 Kew Green, Richmond, Surrey
Alpotels (London), PO Box 388, London SW1X 8LX (send large sae)

Camping
Camping holidays in Austria are increasing in popularity and there are often opportunities available for couriers, camp site attendants etc.

Europcamp Travel Ltd, Edmundson House, Tatton Street, Knutsford,
Cheshire WA16 6BG
Canvas Holidays, Bull Plain, Hertford, Herts SG14 1DY. Tel: 0992 553535

Teaching
Persons seeking employment as a teacher are advised that teachers in the Austrian State School System have civil servant status, and therefore have to be Austrian citizens. A limited programme for the exchange of teachers is being run by the Federal Ministry for Education, Arts and Sport in Vienna and for further information on this scheme the Central Bureau for Educational Visits and Exchanges should be contacted.

It might be possible to get a teaching position in a private school if you speak German.

Central Bureau for Educational Visits and Exchanges, Seymour Mews House, Seymour Mews, London W1H 9PE

Voluntary Work
United Nations Association, Welsh Centre for International Affairs operates camps in Austria from time to time. The work period is for three weeks usually between June and September and most of the work is manual on conservation projects. Send a large sae for details.

The International Voluntary Service and Quaker International Social Projects also have projects involving mainly renovation work for 2-3 weeks in July and August.

United Nations Association, Welsh Centre for International Affairs, Temple of Peace, Cathays Park, Cardiff CF1 3AP

International Voluntary Service, 162 Upper New Walk, Leicester LE1 7QA
Quaker International Social Projects, Friends House, Euston Road, London NW1 2BJ. Tel: 01 387 3601

BAHAMAS, THE
Main language: American English
Capital: Nassau
Industry: Tourism, fishing
Climate: Tropical – Winter (21°C)
Summer (30°C), heavy rainfall from August onwards, sometimes cyclonic

Entry Requirements
High Commission of the Bahamas, Bahamas House, 10 Chesterfield Street, London W1X 8AH. Tel: 01 408 4488

Bahamas Tourist Office, 23 Old Bond Street, London W1X 4PQ

Visas
Immigration formalities for bona fide visitors are minimal. Citizens of the UK and Colonies do not require passports or visas to enter the Bahamas for periods not exceeding three weeks. All visitors are required to have a return or onward ticket and are permitted to remain in the Bahamas for a maximum period of eight months. If they intend to stay in the Bahamas for more than a few days they may be asked to produce evidence of sufficient funds to allow them to do so or indicate relatives or friends with whom they will be staying. Visitors are not allowed to engage in any form of gainful occupation while in the Bahamas.

Annual Residence
Persons wishing to reside in the Bahamas on an annual basis should direct their enquiries to the Director of Immigration, PO Box N-831, Nassau. Applications for annual residence are considered from persons not wishing to engage in gainful employment but wishing to remain in the Bahamas for periods in excess of eight months. A medical certificate is required, plus two written character references, and a police certificate covering the immediate past five years. An annual fee of US$1,000 is payable by the holder of such a permit and a fee of $20 for each of his or her dependents.

Permanent Residence
Application for permanent residence will be entertained for those who meet the statutory requirements, provided they satisfy the following:

(a) they have become domiciled in the Bahamas
(b) they have put down roots in the country
(c) they have either made substantial investment in the country and or have made, or are in the process of making, contributions to the social and or economic welfare of the country. Specific details on whether the applicant is just wanting to retire to the Bahamas or to engage in gainful employment are also required.

Work Permits
Work permits are issued to persons whose employment does not create unfair competition for Bahamians. A person who is not a citizen of the Bahamas and wishes to be employed there must have a prospective employer submit an application on his or her behalf. In addition to the above requirements, a letter from the applicant's prospective employer must be submitted with evidence that the Ministry of Labour in the Bahamas has been notified of the vacancy and that the post

has been advertised locally. These permits are issued for fixed periods and for not more than three years; renewals are based on performance and are not normally given where the total period of time granted to the work permit holder exceeds five years. Applications from persons with considerable experience in specialised fields such as accountancy, education, medicine and engineering are likely to be considered more favourably.

Opening a Business
Persons wishing to open a business or a local branch are required to submit full, specific details of their project to the Director of Immigration. Each application will be subject to scrutiny, with special emphasis on financial standing, on the number of Bahamians to be employed and whether or not it is necessary to bring in expatriate managerial or specialist staff.

Travel
Many discount companies can offer flights to the Bahamas (see Chapter 4). A cheaper way to get there is to fly from Miami or go by boat if you can get work as crew or cook aboard a private yacht.

Accommodation
Contact the Bahamas Tourist Office for information on cheap accommodation in the Bahamas.

Working Holidays

Tourism
One interesting exception to the regulations for work permits is for casino work. This is a very important source of revenue and one which the authorities encourage (American gamblers in particular leave large sums of money in the Bahamas). However, they feel that such establishments would have a corrupting influence on their own people who are not allowed to work in them - thus leaving the opportunity for non-residents.

As there are about 700 islands in the West Indies there are many private and charter yachts plying the waters. It may be possible to pick up work crewing or cooking by asking around on the waterfront. Crewitt may be able to put you in touch with skippers requiring crew for trips to the Caribbean, though you will be expected to pay your share of costs which might well be in the region of £4000! A list of recreational and commercial crew positions wanted and available is available from Marine Data Services in California. It is updated monthly and costs $5 per month plus $8 for the initial set-up.

Crewitt, Cobbs Quay, Hamworthy, Poole, Dorset BH15 4EL. Tel: 0202 678847
Marine Data Services, PO Box 2394, Woodland, CA 95695, USA

Teaching
The League for the Exchange of Commonwealth Teachers organise exchanges in the Bahamas on a post-to-post basis for twelve months though a few exchanges are arranged for one or two terms.

The League for the Exchange of Commonwealth Teachers, Commonwealth House, 7 Lion Yard, Tremadoc Road, Clapham, London SW4 7NF. Tel: 01 498 1101

Voluntary Work

Archaeology
The Archaeological Institute of America publish details of a dig which commenced in January 1989 and which will continue for approximately 5 or 6 seasons at Dundee Bay Site on

Grand Bahama Island. No prior experience or training is necessary and all ages are welcome. Participants must pay all their own expenses and tuition per day is US$75.

The Archaeological Institute of America, 675 Commonwealth Avenue, Boston, MA 02215

Earthwatch Expeditions Inc, 680 Mount Auburn Street, PO Box 403, Watertown, MA 02272

BANGLADESH
Main language: Bengali
Currency: Taka
Capital: Dhaka
Climate: Nov-Mar: mainly cool/dry
Apr-Oct: warm/hot, heavy monsoon rains

Entry Requirements
High Commission for the People's Republic of Bangladesh, 28 Queen's Gate, London SW7 5JA. Tel: 01 584 0081

Visas
All British passport holders require visas for Bangladesh.

Work permits
Work permits are obtainable through the employing agencies in the UK. The organisation who is employing an individual should arrange for the work permit from the Bangladesh authorities in Dhaka.

Permanent Residence
Foreigners can be allowed permanent residence upon application to the Ministry of Home Affairs, Dhaka.

Travel
Many of the discount travel companies offer cheap flights to Bangladesh (see Chapter 4). The cheapest airlines are Eastern European or Middle Eastern airlines. You can also get into Bangladesh overland via Calcutta, India.

Working Holidays
There is no opportunity for working holiday schemes in Bangladesh.

Voluntary Work
Many voluntary organisations, such as Oxfam, War on Want, Save the Children Fund etc can be contacted in the UK for volunteer work in Bangladesh.

Tear Fund is asked from time to time to send a Task Force team to undertake a useful piece of work for projects such as basic repair work, construction of buildings, provision of piped water and specialised installation or repair of equipment. Practical experience in some field such as engineering, plumbing or building is an advantage.

VSO sends volunteers to Bangladesh who are skilled in a variety of fields, such as Agriculture, Business and Social Development, Education, Health, Working with the Disabled, Trades, Crafts and Engineering. Usually VSO volunteers serve for a minimum of 2 years but in Bangladesh there has been a recommendation to support small NGO's that need regular short-term volunteers. Tear Fund, 100 Church Road, Teddington, Middx TW11 8QE. Tel: 01 977 9144

VSO, Enquiries Unit, 317 Putney Bridge Road, London SW15 2PN. Tel: 01 780 1331

IVS 162 Upper New Walk, Leicester LE1 7QA. Tel: 0533 549430

BELGIUM
Main language/s: French, Flemish, German
Currency: Belgian franc
Capital: Brussels
Exports: Iron and steel, Vehicles, Machinery, Non-ferrous metals, Textiles
Climate: Temperate, cool summers, mild winters

Entry Requirements
Belgian Embassy, 103 Eaton Square, London SW1W 9AB. Tel: 01 235 5422

Belgian National Tourist Office, 38 Dover Street, London WIX 3RB

Entry Permit
Nationals of a member country of the EEC do not need an entry permit.

Permanent Residence
If the spouse and children wish to take up residence in Belgium they must have a valid passport or travel document. They do not require a visa if they are nationals of a member country of the EEC. A marriage certificate for the spouse and a birth certificate of the children is needed to register at the local Town Hall in Belgium.

Work Permits
A national of a member country of the EEC does not require a work permit to take up employment in Belgium, and may stay for up to three months whilst looking for work. On arrival in Belgium you are required to report within 8 working days to the Town Hall of your intended place of residence. The local authority will issue you with a certificate of registration (CIRE) valid for 1 year or with a provisional certificate valid for three months which later will be replaced with a CIRE.

A special service has been set up within the EEC to assist European Community nationals who wish to seek employment in another country of the Community. If you wish to work in Belgium you should contact your local job centre and ask for form ES13.

If you are unemployed and go to Belgium to seek employment you should register within 7 days at the Job Centre of the Subregional Employment Bureau of the locality where you have taken up residence. Before leaving Britain you should apply for unemployment benefit at a claims office by means of form E 303.

Social Security
Under EEC regulations British citizens qualify for social security benefits subject to certain conditions. For more information apply to your local DHSS office or the DHSS Overseas Branch.

DHSS Overseas Branch, Newcastle upon Tyne, NE98 1YX. Tel: 0632 793238/857111

Travel

You can fly to Belgium quite cheaply from the UK (see Chapter 4 for discount travel companies), but most people arrive by train from Ostend or Zeebrugge.
Eurotrain offer discount travel to those under 26. YHA Travel can provide many special passes, including the Benelux Tourrail pass which allows unlimited rail travel for 5 days in Belgium, the Netherlands and Luxembourg. Coach travel is another cheap way to get to Belgium.

Belgium is a very flat country and cycling is a good way of getting around. Belgian National Railways lets you hire a bike at some Belgian stations and return it to any station. Brussels has an efficient bus-tram-underground system and multiple-trip cards can be bought from stations and from bus drivers.

Eurotrain, 52 Grosvenor Gardens, London SW1. Tel: 01 730 3402
YHA Travel, 14 Southampton St, London WC2E 7HY. Tel: 01 836 8541
Victoria Coach Station, 164 Buckingham Palace Rd, London SW1. Tel: 01 730 0202
Cyclists' Touring Club, Cotterell House, 69 Meadrow, Godalming, Surrey GU7 3HS. Tel: 04868 7217
Belgian National Railways, 7-11 Kensington High St, London W8 5ND. Tel: 01 938 1721

Accommodation

Tourist offices keep a list of camp-sites, hotels and hostels.
There is a youth information service 'Infor-Jeunes' which gives information on accommodation and travel etc. Acotra World, a budget travel office, offer a free room-finding service.

'Infor-Jeunes', 3 Place Quetelet, Brussels. Tel: 217 40 20
Acotra World, 51 rue de la Madeleine. Tel: 512 55 40
IYHF Hostel, Centre Jacques Brel, 30 rue de la Sablomenniere, Brussels. Tel: 218 01 87
Sleep Well Hostel, 27 rue de la Blanchisserie, Brussels. Tel: 218 50 50

Working Holidays

Job Advertising

Publicitas Ltd, 525 Fulham Road, London SW6 1HF. Tel: 01 385 7723 (represents Le Soir and Het Laatste Nieuws – to place own advertisements)

'The Bulletin', 329 Avenue Moliere, 1060 Brussels, Brussels (Belgian news weekly published in English – carries advertisements for jobs)

Le Soir, UJB, Place de Louvain, 1000 Brussels (carries advertisements for jobs)

Au Pair

There are plenty of opportunities throughout Belgium for Au pairs. Contact any of the following who can make the necessary arrangements:

Students Abroad, Elm House, 21b The Avenue, Hatch End, Middx HA5 4EN. Tel: 01 428 5823

Anglia Agency, 15 Eastern Avenue, Southend-on-Sea, Essex SS2 5QX. Tel: 0702 613888

Universal Care, Chester House, 9 Windsor End, Beaconsfield, Bucks HP9 2JJ. Tel: 0494 678811

Accueil et Orientation Au Pair, 29 rue Faider, 1050 Brussels. Tel: 02 539 35 14

Ahoy, 76 Anselmostraat, 2018 Antwerp. Tel: 03 238 19 34

Secretarial
The chances of finding secretarial work in Belgium is better than in any other European country. Usually contracts are for one year but there is the possibility of longer periods. A knowledge of French is useful.

International Secretaries, 174 New Bond Street, London W1Y 9PT

Addresses for temporary work in Belgium (IT service)

5-7 Jezusstraat, 2000 Antwerp. Tel: 03 232 9860
2 Pensmarkt (Groentenmarkt), 9000 Ghent. Tel: 091 24 09 20
17 Spanjaardstraat, 8000 Bruges. Tel: 050 44 04 70
47 Thonissenlaan, 3500 Hasselt. Tel: 011 22 11 77
22 Rollewagenstraat, 1801 Vilvoorde. Tel: 02 252 20 25
68 Beheerstraat, 8500 Kortrijk. Tel: 056 20 30 79
86 de Merodelei, 2300 Turnhout. Tel: 014 42 27 31
22 Rue de la Province, 4020 Liege. Tel: 041 41 03 10
91 Rue de Montignies, 6000 Charleroi. Tel: 071 31 74 45
14 Rue Borgniet, 5000 Namur. Tel: 081 22 30 12
24 Rue General Molitor, 6700 Arlon. Tel: 063 22 66 45
69 Boulevard Anspach, 1000 Brussels. Tel: 02 511 23 85

Job Service
4 Eikstraat, 3000 Leuven. Tel: 016 23 13 99
53 Rue Childeric, 7500 Tournai. Tel: 069 23 31 41
65 Boulevard Anspach, 1000 Brussels. Tel: 02 513 78 20

Teaching
If you have a knowledge of French, Flemish or German and a teaching qualification you might be able to find a teaching position in one of the English speaking schools in Belgium.

British Primary School, Stationstraat 6, B-1981 Vossem. Tel: 02 767 3098
British School of Brussels, chausee de Louvain 19, B-1980 Tervuren. Tel: 02 767 4700
Brussels English Primary School, avenue Fr Roosevelt, B-1050 Brussels. Tel: 02 648 4311
Brussels European School, avenue du Vert-Chasseur 46, B-1180 Brussels. Tel: 02 374 5847
The International School of Brussels, Kattenburg 19, B-1170 Brussels. Tel: 02 673 6050
St John's International School, dreve de Richelle, B-1410 Waterloo. Tel: 02 354 1138
Brussel's American School, John F Kennedylaan, B-1960 Sterrebeek. Tel: 02 731 5625
British Council, rue Joseph II 30, B-1040 Brussels. Tel: 02 219 3600

Couriers/Camp Sites
Many tour operators offer camping holidays in Belgium and need couriers and camp site attendants to work in the summer months.

Eurocamp, Edmundson House, Tatton Street, Knutsford, Cheshire WA16 6BG

Voluntary Work

Workcamps
Christian Movement for Peace has many projects ranging from recycling organic waste, building,

painting and redecorating, working with the mentally disabled, etc. Although some projects are full by the beginning of June it is often possible to accept volunteers after this date.

The United Nations Association, Welsh Centre for International Affairs organises about 10 camps in Belgium with 'Movements des Jeunes pour la Paix'. The number of participants per camp is 14 and the work is manual mostly concerned with conservation. A knowledge of French is useful.

International Voluntary Service organises camps in July and August – minimum age is 18.

Quaker International Social Projects has agreements with organisations in Belgium who run projects ranging from manual work on environmental or ecological schemes, building playgrounds, working with children and people in disadvantaged areas.

The EYCE organise workcamps from time to time in Belgium. The workcamps have a strong Christian bias and part of the time is devoted to worship and discussion.

CMP, Bethnal Green URC, Pott Street, London E2 0EF. Tel: 01 729 1877

United Nations Association, Welsh Centre for International Affairs, Temple of Peace, Cathays Park, Cardiff

IVS, 162 Upper New Walk, Leicester LE1 7QA. Tel: 0533 549430

QISP, Friends House, Euston Road, London NW1 2BJ. Tel: 01 387 3601

EYCE, 217 Holywood Road, Belfast BT4 2DH, N Ireland. Tel: 44 232 651134/5

BELIZE
Main language: English (official) and Spanish
Currency: BZ$
Capital: Belmopan
Exports: Sugar, citrus fruits, frozen shellfish
Climate: Subtropical – average temp 79oF
Feb-June – dry season
Jun-Oct - wet season

Entry Requirements
Belize High Commission, 200 Sutherland Avenue, London W9 1RX

Belize Tourist Board, PO Box 325, Belize City, Belize

UK nationals and citizens of the USA do not require a visa to enter Belize, if the visit is for less than a period of six months, but must have a valid passport, return or onward ticket and sufficient funds to cover their stay. Usually a passport is stamped for one month and if the visitor wishes to stay longer he should make a personal application to the Police Station, if residing in the Districts. Approximately US$50 per day is sufficient to cover one's stay in Belize including hotel accommodation, transport and meals.

Inoculation against smallpox and malaria is advised.

Work Permits
Working holidays are not encouraged, however it is possible and a temporary Employment Permit must be obtained from the Labour Commissioner prior to arrival in Belize. Student

exchanges are encouraged and should be coordinated through the Ministry of Education in Belize. A visa may be required if the exchange exceeds six months.

Permanent Residence

Anyone wishing to emigrate to Belize must first file an application and receive permission from the Immigration Department, Belmopan, Belize. Necessary application forms can be obtained from the Belize High Commission or directly from the Immigration Department in Belize. Applicants should submit, along with their application form, an Immigration deposit, recent copies of police certificates of character, certificates of health including an AIDS test, three passport sized photographs and a recent local bank statement in case of capital investment. Alternatively applicants can submit a temporary employment permit if they are – or wish to be- engaged in gainful employment. Applicants who are not currently residing in Belize require either an approved work permit or approved plans/proposals for self-employment or business development. Prospective immigrants must secure a work permit which is largely conditional on the applicant's ability to be self-supporting in an approved line of work without displacing a national in employment.

Travel

Regular international services are maintained from the United States (Miami, New Orleans, Houston), Mexico and Central America by Taca and Tan/Sahsa Airways as well as Eastern and Continental Airways and chartered flights by Maya Airways and Tropic Air. Tours are organised regularly from the USA and occasionally from the UK. Your travel agent can update you on these.
Soliman Travel specialises in fares to Spanish-speaking countries.

Overland the journey to Belize by all-weather roads takes 3 to 6 days from Texas, and 5 to 12 days from California. Motorists should bring along their driver's licence and certificate of registration. Third party insurance is mandatory and driving is on the right.

Buses run from Mexico and Guatemala into Belize and fares within Belize are very reasonable (BZ$4-8 to most destinations).

There are occasional sailings from New Orleans, Los Angeles and Tampa, Florida and the Caribbean. You might also be able to work your passage as crew on a private yacht from one of these places.

Eastern Airlines, Tel: 800 327 8376 (US)
Continental Airlines, Tel: 800 231 0856
Taca, Belize Global Travel Services Ltd, 41 Albert Street, Belize City, Belize. Tel: (2) 77185

Soliman Travel, 233 Earls Court Road, London. Tel: 01 370 6446

European-American Travel, 1522 K Street NW, Washington DC 20005.
Tel: 202 789 2255

Maharajah Travels, 518 Fifth Avenue, New York, NY 10036.
Tel: 212 391 0122

Express Discount Travel, 5945 Mission Gorge Road, San Diego, CA 92120.
Tel: 619 283 6324

Greyhound International, 14-16 Cockspur Street, London SW1Y 5BL. Tel: 01 839 5591

Belize Connection, Texas. Tel: 713 486 6993

Triton Tours, 1519 Plymnia Street, New Orleans, LA 70130. Tel: 504 522 3382

Accommodation
As well as hotels, long stay visitors can rent apartments on a monthly basis. If you have your own transport (campervan) there are trailer parks in many parts of Belize though no overnight parking in any public place is allowed.

Apartments - House of the Rising Sun, San Pedro, Ambergris Caye.
Tel: 026 2131/2186

Working Holidays
As already mentioned working holidays are not encouraged and a permit must be obtained from the Labour Commissioner prior to arrival in Belize.

However, as Belize has the world's 2nd largest barrier reef, and there are hundreds of islands called cayes (keys) between the reef and the mainland, the opportunities for diving, snorkelling and fishing abound. There are many charter companies which offer diving and fishing holidays aboard boats and it might be possible to get work on one of these either cooking or crewing by hanging around the waterfront and asking.

You might also be able to get work crewing or cooking on a private yacht. Ports of entry for boats are Belize City, Corozal, Consejo Shores, Dangriga and Punta Gorda.

Student exchanges are encouraged and should be coordinated through the Ministry of Education in Belize. A visa may be required if the exchange exceeds six months.

Voluntary Work
Voluntary work opportunities are available and should be arranged through the appropriate Government Ministry depending on the volunteer's interest. Once approval is received from the Government Ministry obtaining a permit is not difficult.

VSO has 28 volunteers in Belize, with the priority area being technical/vocational education in rural high schools and an increasing involvement in the provision of specialised health postings. VSO assistance to various cultural initiatives is increasing, with other volunteers in planning, agriculture and public works. Posts are for a minimum of 2 years and VSO pays the return fare plus equipment grants. A mid-tour grant is also paid after one year. Accommodation and payment based on local rates is provided by the employer.

VSO, Enquiries Unit, 317 Putney Bridge Road, London SW15 2PN.
Tel: 01 780 1331

Conservation
Belize has a great diversity of natural beauty with the Caribbean Sea and 150 miles of barrier reef on the eastern side and the Maya Mountains, limestone caves and Mayan ruins in the west. As Belize is sparsely populated, much of the country (more than 80%) is covered by tropical forest where wildlife still thrives. The world's only jaguar preserve exists in southern Belize in the Cockscomb Basin and there are more than 500 species of birds and 250 varieties of orchids.

The Belize Audubon Society is the most active conservation organisation in Belize and manages the country's wildlife reserves. The society also publishes and distributes information relevant to wildlife and conservation in Belize. You could contact the Society for any conservation work, as well as the Ministry of Agriculture and Environment.

Belize Audubon Society, 49 Southern Foreshore, Belize City, Belize

Permanent Secretary, Ministry of Agriculture and Environment, Belmopan, Belize

Belize Centre for Environmental Studies, PO Box 666, 55 Eve Street, Belize City, Belize

Archaeology
The Mayan civilisation flourished until about 1000 AD and Mayans were still living in the area when Europeans began colonising in the 17th century. As a result there are numerous archaeological sites throughout Belize including hundreds of caves and cave systems, many of which are actually archaeological reserves as the ancient Mayans were very conscious of the lords of the underworld.

The Archaeological Institute of America publishes details of digs and currently has a project to find and uncover the Spanish Little Armada ships which were sunk in the Bay of St George's Caye in 1798.

The Department of Archaeology, Ministry of Education, Youth and Culture, Belmopan, Belize

Archaeology Abroad, 31-34 Gordon Square, London WC1H OPY

BENIN
Main language: French
Currency: CFA Franc
Capital: Porto Novo
Exports: Palm oil, Oilseeds, Cotton, Cocoa
Climate: Equatorial (20°C-28°C)
Wet, tropical rainstorms July/August

Entry Requirements
Consulate of the People's Republic of Benin, 125/129 High Street, Edgware, Middx HA8 7HS, Tel: 01 951 1234

Visas
All visitors to Benin require a valid passport, visa and Yellow Fever certificate (Cholera, Typhoid and Malaria protection are also recommended).

Visas are issued for a visit of up to 7 days' stay and can normally be extended upon application on arrival in Benin. Cost of a visa is £15.

Work Permits
There is no opportunity for casual work in Benin.

Travel
Apart from flying direct to Benin or driving yourself, Dragoman organises a Trans Africa Expedition from 15 to 28 weeks which leaves the UK for Nairobi or Harare (or vice versa). The expedition goes via North Africa, the Sahara and Sahel, West Africa (including Benin), Equatorial Africa, the East African Plains, the Rift Valley and Southern Africa. Exodus Overland organise an African Explorer expedition from London to Nairobi or Harare following a similar route but spending a few days exploring the mountains in the north of Benin.

Dragoman, 10 Riverside, Framlingham, Suffolk IP13 9AG. Tel: 0728 724184

Exodus Expeditions, 9 Weir Road, London SW12 OLT. Tel: 01 675 7996

Voluntary work
Some of the large relief agencies such as Oxfam, War on Want, Save the Children etc can be contacted for voluntary work in Benin, as well as IVS who can put you in touch with the CCAB in Cotonou.

IVS, 162 Upper New Walk, Leicester. Tel: 0533 549430

BOLIVIA
Main language: Spanish
Currency: Bolivian peso
Capital: La Paz (highest city in the world)
Exports: Tin ore, crude petroleum
Climate: Hot throughout the year (25°C+)
Semi-arid in South east, wet in northern plains

Entry Requirements
Bolivian Consulate, 106 Eaton Square, London SW1W 9AD

Visas
UK nationals do not require a visa if they are going as tourists.

Work Permits
Under current Bolivian Government Policy the employment of foreign nationals is forbidden.

Permanent Residence
For permanent residence and immigration information, write directly to:
Minsterio del Interior, Migracion y Justicia, Av Arce, La Paz

Travel
Apart from flying to Bolivia direct, you can get there by train or bus from the neighbouring countries of Peru, Chile, Paraguay or Brazil.

The following travel companies specialise in holidays for the more adventurous traveller, and arrange overland tours, trekking holidays and expeditions:

Exodus Overland organise overland trips and expeditions lasting about 9 weeks from Bogota in Colombia to Santiago, Chile travelling through Bolivia, as well as trekking in Bolivia.

Dragoman organise 7 week trips from Quito in Ecuador to Santiago, Chile travelling through Bolivia.

Journey Latin America have much personal experience of travel in Latin America and will offer advice to those looking for fares through them. 'Travellers' Packs' with useful tips for people who wish to travel independently in S America are available in addition to a list of publications on S America with valuable comments and criticisms. They also arrange their own trips, eg Peru to Bolivia.

Trailfinders provide an information centre and bookshop for the independent traveller and act as agents for various exploration companies as well as offering discount flights.

Explore Worldwide Ltd organises small group exploratory holidays in Bolivia.

Swan Hellenic organise Art Treasure Tours of Bolivia.

Exodus Expeditions, 9 Weir Road, London SW12 OLT. Tel: 01 675 7996
Dragoman, 10 Riverside, Framlingham, Suffolk IP13 9AG. Tel: 0728 724184

Journey Latin America, 16 Devonshire Road, London W4 2HD. Tel: 01 747 3108

Trailfinders, 194 Kensington High Street, London W8 7RG. Tel: 01 938 3939

Explore Worldwide Ltd, 7 High Street, Aldershot, Hants GU11 1BH. Tel: 0252 319448

Twickers World, 22 Church Street, Twickenham TW1 3NW. Tel: 01 892 7606/8164

Steamond Ltd, 23 Eccleson Street, London SW1 9LX. Tel: 01 730 8646

STA Travel Ltd, 74 Old Brompton Road, London SW7. Tel: 01 937 9962

Swan Hellenic, 77 New Oxford Street, London WC1A 1PP. Tel: 01 831 1616

Working Holidays

Job Advertising
Advertisements may be placed in Latin American newspapers through the following:

Media Universal Services, 34-35 Skylines, Lime Harbour, Docklands, London E14 9TA. Tel: 01 538 5505

Teaching English
It is extremely difficult to find employment other than teaching English in Latin America generally. The British Council recruits a limited number of teachers, lecturers, administrators and educationalists to work in Latin America for periods of 1-3 years. Vacancies occur at primary, secondary and tertiary levels in British type and International schools. All vacancies are advertised in the Guardian and the Times Educational Supplement and a free booklet "The British Council: Teaching Overseas" is obtainable from the British Council.

Gabbitas Thring Services Ltd recruit teaching staff for a number of English medium schools in Latin America and maintain a staff register of over 2000 candidates seeking posts at all levels in education.

There are also many language schools or "culturas" which do not recruit through the British Council but who may be interested in offering you a job if contacted directly. Pay is frequently very low by British standards. There may also be a certain demand for private tuition, especially in large cities. The British Council, Overseas Educational Appointment Dept, 65 Davis Street, London W1Y 2AA. Tel: 01 930 8466

Gabbitas-Thring Services Ltd, Broughton House, 6-8 Sackville Street, Piccadilly, London W1X 2BR. Tel: 01 439 2071

Expedition leaders/drivers
A number of expeditions and overland tour operators require drivers and guides and you might be able to fix up a job with one of these companies before you go. Contact any of the companies listed above offering your services, especially if you have a HGV or PSV licence and/or mechanical skills.

Voluntary Work
There are no workcamps in Bolivia but the United Nations Association International Service has projects in Bolivia which require fully trained health workers, midwives and nurses as well as fully trained and experienced agriculturists, engineers and technicians. There is no salary but volunteers receive an allowance and various grants as well as receiving travelling expenses.

Operation Raleigh has strong links with Latin America, having sent expeditions to Bolivia and other countries in the last 4 years. The expeditions have a strong ingredient of adventure, but are based on community work, scientific research and conservation. A typical expedition consists of 120 young people (aged 17-25 years) split into groups of 5-15 to tackle individual projects normally lasting 10-12 weeks. Anyone may apply provided that they can swim 500 metres and understand basic English.

United Nations Association International Service, 3 Whitehall Court, London SW1. Tel: 01 930 0679/0

Operation Raleigh, Alpha Place, Flood Street, Chelsea, London SW3 5SZ. Tel: 01 351 7541

Archaeology
There are many opportunities each year in South America to go on digs. They are published in the annual edition of the Archaeological Fieldwork Opportunities Bulletin, available from the Archaeological Institute of America and Archaeology Abroad.

Archaeological Institute of America, 675 Commonwealth Avenue, Boston, MA 02215

Archaeology Abroad, 31-34 Gordon Square, London WC1H 0PY

BRAZIL
Main Language: Portuguese
Currency: Cruzado
Capital: Brasilia
Exports: Coffee, Cotton, Iron ore, Machinery
Climate: North/Amazon Basin – hot 25°C +, heavy annual rainfall Round Rio de Janeiro sub-tropical Extreme south – temperate

Entry Requirements
Brazilian Consulate General, 6 St Alban's Street, London SW1Y 4SG. Tel: 01 930 9055

Brazilian Embassy, 32 Green Street, London W1Y 3FD (Information Section)

Visas
Tourists of the UK do not require a visa to enter Brazil. The following documents must be presented to the Brazilian immigration officers:
- a valid passport endorsed for Brazil (the passport must be valid for at least six months;
- smallpox vaccination on an international form (not more than three years old) for travellers who, within the last fourteen days before arrival in Brazil, have been in a country where the disease has not been eradicated;
- Return or onward ticket (or alternatively evidence that sufficient funds are available for a return ticket to the country of origin).

Work Permits
Tourists are not permitted to work in Brazil.

There are two types of visas for those who want to take up employment in Brazil:

1. Temporary visa: when the applicant produces a contract of work with his employer in Brazil, duly certified by the Ministry of

Labour. This visa is given for the duration of the contract and can be extended upon renewal of the contract. Even for applicants who have professions for which there is an unfulfilled demand in Brazil, a visa will only be issued on the presentation of a work contract, duly certified by the Brazilian Ministry of Labour, and an authorisation from the Brazilian Ministry of Foreign Affairs. This means that the task of finding an employer in Brazil is regarded as the personal concern of the applicant, and will depend on his contacts in Brazil.

Those executives or employees seeking transfer to their company's branch in Brazil should have their visa application sent to the Ministry of Labour by the Brazilian affiliate.

2. Permanent visa: when the applicant wishes to establish permanent residence in Brazil.

Permanent Residence
There is no State programme aimed at encouraging immigration. In order to emigrate one of the following conditions must be fulfilled:

(a) An application to the Ministry of Labour, made by a prospective employer in Brazil, for permanent stay of the visa applicant. In this case, the reply is transmitted directly to the Consulate General in the applicant's country of origin and the applicant is informed.

(b) The transfer to US$300,000 to Brazil, in order to establish commercial or industrial activities. Those who wish to do this must call personally at the Consulate General for information before transferring the funds.

Travel
Apart from flying straight to Rio de Janeiro from London (an expensive way to get there), many people work in North America first and then spend some of their earnings travelling around South America. Most of the countries are very cheap to travel in (provided you do it sensibly) with an extensive rail and bus network.

If you are planning your own expedition, the Royal Geographical Society Expedition Advisory Centre will reply to requests from individuals as well as providing information and training for scientific expeditions. The centre offers regularly updated fact sheet for each of the Latin American countries which give addresses and contacts for further advice, and information on visas, climate etc. The centre keeps reports of past expeditions, a register of future expeditions and lists of suppliers.

There are a number of expeditions and overland tours that take in Brazil on the itinerary. The following travel companies specialise in such holidays:

Journey Latin America, 16 Devonshire Road, London W4 2HD. Tel: 01 747 3108

Encounter Overland, 267 Old Brompton Road, London SW5. Tel: 01 370 6845

Explore Worldwide Ltd, 7 High Street, Aldershot, Hants GU11 1BH.
Tel: 0252 319448

Twickers World, 22 Church Street, Twickenham TW1 3NW. Tel: 01 892 7606/8164

Bales Tours Ltd, Bales House, Barrington Road, Dorking, Surrey RH4 3EJ.
Tel: 0306 885991

Dragoman, 10 Riverside, Framlingham, Suffolk IP13 9AG. Tel: 0728 724184

Exodus Expeditions, 9 Weir Road, London SW12 0LT. Tel: 01 675 7996 The Royal Geographical Society Expedition Advisory Centre, Information Officer, 1 Kensington Gore, London SW7 2AR. Tel: 01 581 2057

Working Holidays
There are no official working holiday schemes in Brazil.

Job Advertising
Media Universal Services, 34-35 Skylines, Lime Harbour, Docklands, London E14 9TA. Tel: 01 538 5505

Teaching English
The British Council recruits a limited number of teachers, lecturers, administrators and educationalists to work in Latin America for periods of 1-3 years. British Council branches in Latin America may have addresses of other language schools where English is taught. In addition there are over 40 American/Brazilian Institutes spread throughout Brazil and the US Embassy, while not officially responsible for these, may be able to provide further information on request.

Some international language schools with bases in Britain also have branches in Brazil, eg Linguarama and Berlitz. The European Council of International Schools assists international schools where English is the main language of instruction in the recruitment of suitable teaching and administrative staff with a minimum of two years' teaching experience. Recruitment takes place in London in February. You may also be able to find work as a private tutor especially in the large cities, although well established teachers already on the spot will have a great advantage over newcomers.

British Council, Overseas Educational Appointment Dept, 65 Davis Street, London W1Y 2AA. Tel: 01 930 8466

British Council, 10 Spring Gardens, London SW1 (for branches in Latin America) Linguarama, TEFL Dept, New Oxford House, Waterloo Street, Birmingham B2 6UG

Berlitz, Wells House, 79 Wells Street, London W1A 3BZ

Jose Alvarino, Latin American Division, Berlitz Language Centre, Ejercito Nacional No 530 1er Piso, Col Polanco 11550, Mexico DF (for full-time teaching posts available in some Latin American countries)

European Council of International Schools, Dept IM, 21B Lavant Street, Petersfield, Hants GU32 3EL. Tel: 0730 68244

Business
The Hispanic and Luso Brazilian Council occasionally receives information about jobs available within companies who have business interests in Latin America. Candidates with professional qualifications and fluency in Portuguese or Spanish can register their details with the Council.

The Hispanic and Luso Brazilian Council, Education Department, Canning House, 2 Belgrave Square, London SW1X 8PJ. Tel: 01 235 2303

Expedition Leaders/Drivers
Many overland tour companies require guides and drivers for their expeditions throughout South America. Contact any of the companies listed in the travel section offering your services, especially if you have a HGV or PSV licence.

Voluntary Work

There are no workcamps in Brazil. The main demand is for long term volunteer work (minimum of 2 years) in the fields of engineering and technical subjects as well as health and agriculture.

The United Nations Association International Service at present has projects in Brazil mainly requiring fully trained health workers, midwives and nurses although there may also be requests for those fully trained and experienced in agriculture, engineering and other technical work. There is no salary but volunteers receive an allowance and various grants as well as receiving travelling expenses.

Gap Activity Projects Ltd gives young people the opportunity to spend approximately 6 months overseas working in schools/social services in their "gap" year between school and university or starting a career. There are a few opportunities to go to Latin America.

United Nations Association International Service, 3 Whitehall Court, London SW1.
Tel: 01 930 0679/0

Gap Activity Projects Ltd, 7 Kings Road, Reading, Berks RG1 344

Conservation

Earthwatch supports research into nature conservation, ecology, ornithology etc and from time to time expeditions to Brazil take place which need volunteer assistance. The University Research Expeditions Program need volunteers for assisting field research in the natural and social sciences.

Earthwatch Expeditions Inc, 680 Mount Auburn Street, PO Box 403, Watertown, MA 02272, USA

University Research Expeditions Program, University of California, Desk L-10, Berkeley, CA 94720, USA

BRUNEI

Main language: Malay
Capital: Bandar Seri Bagawan
Exports: Oil, natural gas, rubber
Climate: Coastal plains – humid
Forested mountains (6000ft high) – cooler

Entry Requirements

High Commission of Negara Brunei Darussalam, 49 Cromwell Road, London SW7 2ED
Tel: 01 581 0521

Travel

You can fly to Brunei from Manila, Singapore or Kuala Lumpur. See Chapter 4 for discount travel companies that can offer advice about the cheapest way to fly to Brunei from the UK. If you go from Manila, you can travel from Sabah, Northern Borneo and travel overland through Brunei arriving in Bandar Seri Begawan by boat. From Singapore, you can travel overland through Sarawak.

Working holidays

Brunei, on the north coast of Borneo, is one of the world's richest countries. Half the population is Malay, a quarter are Chinese and the rest include both indigenous people and Europeans. Because of its wealth there is no work for the working traveller; the Europeans who work there are doctors, engineers, etc. It is a very expensive country to stay in and Muslim law is rigidly upheld.

BULGARIA
Main language: Bulgar
Currency: Lev
Capital: Sofia
Exports: Cigarettes, alcoholic drinks, clothing
Climate: Temperate continental/ Mediterranean in South

Entry Requirements
Embassy of the People's Republic of Bulgaria, 188 Queen's Gate, London SW7 5HL
Tel: 01 584 9400/9433

The Bulgarian Tourist Office, 18 Princess Street, London W1. Tel: 01 499 6988

The British Bulgarian Friendship Society, 283 Grays Inn Road, London WC1.
Tel: 01 837 7381

Visas
Tourist entry visas are required when applicants arrange their own holiday and stay longer than 30 hours in Bulgaria. Applications for a visa can be made personally or by post at the Embassy. Tourist entry visas are for a single entry and with a leave to stay up to one month. When applying for a visa you should submit a valid passport, a completed and signed application form, one photograph and a £20 fee.

A visa is NOT required for foreign nationals if they are travelling in organised tourist groups of more than six persons, families with children (a child may be accompanied by only one parent), and persons who have prepaid tourist services (own vouchers). Visas cannot be issued upon entry at the border checkpoints. Visitors staying with relatives or friends as guests in Bulgaria are required to obtain an official invitation from their hosts legalised by the respective Bulgarian local authorities.

Work permits
There are no opportunities for foreigners to obtain employment in the country.

Permanent Residence
Foreigners are permitted to live in Bulgaria but must receive special permission to do so. It will be necessary to provide a list of documents which are required to be legalised, both by the Foreign and Commonwealth Office and the Embassy together with a completed declaration form and two photographs.

Travel
Eurotrain offer discounts to young people under 26. Journeys can be broken and tickets are valid for 2 months. You can also get to Bulgaria by bus.

Eurotrain, 52 Grosvenor Gardens, London SW1. Tel: 01 730 3402
Victoria Coach Station, 164 Buckingham Palace Rd, London SW1. Tel: 01 730 0202

Accommodation
Orbita Chain for Youth Tourism offer accommodation at student hostels in Sofia, Varna, and several other cities in Bulgaria during July and August.

Orbita Chain for Youth Tourism, Boulevard Alexander Stamboliski 45a, Sofia

Working Holidays
Bulgaria has sufficient workers and specialists to meet its requirements and there are no opportunities for short term or seasonal workers.

If, however, a special agreement exists between Bulgaria and any well known British company, employment is possible. There are, for example, some British engineers working in Bulgaria as their company have exchanged contracts with the Bulgarian government.

Teaching English
There are some teaching posts available at English Language schools and information about these posts may be obtained from the British Council. The Central Bureau recruits teachers for one year appointments in teaching English as a Foreign Language.

British Council, Overseas Educational Appointments Dept, 65 Davies Street, London W1Y 2AA. Tel: 01 499 8011

Central Bureau, Seymour Mews House, Seymour Mews, London W1H 9PE

Winter Resorts

Couriers/Reps
The principal skiing resorts of Vitosha, Borovets and Pamporovo are in the south and west – the skiing season starts in early December and ends from mid-April to late May. Tour operators who organise skiing holidays in Bulgaria need couriers, children's couriers, reps etc and it is worth contacting them for possible jobs.

Sports Instructors
Some of the holiday companies also run multi-sport holidays so if you are proficient at sports such as football, rowing, tennis, weightlifting, wrestling, water polo, basketball, volleyball, fencing, boxing, squash to name but a few, it is worth getting in touch with them.

The following tour operators organise skiing holidays and spring and autumn adventure tours in Bulgaria:

Swans, 329 Putney Bridge Road, London SW15 2PL. Tel: 01 789 7081

Global, Glen House, 200 Tottenham Court Road, London W1P 0JP. Tel: 01 637 4261

Balkan Tours, 9A Lombard Street, Belfast BT1 1RB, N Ireland.
Tel: 46795/25902

Ski Scope, Grosvenor Hall, Bolnore Road, Haywards Heath, W Sussex RH16 4BX

Balkan Holidays, Carrington House, 126-130 Regent Street, London W1R 6BD.
Tel: 01 734 8455

Schools Abroad, Grosvenor Hall, Bolnore Road, Haywards Heath, West Sussex RH16 4BX. Tel: 0444 414122

Workcamps
International Voluntary Service can place those with previous workcamp experience. The camp in Bulgaria is organised in association with the National Committee for Voluntary Brigades. Projects involve conservation, restoration and construction.

The United Nations Association organises some 10 camps throughout Bulgaria. Work is manual and the camps very large with up to 100 volunteers from many different countries at each camp.

IVS, 162 Upper New Walk, Leicester LE1 7QA. Tel: 0533 549430

United Nations Association, Welsh Centre for International Affairs, Temple of Peace, Cathays Park, Cardiff CF1 3AP

CANADA
Main language/s: English, French
Currency: Canadian Dollar
Capital: Ottawa
Exports: Vehicles, machinery, paper & cardboard, non-ferrous metals, wood pulp, sawn wood, crude petroleum, wheat
Climate: Winters long and cold, heavy snow
Spring April/May, warm
Summer 10°C-15°C North, 15°C-20°C South

Entry Requirements
Canadian High Commission, Canada House, Trafalgar Square, London SW1Y 5BJ
Immigration Section, MacDonald House, 38 Grosvenor Street, London W1X 0AA.
Tel: 01 409 2071

Canadian Government Office of Tourism, PO Box 9, London SW1Y 5DR

Visas
No visa is required by a UK national to visit Canada. Visitors to Canada must be in good health, have no criminal convictions, and have sufficient funds to maintain themselves and dependents during their stay. Visitors must also have sufficient documentary evidence to establish to the satisfaction of an immigration officer that they will be able to return to the country from which they seek entry or to go to some other country. A valid return airline ticket or evidence of onward transportation is recommended.

Visitors intending to remain in Canada for more than six months may require a medical examination and should contact the Canadian High Commission or the nearest Canadian consulate for further information before proceeding to Canada.

Work Permits
A work authorisation is required for all forms of employment and these are issued by the immigration section once a labour certification has been obtained from Employment Canada to the effect that there is no Canadian resident capable and willing to perform the task for which the visa is required.

Full-time students of universities or other recognised institutions of advanced education of the UK or Republic of Ireland may be authorised to enter Canada for temporary employment provided:

(1) they are British citizens, aged between 18 and 30 years;

(2) they produce written proof that they are bona-fide full-time students of British or Irish universities or similar institutions (including students who have been accepted for admission in the current year), and that they will be returning after the vacation period to continue their courses of study;

Two summer employment programmes are available to British students:

(A) Student General Working Holiday Program
(B) Generic Employment Program

Program A - Students must be in possession of a temporary offer of employment (in writing) in Canada. The job offer, together with evidence of student status and return to course of study should be submitted to the High Commission. On receipt, the appropriate application form will be mailed to the student for completion and return. Should the application prove satisfactory, an employment authorisation may be issued for a maximum duration of 20 weeks. A medical examination is not normally a requirement unless the employment is in food handling, child care, or a related occupation.

Privately arranged employment offers in the Tobacco Harvest cannot be considered under the criteria governing Program A.

Program B - An offer of employment in Canada is NOT required. However, in order to meet the requirements of this Program, in addition to evidence of student status, the student must:
- produce evidence of $1000 to take with them ($500 if they have a relative in Canada)
- produce evidence of return transportation
- undertake a Canadian Government medical examination

All applications for Program B must be submitted through the British Universities North America Club (BUNAC). The maximum duration of an authorisation issued for Program B will be 6 months.
BUNAC, 232 Vauxhall Bridge Road, London SW1V 1AU. Tel: 01 630 0344

The number of students who may be authorised to visit Canada for temporary employment is limited, and permission will be granted on a first come, first served basis. Since the vacation employment programmes in Canada are determined annually, there is no assurance that the programmes authorised for 1989, will be repeated in 1990.

Permanent Residence
The Canadian Immigration Selection Criteria provides for an assessment of most applicants on a point system, with special adjustments being made for people intending to set up in business in Canada. This point system is based on the following factors: education, knowledge of English and/or French, age, area of destination, close relatives residing in Canada, occupational training, occupational demand, occupational experience, arranged employment.

Canadian labour market needs have a very significant influence on the total points which would be awarded to an applicant. The factors concerning occupational experience and demand can be particularly important to the outcome of an assessment. Working experience, excluding training, is mandatory for credit under the experience factor. In addition, limited demand in the occupant's intended occupation due to an adequate supply of Canadian citizens will in the majority of cases result in the application not meeting initial selection criteria.

The classes of admissible immigrants in order of priority are:
(a) Members of the Family Class
(b) Persons who are qualified for and willing to engage in employment in a designated occupation
(c) Persons who have arranged employment in Canada and are able to meet the necessary criteria
(d) Entrepreneurs
(e) Retired persons and self-employed persons

Family Class
Every Canadian citizen and every permanent resident may, if he is residing in Canada and is at least 18 years of age, sponsor the following relatives:
- a husband or wife;

- never-married sons and daughters of any age, and their never-married children of any age;
- a parent or grandparent under the age of 60; (also if widowed or incapable of gainful employment under the age of 60);
- certain orphans;
- a fiance or fiancee (must marry within 90 days of arrival in Canada);
- one relative, regardless of age or relationship, plus accompanying dependents, if the sponsor has no close relatives living in Canada and cannot otherwise sponsor anyone. (Never-married sons and daughters of any age, and their never-married children of any age, may accompany immigrants in any category, as dependents.

The sponsor must accept responsibility for up to ten years to provide housing assistance, living expenses, and financial assistance, should these be necessary.

Assisted Relatives
A Canadian citizen or permanent resident can assist:
- a son or daughter 21 or over;
- a married son or daughter under 21;
- a brother or sister;
- a parent or grandparent under 60;
- a nephew, niece, uncle, aunt or grandchild.

The assistance required to be given is similar to that for sponsors except that the maximum period of time for which assistance must be provided is 5 years. Unlike family class members, assisted relatives have to obtain a certain number of point under the points system selection criteria. These are, however, less than for an independent applicant with no relatives in Canada to assist him.

Independent Applicants
Independent applicants are those who have no relatives in Canada willing and able to sponsor or assist them, and in this class are:

- Entrepreneurs: This is an immigrant who intends and has (a) the ability to establish or to purchase a controlling interest in the ownership of a business in Canada whereby employment opportunities will be created in Canada for more than five Canadians, or more than five Canadians will be continued in employment; and (b) participate in the daily management of that business. Applicants will be required to obtain a minimum of 25 points under the points system.
- Self-employed: A self-employed person is defined as an immigrant who intends to establish a business in Canada that will create opportunities for employment in Canada for himself and up to five Canadians, or who will make a significant contribution to the cultural and artistic life of Canada. It would include small family businesses, professional persons such as doctors, dentists, engineers etc and others without significant capital yet good capabilities. Applicants will be required to obtain at least 30 points under the points system.
- Independent: Independent applicants are the lowest priority of immigrant and are assessed in the full 10 areas of assessment under the point system. They must obtain at least 50 out of the maximum 100 and also have a definite offer of employment or be in a designated category of employment where there is deemed to be a shortage in Canada. The offer of employment must be in a trade or profession acceptable to the authorities as being one where there is a shortage of qualified and willing workers already in Canada. Without such an offer of approved employment there is little chance of an application being accepted.

Travel
If you have an International Student Identity Card (ISIC) you are eligible for discount fares on many international flights and can get up to 45% discount on domestic flights. Bucket shops offer cheap flights to Canada, often on Middle Eastern or Eastern European airlines. Virgin Atlantic also offer cheap flights and air couriers can travel to Montreal, for example, for £175 return (1 or 2 weeks only) or to Toronto for £150 return (7 nights). Travel Cuts (Canadian Universities Travel

Service) specialise in cheap fares to Canada and the USA, especially for those under 26 years of age, using charter flights in peak periods such as summer and Christmas. They are also agents for Goway Adventure holidays which include overland camping trips, activity holidays (rafting, canoeing, snorkelling, gold panning etc).

Once in Canada, bus travel is a cheap way of getting around. If you are planning some long distance travel, you can get a Canrailpass from any Railway station; if you are under 24 you are eligible for a 35% discount. If you are a keen cyclist and wanted to go in summer you could try cycling around (not recommended in the Rockies!).

Poundsavers, 254 Earls Court Rd, London. Tel: 01 373 6465

Trailfinders, 194 Kensington High Street, London W8 7RG. Tel: 01 938 3232

STA Travel, 86 Old Brompton Road, London SW7. Tel: 01 937 9971

Travel Cuts, 295A Regent Street, London W1R 7YA. Tel: 01 637 3161

Greyhound International Travel, 14-16 Cockspur Street, London WC2H OJR. Tel: 01 839 5591

CTC, Cotterell House, 69 Meadrow, Godalming, Surrey GU7 3HS. Tel: 04868 7217

Accommodation
Hostels are the cheapest places to stay and a list of these in Canada can be obtained from The Canadian Hostelling Association. Many hotels charge by the room, not by the number of persons, so a group of four can stay relatively cheaply in a reasonable hotel. In addition many Canadian universities have their residences open during the summer months to the travelling public. Simply write to or phone the university of your choice to make a reservation, as far in advance as possible. Some universities will guarantee a room without a reservation if check-in occurs before 12:00 noon; some only guarantee a room with a reservation. The University of Toronto Housing Service has a list of rates. Below is a list of some of the universities that offer accommodation in the summer:

Nova Scotia:
Mount Saint Vincent University , 166 Bedford Highway, Halifax B3M 2J6.
Tel: (902) 443-4450 (Open May 14 – Aug 26)
Wolfville, Acadia University, Cutten House, Wolfville, BOP 1XO.
Tel: (902) 542-2201 ext 317 (Open May 15-Aug 15)

New Brunswick:
Universite de Moncton, Moncton, E1A 3E9. Tel: (506) 858 4008
(Open May 2-Aug 31)

Quebec:
Bishop's University, Lennoxville VIM 1Z7. Tel: (819) 569 9551 (Open May 18-Aug 28)
McGill University, 3935 University Street, Montreal H3A 2B4
Tel: (514) 398 6367/6365, (Open May 15-Aug1)

Quebec City:
Laval University, Service des residences, Pavillon AM Parent, Cite Universitaire, G1K 7P4. Tel: (418) 656 2921, (Open May 9-Aug 20)

Ontario:
University of Guelph, Room 124, Johnston Hall, Guelph NIG 2W1.
Tel: (519) 824 4120 Ext 2352, (Open April 22-Aug 20)
University of Western Ontario, Alumni House, University Drive, London N6A 5B9.
Tel: (519) 672 5461, (Open May 2-Sept 2)

York University, 4700 Keele Street, North York M3J 1P3. Tel: (416) 736 5020
(Open May 15-July 31)
Carleton University, Tour & Conference Centre, Room 223, Commons Building,
Ottawa K1S 5B7. Tel: (613) 564 3610 (Open May 13-Aug 22)
University of Ottawa, Stanton Residence, 100 Hastey Street, Ottawa KIN 6N5.
Tel: (613) 564 5400 (Open May 7-Aug 21)
Victoria University, 140 Charles St West, Toronto M5S 1K9.
Tel: (416) 585 4524 (Open May 9-Aug 28)

Manitoba:
University of Manitoba, Tache Hill, 26 Maclean Crescent, Winnipeg R3T 2N1.
Tel: (204) 474 9942 (Open May 23-Aug 20)

Saskatchewan:
Luther College, University of Regina, Regina S4S OA2.
Tel: (306) 584 0255 (Open Apr 29-Aug 26)
University of Regina, College West Residence, Regina S4S 0A2.
Tel: (306) 584 4001 (Open Jan 5-Dec 13)

Alberta:
University of Alberta, Room 4, Lister Hall, Edmonton T6G 2H6.
Tel: (403) 432 7200 (Open Apr 29-Sept 1)

Canadian Hostelling Association, National Office, 333 River Road, Vanier, Ottawa,
Ontario K1L 8H9

Working Holidays
Taking formal paid employment in Canada is not possible without a work authorisation.
Immigration officers run spot checks and employers ask for a Social Insurance Number for
deductions to be made. A Canadian employer who knowingly employs workers who are not
Canadian citizens, permanent residents, or who have permission to work in Canada is liable
to a fine of up to $5000 and/or up to 2 years in prison. Knowingly is deemed to be the case
if he has not diligently asked for a social insurance number or other documentation to satisfy
himself that prospective workers have the right to work in Canada. Persons caught working
illegally will almost certainly now be deported and will not be able to return for 5 years without
special permission. However, plenty of people do work illegally and you might get away with it.

BUNAC Work Canada Programme enables you to work in Canada for up to 3 months in the
summer. You may do exactly as you please: work at 1 job for 7-9 weeks and travel afterwards,
take 2 part-time jobs, or travel first and then work, or travel across the country going from
job to job. You have to be a full-time student at HND or degree level, become a member of
BUNAC, attend an orientation course, either know someone in Canada who can sponsor you
or else arrange a job for yourself before departure. The most flexible and independent way is
to apply on the basis of private sponsorship - all you need is a letter from someone living in
Canada offering to sponsor you and look after you in an emergency. If you want to arrange
your job before you go BUNAC publish the Work Canada Directory which contains a listing
of employers who have been recommended by previous Work Canada participants for you to
contact. You could also try going to the library and going through the Canadian Yellow Pages
and writing to individual Chambers of Commerce. The Work Canada Programme is subject to
a quota so the earlier you apply, the better your chances of being accepted.

Fruit picking
Apples: The main commercial cultivation of apples is in the Annapolis Valley of Nova Scotia,
the southern portion of Quebec within a 75 mile radius of Montreal, several portions of Old
Ontario, and the Okanagan Valley of British Columbia. At present BC is the largest producer,

Ontario second, Quebec third, Nova Scotia fourth, and New Brunswick fifth. There is smaller commercial production in the Kootenay Valley of British Columbia and the St John Valley in New Brunswick.

Apricots: These are grown commercially in the Okanagan Valley of BC and to a limited extent in the Niagara Peninsula of Ontario.

Cherries: Cherries are grown for commercial use in BC and in favoured parts of Ontario and Nova Scotia.

Peaches: The second most important tree in Canada. Commercial production is confined to the Niagara Peninsula and the Essex Peninsula of Ontario and the Okanagan Valley of BC, except for a small production in the Annapolis Valley of Nova Scotia.

Pears: The main areas of production are the Okanagan Valley, the Ontario fruit belt and the Annapolis Valley in Nova Scotia.

Plums: The plum is cultivated in every province. Commercial production is not large but is well distributed in the Okanagan, Kootenay and Fraser Valleys of BC, on Vancouver Island and the fruit areas of Ontario, Quebec, New Brunswick, Nova Scotia, Prince Edward Island and Newfoundland.

Grapes: Commercial cultivation of grapes is practically limited to the Okanagan Valley and the Niagara Peninsula of Ontario.

The Okanagan and Creston Area
Keremeos, Oliver Creston, Penticton Kelowna, Rutland
Osoyoos Naramata, Summerland Winfield, Oyama
Vernon

Cherries mid June late June late June
Apricots mid July mid July late July
Peaches mid July late July late July
Prunes early August mid August late August
Pears mid August late August late August
Apples late August early September early September
Grapes early September late September late September
Strawberries late June early July mid July
Raspberries early July mid July late July

Highway 97 which runs through the valley, has orchards either side between Osoyoos and Penticton, and some on as far up as Kelowna. The southern end between Osoyoos and Oliver has the greatest concentration and is the best area to start out on. Keremeos, which is just to the west of the Okanagan also has orchards. This can be reached via the Richter Pass Highway from Osoyoos or Highway 3A from Kaleden Junction.

Most orchards are small family concerns of about 10 acres and support about 2 pickers for much of the season. Larger orchards are usually a combination of several smaller units. There will be spells between the different fruit varieties but there is generally other work to be done such as grass mowing, cutting props etc. In addition to this, the fruits vary from orchard to orchard and, as ripening dates are different throughout the region, when a particular fruit finishes in the orchard in which you are working, there will be work available at some other orchard nearby. It is common to work for friends and neighbours of the orchard owner.

Many orchards have accommodation for workers and these are usually small cabins situated right in the orchard. Some have trailers or cottages. Normally pickers start at about 7 am or earlier, to take advantage of the lower temperature (it can be very hot during the daytime with temperatures in the 90's). Fruit picking is hard work – a single picking bag of fruit can weigh 30-45 pounds, the hours are long and the heat can be intense. Most fruits are picked on a 'piece work' basis (by the bin, box) though peaches are usually picked on an hourly rate. Accommodation is provided and fruit (sometimes vegetables) is grown on the farm, so it is possible to live quite cheaply.

Hiring for this type of work is generally by applying direct at the farm – there are so many of them in a continuous chain that it is simply a matter of walking from one to another until an opportunity is found. Alternatively you could try asking farmers delivering their produce at the local fruit packing shed.

See Chris Cox's account of fruit picking in Chapter 10.

If you have some documentation agricultural information for the Okanagan area can be obtained by phoning any of the following Canada Farm Labour offices:

Manager, 212 Main Street, Penticton, BC V2A 5B2. Tel: (604) 493 3727
Manager, 591 Lawrence Avenue, Kelowna, BC V1Y 6L8. Tel: (604) 860 8384
Manager, 3380 Okanagan Street, Armstrong, BC VOE 1BO. Tel: (604) 546 9626
Manager, Federal Building, 7th St West, Oliver
Manager, 8521 Main St, Osoyoos

Tobacco Harvesting
The principal tobacco growing regions in Canada are located in Ontario and Quebec. In Ontario, tobacco is grown in the southwest area or Old Belt, primarily in Essex and Kent counties, and in the New Belt, farther east, in the counties of Norfolk, Elgin, Middlesex, Oxford and Brant. The towns of Delhi and Tilsonberg are the centre of the industry. Small areas of tobacco cultivation are also found in Durham and Simcoe counties.

In Quebec, the major growing area are located north of Montreal in Montcalm and Joliette counties. Another large area is situated to the southeast of Montreal along the Yamaska Valley in and around the county of Rouville.

There is a heavy demand for labour during August, with many people flocking to the growing areas in Quebec and Ontario to participate. While the harvest does not last more than a few weeks it is possible to stretch this out by starting in the earlier areas and finishing in the latest. Ontario is the most attractive, whilst the growing areas of Quebec are predominantly French and somewhat poorer.

Tobacco picking is hard work with longish hours. However, as the harvest is short (end of July to the middle of September) and the money good (about $50 a day), there is never a shortage of pickers. BUNAC no longer include tobacco picking on their Work Canada Program, so arrangements should be made well in advance through a 'personal contact' in the area, as the chances now of obtaining work simply by arriving there at the start of the harvest are not as good as they used to be.

Tree Planting
One opportunity that has increased tremendously in the past few years is that of tree planting. Everyone knows that Canada is a country of vast forest resources and it is a condition of many cutting contracts now that the areas being cut down are replanted. There are planting contractors in most locations from Nova Scotia to British Columbia; British Columbia offers the best prospects.

The planting season is fairly short: planting operations generally start in lower coastal areas in February or early March and in interior regions in April. Planting is normally completed in all areas by July, though some regions also undertake summer (hot planting) and/or fall planting programmes.

Conditions for tree planting vary greatly depending on the location. As British Columbia is a mountainous province, it is inevitable that some planting takes place on steep slopes. Climate also varies greatly – there is tropical rainforest in coastal areas, and desert regions in the interior. Mosquitoes and black flies can drive you almost to suicide in one location, yet be scarcely in evidence in another.

The rates of pay vary depending on the site to be planted. For example, in a fairly good location of mildly undulating ground, the rate will be somewhere in the region of 12 cents per tree planted and an average worker should have no problem in planting 1,000 trees per day, thus earning $120. In areas where slopes are steeper and undergrowth causes a problem the rate per tree can run to 25 cents. Generally a planter is expected to put in a 10-hour day on 6-day shifts.

Tree planting is responsible work. The trees have to be spaced properly within a given area and the work is checked. The contractor has to make sure that every planter is doing his/her job properly, because the Department of Land & Forests also do a check, and if all is not well the contractor doesn't get paid.

Each planter provides his/her accommodation, either in tents or trailers and campers, and have to pay camp costs of approximately $15 a day, which includes meals.

Tree planting is tiring work, the conditions may be tedious, some camps remote, the mosquitoes can be a real problem, but for those interested in earning good money and working outdoors this is one way to get out in the wilderness and get paid for it.

The Western Silviculture Contractor's Association represents some of the silviculture contractors in the Province and may be able to supply information of employment opportunities.

The Pacific Reforestation Workers' Association represents some of the tree planting and stand tending workers employed by silviculture contractors, and can provide information on typical salary, living and working conditions, planting, stand tending, etc.

There are six Ministry of Forests and Lands regional offices which, together with the district offices (located within each forest regions) are responsible for the entire administration of Ministry silviculture contracts within their region. They will be able to provide information on contract projects and locations, and the companies who have been awarded the contracts.

Western Silviculture Contractor's Association, №310-1070 West Broadway, Vancouver, BC V6H 1E7

The Pacific Reforestation Workers' Association, PO Box 65361, Station F, Vancouver, BC V5N 5P3

Ministry of Forests and Lands Regional Offices:

Nelson Region – 518 Lake Street, Nelson, BC V1L 4C6. Tel: 354 6200
Kamloops Region – 515 Columbia Street, Kamloops, BC V2C 2T7. Tel: 828 4131
Cariboo Region – 540 Borland St, Williams Lake, BC V2G 1R8. Tel: 398 4345
Prince George Region – 1011 Fourth Ave, Prince George, BC V2L 3H9.
Tel: 565 6100
Prince Rupert Region – Bag 5000, 3726 Alfred St, Smithers, BC VOJ 2NO. Tel: 847 7500
Vancouver Region – 4595 Canada Way, Burnaby, BC V5G 4L9. Tel: 660 7500

Agriculture
The International Farm Experience Programme (IFEP) organises work-experience in Ontario and if you already have a job in Ontario they can help you obtain your work permit. They offer six

to twelve months practical training on dairy farms and the pay is approximately Can$ 900 per month, less board and lodging. You have to pay a registration fee, your own travel costs, plus medical and personal insurance, but the pay should enable you to cover all your costs as there is little to spend your wages on. To qualify for a place on the programme you must have at least two years of experience in agriculture (one of which may be at college) and be aged from 18 to 26.

The International Agricultural Exchange Association (IAEA) operates exchange study tours in agriculture in Canada and offers trainee placements in BC, Alberta, Saskatchewan, Manitoba and southern Ontario. Direct programmes to Canada last for 7 months from April to November and trainees are paid approximately £100 per week gross, with deductions for income tax, board and lodging. They also offer Around the World Programmes which involve combining Australia and Canada (13 months) or New Zealand and Canada (13 months) from October to November. Applicants for the programmes should be over 19 years of age and have at least one year's experience in agriculture. They can choose the type of farming they wish to work in and are placed with selected host families where in most cases they live and work as a member of that family.

Working Weekends on Organic Farms (WWOOF) offer work on organic farms without the necessary experience. Upon membership of WWOOF you will receive the current list of holdings where volunteers are welcome. Membership is £6.

International Farm Experience Programme, YFC Centre, National Agricultural Centre, Stoneleigh, Warwickshire CV8 2LG

IAEA, YFC Centre, National Agricultural Centre, Kenilworth, Warwickshire CV8 2LG

WWOOF, 19 Bradford Road, Lewes, Sussex BN7 1RB

Working with Children

Au Pair/Mothers' Helps
The Au Pair classification is not recognised in Canada, but there are opportunities for mothers' helps and nannies in a number of locations across Canada, the most popular cities being Toronto and Vancouver. Mothers' helps must be 18 years of age or over and have a minimum of 6 months' residential experience and/or qualifications. Nannies should have at least 1 year's experience and be able to show relevant references. Wages can vary from £175 to £300 a month. Because of the Canadian Government's requirements, the procedures take between 3/4 months so you should apply in plenty of time.

Universal Care, Chester House, 9 Windsor End, Beaconsfield, Bucks HP9 2JJ.
Tel: 0494 678811

Anglia Agency, 15 Eastern Avenue, Southend-on-Sea, Essex SS2 5QX. Tel: 0702 613888

Students Abroad, Elm House, 21b The Avenue, Hatch End, Middx HA5 4EN. Tel: 01 428 5823

Camp Counselling
BUNACAMP organises summer jobs working in children's camps throughout Canada. The counselling jobs are open to anyone between the ages of 19 and 35 who positively likes working with children and who is free for at least 9 weeks between mid-June and the end of August. You should also be able to offer some skill or experience in one or more activities. You have to pay a registration fee of £48. Your flight is advanced by BUNAC and recouped from your salary at camp. At the end of your service you should have between $360 and $420 and you receive free food and lodging while at camp.

BUNACAMP, 16 Bowling Green Lane, London EC1R OBD. Tel: 01 251 3472

Voluntary Work
The Canadian Parks Service runs a volunteer programme in Alberta and British Columbia. Every three months, in January, April, July and October, it circulates a list of current volunteer applicants to the national parks and national historic parks in Alberta and British Columbia. The Parks Service can put volunteers in touch with a park project that matches their interests. Primarily, of course, for Canadians, non-Canadians might be considered for positions based on their qualifications and what they may offer the Canadian Parks Service.

The Alberta Wilderness Association has volunteer programmes in the summer. The programmes depend on grants and for 1989 its only grant was for summer office help. However, if you are willing to live in the Calgary area the Association might be able to find you some voluntary work outdoors.

Canadian Parks Service, 552, 220-4 Avenue SE, PO Box 2989, Station M, Calgary, Alberta, Canada T2P 3H8

Alberta Wilderness Association, Box 6398, Station D, Calgary, Alberta, Canada T2P 2EI

Work Camps
Christian Movement for Peace has workcamps in Canada each year. Camps include working with children in a variety of activities from swimming, arts and crafts, drama as well as maintenance work.

United Nations Association for International Affairs organises a number of manual, social and work/study camps. The average number of volunteers per camp is 15, with plenty of opportunities for outdoor recreation.

International Voluntary Service organises several camps in Canada assisting the Canadian Bureau for International Education. The application deadline is 1st April each year. Most of the workcamps are in July and August and last for two to four weeks (Quebec 4-12 weeks). Applicants must be 18 years of age or over (16 years + for Quebec). You will work about 30 to 40 hours a week and room and board will be provided at the workcamp. Projects include manual or social work and archaeology. Volunteers are responsible for arranging and paying for their travel to and from the workcamp and should take along some pocket money.

GAP Activity Projects offers school leavers the chance to spend at least six months in Canada, working as volunteers and living with a host family. The hosts provide board, accommodation and in most cases pocket money. Volunteers must pay the return air fare, insurance, registration fee and take money with them for further travel if they wish.

Operation Beaver are interested in volunteers willing to offer their services for 3 months up to 18 months to work on community projects in co-operation with the local people. Volunteers with previous camp experience or construction skills are preferred and the minimum age is 18 years of age. The summer season of service on their projects is from the last week-end of June until the last week of August. However, volunteers can start before this and can continue or commence after this. They will pay for all your food, accommodation and travel expenses inside Canada during your term of service and after two months' service, extended volunteers are eligible for a living allowance ($35 per week to start) and vacation allowance programmes.

CMP, Bethnal Green URC, Pott St, London E2 OEF. Tel: 01 729 1877

United Nations Association for International Affairs, Temple of Peace, Cathays Park, Cardiff CFI 3AP

IVS, 162 Upper New Walk, Leicester LE1 7QA. Tel: 0533 549430

GAP Activity Projects (GAP) Ltd, 7 King's Road, Reading RG1 3AA. Tel: 0734 594914

Operation Beaver, 2615 Danforth Ave #203, Toronto, Ontario, Canada M4C IL6. Tel: (416) 690 3930

Archaeology
The Archaeological Institute of America publishes details of digs in its quarterly bulletin. On many digs no experience is necessary as volunteers are taught various techniques. Digs have taken place in Alberta; Ontario, where participants are taught rock art recording techniques; and Saskatchewan where there is a field school which gives instruction in archaeological techniques. Archaeology Abroad publishes details of excavations in Canada from time to time.

The Archaeological Institute of America, 675 Commonwealth Avenue, Boston, MA 02215

Archaeology Abroad, 31-34 Gordon Square, London WC1H OPY

Conservation
Earthwatch have details of projects in Canada, though mainly these are in Alaska, studying the Alaskan watershed, the Alaskan Musk Ox or Ice Age seeds for example.

Earthwatch Expeditions Inc, 680 Mount Auburn Street, PO Box 403, Watertown, MA 02272

CHILE
Main Language: Spanish
Currency: Chilean Peso
Capital: Santiago
Exports: Copper, Iron ore, Fishmeal, Saltpeter.
Climate: North – desert; centre – warm/temperate;
South – cool/temperate. Jan 20°C, Jul 8°C in Santiago

Entry Requirements
Chilean Consulate General, 12 Devonshire St, London W1N 2DS.
Tel: 01 580 1023

Direccion de Turismo, Catedra 1165 P3o, Santiago

Visas
With very few exceptions, short-term visitors from countries that have diplomatic relations with Chile may enter the Republic for a period of stay not exceeding 90 days without a consular visa, the only document required upon entry being a valid passport and an outward ticket. This period of 90 days may be extended only once, for another 90 days. Included in this category are all persons travelling for reasons of tourism, sport, health, business, attending congresses, family affairs, religious pilgrimages or similar purposes, without the intentions of immigrating, residing or carrying out remunerated paid employment.

Work Permits
Visitors to Chile are not permitted to carry out paid employment. If you wish to work in Chile you must first find an employer who must apply to the Foreign Office in Santiago for a visa. The Consulate General of Chile in London will issue this visa when instructed to do so by the Foreign Office.

Permanent Residence
Persons wishing to reside in Chile in order to carry out paid employment or to study do need a visa. To obtain this, each case should be dealt with and arranged personally at the Consulate General by the interested person himself. There are no health requirements.

Travel
Some travel companies can arrange a flight via one country, eg Chile and leave by another, eg Peru.

The following travel companies offer cheap flights to Chile:

Soliman Travel, 233 Earls Court Road, London. Tel: 01 370 6446
Travel Cuts, 295A Regent Street, London W1R 7YA. Tel: 01 637 3161
Trailfinders, 194 Kensington High Street, London W8 7RG. Tel: 01 938 3939
STA Travel, 86 Old Brompton Rd, London SW7. Tel: 01 937 9921
Steamond Ltd, 23 Eccleson St, London SW1 9LX. Tel: 01 730 8646

With an ISIC students can get a 20% discount on state railways between Santiago and Puerto Montt, and a 50% discount on the ferry from Isla de Chiloe to Puerto Chacabuco.

The following travel companies specialise in holidays for the more adventurous traveller, and arrange overland tours, trekking holidays and expeditions in Chile.

Journey Latin America, 16 Devonshire Rd, London W4 2HD. Tel: 01 747 3108
Encounter Overland, 267 Old Brompton Rd, London SW5. Tel: 01 370 6845
Exodus Expeditions, 9 Weir Rd, London SW12 OLT. Tel: 01 675 5550
Inca Tours, c/o Top Deck Travel, 133-135 Earls Court Road, London SW5 9RH. Tel: 01 370 4555
Twickers World, 22 Church Street, Twickenham TW1 3NW. Tel: 01 892 7606
Dragoman, 10 Riverside, Framlingham, Suffolk IP13 9AG

If you are interested in planning your own expedition, the Royal Geographical Society provides an information and training service, and although it caters mainly for scientific expeditions will also reply to requests for information from the individual. The centre offers regularly updated fact sheets for each of the Latin American countries which give addresses and contacts for further advice. The centre also keeps reports of past expeditions and a register of future expeditions and lists of suppliers.

Royal Geographical Society Expedition Advisory Centre, 1 Kensington Gore, London SW7 2AR. Tel: 01 581 2057

Working Holidays

Job Advertising
Media Universal Services, 34-35 Skylines, Lime Harbour, Docklands, London E14 9TA. Tel: 01 538 5505

There are very few opportunities for the working traveller in Chile. You could contact any of the travel companies listed above for a job as a guide, tour leader or driver before you go.

Teaching English
The British Council recruits a limited number of teachers for Latin America for periods of 1-3 years. It is normally necessary to be a graduate with teaching qualifications and at least 3 years' experience. All vacancies are advertised in the Guardian and The Times Educational Supplement and The Council publishes a free booklet "The British Council: Teaching Overseas" with details of terms of employment and types of posts available.

The European Council of International Schools assists international schools (where English is the main language of instruction) in the recruitment of suitable teaching staff with a minimum of two years' teaching experience. There is an all year-round placement service as well as a recruitment in London in February.

Language schools may be contacted directly: either look the addresses up in the local telephone directory in Chile, or get the addresses of British Council branches in Latin America who may have addresses of centres where English is taught. Some international language schools with bases in Britain also have branches in Chile, eg Berlitz.

The Overseas Educational Appointment Dept, The British Council, 65 Davis St, London W1Y 2AA.
Tel: 01 930 8466
The British Council, 10 Spring Gardens, London SW1 (for LA Branches)
European Council of International Schools,(Dept IM), 21B Lavant St, Petersfield, Hants GU32 3EL.
Tel: 0730 68244
Berlitz, Wells House, 79 Wells Street, London W1A 3BZ

Voluntary Work

Conservation
From time to time The University Research Expedition Programme in California requires volunteers to provide field assistance on a number of different projects in Latin America. Applicants can be aged between 16 and 75, be physically fit, with a willingness to undertake rigorous but rewarding work.

Operation Raleigh sends expeditions to Chile which are based on community work, scientific research and conservation. A typical expedition consists of 120 young people split into groups of 5-15 to tackle individual projects normally lasting 10-12 weeks. Anyone aged 17-25 may apply provided that they can swim 500 metres and understand basic English.

The University Research Expedition Program, University of California, Berkeley, California 94720
Operation Raleigh, Alpha Place, Flood St, Chelsea, London SW3 5SZ.
Tel: 01 351 7541

Archaeology
There are many opportunities each year for those interested in archaeology in Latin America.

The Archaeological Institute of America, 675 Commonwealth Ave, Boston, MA 02215
Archaeology Abroad, 31-34 Gordon Square, London WC1H OPY
Earthwatch Expeditions Inc, 680 Mount Auburn St, PO Box 403, Watertown, MA 02272

CHINA
Main language: Han Chinese
Currency: Yuan (Renminbi)
Capital: Beijing
Exports: Agricultural products, textiles, minerals.
Climate: Winter: cold and dry in North, temperate in South.
Summer: hot and dusty in North, sub tropical in South.

Entry Requirements
Chinese Embassy, Portland Place, London W1N 3AH. Tel: 01 636 1835.

Visas
All foreigners require a visa. These can be obtained from the Embassy or, if you are travelling that way, in Hong Kong. Regulations governing foreign visitors change very frequently.

Occasionally individual travellers can obtain visas but more often you must be part of a group. Up to date information is available from the Anglo-Chinese Friendship Society.

Work Permits
Applicants for jobs in China will, if accepted, be issued with a work permit by the Embassy. All appointments must be obtained before entering the country.

Travel
Some of the expedition travel companies organise trips to China, either flying to Peking and travelling round China, or travelling on the Trans-Siberian express. If you can get into China via Hong Kong, it is much cheaper either going into China by train or taking the boat to Shanghai. Regulations concerning entry into China by individuals keep changing. Contact the Chinese Embassy for up-to-date information. It is easier to get a visa in Hong Kong for China than it is from the UK. If you decide to go via Hong Kong contact the Hong Kong Student Travel Bureau at Star House, Tsimshatsui, Hong Kong (not just for students).

Exodus Expeditions, 9 Weir Rd, London SW12 OLT. Tel: 01 675 7996
Trailfinders, 194 Kensington High St, London W8 7RG.

Accommodation
If you travel independently in China you must stay in government approved hotels in certain cities in China. Most cities have only one hotel where foreigners can stay. Many of these hotels have old annexes that have been converted into dormitories where Chinese students and Hong Kong students may stay. Some let foreigners stay in them (dormitories are one third of the price of the government hotels), but most refuse to allow foreigners to use them. It is always worth asking, otherwise be prepared to pay upwards of £10 per night.

Teaching
Virtually the only work available in China is English teaching in Higher Education Establishments. Most places are filled through the British Council but it is possible to apply direct to the Education Section of the Chinese Embassy.

Overseas Education Appointments Dept, The British Council, 65 Davis Street, London W1Y 2AA. Tel:01 930 8466.

Chinese Embassy Education Section, 51 Drayton Green, Ealing, London W13. Tel: 01 991 1730.

Voluntary Work
VSO has 42 volunteers currently working in China. They are hoping to send more in 1990/91 but this will depend on the political situation.

VSO, 317 Putney Bridge Road, London SW15 2PN. Tel: 01 780 2266.

Warning. Since the incidents in Tianmen Square in mid 1989 the situation in China has been even more volatile than usual and we advise potential travellers to exercise great caution.

COLOMBIA
Main Language: Spanish
Currency: Colombian Peso
Capital: Bogota
Exports: Coffee, Crude petroleum, Cotton, Bananas, Sugar and honey.
Climate: Plains & Coastal regions – warm and tropical.
Central highlands - temperate (66oF)

Entry Requirements
Consulate General of Colombia, Suite 10, 140 Park Lane, London W1Y 3DF.
Tel: 01 493 4565

The Colombian Embassy, 3 Hans Crescent, London SW1X OLR

Visas
Nationals of Great Britain do not need a tourist visa. On entry to Colombia a valid passport and a return or onward journey ticket must be produced. Visas will be granted for 90 days at the port of arrival. Extensions may be requested from immigrations authorities at DAS headquarters in Bogota or at DAS offices in other cities.

Work permits
Tourists are not allowed to engage in paid or unpaid employment during their stay in Colombia.

Applicants with a work contract in Colombia may apply for a work visa. They need to submit a police clearance certificate; a medical certificate; birth and marriage certificates; work contract in triplicate; certificates of academic or professional qualifications or work experience; a valid passport. All documents must be authenticated and translated into Spanish.

Transitory business visas are issued to those travelling to Colombia for short business visits. They are valid for up to 1 year and for visits of 90 days each time. Applicants need to submit a medical certificate; letter from sponsoring company, stating their responsibility for the activities of their agent, and reasons for requesting the visa; documentary evidence of financial solvency of the company; police clearance certificate. Applications must be sponsored by the company that wants to send a representative to Colombia, and the applicant must produce a valid passport and three photographs.

Permanent business visas are issued to those who have to travel frequently to Colombia on business, on a permanent basis. In addition to the documents mentioned above, the applicant must also produce birth and marriage certificates; academic and/or work experience certificates; letter of support of the company stating in which capacity the applicant will work in Colombia, including a clause showing his salary, and a certification that they are providing return tickets and expenses.

Travel
Soliman Travel specialises in fares to Latin America from London but try any of the other cheap discount travel companies already listed. Dragoman and Exodus Overland organise expeditions that take in Colombia.

Colombia is bordered on the east by Venezuela and Brazil, on the northwest by Panama, on the north by the Caribbean, on the west by the Pacific Ocean and on the south by Peru and Ecuador. There are therefore many routes by which you can enter the country.

Land transportation is difficult because of the three chains of mountains and the broad strip of jungle that separates the Pacific Ocean and Panama from the western range of the Andes; some regions are only accessible by air. However the Pan American highway crosses the country from north to south and the Atlantic Railway connects Atlantic and Pacific ports with the capital, Bogota, and other major cities. The railways are reserved mainly for cargo, however, though there is a passenger service on some trains. The best way to get about the country is either by bus or air.

Accommodation
Apart from Youth hostels, some hotels are not too expensive (rates vary from US$10 to US$170). Colombia also has several fully equipped campgrounds. Permission should be requested from

INDERENA (The National Institute for Preservation of Natural Resources and the Environment) for camping at national parks.

Working Holidays

Job Advertising
Media Universal Services, 34-35 Skylines, Lime Harbour, Docklands, London E14 9TA. Tel: 01 538 5505

There are very few opportunities for the working traveller in Colombia and we would strongly advise travellers to take into account the political/social situation before planning a visit to Colombia.

Teaching
The British Council recruits a limited number of teachers for Latin America for periods of 1-3 years. The European Council of International Schools assists international schools where English is the main language of instruction in the recruitment of suitable teaching and administrative staff. They recruit in London in February as well as having an all year round placement service. Private tuition may be available in large cities.

Overseas Educational Appointment Dept, The British Council, 65 Davis Street, London W1Y 2AA. Tel: 01 930 8466

European Council of International Schools, Dept IM, 21B Lavant St, Petersfield, Hants GU32 3EL. Tel: 0730 68244

CONGO
Main Language: French
Currency: CFA Franc
Capital: Brazzaville
Exports: Timber
Climate: Equatorial, hot 20°C-28°C throughout the year; round the year rainfall, heavy in summer (Jul-Aug)

Entry Requirements
Honorary Consulate of the People's Republic of Congo, Livingstone House, 11 Carteret St, London SW1H 9DJ. Tel: 01 222 7575

Visas
UK nationals are required to complete a visa application form and one passport sized photograph together with a fee of £20. They must also have a valid passport.

Work Permits
Tourists are not allowed to engage in paid employment while in the Congo and must have sufficient funds to support themselves.

Work permits for UK nationals must be obtained from the Congolese based company, through the Ministry of Foreign Affairs and the Immigration Dept.

If you are travelling to the Congo on business you must send a letter on the company headed paper stating the nature of business in the Congo, or a telex or letter of Invitation from the Congolese organisation or the name and address of the company in the Congo.

Ministry of Foreign Affairs, BP 2070, Brazzaville, RP du Congo

Immigration Dept, Quartier des Arcades, BP 2088, Near Town Hall, Brazzaville, RP du Congo

Travel
There are daily air services between Brazzaville and Europe on Air Afrique or Ethiopian Airlines. Travelling to one African destination is expensive though, and it is cheaper as well as much more interesting and exciting to travel overland, taking in whichever African countries you like the look of. Exodus Overland organise an African Discoverer expedition travelling on little used routes which include the Congo.

Accommodation
Hotels are generally international class hotels and therefore expensive, another good reason to go for an overland trip which includes accommodation as part of the expedition.

Working Holidays
You are unlikely to find opportunities for casual work in the Congo.

Teaching
The British Council organise the Key English Language Teaching (KELT) project in support of English language teaching in developing countries, the Congo being one of them. Qualifications are high for these posts – a degree, and at least three years' teaching experience of which two years will have been spent in an appropriate overseas country.

The British Council, 10 Spring Gardens, London SW1A 2BN

Voluntary Work
All enquiries regarding voluntary work should be made through the British Embassy in the Congo.

COSTA RICA
Main Language: Spanish (English is widely spoken)
Currency: Colon
Capital: San Jose
Exports: Coffee, Ceramics, Pre-Colombian gold pieces, wooden carvings.
Climate: 70oF in highlands; high 70's-low 90's in lowlands
Rainy season – May to Nov
Summer - Dec to Apr

Entry Requirements
Consulate General of Costa Rica, Flat 1, 14 Lancaster Gate, London W2 3LH.
Tel: 01 723 9630

Visas
British subjects, and citizens of Canada and the United States do not require a visa to enter Costa Rica. The maximum stay is up to 90 days and if a longer period of stay is required, contact the Migration Authorities in San Jose. A valid UK passport is necessary plus a return or onward ticket.

Work Permits

For a work permit in Costa Rica you will need the following documents:
- work contract
- birth certificate
- marriage certificate
- good conduct sworn declaration signed by 3 witnesses
- professional references
- educational references and certificates
- medical examinations – chest X-ray and blood tests
- photocopies of all the used pages of passport
- 5 passport photographs
- letter of application for permit giving type of work intended, name, address and any other useful information
- International Money Order for US$20 payable to "Consejo Nacional de Migracion"

Permanent Residence

For a permanent residence permit you will need the same documents as outlined above. All documents must be translated into Spanish, legalised by a solicitor/Foreign Office and by the Consulate in London.

Travel

Daily and regular flights are available from six cities in the United States: New York, Miami, New Orleans, Los Angeles, Houston and San Juan (Puerto Rico). Some airlines servicing these routes are: Lacsa (the airline of Costa Rica), Eastern, Pan American, Tan/Sahsa, Taca, Iberia and Mexicana. Some discount travel agencies in America specialise in cheap fares to South America, eg Express Discount Travel and Sunline Express Holidays (see Chapter 4 for addresses). In London, try Soliman Travel. If you have an ISIC you are entitled to reduced airfares from many destinations in North and South America and Europe to San Jose.

Within Costa Rica buses are efficient and inexpensive. If you hire a taxi it is best to negotiate with the driver beforehand.

Accommodation

If you have an ISIC there are several youth hostels where you can stay for around US$2-US$3.30 and some include meals and laundry in the cost. In addition you can get up to 40% discount in local hotels.

Youth Hostel Toruma. Tel: 244085
Residencia Juvenil.
OTEC, Av 3 calle 3 y 5, Edif Victoria, 2 do piso, San Jose. Tel: 220866 (for student information)

Another way of staying in Costa Rica involves combining a Spanish language course with a holiday. The following schools place students with Costa Rican families and usually private room, board, laundry and airport pick up are included in the cost. Class size is two to five students and intensive conversational methods are used for four to six hours per day.

American Institue for Language and Culture, Apdo 200, 1001 San Jose.
Tel: 254313 ($15 per hour/group. Room & board $45 a week)

Centro Cultural Costarricense-Norteamericano, Apdo 1489, San Jose.
Tel: 259433 ($100 for 2-month course. Optional room & board $175 per month)

Instituto de Lengua Espanola, Apdo 100, 2350 San Francisco de Dos Rios, San Jose. Tel: 269222
($615 for 3 months. Optional room & board $150-175 pm)

Instituto Internacional Forester, 75 m south of Automercado Los Yoses, SJ.
Tel: 251649 ($1010 for 4 weeks including room & board)

Central American Institute for International Affairs School of Languages,
3540 Wilshire Blvd, Suite 100-C, Los Angeles, CA 90010. Tel: (213) 383-1218
or 338571 (San Jose) ($800 pm, $400 without room & board. Optional tour and culture program extra)

Centro Linguistico Conversa, Apdo 17 Centro Colon, SJ. Tel: 217649/332418
($1080 – on a farm in Santa Ana)

Centro Linguistico Latinoamericano, Apdo 151, Alajuela, CR. Tel: 410261
($900 – in San Antonio de Belen, rural area 25 km from SJ)

Working Holidays
There are few opportunities for the working traveller. You might be able to find some work teaching English by contacting local language schools or arranging private tuition. Look on youth hostel boards for any jobs that might be going.

Voluntary Work
Most of the voluntary work schemes to Costa Rica are based in The United States. Amigos de las Americas sends volunteers to Costa Rica each year for one or two months. Volunteers work in teams in schools, health clinics etc and must complete a training course either in the United States or by correspondence. The cost is US$2100-2500; international return flight costs are covered.

Peace Brigades International works in various places around the world, encouraging the use of non-violent action for peace and justice. It has worked with the United Nations University for Peace to develop and implement models for training in nonviolent conflict resolution, effective group process and negotiation skills. You must attend a training session usually held over a weekend and a good knowledge of Spanish is essential.

Amigos de las Americas, 5618 Star Lane, Houston, Texas 77057

Peace Brigages International, Central America Project Office,
345 Adelaide St W, Suite 606, Toronto, Ontario, Canada M5V 1RS
Tel: (416) 595-9484

Conservation
Genesis II is a privately owned cloud forest at the 7500 foot level in the Talamanca Mountains of Central Costa Rica and covers an area of 75 acres. It is operated as a preserve for academic research and recreational (non-hunting) pleasure. Volunteers help to maintain and construct new trails to provide access to the forest for bird-watchers, ornithologists and day-hikers. Experience is preferable but not essential as training can be given. On occasions when it is not appropriate to work on the trails, volunteers help in the house or the gardens. Volunteers are required to stay for at least one month and pay a contribution of £30 per week which includes full board, room and laundry. Volunteers work the first 20 days (5 hours per day) and then can take the next 8 days off, though after the first 28 days they are free to take days off as they are accumulated (2 days off for every 5 days worked). Days off can be spent travelling around Costa Rica or even visiting nearby Panama and Nicaragua.

Earthwatch publish details of expeditions to Costa Rica – in 1989 projects included following ant trails, recording bird behaviour, collecting fruit and studying birds.

The University Research Expeditions Program needs volunteers to provide field assistance on a number of different projects, some of which are in Costa Rica. Applicants can be aged between 16 and 75, be physically fit and be willing to undertake rigorous but rewarding work.

Steve and Paula Friedman, Genesis II Cloudforest, Apdo 655, 7.050 Cartago, Costa Rica

Earthwatch Expeditions Inc, 680 Mount Auburn St, PO Box 403, Watertown, MA 02272

University Research Expeditions Program, University of California, Berkeley, CA 94720, USA

CUBA
Main language: Spanish
Currency: Cuban peso
Capital: Havana
Exports: Sugar cane
Climate: Dry Season: Nov-Apr, 25°C
Wet Season: May-Oct

Entry Requirements
Cuban Consulate, 15 Grape Street, London WC1. Tel: 01 240 2488
Cuban Tourist Office, Museum House, 25 Museum St, London WC1A IJT.
Tel: 01 580 2942/3

Visas
British Nationals require Tourist cards if they go as tourists. These can be obtained from the Cuban Consulate or through one of the tour operators mentioned below.

Work Permits
Cuba does not issue work permits to British nationals.

Travel
There are regular direct flights to Cuba from Berlin, Barbados, Mexico, Guyana, Jamaica, Peru, Angola, Spain, Nicaragua, Canada, USSR, Panama, France, Trinidad and Tobago and Czechoslovakia. Seasonal charters also fly directly from Cologne, Milan and Miami.

The following tour operators specialise in holidays in Cuba:

Package Tours:
Melia Travel Ltd, 12 Dover St, London W1X 4NS. Tel: 01 491 3881
Thomson Worldwide, Greater London House, Hampstead Rd, London NW1 7SD.
Tel: 01 387 8484
Balkan Holidays Ltd, Sofia House, 19 Conduit St, London W1R 9TD. Tel: 01 493 8612
Progressive Tours, London. Tel: 01 262 1676

Individual Tours:
Regent Holidays,, 13 Small St, Bristol, Avon BS1 1DE. Tel: Bristol 2117111
Europe Air Promotion (Cubana Airline Agents), London: Tel: 01 930 1138

Accommodation
In the capital, Havana, the accommodation is mainly in hotels, but in the beach resorts you can stay in villas, houses or cabanas. Prices for cabanas range from US$7 to US$14 per day.

Working Holidays
There are no opportunities for working holidays in Cuba.

Voluntary Work
The Britain-Cuba Resource Centre organise voluntary work experience in Cuba once a year from September to October. Applications must be received by the end of March.

EYCE organise workcamps in Cuba in conjunction with the Workers' and Students' Baptist Coordination of Cuba (COEBAC). They run field-work camps which give volunteers the opportunity for involvement in agricultural projects, and study camps which gives volunteers the opportunity to participate in Christian-Marxist dialogue, bible studies, discussions, trips and the worship of local congregations. Accommodation is provided in church properties and family homes. A knowledge of Spanish is an advantage.

Britain-Cuba Resource Centre, 29 Islington Park St, London N1.
Tel: 01 359 2270
EYCE Secretariat, 217 Holywood Rd, Belfast BT4 2DH, N Ireland.
Tel: 44 232 651134

CYPRUS
Main Languages: Greek, Turkish and English
Currency: Cypriot Pound
Capital: Nicosia
Exports: Vegetables, Citrus fruits, Copper
Climate: Mediterranean

Entry Requirements
Cyprus High Commission, 93 Park Street, London W1Y 4ET. Tel: 01 499 8272

Visas
A tourist visa lasts for 3 months but may be renewed if you have sufficient funds to support yourself.

Work Permits
Non-Cypriot citizens must obtain a work permit before entering the Republic of Cyprus in order to work. A work permit is obtained, on behalf of the prospective employee, by the Company or employing organisation in Cyprus.

Travel
You can either fly direct to Cyprus or get there by sea from Greece or Israel.

Accommodation
The cost of living in Cyprus is quite high and sleeping on beaches, as in Greece, is not permitted. Youth hostels or campsites are the best bet; the Cyprus Tourism Organisation has information on official campsites and other accommodation.

The Cyprus Tourism Organisation, 213 Regent St, London W1R 8DA.
Tel: 01 734 9822

Cyprus Youth Hostel Association, 13 Prince Charles St, Ay Dometios, Nicosia

Working Holidays
Officially it is not possible to work in Cyprus. However, between August and October you may be able to find work grape picking, and in September the olives are harvested. Oranges are grown

around Limassol. As with most places, word of mouth is the best way to find such work, though it is as well to keep a low profile and keep out of the way of the police. You might also be able to find work in cafes/bars by asking around.

Teaching

As there are a large number of British forces stationed in Cyprus, the army have schools for service men's children to attend there. If you have teaching qualifications at primary, middle or secondary level, the Directorate of Army Education has information on job vacancies at army schools.

The European Council of International Schools assists international English-medium schools (pupils 3-19 years) throughout the world with staff recruitments and offer a year round placement service.

Service Children's Education Authority 2a, Directorate of Army Education, Ministry of Defence, Court Road, Eltham, London SE9 5NR. Tel: 01 854 2242 ext 4206/4224

European Council of International Schools, 21b Lavant St, Petersfield, Hants GU32 3EL. Tel: 0730 68244

Voluntary Work

Workcamps

The World Council of Churches organises workcamps in Cyprus from time to time. In 1989 for example the camp was mainly a study camp near the border of Famagusta which is under occupation.

Middle East Council of Churches, Ayia Napa Conference Centre, Box 48, Ayia Napa, Cyprus. Tel: 037 21284

Archaeology

Earthwatch publish details of digs in Cyprus from time to time. Contact also Archaeology Abroad for possible excavations in Cyprus requiring volunteers.
Earthwatch Expeditions Inc, 680 Mount Auburn St, PO Box 403, Watertown, MA 02272, USA
Archaeology Abroad, 31-34 Gordon Square, London WC1H OPY

CZECHOSLOVAKIA

Main Language: Czech, Slovak
Currency: Koruna
Capital: Prague
Exports: Machinery, Manufactured goods, Iron and steel, Vehicles.
Climate: Cold winters, hot summers

Entry Requirements

Czechoslovak Embassy, 28 Kensington Palace Gardens, London W8 4QY
Tel: 01 727 3966

Czechoslovak Travel Bureau, 17/18 Old Bond Street, London W1X 3DA
Tel: 01 629 6058

Visas
UK nationals need a visa to visit Czechoslovakia. Visas for workcamps are easily obtained; they are usually obtained by the organisation concerned.

Travel
STA Travel arranges low cost flights to Prague. Try also any of the cheap discount travel companies listed in Chapter 4. If you are travelling overland, from May to September, the Raketa boats of the Czechoslovak Danube Shipping Company link Bratislava with Budapest and Vienna. There are also direct bus connections with Budapest and Vienna, as well as long distance express buses to Prague.

Rail travel in Czechoslovakia is cheap, with connections to most major towns and cities. Trains are frequent and tickets are priced according to the speed of the train. The fastest sometimes require a seat reservation. Service is good on the Ostend-Prague line, linking Paris, Strasbourg, Stuttgart and Nuremburg. Departures are frequent from Frankfurt, Munich and Vienna, less so from Rotterdam. Travellers from London will have to change trains in one of the above cities.

Cedok (London) can book rail tickets for people who have already pre-booked services such as accommodation, but only for internal rail travel. Inter-rail cards are not valid for Czechoslovakia but if you are travelling from any of the Eastern bloc countries you can get a 25% reduction with an IUS card.

If you want to visit Czechoslovakia as a tourist/traveller it seems that the easiest (if not the only) way you can do so is by going through CEDOK. If your visit has not been prepaid you will have to pay approximately £10 for each day of your visit on arrival at the Czechoslovak border.

For those interested in cycling in Europe, the CTC Touring Department has quite recently revised information sheets on Czechoslovakia together with the rest of Eastern Europe, which explain general travel procedures as well as covering problems specific to bicycle travel.

STA Travel, 86 Old Brompton Road, London SW7. Tel: 01 937 9921

International Rail Centre, PO Box 303, Victoria Station, London SW1V 1JY.
Tel: 01 834 2345

CEDOK, 17/18 Old Bond Street, London W1X 4RB. Tel: 01 629 6058

CTC, Cotterell House, 69 Meadrow, Godalming, Surrey GU7 3HS.
Tel: 04868 7217

Accommodation
You can obtain temporary accommodation directly at hotels, motels, chalet camps etc or through CEDOK. In some places where there is a large concentration of tourists, rooms can be booked in private houses through a travel office (CEDOK). Accommodation facilities such as student hostels, dormitories and camps are provided exclusively by CKM Travel Agency (Youth Travel Bureau). CKM can arrange accommodation for its members and holders of student cards from country members of the IYHF. Reservations in student hostels, Junior Hotels or junior camps are made either through the CKM office in Prague, or directly on the spot on arrival. With an ISIC students can get special rates for accommodation in CKM Junior Hotels or student dormitories.

CKM, 12 Zitna Ulice, 12105 Prague 2. Tel: 299941

Working Holidays
There are no opportunities for paid employment in Czechoslovakia. However, some tour operators organise holidays in Czechoslovakia and you might be able to get work before you

go as a courier. Explore Worldwide specialise in small group exploratory holidays, walking and rambling etc. Ski Thomson organise ski holidays in the Tatras Mountains.

Explore Worldwide (CZ), 7 High Street, Aldershot, Hants GU11 IBH.
Tel: 0252 319448
Thomson Holidays Ltd, Greater London House, Hampstead Rd, London NW1 7SD.
Tel: 01 387 9321

Voluntary Work

Workcamps
There is a good programme of workcamps in Czechoslovakia. The workcamps are organised by CKM but you must apply through the organisation in your home country in April or May. The workcamps are held each year, mostly in July and August and last for 2 or 3 weeks. The work is usually in forests, gardens and helping with construction projects. Participants must obtain a visa but may stay on in Czechoslovakia for the rest of the month and are exempted from the compulsory exchange requirements. Previous workcamp experience or similar voluntary work is essential.

IVS, 162 Upper New Walk, Leicester LE1 7QA. Tel: 0533 549430
CMP, Bethnal Green URC, Pott St, London E2 OEF. Tel: 01 729 1877
United Nations Association, Welsh Centre for International Affairs, Temple of Peace, Cathays Park, Cardiff CF1 3AP

DENMARK
Main Language: Danish
Currency: Danish Krone
Capital: Copenhagen
Exports: Machinery, Pork, Other meat, Fish.
Climate: Cold winters (0.5°C); warm summers (17°C)

Entry Requirements
Royal Danish Embassy, 55 Sloane St, London SW1X 9SR. Tel: 01 235 1255
Danish Tourist Board, Sceptre House, 169/173 Regent St, London W1R 8PY.
Tel: 01 734 2637

Visas
Holders of a valid national passport/travel document from the UK do not need an entry visa and may stay for up to 3 months in Denmark in order to seek employment.

Work Permits
Once a job has been found it is necessary to obtain a personal registration number within 5 days. This can be done by taking personal identification and a statement from the new employer to the nearest Folkeregistret. A personal registration number entitles the employee to use the National Health Service. Legal permission to stay for more than 3 months must be obtained from the local police. This is usually just a formality for citizens of EEC countries if they have a job.

Permanent Residence
EEC Nationals, including British nationals, who wish to remain longer than 3 months in Denmark can apply for a residence permit after arrival. Apply to the Directorate for Aliens (Direktoratet for Udlaendinge) or the local police not later than 15 days before the expiry of the 3-month period.

Travel

The Travellers Guide to Denmark is produced by the Danish Tourist Board and includes information on accommodation, travel as well as maps and suggested tours and excursions.

About 40 airlines have regular flights to Copenhagen Airport Kastrup. Copenhagen is also the "gate way" to Europe for travellers from the United States, the Far East, Near East and Africa. Because of this there are many discount flights to Copenhagen – contact the travel companies listed in Chapter 4 as well as Air Courier companies. If you hold an ISIC you are entitled to reduced airfares from Copenhagen to numerous destinations all over the world.

International through trains connect Britain and the Continent with Denmark, Norway and Sweden via Copenhagen, eg 4 times daily via Ostende or Hook of Holland, from London (22-24 hours). The Scandinavian from Liverpool Street Station (London) to Harwich and DFDS Danish Seaways connect with the boat train to Copenhagen (27 hours). Nordic Tourist Tickets can be purchased which allow you unlimited travel by rail and to a certain extent by sea in Denmark, Norway, Sweden and Finland for 21 days. If you are under the age of 26, you can purchase an Inter-Rail ticket which is valid for one month. With an ISIC students can get up to 40% discount on train fares from Denmark to many parts of Europe.

Norwegian State Railways, 21-24 Cockspur St, London SW1Y 5DA.
Tel: 01 930 6666

There are car ferries from Harwich or Newcastle to Esbjerg and also connections from Germany, Poland, Sweden, Norway and the Faroes. You should, if possible, always make advance bookings through travel agents as a number of the ferry companies offer special discounts at varying times of the year. Special circular tour tickets may also be available on domestic as well as international ferry routes. With an ISIC you can get discounts on ferries to Norway and the UK.

DFDS Travel Centre, 15 Hanover St, London W1R 9HG. Tel: 01493 6696
Fred Olsen Lines, Crown House, Crown Street, Ipswich. Tel: 0473 233022

Accommodation

"Use It", The Youth Information Centre in Copenhagen produce a magazine, Playtime, which gives details of cheap accommodation in hostels, pensions, sleep-ins, hotels and private rooms as well as information on cheap places to eat, music etc.

Use It Youth Information Centre, Radhusstraede 13, 1466 Copenhagen K.
Tel: 156518

Working Holidays

Job Advertising

Frank L Crane Ltd, 5-15 Cromer St, London WC1H 8LS. Tel: 01 837 3330
(Agents for Politiken and Ekstrabladet for which they can accept job advertisements)

The Youth Information Centre, Use It, issues an information sheet "Working in Denmark" for EEC citizens which lists the procedures to follow when looking for a job and after work has been found. There is information on how to find a job, obtaining a personal registration number, income tax, legal permission to stay after a 3-month period and becoming a member of the union and unemployment fund.

Use It Youth Information Centre, Radhusstraede 13, 1466 Copenhagen K.
Tel: 156518

Wages are very high in Denmark (as is the cost of living). There is generally work to be found in the more menial occupations (such as dishwashing etc) as the pay is much lower and the local people not so keen to do it.

Agriculture
Tomatoes are picked in Denmark throughout the summer, strawberries in June and July, cherries in July and August and apples in September and October. Farms are scattered all over Denmark so a bicycle would be useful to get from place to place in search of work. There are a number of organic farms. Membership of WWOOF (£6) entitles you to receive a current list of holdings on completion of two successful weekends on a farm in the UK. The International Farm Experience Programme organises work experience exchanges for young farmers and horticulturists in Denmark. Girls are also accepted for work in the house. The training is from 3-12 months at any time of the year and wages are £30 plus board and lodging. You should apply at least four months before your intended starting date.

WWOOF, 19 Bradford Road, Lewes, Sussex BN7 1RB
IFEP, YFC Centre, National Agricultural Centre, Stoneleigh, Warwickshire CV8 2LG.

Au Pair
Universal Care have vacancies for Au pairs in Denmark. Most Danish families speak good English and the usual post offers the chance to take evening classes in Danish. Most girls work on a full time basis and the duties are housework and child care. Student's Abroad occasionally have vacancies in Denmark.

Universal Care, Chester House, Windsor End, Beaconsfield, Bucks HP9 2JJ.
Tel: 0494 678811
Student's Abroad, Elm House, 21b The Avenue, Hatch End, Middx HA5 4EN.
Tel: 01 428 5823

Teaching
The Central Bureau administers a scheme for the interchange of qualified, experienced teachers of Modern Languages and related subjects for 3 weeks, 6 weeks, one term or one year with Denmark. It also recruits teachers for one year appointments in Teaching English as a Foreign Language.

Central Bureau, Seymour Mews House, Seymour Mews, London W1H 9PE.
Tel: 01 486 5101

Voluntary Work

Workcamps/Conservation
Workcamps are mainly situated in or near the larger Danish towns. If you are in Denmark already, contact the Mellemfolkeligt Samvirke (Danish Association for International Cooperation) who organise projects in Greenland and the Faroes. Applicants should either have previous workcamp/voluntary work experience or should at least have significant experience of foreign travel. Volunteers receive free board and lodging in schools/tents and insurance. Places are also available for families.

The organisations listed also have information on conservation workcamps as well as study camps.

IVS, 162 Upper New Walk, Leicester LE1 7QA. Tel: 0533 549430

Quaker International Social Projects, Friends House, Euston Road,
London NW1 2BJ. Tel: 01 387 3601

EYCE, 217 Holywood Road, Belfast BT4 2DH, N Ireland. Tel: 44 232 6511

CMP, Bethnal Green URC, Pott Street, London E2 OEF. Tel: 01 729 1877

Mellemfolkeligt Samvirke, Borgergade 10-14, 1300 Copenhagen K

BTCV, 36 St Mary's Street, Wallingford, Oxon OX10 0EU. Tel: 0491 39766

EL SALVADOR
Main Language: Spanish
Capital: San Salvador
Exports: Coffee
Climate: Tropical (20°C-25°C)

Entry Requirements
Consulate General of El Salvador, 9 Welbeck House, 62 Welbeck St, London W1M 7HB. Tel: 01 486 8182/3

Visas
British passport holders do not require a visa to travel to El Salvador.

Work Permits
Aliens wishing to engage in technical or specialised work may obtain a temporary residence visa through a Salvadorean consulate. Visa requirements are a passport and a work permit for which the employer must apply at the Ministry of the Interior. The employer must also submit on behalf of the employee one photograph and a copy of the proposed service contract as well as, duly authenticated (by the Foreign Office and the Salvadorean Consulate): birth certificate, good conduct certificate from police authorities during the last two years, and health certificate. Temporary residence can be for up to one year, but can be renewed periodically, not exceeding a total period of five years. In special cases, and if requested by the employer, after a period of five years a permanent visa may be granted upon payment of a $800 fee.

Aliens entering the country with a tourist visa (valid for up to 90 days), can change their migratory status to that of temporary residence at the discretion of the Ministry of the Interior and by a prior designated payment ($100). Aliens eligible for this change of status are the following:

- Technicians and specialised workers who are contracted by industrial or commercial enterprises based in the Republic, by written application of the party concerned;

- Those members of a religious order dedicated to teaching in any educational centre, or to activities of their cult, by written application of the party concerned;

- The wives, sons and daughters of the technicians or specialised workers when accompanying them.

Travel
Try the discount travel companies listed in Chapter 4 for cheap flights to El Salvador. Encounter Overland organise expeditions to Central America. If you are in the United States or Mexico you might find cheap flights to El Salvador. Bus travel is the cheapest, most comfortable and convenient way of travelling in El Salvador (as in most of Central and South America). Trains are to be avoided unless you can go first class! We would strongly advise taking the political situation into account before travelling in El Salvador.

Accommodation
"Central America by Chicken Bus" is recommended. It has up-to-date information on where to stay, what to do, eat etc.

"Central America by Chicken Bus", Vivien Lougheed, £7.95

Working Holidays
There are very few opportunities for the working traveller in El Salvador. It has a dense population centred around San Salvador, Santa Ana and Santa Tecla and civil unrest is destroying the economy. You might be able to find some teaching work in the cities by contacting language schools or through private contacts.

Voluntary Work
Peace Brigades International seeks to establish international and nonpartisan approaches to peacemaking and to the support of basic human rights. They seek to demonstrate that as international volunteers, citizens can act as peacemakers when their governments cannot.

Peace Brigades sends unarmed peace teams into areas of violent repression or conflict. In El Salvador, PBI volunteers provide protective accompaniment for threatened leaders of unions, human rights and peasant organisations, and a watchful presence at demonstrations and in workplaces. This accompaniment is supported by the PBI Emergency Response Network of concerned organisations and individuals who send telegrams when a kidnapping or other crisis occurs. In addition the El Salvador team is developing curriculum materials and conducting teacher training in conflict resolution and cooperative skills for use in Salvadorean schools.

A great deal of commitment is necessary in order to join PBI as well as a good working knowledge of Spanish. The job is also dangerous and not to be applied for lightly.

PBI, Central America Projects Office, 345 Adelaide St W, Suite 606, Toronto, Canada M5V 1R5.
Tel: (416) 595 9484

ETHIOPIA
Main Language: Amharic (English, Italian, Arabic are widely spoken)
Currency: Ethiopian Birr
Capital: Addis-Ababa
Exports: Coffee, Hides.
Climate: Dry season – Oct-May
Wet season – Jun-Sept
16oc (Addis-Ababa) – 30°C lowlands

Entry Requirements
Ethiopian Embassy, 17 Princes Gate, London SW7 1PZ. Tel: 01 589 7212

Visas
In order to visit Ethiopia as a tourist or on business an application for a visa must be made. Application for a visa should be accompanied by a valid passport, two photographs, a return or onward ticket, and a vaccination certificate for Yellow Fever and Cholera. Tourist and Business visas are valid for two months, and further extension can be obtained by applying to the Immigration and Consular Department of the Ministry of Public and State Security, Addis-Ababa. The fee for a tourist or business visa is £7.

Work Permits
Applicants desiring to stay for a longer period and desiring to work in Ethiopia must apply for an Entry visa which can be issued only upon instruction from Addis Ababa. They should send their request for an Entry visa directly to the Ministry of Foreign Affairs, Passport and Visa Section, Addis Ababa or to persons residing in Ethiopia. The fee for an entry visa is $10.

Travel
You can fly to Ethiopia from London using one of the cheap discount travel companies listed in Chapter 4 or on Ethiopian Airlines. Ethiopia is bordered by the Sudan to the north and west, Djibouti and Somalia to the east and Kenya to the south, and has an 800 kilometre long coastline on the Red Sea. A 778 kilometre long railway line links Addis Ababa with Djibouti and there are two major ports on the Red Sea, Assab and Massawa. The port of Djibouti is also much used.

Working Holidays
There are no opportunities for the working traveller in Ethiopia. 90% of the population earn their living from the land, mainly as subsistence farmers. Teaching is the only paid work you are likely to find.

Teaching
Christians Abroad recruits graduate teachers for service abroad in church related schools and colleges in the developing countries of Africa. Gabbitas-Thring recruits staff at all levels for English-medium schools overseas, one of the major areas being Africa. The Committee for International Cooperation in Higher Education assists in the recruitment of academic, technical, library and administrative staff to universities and colleges in Ethiopia. The British Council operate the Key English Language Teaching (KELT) project in Ethiopia which is aimed at increasing the potential of local teaching centres and at improving the English proficiency of students and trainees in developmental sectors of the economy.

Christians Abroad, Livingstone House, 11 Carteret St, London SW1H 9DL. Tel: 01 222 2165

Gabbitas-Thring Service Ltd, 6-8 Sackville St, Piccadilly, London W1X 2BR. Tel: 01 439 2071

Committee for International Cooperation in Higher Education, Higher Education Division, 10 Spring Gardens, London SW1A 2BN. Tel: 01 930 8466

British Council Overseas Educational Appointments Dept, 65 Davies St, London W1Y 2AA. Tel: 01 499 8011

EGYPT
Main language: Arabic
Currency: Egyptian pound
Capital: Cairo
Exports: Textiles, esp cotton
Climate: Dry, hot in summer – 24°C; cool in north in winter 10°C, warmer in south

Entry Requirements
Egyptian Embassy, 26 South Street, London W1Y 8EL. Tel: 01 499 2401
Egyptian State Tourist Office, 168 Piccadilly, London W1V 9DE. Tel: 01 493 5282

Visas
All visitors to Egypt require a tourist visa which is valid for one month from the date of arrival. Don't get a visa in Israel if you want to travel in the Arab world; get the Israelis to stamp a separate card instead. You must register with the police within seven days of arrival. Usually hotels do this for you but if not, then go to the passport office in Tahrir Square in Cairo.

Work Permits
A work permit is required for employment in Egypt but can only be applied for in Egypt. If you are planning to work in Egypt you must register at the Ministry of the Interior within 1 week of arrival.

Travel
Many discount travel companies offer low cost flights to Cairo (see Chapter 4 for addresses). CPJ Travel offer a £200 open dated ticket to Cairo as an air courier. Exodus Expeditions and Dragoman travel through Egypt on their expeditions to Africa and Asia. Transglobal offer camping tours for budget travellers in Egypt. The Egyptian Tourist Office produce a leaflet giving information on travel, passport and visa regulations, climate, accommodation etc. With an ISIC you can get up to 45% off many international air fares.

Travelling by train is the best way to see the country. There are air-conditioned, non-airconditioned and third class carriages, the latter having no facilities and being extremely crowded. With an ISIC you can get up to 50% off domestic rail fares, though not on 1st class, and cheap ferries from Egypt to the Mediterranean and Red Sea ports.

CPJ Travel, Orbital Park, 178-188 Great South West Rd, Hounslow, Middx TW4 6JS
Tel: 01 890 9393 Ext 3407
Exodus Expeditions, 9 Weir Rd, London SW12 OLT. Tel: 01 675 7996
Dragoman, 10 Riverside, Framlingham, Suffolk IP13 9AG. Tel: 0728 724184
Transglobal, 64 Kenway Rd, London SW5 ORD. Tel: 01 244 8571
ESC/STSD (Student Information) Medical Faculty, Egyptian Scientific Centre,
PO Box 58, El Malek El Saleh, Cairo. Tel: 3622735 (4pm-7pm)

Accommodation
The Egyptian Tourist Office produce an information sheet listing all the youth hostels in Egypt. There are cheap hotels in the New City area, behind Rameses station. You can hire tents at some campsites in Egypt if you haven't got one of your own. Contact Pan Arab Tours in Cairo for information on campsites.

YMCA, 27 El Coumhouria St, Cairo. Tel: 917360
Pan Arab Tours. Tel: Cairo 902133

Working Holidays
Tour leaders and drivers are needed by the tour companies that offer expeditions to/through Egypt. Transglobal specialise in tours within Egypt, ranging from camping holidays for the budget traveller to first class hotel programmes and most tours incorporate a felucca sailing trip down the Nile. They also have small motor yacht tours on the Nile.

Exodus Expeditions, 9 Weir Rd, London SW12 OLT. Tel: 01 675 7996
Dragoman, 10 Riverside, Framlingham, Suffolk 1P13 9AG. Tel: 0728 724184
Transglobal, 64 Kenway Rd, London SW5 ORD. Tel: 01 244 8571

Teaching
The British Council has two centres in Egypt for teaching EFL and often positions fall vacant each year. If you haven't got the necessary qualifications and experience to teach in one of their schools, they may have lists of other language schools you can contact. Try the University notice boards for private tuition as well as youth hostels.

British Council, Overseas Educational Appointments Dept, 65 Davies Street, London W1Y 2AA.
Tel: 01 499 8011

Voluntary Work
VSO are involved in large development projects and technical and vocational training in Egypt, as well as English teacher training, electronics engineering and rehabilitation. Posts are for a minimum of two years and VSO pays the return fare plus a mid-tour grant after one year. Accommodation is provided by the employer and payment is based on local rates.

VSO, Enquiries Unit, 317 Putney Bridge Road, London SW15 2PN.
Tel: 01 780 1331

Workcamps
The Youth Exchange Centre has arranged for volunteers to participate in international youth workcamps in northern Sinai organised by the Supreme Council for Youth and Sport in Cairo. Participants pay for their own travel and food, accommodation and transport within Egypt is provided.

The World Council of Churches organises workcamps in Egypt. Last year the camp was held at a monastery near Beni Sweif and volunteers helped the community of nuns and farmers in its agricultural work as well as sharing the community life. The age limit for workcamps is 18-30 years and volunteers have to pay their own travel costs and insurance. They are also expected to make a small contribution towards general living expenses in the camp.

Youth Exchange Centre, Seymour Mews House, Seymour Mews, London W1H 9PE.
Tel: 01 486 5101

Middle East Council of Churches, Ayia Napa Conference Centre, Box 48,
Ayia Napa, Cyprus. Tel: 037 21284

Archaeology
The Archaeological Institute of America has details of digs in Egypt. In particular, for mid-winter 1991 up to three volunteers are needed with field experience, aged at least 21, who can stay for one or two months for an excavation at Bahariya Oasis. Lodging, meals and local travel to the site are provided but not travel to Egypt or insurance. Applications for this dig have to be submitted at least six months in advance as the work is taking place in a high security military zone and a lot of paper work is involved.

Archaeological Institute of America, 675 Commonwealth Ave, Boston,
MA 02215. Tel: (617) 353 9361

FINLAND
Main Language: Finnish, Swedish
Currency: Markka
Capital: Helsinki
Exports: Paper and cardboard, Wood pulp, Sawn wood, Machinery, Ships and boats, Clothing.
Climate: Winter - Oct-May (min temp - 30°C)
Summer - Jun-Sep (max temp - 30°C)

Entry Requirements
Embassy of Finland, 38 Chesham Place, London SW1X 8HW. Tel: 01 235 9531
Finnish Tourist Board, 66/68 Haymarket, London SW1Y 4RF. Tel: 01 839 4048

Visa
UK citizens holding a valid passport do not require a visa for a tourist or business visit to Finland for a period not exceeding 3 months.

Work Permits
It is strongly emphasised by the Finnish Embassy that a person intending to work in Finland should not enter the country before the following formalities have been completed:

- employment must first be found in Finland;
- the applicant must complete the work permit and visa forms and attach to the work permit application (a) the Finnish employer's certificate, giving precise details of salary, type and duration of work; (b) all possible qualification certificates; (c) three passport photographs.

Applications will be forwarded to the Finnish Ministry of the Interior. If the application is successful the applicant's passport is stamped for three months which may or may not be extended in Finland.

Permanent Residence
Foreign nationals wishing to reside permanently in Finland require a residence permit. This also applies to those married to Finnish citizens, former Finnish citizens and children not having Finnish nationality.

Travel
Air fares to Finland tend to be expensive. However, if you have an ISIC you are entitled to reduced fares on international flights. Try also the cheap discount travel companies mentioned in Chapter 4. Students and those under 26 can get a 50% discount on ferries to Sweden and a 50% discount on ferries from Sweden to Finland. They can also get up to 50% discount on rail fares to Finland through Eurotrain. The Nordic Tourist Ticket entitles you to unlimited travel on trains in Finland and the rest of Scandinavia and is valid for 21 days (you must purchase it before you enter Finland). The Helsinki Card is valid for 1, 2 or 3 days and is designed to help you get to know the city. The card entitles you to fee travel on city buses, trams and the metro; free boat trips and tours; city tour reductions; special benefits for saunas, swimming baths, bicycle rental etc and free admittance to some museums and sights.

FSTS Travela, Kaivokatu 10b 8th floor, 00100 Helsinki. Tel: (90) 624101

Norwegian State Railways, 21-24 Cockspur Street, London SW1Y 5DA.
Tel: 01 930 6666

Eurotrain, 52 Grosvenor Gardens, London SW1. Tel: 01 730 3402

Accommodation
ISTC produce a "Sleep Cheap Guide to Europe" which is available from student travel office and which gives information on accommodation in Finland The Finnish Tourist Board also have details of campsites and youth hostels.

Working Holidays

Job Advertising
Frank L Crane Ltd, 8 Salisbury Square, London EC4Y 8HR (agents for Helsingin Sanomat)

Joshua B Powers Ltd, 46 Keyes House, Dolphin Square, London SW1V 3NA

Opportunities for the working traveller in Finland are not good. It is one of those countries better to pass through between work spells in other countries where the opportunities are better. This doesn't mean that you can't pick up casual work in hotels or on farms but the chances are much better and easier in other countries. There are, however, a number of international trainee exchange programmes supervised by the Ministry of Labour in Finland which you can set up before you go.

Exchange Programmes

The Ministry of Labour organise The Family Programme which gives you a chance to get to know the Finnish way of life as a member of a family. Many Finnish families want to improve their knowledge of foreign languages, mainly English, German and French and therefore language teaching is the main purpose of the programme. The programme is open to 18-23 year olds and the training period varies from one month to three months in the summer. You can also apply for a longer training period outside the summer season which lasts from 6 to 12 months. Besides teaching your mother tongue to the family, you will be expected to share the family's daily tasks, such as child care, light housework etc. If you prefer a placement in a family engaged in farming or cattle raising, you should mention this in your application. You will be expected to work for 5-6 hours per day, five days per week which includes both language teaching and housework. Besides free board and lodging the trainee will have, depending on the district, at least FIM 150-200 pocket money per week.

Applicants for the summer period should have their applications in the Finnish Ministry of Labour at the beginning of March. Applications for a longer training period can be sent in throughout the year. Allow 2-3 months to arrange a placement. Information and application forms are available from The Central Bureau for Educational Visits and Exchanges.

IAESTE (International Association for the Exchange of Students for Technical Experience) handles student exchanges for universities of technology, technical colleges and institutes, and faculties of agronomy, forestry, mathematics, science, architecture, etc. Age limits are 18-30. Training in Finland usually lasts one to three months between May and October, inclusive.

Openings also exist in commerce, economics, tourism, services, forestry, agriculture, horticulture etc. Students of Finnish who want to improve their knowledge of the language are welcome to jobs involving customer service. Training periods are 2-4 months from May to October. You must be aged between 18 and 30, have studied for at least one year and have some experience in the field. Male agricultural trainees require a driving license for a tractor. Also accepted are agricultural trainees who have had practical experience on the farm, but no theoretical instruction.

There are limited openings for graduates in technical and commercial branches, catering, agronomy, horticulture, and for assistant language teachers at school (mother tongue only). Training periods are for 6 to 18 months. Applicants should be under 30. Schools also accept non-graduate students for mother-language teaching.

Trainees are usually paid the normal rates for the job in Finland and work a normal 40-hour, five-day week. The local manpower office will help you find housing. Trainees arrange their own travel and pay for it themselves.

If you are interested in any of these programmes and meet the qualifications, you should get in touch with one of the organisations listed below. One to three months will be needed for organising the arrangements.

The International Farm Experience Programme organises work experience exchanges for young farmers and horticulturists in Finland. It involves practical work on farms and nurseries. Almost all placements are for the Spring and Summer months. Wages are £30 per week plus board and lodging.

The Central Bureau for Educational Visits and Exchanges, Seymour Mews House, Seymour Mews, London W1H 9PE

United Kingdom Sponsoring Authority (UKSA) for the International Exchange of Young Agriculturists, Agriculture House, Knightsbridge, London SW1X 7NJ

IFEP, YFC Centre, National Agricultural Centre, Stoneleigh, Warwickshire CV8 2LG

Voluntary Work

Workcamps

IVS organise workcamps in Finland in the summer months. Details of summer camps are available from January. On receipt of £3 you will be put on their mailing list.

The EYCE organise workcamps in Finland. In 1989 workcamps were based at Valamo Monastery in Eastern Finland, the centre of Orthodox worship in Finland. Work included gardening and general household tasks. The camp also offers the opportunity to experience the Orthodox faith in the context of monastery life.

IVS, 162 Upper New Walk, Leicester LE1 7QA. Tel: 0533 549430

EYCE Secretariat, 217 Holywood Road, Belfast BT4 2DH, N Ireland. Tel: 44 232 651134

FRANCE
Main Language: French
Currency: French Franc
Capital: Paris
Exports: Machinery, Vehicles, Iron and steel, Textiles, Non-ferrous metals, Petroleum products, Petrol, Wine, Wheat.
Climate: South: hot and dry in summer (23°C+), winter mild and damp, mistral (strong cold winds) in autumn and winter
North: unpredictable, rain throughout year, cold winters, warm summers

Entry Requirements
French Consulate General, PO Box 57, 6A Cromwell Place, London SW7 2EW
French Embassy, 58 Knightsbridge, London SW1X 7JT

French Government Tourist Office, 178 Piccadilly, London W1V OAL

Visas
British citizens do not require a visa to go to France as tourists for a period of three months maximum and in this time may seek employment.

Work Permits
Nationals of the EEC member states, including the UK, do not need to obtain a work permit prior to their departure. A person who wishes to work in France should apply, within the first three months of arrival for a "carte de sejour" (residence permit) at the "mairie" (townhall) or "Prefecture" of the place of residence. This permit will be granted upon production of a valid passport, birth certificate, marriage certificate, three passport photographs, a proof of accommodation and a contract of work or the necessary authorisations from the Chamber of Commerce in case of self-employment/business.

Permanent Residence
Foreigners who wish to establish residence in France without working there or setting up commercial or industrial business should make an application for a visa at least 3 or 4

months before departure. They should complete six application forms in French. The following documents are required:

- an affidavit drawn up in the presence of a Commissioner for Oaths or a solicitor;
- a letter from their bank, solicitor or accountant, confirming the capital they possess and their yearly income once in France;
- the title of ownership (for people owning a property in France);
- a copy of the marriage certificate with the French passport of the French spouse (for spouses of French nationals):

The visa fee is at present £10.

Travel
France is expensive to get to by ferry (comparatively) unless you buy a through ticket, or have an ISIC which entitles you to a discount. Trains are a much cheaper alternative especially if you qualify for an Inter Rail Pass (ie if you are under 26 years of age). Try Top Deck Travel, which not only arranges double-decker tours of Europe but also sells discounted air tickets. Try also the other cheap discount travel companies listed in Chapter 4.

Within France if you have an ISIC you are entitled to up to 50% off domestic flights on Air Inter; 25% discount on some domestic rail routes and up to 40% off non-domestic rail travel. SNCF French Railways Ltd produce an information pack on various rail passes. You can also get discount bus fares to other European destinations as well as discounts on ferries to Greece.

You can purchase rail passes at train stations (bring a photo). There are two kinds – the Carte Jeune and the Carre Jeune, depending on when you want to travel. The Accueil des Jeunes en France (AJF) at the Gare du Nord can provide cheap rail and coach tickets. If you want to travel by train-plus-rent-a-bike SNCF produce a pamphlet 'Train + Velo' containing information; it costs about £4.50 per day. If hitching doesn't appeal, a good way to cover distance cheaply is with Allostop, a national service which pairs drivers and passengers on payment of a small registration fee.

Top Deck Travel, 131 Earls Court Rd, London. Tel: 01 373 8406

SNCF French Railways Ltd, French Railways House, 179 Piccadilly,
London WIV OBA

French Government Office, 178 Piccadilly, London W1V OBA

Eurotrain, 52 Grosvenor Gardens, London SW1. Tel: 01 730 3402

Allostop, 84 passage Brady, 10eme, 75010 Paris

AJF Gare du Nord, Arrival Hall, 75010 Paris

Accommodation
If you haven't booked in advance in Paris, try the Accueil des Jeunes en France (AJF) kiosk at the Gare du Nord (the main arrival station from the UK).
It is a youth information centre and arranges cheap accommodation as well as cheap rail and coach tickets. There are four other AJF offices in Paris – try also the one at 119 rue St Martin

in front of the Pompidou Centre. The five youth Hostels are all out of town and tend to get booked up months in advance. 'Foyers' are like hostels but don't take reservations – try to get there before 10am. Lists of these are available from the AJF office. The most popular one is the Foyer International des Edudiantes, 93 bvd St Michel, 6eme, but only from June to October. Make a reservation in writing or take a chance in person before 10am. The OTU (French Student Travel Office) has details of other cheap accommodation throughout France.

Camping is easy in Paris as in the rest of France. The most central one is the Bois de Boulogne site, alle du Bord de l'Eau, 775016 Paris.

AJF Gare du Nord, Arrival Hall, 75010 Paris
AJF Beaubourg, 119 rue St-Martin, 75004 Paris. Tel: 42 77 87 80
AJF Hotel de Ville, 16 rue du Pont Louis-Philippe, 75004 Paris
AJF Quartier Latin, 139 bvd St Michel, 75005 Paris
AJF, 12 rue des Barres, 75004 Paris

OTU, 137 bvd St Michel, 75005 Paris. Tel: (01) 43 29 12 88

Working Holidays

Job Advertising
French Publishing Group, 171 Fleet St, London EC4. Tel: 01 353 4418
(agency for many French newspapers including 'Le Figaro')

International Herald Tribune, 63 Long Acre, London WC2. Tel: 01 836 4802
(advertisements can be inserted in the Paris edition through this office)

Publicitas Ltd, 525 Fulham Rd, London SW6 IHF (agents for 'Le Monde')

Chambre de Commerce Franco-Britannique, 26 avenue Victor Hugo, 75016 Paris.
Tel: 1 45 01 55 00

There is a good working relationship between the British Employment Service Agency and the French "Agence Nationale pour l'Emploi". The Employment Service Agency issues a leaflet "Working in Europe" which gives useful information on how to get a job which is available from any Employment Office.

The Cultural Services of the French Embassy provide information on the opportunities for vacation work, paid or unpaid, and on courses. The Centre d'Information et de Documentation Jeunesse (CIDJ) can provide practical help in finding work and produce many information sheets and booklets giving practical advice.

Agriculture
In France there are opportunities for grape picking. The vendage (harvest) starts in mid-September and goes on until the end of October in Beaujolais, Aquitaine, the Loire Valley, Central France, Burgundy, Midi-Pyrenees and Champagne. The work is back-breaking and consists of either picking the grapes or emptying the baskets which weigh up to 100 lbs. You generally work for 8 hours a day with a 2 hour lunch break and you may have to work on Sundays. If the weather is bad, only the hours actually worked are paid. Accommodation is sometimes provided by the vineyard, sometimes the cost is deducted from your earnings; living conditions can be primitive. You generally have to provide your own food so take camping

equipment with you as well as a sleeping bag. Wages are approximatley FF36 per hour, more if you work as a porter.

You can find work by visiting all the vineyards in the region well before the start of the vendage or by applying to the local employment agencies (ANPEs) or the Centre d'Information et de Documentation Jeunesse (CIDJ) in Paris. A working knowledge of French is an advantage.

'Vacation Work' arrange grape picking for groups of young people in the South of France from the middle of September to the end of September. All arrangements are made for you: your job with work permit, travel orientation, insurance etc and in most cases there is a back-up service which you may call on if you have problems. Return travel is not included in the cost.

There are also opportunities in France for fruit picking in the Rhone Valley, Brittany, Languedoc-Roussillon, Dordogne, Medoc, Normandy and around Paris. In the South west and in the Auvergne area maize is grown and from mid-July to mid-August needs to be "topped" (picking off the male flowers to produce a better cob). Apply to the local ANPEs.

The International Farm Experience Programme offers a combined work-experience and language course through CEJA, the European Council of Young Farmers. A five week course of French or German is held in France, followed by 4 1/2 months of practical training in any of the EEC countries. Courses begin in February and July and wages and free board and lodging are provided during the practical training. Pocket money and board are provided during the course. They also offer a three month training course, beginning in June and 2-8 week courses on Computer business, landscape gardening, tourism, butter and cheese, forestry and others.

If you have no experience but would like to help out on an organic farm, WWOOF will send you details of organic farms in France when you become a member (membership is £6).

Centre D'Information et de Documentation Jeunesse (CIDJ), 101 quai Branly, 75740 Paris 15

Vacation Work International Club, 9 Park End Street, Oxford OX1 1HJ

IFEP, International Farm Experience Programme, YFC Centre, National Agricultural Centre, Stoneleigh, Warwickshire CV8 2LG

WWOOF, 19 Bradford Road, Lewes, Sussex BN7 1RB

Au Pair
A basic knowledge of French is usually required. Departures after early July are often difficult as families are frequently away until at least September and French offices are often closed for at least the whole month of August, so it is a good idea to apply early on in the year if you want to work in France during the summer. It is preferred for girls to stay at least three months in France.

Universal Care, Chester House, 9 Windsor End, Beaconsfield, Bucks HP9 2JJ.
Tel: 0494 678811

Students Abroad, Elm House, 21b The Avenue, Hatch End, Middx HA5 4EN.
Tel: 01 428 5823

Anglia Agency, 15 Eastern Avenue, Southend-on-Sea, Essex SS2 5QX. Tel: 0702 613888

Helping Hands Au Pair and Domestic Agency, 10 Hertford Rd, Newbury Park, Ilford, Essex IG2 7HQ. Tel: 01 597 3138

Accueil Familial des Jeunes Etrangers, 23 rue du Cherche Midi, 75006 Paris

Comite Parisien de l'Association Catholique des Services de Jeunesse Feminine, 65 rue Monsieur le Prince, 75006 Paris

Alliance Francaise, 101 Boulevard Raspail, 75006 Paris

Tourism

Many tour companies organise holidays in France – some in hotels, some in winter resorts and others on campsites. It is worth visiting your local travel agent and picking up brochures from which you can get the names and addresses of companies to apply to for courier, ski instructor, watersports jobs.

Hotels

British subjects over 18 and under 30 who have at least two years' experience of hotel work and wish to find work for a few months as "stagiaire" in a hotel or restaurant in France should contact the British Hotel, Restaurant and Caterer Association.

Jobs as waiters, kitchen staff, hall porters, night porters, chambermaids, barmaids, receptionists, swimming pool attendants etc are available for those who do not speak French by applying to British Tour Operators. An increasing number of hotels in France have been taken over to be run by an entirely British team for entirely British guests. The standards are generally much lower and the ambiance more informal than in a National hotel. British workers are paid only 1/3 of the minimum legal wage in France, so the Tour Operators can offer cheaper holidays.

At any National hotel in France, a good working knowledge of French is essential and there is every opportunity to speak French. The standards are high and the discipline is strict and the salaries are therefore three times those paid in the British Tour Operators' Hotels. Days off are limited and may be missed in the high season, as French hotels employ the minimum staff.

The JITA Club (Jobs in the Alps) offers benefits and assurance to British workers who work in winter resorts in France, though there are opportunities for summer jobs at these resorts as well. Most winter jobs start early to mid-December and last until mid-April though there a few in January when replacements may be needed. Most summer jobs are for three months, from mid-end June to mid-end September. Alpotels produce a booklet (£5) which gives guidance on how to set about finding work in hotels and lists 30 resorts in France which have seasonal hotels. They also produce lists (50p each) hotels in these resorts to which you can write (in French) or which you can visit in search of work.

The British Hotel, Restaurant and Caterer Association, 40 Duke Street, London W1M 6HR. Tel: 01 499 6641

Jobs in the Alps, PO Box 388, London SW1X 8LX. Tel: 01 235 8205

Alpotels (London), PO Box 388, London SW1X 8LX

Couriers/Reps

Many holiday companies require a large number of staff to supervise their operations in France mainly on campsites. At each site campsite couriers are needed (including children's couriers), as well as activity instructors whose job it is to teach watersports, climbing etc. Some companies, such as PGL and Quest Adventure, need cooks, nurses, administrative assistants, cashiers etc at their Activity Centres in France. Generally you must be over 20 for positions abroad and must enjoy working as a team, as well as being prepared to lend a hand with any job that needs doing. Return travel is usually provided, as well as accommodation. Wages are approximately £75 per week. The season usually starts in April and finishes in September/October.

Thomson Holidays need Overseas Reps to meet clients at the airport and give them advice and assistance while on holiday. EF Educational Tours require Tour Directors to lead groups of visiting American and Canadian school students on tours of Europe. World Wine Tours organise tours to France's wine regions with expert wine guides to accompany them. They also operate wine tours through France by barge which require couriers.

British students over the age of 16 looking for work in summer camps in France can contact the Central Bureau.

PGL Young Adventure Ltd, Personnel Dept, Station St, Ross-on-Wye, HR9 7AH.
Tel: 0989 767833

Quest Adventure, Grosvenor Hall Leisure, Bolnore Road, Haywards Heath, West Sussex RH16 4BX. Tel: 0444 441300

Eurocamp Travel, Edmundson House, Tatton St, Knutsford, Cheshire WA16 6BG

Canvas Holidays Ltd, Bull Plain, Hertford, Hertfordshire SG14 1DY.
Tel: 0992 553535

Club Cantabrica, Holidays Ltd, Overseas Dept, Holiday House, 146-148 London Rd, St Albans, Hertfordshire AL1 1PQ. Tel: 0727 33141

Intasun Camping, Intasun House, 2 Cromwell Avenue, Bromley, Kent BR2 9AQ.
Tel: 01 290 1900

Thomson Holidays Ltd, Greater London House, Hampstead Rd, London NW1 7SD.
Tel: 01 387 9321

EF Educational Tours, EF House, 1 Farman St, Hove, Brighton BN3 1AL.
Tel: 0273 723651

World Wine Tours Ltd, 4 Dorchester Rd, Drayton St Leonard, Oxfordshire OX9 8BH
Tel: 0865 891919

Central Bureau, Seymour Mews House, Seymour Mews, London W1.
Tel: 01 486 5101

Teaching English
The French Embassy Cultural Service publishes an information sheet "Teaching Posts in France" which gives information on how to obtain posts as teachers and assistants in both state and private schools.

Casual teaching jobs in Paris are hard to come by as there is an abundance of qualified teachers who want to work there.

The British Council in Paris publishes a list of language schools which you could try contacting. You could try placing advertisements in the papers for private tuition (as well as reading papers for tuition wanted) or putting up notices advertising your services on youth hostel boards or at the Alliance Francaise.

The Central Bureau administers a scheme for the interchange of qualified, experienced teachers of Modern Languages and related subjects for 3 weeks, 6 weeks, one term or one year with France. International House recruits and trains teachers for its affiliated schools in France.

PGL Young Adventure require both teachers and senior teachers, preferably with TEFL qualifications and relevant experience, for their activity centres in France. Wages are £60-£90 per week depending on qualifications and experience.

French Embassy Cultural Service, 23 Cromwell Rd, London SW7. Tel: 01 581 5292

Alliance Francaise, 101 Boulevard Raspail, 75006 Paris

British Council, Overseas Educational Appointments Dept, 65 Davies St, London W1Y 2AA. Tel: 01 499 8011

Central Bureau, Seymour Mews House, Seymour Mews, London W1H 9PE. Tel: 01 486 5101

International House, Teacher Selection Dept, 106 Piccadilly, London W1V 9FL. Tel: 01 491 2598

PGL Young Adventure Ltd, Station St, Ross-on-Wye, HR9 7AH. Tel: 0989 767833

Voluntary Work

Work Camps
There are a great many opportunities for workcamps throughout France, and they cover a range of activities from restoration work, and general manual labour, to ecology and study camps.

CMP, Bethnal Green URC, Pott St, London E2 0EF. Tel: 01 729 1877

IVS, 162 Upper New Walk, Leicester LE1 7QA. Tel 0533 549430

Quaker International Social Projects, Friends House, Euston Rd, London NW1 2BJ Tel: 01 387 3601

EYCE Secretariat, 217 Holywood Rd, Belfast BT4 2DH, N Ireland. Tel: 44 232 651134/5

GAP Activity Projects (GAP) Ltd, 7 King's Road, Reading RG1 3AA. Tel: 0734 594914

Concordia, 8 Brunswick Place, Hove, East Sussex (summer camps)

Archaeology
The Archaeological Institute of America publishes details of digs in France in its Fieldwork Opportunities Bulletin. Excavations abroad requiring volunteers are also published in a booklet called 'Archaeology Abroad'. Earthwatch publish details of digs in France in their monthly magazine.

Volunteers always have to pay their own travel expenses to the site. In some cases accommodation and food is provided, and on some digs you have to pay a contribution towards costs. Volunteers in France have to be at least eighteen in most cases.

Archaeological Institute of America, 675 Commonwealth Ave, Boston, MA 02215, USA

Archaeology Abroad, 31-34 Gordon Square, London WC1H OPY

Earthwatch Expeditions Inc, 680 Mount Auburn St, PO Box 403, Watertown, MA 02272, USA

Conservation

BTCV organise conservation projects in France in the summer. The cost is £70 for ten days (1989) and includes accommodation, food, transport from the pre-arranged pick-up point and holiday insurance. You have to make your own travel arrangements, but BTCV can provide you with advice. The project leader is bilingual so a knowledge of the language is not essential. In 1989 the project took place near le Touquet on a coastal access project for the disabled.

BCTV, 36 St Mary's Street, Wallingford, Oxfordshire OX10 0EU. Tel: 0491 39766

Germany (Federal Republic)
Main Language: German
Currency: Deutschmark
Capital: Bonn
Exports: Machinery, Vehicles, Iron and steel, Textiles, Organic chemicals.
Climate: Similar to UK though colder in winter especially in the mountains

Entry Requirements

Embassy of the Federal Republic of Germany, 23 Belgrave Sq, Chesham Place, London SW1X 8PZ. Tel: 01 235 0165

German National Tourist Office, Nightingale House, 65 Curzon St, London W1Y 7PE. Tel: 01 495 3990/91

Visas

Holders of British passports with the endorsement "British Citizen" or "Holder has the right of abode in the UK" do not need a visa for entry in the Federal Republic of Germany.

Work Permits

European Community nationals who wish to be gainfully employed either as wage-earners or in a self-employed capacity are granted liberty of movement and may enter the Federal Republic of Germany without entry visa or work permit. They may enter and stay in Germany for up to 3 months seeking employment.

Following their entry, European Community Nationals and their families must obtain a Residence Permit (Aufenthaltserlaubnis) from the local Foreign Nationals Authority (Auslanderamt) as soon as employment has been taken up but not later than three months after arrival. A Residence Permit will not be granted if no employment has been taken up by the end of the three months' period.

Travel

Many of the discount travel companies offer cheap fares to Germany. The fare from London to Munich for example with STA Travel is from £82 return (low season) to £122 return (high season). If you are travelling by train Eurotrain offer cheap rail passes to those under 26. Try Top Deck Travel for bus travel.

For rail travel within Germany, you can buy a Germanrail Tourist Pass outside Germany. It is pricey and you need to travel at least 1000km to make a saving. Students can get reductions on 9 and 16-day passes. If you are under 26 you are entitled to up to 40% discount on rail fares from Germany to other European destinations.

Bikes can be hired at the railway station in West Berlin, cheaper if you have a current rail ticket. The major cities have a system of day tickets for travel on all inner-city transport systems, as well as weekly and monthly travel passes which are available from the railway stations.

Accommodation

The tourist offices in the cities have free maps and leaflets listing cheap accommodation. The Munich tourist office is reportedly very helpful and books rooms, but be prepared to queue. In West Berlin there is a university residence open to travellers in the summer which is cheap but fairly difficult to get to. The BBS tour agency also has cheap accommodation in Berlin but it is advisable to contact them in advance in the summer. Camping is popular in Germany, but generally you have to book in advance in the summer to be able to stay when you want to.

Studentenwohnheim Schlachtensee (University Accomm), Wasgenstr 75, 1000 Berlin 38. Tel: 80 10 71

BBS Tour Agency, West Berlin. Tel: 01049 302 13 90 31

Deutscher Camping Club, Geisbergstr 11, 1000 Berlin. Tel: 24 60 71

Burg Schwaneck Hostel, Burgweg 4-6, Munich. Tel: 793 06 44

CVJM (YMCA), Landwehrstr 13, Munich. Tel: 55 59 41

Working Holidays

Job Advertising

The Axel Springer Group, 58 Jermyn St, London SW1Y 6PA (places advertisements in 'Die Welt' and other papers)
Frankfurter Allgemeine Zeitung, 10 Hans Crescent, London SW1X OLJ (places advertisements in the leading German daily FAZ)
International Graphic Press, 6 Welbeck St, London W1M 7PB (represents a number of German newspapers)

For help in finding employment in Germany, you can contact your nearest Employment Office which liaises with its German counterparts or the local German Employment Office (Arbetisamt) which will provide the same facilities as given to German nationals. For temporary work during holidays contact the Central Placement Office in Frankfurt.

The Youth Exchange Centre can arrange opportunities on a 'Live and Work' basis. Successful applicants aged between 18 and 22 with good spoken German, can spend between 4 and 6 months working in Germany in offices, banks, supermarkets, department stores, factories etc. Salary is in the region of £100 per week. The main idea behind this scheme is cultural exchange.

There are great numbers of American Servicemen based in West Germany. The main bases are at Heidelberg, Frankfurt, Berlin and Augsberg, but there are many smaller ones. You will not be allowed on the bases to look for work but should approach the local state employment office (arbeitsamt).

Zentralstelle fur Arbeitsvermittlung (Central Placement Office), Feuerbachstrasse 42, D-6000 Frankfurt/Main

The Youth Exchange Centre, Seymour Mews House, Seymour Mews, London W1H 9PE

Agriculture

Whilst most German farms tend to be small family-run affairs there are opportunities for those in the area at harvesting time. Fruit is grown in many areas, but the principal production area is south of the River Elbe (try Jork and Horneburg). The Lake Constance area is also worth a try. The main fruits grown in the country are apples (harvested during September and October), pears, plums and cherries.

The grape harvest starts from early October and ends in mid-November which means that there are fewer students competing for work. Grapes are grown in the Rhinegau, Rheinhessen, Mosel, Baden Wurttemburg and Franconia regions, often on steep hillsides so the work is hard. You will have to pay the cost of your own travel and food and accommodation in most cases.

For work on organic farms contact WWOOF who will send you the current list of holdings upon membership (£6).

The International Farm Experience Programme organises work experience exchanges for young farmers and horticulturists in Germany. The training lasts from three to twelve months and wages are £30 per week plus board and lodging with a host family. Applicants have to pay their own travel costs, plus registration fee and insurance.

WWOOF, 19 Bradford Road, Lewes, Sussex BN7 1RB

IFEP, YFC Centre, National Agricultural Centre, Stoneleigh, Warwickshire CV8 2LG

Au Pair
There are plenty of opportunities for au pairs and mother's helps. The minimum age requirement is 18 years up to about 30. Most positions are for between 6 and 12 months and a knowledge of spoken German is an advantage, though most Germans speak excellent English.

Verein fur Internationale Jugendarbeit, 39 Craven Road, London W2 3BX.
Tel: 01 723 0216 (affiliated to the World Young Women's Association, Employment Service)

German Catholic Social Centre, Haus Lioba, 40 Exeter Road, London NW2 4SB.
Tel: 01 452 8566

Helping Hands Au Pair & Domestic Agency, 10 Hertford Rd, Newbury Park, Ilford,
Essex 1G2 7HQ. Tel: 01 597 3138

Students Abroad, Elm House, 21b The Avenue, Hatch End, Middx HA5 4EN.
Tel: 01 428 5823

Universal Care, Chester House, 9 Windsor End, Beaconsfield, Bucks HP9 2JJ.
Tel: 0494 678811

Anglia Agency, 15 Eastern Ave, Southend-on-Sea, Essex SS2 5QX.
Tel: 0702 613888

Tourism

Hotels
The summer tourist season in Germany generally runs from May to early October; the winter season from December to May. For those in the area at the beginning of the season, and prepared to work for the whole season, there is a good chance of picking up work on the spot. Opportunities are available in hotels, resorts, restaurants etc and if you don't mind making beds or washing up you should be able to spend the summer in Germany without too much trouble. The best areas for picking up casual work are the Black Forest, the coast, the Bavarian Alps and the Bohmer Wald. Wages are approximately £50 per week with board and lodging provided in most cases. English is widely spoken in Germany so a knowledge of the language is not essential.

Jobs in the Alps organise ALPOTELS aptitude tests which are accepted by German employers who wish to recruit suitable British workers. If you join their JITA Club you are entitled to benefits and assurance when you find employment. ALPOTELS also publish a booklet giving guidance on how to set about finding work in hotels in Germany and lists of the main hotels in resorts in Germany to which you can write or visit in search of work.

Vacation Work arranges work in German hotels, restaurants and sometimes factories. About 48-54 hours are worked per week. Job arrangements are made through the central government agency and jobs last for 2-3 months in July/August. Applicants must have a sound knowledge of German and apply before February each year.

Jobs in the Alps, PO Box 388, London SW1X 8LX

ALPOTELS, PO Box 388, London SW1X 8LX

Vacation Work International Club, 9 Park End St, Oxford OX1 1HJ.
Tel: 0865 241978

Couriers/Reps

Camping and self-catering holidays are popular in Germany and many British travel companies recruit couriers, site attendants, water sport instructors and drivers etc from this country for their sites in Germany. The working period is generally from late April/early May until the end of September. You must be over 18 and have a good knowledge of German. Accommodation in tents or caravans is provided as well as travel costs to the site.

Reps are required for companies like Thomson Holidays to meet clients at the airport and offer advice and assistance whilst they are on holiday. Applicants should be aged between 21 and 30 and have a good knowledge of German. The work is on a seasonal basis usually from April to October with the possibility of winter employment. Salary is paid monthly and a commission is paid on excursion sales. After 9 months' service (cumulative) generous holiday concessions are available.

A company that requires a good knowledge of German plus a working knowledge of major European cities is EF Educational Tours. EF Tour Directors lead groups of visiting American and Canadian school students on tours of Europe, ranging from 9-35 days in length.

If you have a knowledge of the wine regions of Europe, including West Germany, World Wine Tours recruit couriers to lead wine tours from March to October. Couriers must speak French and a knowledge of another European language is an advantage. Accommodation is provided.

Eurocamp Travel, Edmundson House, Tatton St, Knutsford, Cheshire WA16 6BG.

Canvas Holidays Ltd, Bull Plain, Hertford, Herts SG14 1DY. Tel: 0992 553535

Thomson Holidays Ltd, Greater London House, Hampstead Rd, London NW1 7SD.
Tel: 01 387 9321

EF Educational Tours, EF House, 1 Farman St, Hove, Brighton BN3 1AL.
Tel: 0273 723651

World Wine Tours Ltd, 4 Dorchester Rd, Drayton St Leonard, Oxon OX9 8BH.
Tel: 0865 891919

Teaching

It may be possible to pick up teaching work in Germany at a language school or by teaching privately. A thriving 'industry' in teaching English is that of Business English and many companies run 'in-house' Business English courses. Try advertising your services in a local paper or look at notice boards in Youth Hostels or at the Universities. The British Council can supply you with a list of language schools recognised by them before you go. Standards are high in Germany so make sure you take with you all your qualifications and references. Some language schools in Britain have affiliated schools in Germany which can be contacted.

The Central Bureau administers a scheme for the interchange with Germany of qualified, experienced teachers of Modern Languages, and related subjects for 3 weeks, 6 weeks, one term or one year.

As there are many British soldiers stationed in Germany, there are also British schools attached to the bases. The European Council of International Schools assists international English-medium schools (pupils 3-19 years) throughout the world with staff recruitments. It provides a year round placement service for teachers/administrators with a minimum of 2 years' teaching experience who register with the Council as individual members, as well as organising an annual two day Recruitment Centre held in London.

For primary, middle and secondary posts in all service children's schools overseas contact also the Service Children's Education Authority at the Ministry of Defence.

International House, 106 Piccadilly, London W1V 9FL. Tel: 01 491 2598

Central Bureau, Seymour Mews House, Seymour Mews, London W1H 9PE. Tel: 01 486 5101

British Council Overseas Educational Appointments Dept, 65 Davies St, London W1Y 2AA. Tel: 01 499 8011

European Council of International Schools, 21b Lavant St, Petersfield, Hants GU32 3EL. Tel: 0730 68244

Service Children's Education Authority 2a, Directorate of Army Education, Ministry of Defence, Court Rd, Eltham, London SE9 5NR. Tel: 01 854 2242 ext 4206/4224

Voluntary Work
IVS organises a large number of camps in Germany, mostly engaged in renovation, work, forestry and conservation. They are situated throughout the country with 12-15 volunteers at each. You must be over 18 and a knowledge of German is preferable. The camps operate for 2-3 weeks between May and October.

CMP has projects at many camps in Germany each year that involve mostly renovation and social work. You must be over 18 and preferably able to speak some German. Camps take place from July to September for 2-4 weeks.

The United Nations Association organises camps in association with IBG. These camps have comparatively comfortable conditions and are located mostly in Southern Germany. About 12 volunteers at each camp are engaged in manual, conservation and forestry work. Further camps are organised with IJGD in Berlin, northern, southern and central Germany. A similar number of volunteers engage in manual, conservation, and social work with children and the elderly. You must be aged between 16 and 25 and previous workcamp experience is preferable. Camps run for 3 weeks from June to September.

EYCE organise camps working with mental and multiple handicapped people in small home groups for 6-7 hours a day for 12-14 days. The camps run for 3 weeks. Special trips and programmes are organised for your free week. You must be over 17 and speak German.

GAP Activity Projects offers school leavers the chance to spend at least six months in Germany staying with a host family. Volunteers can teach English, help with the sick and handicapped, assist in schools, work on a farm or in an office. Interviews begin in December and the closing date for applications is March.

IVS, 162 Upper New Walk, Leicester LE1 7QA. Tel: 0533 549430

CMP, Bethnal Green URC, Pott St, London E2 OEF. Tel: 01 729 1877

United Nations Association, Welsh Centre for International Affairs, Temple of Peace, Cathays Park, Cardiff CF1 3AP

EYCE Secretariat, 217 Holywood Rd, Belfast BT4 2DH, N Ireland. Tel: 44 232 651134/5

GAP Activity Projects (UK) Ltd, 7 King's Rd, Reading RG1 3AA. Tel: 0734 594914

Archaeology
Archaeology Abroad publish a booklet with excavations abroad that require volunteers. In Germany contact the Internationale Jugendgemeinschaftdienste for information on digs.

Archaeology Abroad, 31-34 Gordon Square, London WC1H OPY

Internationale Jugendgemeinschaftdienste, Geschaftsstelle Nord, Katharinenstrasse 13, D-3200 Hildesheim, W Germany

GIBRALTAR
Main Language: English
Currency: UK£/Gibraltar Govt £
Capital: Gibraltar
Climate: Summer – Generally hot and dry
Winter – Warm (60°F +)

Entry Requirements
UK Passport Office, Petty France, London. Tel: 01 279 3434 (passport) 01 271 8560 (Visa)

Gibraltar Government Tourist Office, Arundel Great Court, 179 Strand, London WC2R 1EH. Tel: 01 836 0777/01 240 6611

Visa
Only a valid passport or other acceptable travel document is required to visit Gibraltar. Visas are only required for nationals of 'Eastern Bloc' countries, Argentina, Libya, People's Democratic Republic of Yemen and Cuba.

Work Permits
The issue of work permits is governed by the Employment Ordinance which prohibits non-residents of Gibraltar (excepting EEC nationals) from gaining employment unless they obtain a work permit issued by the Director of Labour and Social Security and procured for them by their prospective employer. To obtain a work permit, the following conditions must be met:

1. that there is a genuine vacancy for which there is no Gibraltarian available;
2. that the employer will undertake to repatriate the worker if and when his/her services are no longer required;
3. acceptable arrangements for accommodation are made.

EEC nationals may enter Gibraltar to find or take up or set up in business for six months. If after this time they have gained employment or established a business, they may obtain a residence permit valid for the duration of the business of employment or for renewable periods of five years at a time.

Permanent Residence
Citizens of the UK may be granted (on application and at the Governor's discretion) a permanent certificate of residence if they are of good standing and an asset to the community.

Intending residents are advised to consult the Principal Immigration Officer, 124 Irish Town, Gibraltar. Tel: 71543

Travel
Air Europe, British Airways and GB Airways operate scheduled flights from London. From Spain the border is open 24 hours a day and you can easily walk or drive into Gibraltar. La Linea crossing point is two hour drive from either Malaga or Cadiz. From Morocco you can get to Gibraltar by sea (1 hour) or by air (20 mins).

Accommodation
Accommodation is scarce and therefore difficult and expensive to obtain. There are no camping facilities in Gibraltar but there are a number of good camp sites in Spain within 20 miles of Gibraltar so it would be possible to camp in Spain and go into Gibraltar for work each day.

Working Holidays

Tourism
Many tour operators organise holidays in Gibraltar and require couriers and reps. Some of the companies that operate in Gibraltar are:

Gibraltar Travel Ltd, 251 Northfields Ave, London W13 9QU. Tel: 01 579 0307

Cadogan Travel Ltd, Cadogan House, 9-10 Portland St, Southampton SO9 1ZP. Tel: 0703 332661

Intasun, Intasun House, 2 Cromwell Ave, Bromley, Kent BR2 9AQ. Tel: 01 290 1900

Marshall Sutton's Yorkshire Travel, 9 Butcher Row, Beverley, E Yorks, HU17 7BR. Tel: 0482 882638

Sovereign Holidays, Groundstar House, London Rd, Crawley, W Sussex RH10 2TB Tel: 0293 560 777

Teaching
The Ministry of Defence runs two primary schools for the children of UK services personnel to which a considerable number of local Anglican children are admitted by arrangement with the Gibraltar government. There is also a private school at Loreto Convent providing education at both Infant and Junior level. There are two single sex comprehensive schools as well as a Technical College.

Director of Education, Dept of Educaucation, 40 Town Range, Gibraltar

Officer in Charge, Services Children's School, c/o Gibraltar & Dockyard

Technical College, Queensway, Gibraltar

The Headmistress, Loreto Convent School, Europa Rd, Gibraltar

124

Other Employment
For details of other types of employment in Gibraltar contact the following:
The Senior Labour Officer, Dept of Labour and Social Security,
23 John Mackintosh Sq, Gibraltar. Tel: (010 350) 78583
Main Employment Agency, 21 Horse Barrack Lane, Gibraltar.
Tel: (010 350) 73733
Career Moves Ltd, 104/106 Irish Town, Gibraltar. Tel: (010 350) 79697
Ariadne Pershing & Executive Services Ltd, PO Box 684, Suite 43,
Victoria House, 26 Main St, Gibraltar. Tel: (010 350) 79358
Acira (Nursing & Secretarial), 27 City Mill Lane, Gibraltar.
Tel: (010 350) 76678/79849

GREECE
Main Language: Greek
Currency: Drachma
Capital: Athens
Exports: Tobacco, Iron and steel, Raisins, Aluminium, Cotton.
Climate: Summer – Warm to hot, arid.
Winter – mild, snow in mountains

Entry Requirements
Embassy of Greece, 1A Holland Park, London W11 3TP.
Tel: 01 727 8040

National Tourist Organisation of Greece, 195/197 Regent St, London W1R 8DL.

Visas
British subjects who are holders of valid passports can enter Greece without a visa for up to three months to take up or look for employment.

Work Permits
A work permit is not needed for EEC nationals who come to Greece to take up or look for employment and they can remain in Greece for up to three months. If you wish to stay longer a Residence Permit will be issued if you present yourself at the Aliens Department of the Ministry of Public Order in Athens, or the local police station if you are outside Athens. You should present your passport, a letter of intent of employment, and a Medical Certificate from a local hospital in Greece. Initially a six months' residence permit will be issued. After that the person concerned will be granted a five year residence permit.

Permanent Residence
Foreign nationals who are permanent residents abroad may be issued with a certificate of transfer of usual residence, provided they have been residing permanently in the UK for the last two 12-month periods before they transfer their usual residence to Greece.

Travel
There are many cheap flights offered by discount travel companies to Greece (see Chapter 4 for addresses). Air Courier companies also offer cheap fares to Athens, CTS for example offer £80 return, Polo Express from £60 to £85 for a one week return. With an ISIC you can get up to 50% discount off regular fares depending on the route and the season.

By rail you can get a discount of 20%-40% off regular train fares if you are under 26. Tickets are valid for two months, and stopovers en route are permitted. You can also get cheap bus fares from London to Athens.

Most ferry lines from Greece to various Mediterranean ports offer a discount of between 10%-25% to holders of an ISIC if you are under 27. If you are heading for Piraeus to catch an island ferry go direct from the airport by bus. There are no special fares for students on rail fares within Greece but train fares in Greece are reasonable and you are entitled to unlimited travel on bus and rail services of the Greek State Railways with a Greek Tourist Card. Buses in Greece are cheap and are a good way to get around. The ISYTS (International Student and Youth Travel Service) is also the office for Eurotrain for cheap rail travel out of Greece.

Make sure you receive a pink slip when changing foreign currency into drachmas; without this slip you may not be allowed to pay in drachmas for student tickets for travel outside Greece.

YHA Travel, 14 Southampton Street, London WC2E 7HY. Tel: 01 240 5236
ISYTS, 11 Nikis Street (2nd floor), Syntagma Square, Athens 105 57. Tel: 322 1267
CTS (Student Travel Centre), c/o Hello Travel, 62 Akadimias, Athens.
Tel: 360 4450

Accommodation
Rail station touts abound, but finding somewhere cheap to stay is fairly easy. Omonia Square which is a short walk from the station and Sintagma has lots of cheap accommodation in the streets behind it. Private students hostels are more comfortable than the official Youth Hostels and most are in the streets leading from Sintagma to the Acropolis. It is a good idea to take the first reasonable offer for the night and then look around. The ISYTS office also offers special reduction for numerous hotels in Athens and on the islands.

There are many campsites in Greece. The Greek Tourist Office also publishes 'Camping' which gives information on campsites run by them. It is still possible to sleep on beaches off the beaten track in Greece, though not in the more popular resorts or islands where you are likely to be moved on.

Working Holidays

Job Advertising
Athens Daily Post, 57 Stadiou Street, Athens
Athens Daily News, 5 Chavriou Street, Athens
Publicitas, 525 Fulham Rd, London SW6 1HF (agents for a number of Greek papers)

There are plenty of opportunities for casual work in Greece. The pay is generally quite low compared to the more affluent North and it might not be possible to earn enough money in Greece to fund further travel, but it is easy to earn enough to live on and have a good time.

Agriculture
Agricultural work in Greece is principally confined (as far as the foreigner is concerned) to the orange harvest. The principle area, and certainly the best to look for work, is the Peloponnese. Try the area between Corinth, Argos and Navplion. Work can be found with individual farmers, although the larger processing plants have 'agents' who recruit pickers on a daily basis in Navplion. Rates of pay vary and depend on a number of factors, as with all harvest work, but it is possible to earn up to £20 or more a day. Harvesting is from early December through to the end of February, with Christmas being the peak period.

In addition to oranges there are harvests for olives, cherries, apricots, pears, grapes and apples virtually throughout the year – there's nearly always something to be harvested except during the summer months of July/August. Ask taverna owners, who are likely to speak some English, if they know of any work going. Farmers are unlikely to speak English so you could either get a Greek to translate your request for work or use sign language if you want to approach them directly.

Au Pairs/English Conversation
There are opportunities for au pairs and mother's helps throughout Greece, but not always in the tourist areas. Applicants must be over 18 years of age and be prepared to work from between 3 and 12 months. With some agencies it is possible to stay with a family in the summer and give the family practice in English conversation in exchange for board and lodging. Applicants usually have to pay their own travel costs.

Universal Care, Chester House, 9 Windsor End, Beaconsfield, Bucks HP9 2JJ
Tel: 0494 678811
Anglia Agency, 15 Eastern Ave, Southend-on-Sea, Essex SS2 5QX. Tel: 0702 613888
Helping Hands Au Pair & Domestic Agency, 10 Hertford Rd, Newbury Park, Ilford, Essex 1G2 7HQ. Tel: 01 597 3138
Students Abroad, Elm House, 21b The Avenue, Hatch End, Middx HA5 4EN.
Tel: 01 428 5823
Theodoris Cammenos, 12 Batasi Street, Athens 10682 (Enclose 2 IRCs)
Messrs Miterna, Ermou 28, Journarou 2, Athens
Homer Schools, 91-93 Academias St, 4th floor, Athens. Tel: (010 301) 364 2194

Tourism
The tourist industry in Greece is vast and there are always opportunities for picking up casual work in bars and clubs. The best places to pick up bar work etc are in the up-market establishments or those that are trendy in the large resorts. You won't get any joy from looking for such work in small villages or local tavernas. The tourist season starts in late April and finishes in September. Make sure that you are paid at the end of every working day and that from the outset you know what your pay is going to be.

The Greek Tourist Board publishes an annual guide of UK tour companies operating in Greece, including student travel and educational organisations which is a useful source of addresses for setting up work before you go. Camping holiday companies need couriers, supervisors, drivers, water sports instructors, etc while the regular holiday companies need reps to meet clients at the airport. Some companies like CV Travel (Corfu Villas Ltd) need experienced cooks to look after guests renting private villas during the summer.

National Tourist Organisation of Greece, 195/197 Regent Street, London W1R 8DL. Tel: 01 734 5997
CV Travel, 43 Cadogan St, London SW3. Tel: 01 581 0851
Xenodochiakon Erimel Itirion Ellados (Chamber of Hotels of Greece),
3 Plateia Kolokotroni, Athens
Intercom, 24-26 Halkokondili Street, 8th floor, Athens.
Tel: (010 301) 523 9551/9470

Crewing
Many yachts ply the islands of Greece and you can pick up work by being in the right place at the right time. Visit the harbours where you see large yachts and frequent the tavernas where you see the 'yachties' drinking. If you don't get offered a job as a crew member, you may be able to find work as a cook or cleaner, or even as a babysitter, aboard.

Some companies such as 'Sunsail' operate Flotilla Sailing holidays in Greece. They require 3 staff to run these holidays: an experienced skipper in charge of all sailing matters, a hostess to run the social side of the trips, organising excursions, BBQ's etc, and a mechanic bosun with diesel experience to service and maintain the engines on the thirteen flotilla yachts. These three people live aboard their own pilot yacht and are paid from £80 per week together with flights to and from the UK.

In addition they operate watersports centres, Sunsail Clubs, in Greece and require a wide range of staff for these hotels: dinghy sailing/windsurfing instructors, cruising instructors, bar staff, nannies, cooks and catering assistants. The pay is from £50 per week, plus accommodation, half board and flights to and from the UK.

Crewitt deliver boats to Greece and cater for novices as well as experienced sailors. Private boat owners and delivery companies also contact them for crew. You have to share expenses such as food, sometimes moorings and fuel.
The Crewing Service puts potential crew in touch with skippers and publish the details you provide them with at various times during the year.

Dragon Yachts operate luxury charter yachts in the Mediterranean, including Greece. They employ many young people for varying periods and as well as crew members, need water sports and entertainment officers, cooks and domestic staff.

Sunsail, The Port House, Port Solent, Portsmouth, Hants PO6 4TH.
Tel: 0705 219847
Crewitt Services, Cobbs Quay, Hamworthy, Poole, Dorset BH15 4EL.
Tel: 0202 678847
The Cruising Association, The Port House, Port Solent, Portsmouth,
Hants PO6 4TH. Tel: 0705 219847
Dragon Yachts (Worldwide) Ltd, 788 Bath Rd, Cranford, Middx TW5 9UL.
Tel: 01 897 9995

Teaching
It is still possible to get teaching work in Greece without the necessary qualifications or experience, just so long as you speak English.
There are hundreds of language schools in Greece, some reputable, some not, mainly in Athens but in other big centres too. Try contacting them in person, remembering to take with you your relevant qualifications, certificates etc. You could check youth hostel notice boards and the local papers or contact the British Council in Athens. If you can be in Greece before the start of the school term ie August/September for October or at the beginning of January for the Spring Term you stand a better chance.

Some language schools in England recruit teachers for Greece. Qualifications and/or experience are required.
Surrey Language Centre, Sandford House, 39 West Street, Farnham, Surrey GU9 7DR. Tel: 0252 723494
International House, 106 Piccadilly, London W1V 9FL. Tel: 01 491 2598
British Council, Overseas Educational Appointments Dept, 65 Davies St, London W1Y 2AA.
Tel: 01 499 8011
British Council, 17 Falkis Etairias, Kolonaki, Athens
Hambakis Schools, 1 Philellinon Street, Syntagma Square, Athens.

Voluntary Work

Workcamps
IVS operates a number of workcamps in Greece. Projects and locations vary from year to year but are always interesting. Applicants must be over 18 and have previous workcamp experience. Food and accommodation is provided but volunteers must pay their own travel costs. Most camps are for 2-3 weeks from July to September.

CMP have projects in Greece from time to time. Last year the project was based at a Peace Centre in Crete offering professional training for young handicapped people. Work involved restoration of the buildings.

IVS, 162 Upper New Walk, Leicester LEI 7QA. Tel: 0533 549430
CMP, Bethnal Green URC, Pott St, London E2 OEF. Tel: 01 729 1877
QISP, Friends House, Euston Rd, London NW1 2BJ. Tel: 01 387 3601

Archaeology
As you would expect, Greece is crawling with archaeological sites and digs. Archaeology Abroad has information on excavations in Greece and can put you in touch with the British School in Athens and the American School of Classical Studies for details of digs they organise.

The Archaeological Institute of America publishes details of many digs in Greece and Crete in its Fieldwork Opportunities Bulletin.

Archaeology Abroad, 31-34 Gordon Square, London WC1H OPY.
Archaeological Institute of America, 675 Commonwealth Ave, Boston, MA 02215. Tel: (617) 353 9361

Conservation
BTCV are offered places on international conservation working holidays in various parts of Greece and Corfu in July, August and September. The work varies from year to year and can involve restoration of monasteries, drystone walling and forest management. Accommodation is camping or sleeping in a dormitory and the cost is approximately £100, including insurance, food and transport from the pre-arranged pick-up point. You have to make your own travel arrangements.

BTCV, 36 St Mary's Street, Wallingford, Oxon OX10 0EU. Tel: 0491 39766

GUYANA

Main Language: Spanish, English
Capital: Georgetown
Exports: Sugar, rice, bauxite
Climate: Hot throughout the year. Heavy annual rainfall.

Entry Requirements
Guyana High Commission, 3 Palace Court, Bayswater Rd, London W2 4LP.
Tel: 01 229 768418

Visas
UK nationals do not require a visa to visit Guyana.

Work Permits
Officially, it is not possible to obtain employment while holidaying in Guyana.
Obtaining a work permit is the responsibility of the employer on behalf of the prospective employee following offer and acceptance of employment. Applications for employment are processed by the relevant authority in Guyana.

Permanent Residence
Persons wishing to emigrate to Guyana are required to write, giving details regarding their financial status and how they propose to support themselves in the country, to:

Ministry of Home Affairs, 6 Brickdam, Georgetown, Guyana, South America

Travel
The following companies are specialists in discount travel to Latin America:

Journey Latin America, 16 Devonshire Road, London W4 2HD. Tel: 01 747 3108

Steamond Ltd, 23 Eccleson St, London SW1 9LX. Tel: 01 730 8646
Trailfinders Ltd, 194 Kensington High Street, London W8 7RG.
Tel: 01 938 3939
Wexas, 45 Brompton Rd, Knightsbridge, London SW3 1BR. Tel: 01 589 3315
STA Travel Ltd, 74 Old Brompton Rd, London SW7. Tel: 01 581 4751
Encounter Overland, 267 Old Brompton Rd, London SW5. Tel: 01 370 6845

Voluntary Work
There are no work camps or conservation organisations in Guyana. VSO have recently returned to Guyana after a 16 year gap and are assisting in the regeneration of the infrastructure and supporting economic activities, such as food-crop diversification, small business development and pharmaceutical manufacturing.

VSO, Enquiries Unit, 317 Putney Bridge Road, London SW15 2PN.
Tel: 01 780 1331

HONDURAS
Main Language: Spanish, English
Currency: Lempira
Capital: Tegucigalpa
Exports: Bananas, coconuts, coffee, timber, silver
Climate: Dry season (Nov-Apr) – Temperatures around 30°C. Also cyclonic storms mainly from August onwards. Wet season (May-Oct) – Temperatures seldom fall below 21°C

Entry Requirements
Honduran Embassy, 47 Manchester Street, London W1M 5PB
Tel: 01-486 3380

Visas
Visas are not required for tourist visits. Business travellers require a visa. Visas cost £10. 30 days permit is granted by Immigration at the time of entry and can be extended for periods of 30 days each. The stay is no longer than six months.

Work Permits
Applications to both the Honduras Ministry of the Interior and Honduras Ministry of Labour are needed. Contact any Honduran Consulate.

Permanent Residence
Individuals looking for work in Honduras on a permanent basis must apply for a resident visa at their local Honduran Consulate. You will need to supply:
1) Sworn declaration which states that the individual will comply with Honduran law, denounce communism, and does not oppose a democratic, representative form of government.
2) A certified letter stating that the applicant does not have a police record.
3) A health certificate.

Travel
You can fly from Miami, New Orleans or Houston to Honduras on airlines such as Tan, Sahsa, Taca and Challenger (see Chapter 4 for discount travel companies in the US). Honduras is bounded by Guatemala, El Salvador and Nicaragua so you could also get there by bus. Encounter Overland organise expeditions to Central America.

Encounter Overland, 267 Old Brompton Rd, London SW5. Tel: 01 370 6845

Working Holidays
As Honduras shares its borders with two of the most unstable countries in Central America, El Salvador and Guatemala, we would strongly advise you to take in the political situation in these countries before planning a trip to this area.

There are very few opportunities for casual work in Honduras as labour is so cheap and the population fairly small. You could try teaching English in the capital; look in the local newspapers for advertisements for language schools or private tuition.

Voluntary Work
The Catholic Institute for International Relations, (CIIR), recruits professionally qualified people with a minimum of 1-2 years' work experience, particularly in the fields of health and agriculture for Central America. Their stated aim is to provide technical support for community projects which tackle the causes of poverty and at present they have workers in Honduras. It is a secular programme and religious commitment is not a prerequisite.

Catholic Institute for International Relations, (CIIR), Recruitment Coordinator, 22 Coleman Fields, London N1 7AF. Tel: 01 354 0883

HONG KONG
Main Language: English, Chinese
Currency: Hong Kong Dollar
Capital: Hong Kong
Exports: Clothing, Textiles, Toys and games, Radios.
Climate: Summer May-Sept (rainy season) 31°C, humid, tropical cyclones
Autumn Sept-Jan (dry season)
Winter monsoon Feb-March 15°C, foggy, cool

Entry Requirements
Chief British Passport Office, Clive House, Petty France, London SW1.
Tel: 01-214 5010

Visas
British nationals do not require a visa. You will normally be allowed to stay for six months initially. On arrival in Hong Kong you may have to satisfy the immigration officer that you have sufficient means of support for your stay in Hong Kong without working. You should also hold return or onward tickets, or evidence of definite employment in Hong Kong. Extensions of stay will be granted on individual merits and in practice are easy to obtain.

Work Permits
British citizens who wish to work in Hong Kong are advised to secure some firm assurance of employment before they arrive in Hong Kong. No work permit is required if you are a Hong Kong permanent resident, a resident British citizen or a resident UK belonger.

Permanent Residence
All newcomers, who have obtained permission from the Director of Immigration to stay in Hong Kong for more than 180 days are required to register with the Registration of Persons Office for Identity Cards within 30 days of arrival.

Travel
Many of the discount travel companies offer cheap flights to Hong Kong (see Chapter 4 for addresses). It is often included on a round-the-world ticket. CTS (Air Courier Club) offer a £350

return ticket to Hong Kong without suitcase or £425 return with suitcase. With an ISIC you are entitled to reduced airfares on international flights.

Within Hong Kong there is a comprehensive transport system that is very cheap: trams on Hong Kong side, buses, Public Light Buses (hail and ride), and the MTR (Mass Transit Railway or underground) as well as the ferry to Kowloon and the outlying islands. Try and avoid travelling at peak times! Taxis, too, are inexpensive.

The Kowloon-Canton Railway runs through Kowloon and the New Territories serving local passengers and also providing a direct rail link between Hong Kong and China. There is a boat service to Canton as well as to Shanghai. Hydrofoils and ferries also link Hong Kong with Macau.

HK Student Travel Bureau, Room 1021, Star House, 3 Salisbury Rd, Tsimshatshui, Kowloon. Tel: (3) 721 3269

Accommodation
Accommodation is very expensive in Hong Kong and difficult to find. The cheapest places to stay are the YMCAs and Youth Hostels and, on arrival, it is better and more convenient to stay on Kowloon side. There are cheap dormitory hostels in the Nathan Road area round Chung Kiu and King's Park and the harbour.

If you are planning to stay for any length of time, you could try advertising in the 'wanted' section of the local newspaper for a room to rent as well as checking the papers for rooms or flat share. Another place to look is the MacDonald's notice board on Hong Kong side. If you can rent a flat or room on one of the outlying islands such as Lamma or Lantau, you get the best of both worlds – the peace and quiet of an island community and the bustle and work in the big city. Rents are very high in Hong Kong, rents are cheaper on the islands and in the New Territories (in fact, the further you go from the centre of Hong Kong).

YMCA, 41 Salisbury Road, Kowloon. Tel: (3) 692 211
YMCA, 23 Waterloo Road, Yau Ma Tei, Kowloon. Tel: (3) 771 9111
HKSTB Hostel, 255-261 Reclamation St, 2/F Gt Eastern Mansion, Yau Ma Tei, Kowloon
Chung King House, 4-5 Floor, Block A, Chung King Mansion, 36-44 Nathan Rd, Kowloon. Tel: (3) 665 362
Travellers Hostel, Chung King Mansion, 40 Nathan Rd, Kowloon
HKYHA, Room 1408, Block A, Watson's Estate, North Point, Hong Kong. Tel: (5) 706 222/3

Working Holidays
There are many opportunities for the working traveller in Hong Kong. The most difficult obstacle to overcome is accommodation as already mentioned, as once you have found somewhere to stay, you have to work for a few months in order to pay the rent before you can save up enough money for further travel.

Try the local newspapers for job advertisements, The South China Morning Post and the Hong Kong Standard, especially the Saturday edition of the Morning Post. Check the notice boards at Chung King Mansions and the other youth hostels as well as the Yellow Pages for language schools.

There are a great many journalists and radio journalists in Hong Kong and if you have any talent in writing, try hawking your wares round the papers or glossy magazines (addresses from the inside covers) or approach Hong Kong Radio. Another advantage of living on one of the outlying islands is that it is much easier to make contact with such people as they tend to live out of Hong Kong. As anywhere, once you have contacts jobs are easier to come by. It is possible to get fairly lucrative work doing 'voice overs' for radio or for TV commercials, or even a part in a Chinese soap opera (not recommended!).

Hong Kong abounds in English pubs and many employ 'foreigners', especially women, as barmaids or waitresses. The direct approach is the best way to get such work. Avoid the clubs, which use 'hostesses' to serve customers.

If you have some skill or expertise to offer, belly dancing or batik for example, it might be worth getting in touch with the Adult Education Department at Hong Kong University to see if you can teach a class.

Teaching English
English language teaching jobs are easy to find in Hong Kong, especially if you have qualifications and/or experience, either through the Yellow Pages or the paper. In spite of the fact that Hong Kong is a British colony, the standard of English is very poor and many students want to improve their English to further their careers. The language schools vary, from hole-in-the-wall establishments to large, well-equipped concerns which pay well, and needless to say the latter are the ones which require qualifications and experience. It is still possible to teach English in Hong Kong without any qualifications, especially 'conversation' classes but the pay is generally very low and barely enough to pay the rent.

One popular subject now is 'Business English' and many language schools offer 'in-house' language teaching to companies which pays well. Teaching Business English to secretaries is also popular in Hong Kong.

In addition to the Hong Kong Education Department and English Schools Foundation, there are a number of organisations who recruit staff in the UK for universities or English-medium schools in Hong Kong.

Education Dept, Lee Gardens, 3/F, Hysan Avenue, Hong Kong
English Schools Foundation, GPO Box 11284, Hong Kong
Association of Commonwealth Universities, 36 Gordon Square, London WC1H OPF
Tel: 01 387 8572
European Council of International Schools, 21b Lavant St, Petersfield, Hants GU32 3EL. Tel: 0730 68244
Gabbitas-Thring Service Ltd, 6-8 Sackville St, Piccadilly, London W1X 2BR
Tel: 01 439 2071
Committee for International Cooperation in Higher Education, Higher Education Division, 10 Spring Gardens, London SW1A 2BN. Tel: 01 930 8466
Service Children's Education Authority 2a, Directorate of Army Education,
Ministry of Defence, Court Road, Eltham, London SE9 5NR. Tel: 01 854 2242
Ext 4206/4224
British Council, Overseas Educational Appointments Dept, 65 Davies Street, London W1Y 2AA.
Tel: 01 499 8011

Voluntary Work
There are no work camps as such in Hong Kong, but there are possibilities to help with the Vietnamese refugees who are held in camps there, usually teaching English or, if you speak Vietnamese, helping in a social worker capacity. Get in touch with the local Red Cross or relief agencies or enquire at the British Consulate.

Archaeology
The Archaeological Institute of America have details of a dig in Lung Kwu Tan, one of the last remaining undisturbed prehistoric sites in the rapidly developing city. Volunteers who are at least high school graduates are needed for a minimum stay of two weeks. They are responsible for food, lodging and insurance. The deadline for application on this excavation was June 1989 but the work is continuing until March/April 1990, so it is still worth applying if you are interested.

Archaeological Institute of America, 675 Commonwealth Avenue, Boston, MA 02215. Tel: (617) 353 9361

HUNGARY
Main language: Magyar (German understood)
Capital: Budapest
Climate: Cold winters (-1°C Jan); long hot summers.

Entry Requirements
Hungarian Embassy, 35B Eaton Place, London SW1X 8BY
Danube Travel, 6 Conduit Street, London W1R 9TG

Visas
The tourist office of Danube Travel has information on how to obtain a visa for Hungary, as well as details of accommodation, travel, insurance etc. A Hungarian entry visa may be obtained on border stations, Budapest Airport, Budapest Danube ship station or road frontier posts. You will need 2 photos. A stamp on your visa is required for each night's stay.

Work Permits
Visas/work permits can be obtained for workcamps in Hungary and the appropriate organisation will inform you as to how to obtain one.

Travel
With an ISIC students can get discounts on flights to Hungary and some discount travel companies (see Chapter 4) offer cheap fares to Budapest. Trains run from Vienna to Budapest.

The Cycling Touring Club Touring Department has quite recently-revised information sheets on Hungary which explain general travel procedures as well as covering problems specific to bicycle travel. Trains have an excellent system for carrying bikes and fares are cheaper if your bike is accompanied.

Accommodation
There is a good distribution of campsites in Hungary, and whilst facilities are fairly basic, most campsites have excellent cafes. ISIC holders are entitled to a 50% discount in camping sites. Express, the Hungarian student travel bureau, is also the Hungarian Youth Hostels Association and with an ISIC give a 25% discount in youth hostels and centres. If you are arriving by train the Express Sales Office at Keleti Pu Railway Station is open 24 hours every day.

Danube Travel Ltd, 6 Conduit Street, London W1R 9TG. Tel: 01 493 0263
Express, Semmelweis utca 4, Budapest 5. Tel: 178600
Express (National Head Office), Szabadsag ter 16, 1395 Budapest 5. Tel: 317777

Working Holidays
There are no opportunities for the working traveller in Hungary. Some of the tour operators organise holidays in Hungary and require couriers/reps. Contact Danube Travel for companies that operate in Hungary and apply direct to them before you go.

Teaching
The Central Bureau recruits teachers for one year appointments in teaching English as a Foreign Language in Hungary and also teachers of Maths, Physics and Biology.

134

Central Bureau, Seymour Mews House, Seymour Mews, London W1H 9PE.
Tel: 01 486 5101

Voluntary Work
There are several opportunities for work/study camps in Hungary. Previous workcamp experience is essential and applicants must be at least 18 years old.

CMP, Bethnal Green URC, Pott Street, London E2 OEF. Tel: 01 729 1877
IVS, 162 Upper New Walk, Leicester LE1 7QA. Tel: 0533 549430
QISP, Friends House, Euston Rd, London NW1 2BJ. Tel: 01 387 3601
United Nations Association, Welsh Centre for International Affairs, Temple of Peace, Cathays Park, Cardiff CH1 3AP

ICELAND
Main Language: Icelandic
Currency: Icelandic Krona
Capital: Reykjavik
Exports: Fish, frozen and fresh, Fish, salted and smoked, Cod liver oil
Climate: Summer – Cool, 10°C and 15°C; generally mild, warmer in SW
Winter – Cold (-0.3°C)

Entry Requirements
Icelandic Embassy, 1 Eaton Terrace, London SW1
Tel: 01-730 5131-2

Tourist Office, Icelandair, 172 Tottenham Court Road, London W1P 9LG Tel: 01-388 5599

Visas
UK nationals do not require a visa in order to visit Iceland for up to three months, but must be in possession of a return travel ticket from Iceland and show upon arrival in Iceland sufficient funds for their support during their stay. If a visitor wishes to stay longer than three months he must apply for an extension of his visitor's permit to the nearest police authority.

Work Permits
A foreign national may not seek or accept employment in Iceland after his arrival in the country unless he has a prior working permit. Such permits must be applied for from the Ministry of Social Affairs by the prospective Icelandic employer on behalf of the foreign national, who must show sufficient proof that the foreign national will fill a position for which no skilled Icelander is presently available. Working permits must be renewed at least once a year.

Permanent Residence
You are not as a rule eligible to apply for Icelandic citizenship before you have been a permanent resident in Iceland for 10 years. Applications for citizenship are considered by Parliament following the above time limit and are validated by law.

Travel
Iceland is an expensive place to fly to, though it would seem to be cheaper to fly from Glasgow than from, say, Copenhagen or Oslo. Students should be entitled to reductions on international flights and some discount travel companies may be able to offer cheap flights (see Chapter 4).

In Reykjavik you can buy two types of bus pass: (1) the full circle passport is valid for travel on the main road (ring route). There is no time limit on the passport, but you have to keep in a continuous direction; (2) omnibus passport which is valid for unlimited travel on all scheduled coach routes, main roads and secondary roads, but with the time limit you choose. ISIC holders are entitled to a 5% discount from June to the middle of September.

Hitching is a good way to travel in Iceland – crime is virtually unknown so it is safe, both by day and by night and the locals use hitching as a means to get about.

Iceland Student Travel, University Student Centre, Hringbraut, 101 Reykjavik,
Tel: 16850

Accommodation
Contact Icelandair, the tourist office, for details of accommodation in Iceland. Youth hostel information can be obtained from the Iceland Student Travel Centre in Reykjavik or from the Icelandic YHA.

Icelandair, 172 Tottenham Court Road, London W1P 9LG. Tel: 01 388 5599
Iceland Student Travel, University Student Centre, Hringbraut, 101 Reykjavik,
Icelandic YHA, Bandalag Islenskra Farfugla, Laufasvegur 41, 101 Reykjavik

Working Holidays
There are not many opportunities for the working traveller in Iceland. There are farms but these are scattered very widely and it is therefore difficult to get around them. The fish processing industry might provide you with work (see Chapter 8 for personal experience of this), but be prepared for long hours and the smell.

Voluntary Work
The British Trust for Conservation Volunteers are offered places on workcamps in Iceland for volunteers. Sites have included Porsmork in Southern Iceland and the Jokulsarglijufur National Park. Work includes path construction and maintenance. Volunteers either camp or stay in touring huts and must pay for their own travel and food. There is plenty of time to explore the region.

BTCV, 36 St Mary's Street, Wallingford, Oxon OX10 0EU. Tel: 0491 39766

INDIA
Main Language: Hindi, English
Currency: Indian Rupee
Capital: Delhi
Exports: Jute productions, Tea, Iron ore, Iron and steel, Cotton goods.
Climate: Nov-Mar: Cooler & dry (10°C in North – 25°C in South)
Mar-Jun: Very hot
Jun-Oct: Monsoon season

Entry Requirements
The High Commission of India, India House, Aldwych, London SC2B 4NA
Tel: 01-836 8484

India Tourist Office, 7 Cork St, London W1X QAB

Visas
British nationals require a valid passport for at least 9 months, a completed visa application form, 3 photographs and the entry fee. Visas are valid for 90 days; if possible try and get a multiple-entry one. If you are staying longer than 90 days, allow a few extra days before the expiry date because of the red tape.

Work Permits
There is no work permit system in India. Foreign nationals require the permission of the Reserve Bank of India to take up any employment if they desire remittance of their earnings outside India.

Permanent Residence
For permanent settlement in India prior sanction of Government of India is required.

Travel
Most people fly to India, either directly or as part of a discount round-the-world ticket. The cheapest airlines are the Eastern European or Middle Eastern ones, but be prepared for delays and little explanation if schedules go awry. There are also many overland expeditions to India (see Chapter 4).

India has an excellent rail system and while fares are cheap, it is possible to buy an Indrail pass, for various lengths of time, which is available only to foreign nationals and must be paid for in US dollars. The Pass can be bought from the foreign tourist bookings office at Delhi Railway Station and is valid for unlimited travel throughout India, and will save you hours of patient queuing. Holders of ISICs can purchase a 21-day unlimited travel pass on Indian Airlines 'Discover India Fare', but it must be purchased outside India.

While the railways are the best way to travel long distances in India, sometimes the only way to get around is on the bus, for example, if you are going from Jammu in the north to Kashmir.

Trailfinders, 194 Kensington High St, London W8 7RG. Tel: 01 938 3939
STA Travel, 86 Old Brompton Rd, London SW7. Tel: 01 937 9921
Encounter Overland, 267 Old Brompton Rd, London SW5 9JA. Tel: 01 370 6845
Hann Overland, 201-203 Vauxhall Bridge Rd, London SW1V 1ER. Tel: 01 834 7337
Exodus Expeditions, 9 Weir Rd, London SW12 OLT. Tel: 01 675 7996
Transglobal, 64 Kenway Rd, Earls Court, London SW5 ORD. Tel: 01 244 8571
Pleasureseekers Ltd, 52 Haymarket, London SW1Y 4RP. Tel: 01 930 3803

Accommodation
There are plenty of cheap places to stay in India in guest houses or lodges and they vary from the bed bug variety to the quite adequate. Airports and all main rail stations have Retiring Rooms where you can rent a bed if you have a current ticket. YMCAs generally have very good facilities but tend to get booked up months in advance. The India Tourist Office has a great deal of useful information on accommodation and travel and ISIC holders are entitled to accommodation discounts in India.

India Tourist Office, 7 Cork St, London W1X QAB
STIC Travels, Room 6, Hotel Imperial, Janpath, New Delhi 110001.
Youth Hostels Association of India, 5 Nyaya Marg, Chanakyapuri, New Delhi

Working Holidays
As you can imagine, there are very few opportunities for the working traveller in India, but it is so cheap to live there that you should be able to spend a few months on the money you saved in the more affluent parts of the world.

Voluntary Work
There are plenty of opportunities for community and voluntary work in India. The Indian High Commission produces a detailed information sheet giving the names and addresses of voluntary organisations with whom the Youth Service is connected. IVS operates camps in India

in association with Service Civil International and the United Nations Association organises some 30 camps in India. About 10 volunteers attend each camp and the work is mainly manual, agricultural and social. The accommodation can be very primitive depending on the particular area in India where the camp is located.

IVS, 162 Upper New Walk, Leicester LE1 7QA. Tel: 0533 549430
SCI, K-5, Green Park, New Delhi 110016
United Nations Association, Welsh Centre for International Affairs, Temple of Peace, Cathays Park, Cardiff CF1 3AP

IRELAND
Main Language: Irish, English
Currency: Irish pound (Punt)
Capital: Dublin
Exports: Cattle, Beef, Dairy products, Non-ferrous metals, Machinery.
Climate: Unpredictable. Generally winters are cold with warm to hot summers. Rain throughout the year.

Entry Requirements
Irish Embassy, 17 Grosvenor Place, London SW1X 7HR
Tel: 01-235 2171

Irish Tourist Office, Ireland House, 150 New Bond Street, London W1Y 0AQ Tel: 01-493 3201

Visas
UK citizens do not require a visa/passport.

Work Permits
Citizens of member states of the EEC do not need work permits to work in Ireland, but should produce evidence of their place of birth.

Permanent Residence
There are no restrictions on EEC citizens purchasing land in Ireland. In certain circumstances, however, the authorities may insist that farm land is retained in that form and not purchased for any other purposes, ie for conversion into large scale residential or commercial property. Persons who wish to buy property should consult a house agent, estate agent, auctioneer or solicitor. The Irish Auctioneers' and Valuers' Institute and the Incorporated Law Society of Ireland can be of assistance in this regard.

The Irish Auctioneers' and Valuers' Institute, 38 Merrion Sq, Dublin 2. Tel: (0001) 611794
The Incorporated Law Society of Ireland, Blackhall Place, Dublin 7. Tel: (0001) 710711

Travel
There are flights to Dublin and Cork, but most people travel to Ireland by ferry to Dun Laoghaire or Rosslare. Holders of ISICs can get discounts on ferries and on international flights.

There are numerous bus and rail passes within Ireland so check at bus/rail stations for the most appropriate deal and special offers. If you get a Travelsave stamp affixed to your ISIC you are entitled to a 50% discount on all rail and bus travel in Ireland, except on local runs costing less than £2. The public transport system is not very efficient, however, and trains are very slow.

Ireland is a good place for cycling. Even in Connemara, with its mountains and lakes, the roads generally follow the lakes in the valleys and its recent Irish Cycling champions have made cycling a popular sport. The Cyclists' Touring Club has information on cycling in Ireland. An Oige (Irish Youth Hostel Association) organises Rail Cycling holidays which include return rail fare to the starting point from any railway station in Ireland, hire of bicycle for one/two or three weeks, and youth hostel overnight accommodation vouchers, plus youth hostel handbook and map.

Hitching is commonplace and everyone does it (locals think nothing of hitching a two hour ride to work every day and back).

USIT, 7 Anglesea St, Dublin 2. Tel: (0001) 778117
CTC, Cotterell House, 69 Meadrow, Godalming, Surrey GU7 3HS. Tel: (04868) 7217
An Oige, 39 Mountjoy Sq, Dublin 1. Tel: 363111

Accommodation
The Irish Youth Hostel Association (An Oige) has details of all the youth hostels in Ireland as well as information on different hostelling passes. For example, a rambler/hostelling eight day journey pass includes an eight day bus/rail pass, youth hostel accommodation vouchers, plus handbook and map for IR£85 (under 18) or IR£95 (over 18).

There are also many private hostels which are more easy-going but more expensive. Trinity Hall offers university dormitory accommodation in the summer.

An Oige, 39 Mountjoy Sq, Dublin 1. Tel: 363111
Trinity Hall, Dartry Rd, Dublin. Tel: 971772

Working Holidays

Job Advertising
The Evening Press/ Tara House, Tara St, Dublin 2.
The Irish Press Tel: (0001) 713333
72 Fleet St, London EC4
Tel: 01 353 4539
Irish Independent/ 90 Middle Abbey St, Dublin 1
Evening Herald Tel: (0001) 731333
1st floor, Gotch House,
30 St Bride St, London EC4A 4BA
Tel: 01 353 4325
The Irish Times 11 D'Olier St, Dublin 2
Tel: (0001) 792022
85 Fleet St, London EC49 1LB
Cork Examiner/ 95 Patrick St, Cork
Evening Echo Tel: (010 353 21) 963300

If you are interested in working in Ireland, contact FAS, the Training and Employment Agency or try advertising in one of the papers. The Youth Exchange Bureau and the Irish Tourist Board in Dublin can give you information on working holidays or student exchanges.

Tourism offers the best opportunities for casual work, especially in areas such as Cork and Kerry. It is better to stick to the bigger centres, as in the rural areas especially, school children are often employed in the summer holidays in the hotels, pubs etc, and preference is generally given to locals. The Irish Tourist Board will be able to provide a list of hotels, resorts, restaurants etc.

There are very few opportunities for farm work in Ireland. Unemployment is quite high and local people are always given work in preference to outsiders. However, many farms and small holdings in Ireland offer the chance of first-hand experience of organic gardening and farming which is labour intensive. Upon membership of WWOOF you will receive a current list of holdings, and it is up to you to get in touch with your prospective host and make the arrangements. In return for your help with the work you receive board and lodging and your stay can be a weekend, week, month or longer by mutual agreement.

FAS, 27-33 Upper Baggot Street, Dublin 4. Tel: (0001) 685777
Youth Exchange Bureau, 10 Lower Hatch St, Dublin 2
Irish Tourist Board, Baggot St Bridge, Dublin 2
WWOOF, Annie Sampson, Crowhill, Newgrove, Tulla, Clare, Eire

Voluntary Work

There are many interesting opportunities for voluntary work in Ireland, from workcamps to conservation and preservation.

Workcamps

IVS organise a number of camps in Ireland each year which are run by Voluntary Service International. Applicants must be 18 years or over and preferably have previous workcamp experience. The work period is from 1-3 weeks between May and September and involves mostly outdoor renovation, restoration, conservation and labouring.

Comhchairdeas, the Irish Workcamp Movement organises workcamps involving manual, conservation and social work.

EYCE organise study camps in Ireland from time to time.

IVS, 162 Upper New Walk, Leicester LE1 7QA. Tel: 0533 549430
Voluntary Service International, 4/5 Eustace St, Dublin 2
Comhchairdeas, 2 Belvedere Place, Dublin 1
EYCE Secretariat, 217 Holywood Rd, Belfast BT4 2DH, N Ireland

Conservation

'Groundwork', part of the Irish Wildlife Federation, organises conservation workcamps at two National Parks in Ireland. Work involves clearing Rhododendron from wild oak forests. The cost for one week is £10 or £15 for two weeks and includes food and accommodation in the National Park Hostel. The working holidays begin on Sundays and consist of 5 days work, with evenings and the weekend free. Volunteers should be in good health and between 17 and 65 years of age.

The Irish Georgian Society organise volunteers to help restore old houses in Ireland. The programme runs from May until September and you may go for a minimum of two weeks during that time. Accommodation is provided, but you are asked to contribute IR£20 per week towards food and you need to bring a sleeping bag. Work involves painting, stripping and reglazing and cleaning windows, removing rubble, removing old wallpaper, oil treating doors etc. The minimum age for applicants is 17 years.

Sherkin Island Marine Station in County Cork need volunteers to help with various research projects including sea shore monitoring, plankton research, seals, birds, insects, plants, butterflies and moths. Volunteers are expected to help with the centre's garden which provides vegetables, and to help with cooking and washing up. Accommodation is in a bunkhouse with sleeping bags in rooms of 4 or 8 persons. Volunteers are asked to come on a month's trial. The weekly grant offered at the Marine Station is IR£10 together with free accommodation and board.

Groundwork, c/o Knockreer House, Killarney National Park, County Kerry, Ireland. Tel: (064) 31246
Groundwork, c/o Glenveagh National Park, Churchill, Letterkenny, Co Donegal, Ireland. Tel: (074) 37088
Irish Georgian Society, Leixlip Castle, Leixlip, Co Kildare, Ireland. Tel: (0001) 244211
Sherkin Island Marine Station, Sherkin Island, Co Cork, Ireland.
Tel: 028 20187

ISRAEL
Main Language: Hebrew, Arabic
Currency: Shekel
Capital: Jerusalem
Exports: Diamonds, Fruit, Clothing.
Climate: Summer – Hot (23°C)
Winter – Rainy, cool (8°C)

Entry Requirements
Israeli Embassy, 2 Palace Green, London W8 4QB. Tel: 01-937 8050
Israel Government Tourist Office, 18 Great Marlborough Street, London W1V 1AF
Tel: 01-434 3651

Visas
If you hold a full British passport valid for at least six months beyond the period of your intended stay you do not require a visa for Israel for a stay up to 90 days. If you want to stay longer you must apply for an extension. If you are not a British subject you should consult the Consular section of the Israeli Embassy. British Visitors passports are not accepted for entry into Israel. You should have a return or open ticket and proof of sufficient funds to cover your stay in Israel.

Work Permits
Work permits are required for work in Israel, and must be obtained by the prospective employer on application to the Ministry of the Interior. It is important that a permit is obtained before leaving for Israel. A work permit will only be granted if a vacancy cannot be filled by local manpower. Visas are given on arrival to those going to work on a kibbutz, moshav or on a archaeological excavation.

Travel
Many discount travel companies offer cheap flights to Israel (see Chapter 4). Some companies, such as WST have charter flights to Israel and also offer a London-Tel Aviv-Athens/Cairo/Istanbul ticket for the price of one, eg London-Tel Aviv-Athens £148 one way. Holders of an ISIC are eligible for discounts. Many people prefer to fly to Israel and return overland by train.

It is also possible to get to Israel by boat from Cyprus, Crete, Piraeus (Greece) and Rhodes, and ISIC holders can get a 20% discount on deck class fares. Getting to Israel overland presents more of a problem. You can go overland through Turkey, but it could be a bit dodgy because of Lebanon, or you could go via North Africa and Egypt but then you might have problems with an Arab stamp in your passport on entering Israel.

Students can get a 10% discount on EGGED buses throughout the country, and 20% discount on national railways.

WST, Priory House, 6 Wrights Lane, London W8 6TA.
STA Travel, 86 Old Brompton Rd, London SW7, 01 937 9921
ISSTA Lines, 109 Ben Yehuda St, Tel Aviv 63401.
Tel: (03) 247164

Accommodation
The Youth Hostel in Tel Aviv offers good accommodation and is popular so you need to book in advance. There are also good private hostels; the beach area is the best place to look for accommodation. The YMCA in Jerusalem is cheap and has excellent facilities and there are two good Youth Hostels. The Israel Government Tourist Office has information on campsites, inns and guest houses and Christian Hospices offering accommodation throughout Israel.

Israel Government Tourist Office, 18 Great Marlborough St, London W1V 1AF.
Tel: 01 434 3651

Working Holidays

There are quite a number of opportunities for casual work in Israel, especially in the cities and resorts like Eilat on the Red Sea. Ask in bars, hotels, youth hostels etc.

Club Mediterranee operates holiday villages on the Red Sea. Positions are available for receptionists, secretaries, couriers, computer operators, hostesses, cashiers, entertainment organisers, musicians, hairdressers, electricians, plumbers, nurses, housekeepers, kitchen, laundry and bar staff, chefs, qualified instructors in tennis, riding, golf, judo, cycling, skiing, sailboarding, kayaking, swimming, archery, yoga, scuba diving, water skiing, sailing, the arts, children's activities etc. Not all the vacancies are available at every resort, nor can applicants specify in which country they wish to work. All applicants must speak French, be aged between 21 and 30 and be available for work from May to October. Applications for the following year can only be made in November and December. Try contacting other tour operators for similar work with them.

There is little agricultural work, indeed rural work of any kind outside
the kibbutz/moshav system.

Kibbutz/Moshav

The official line is that it is very hard now to find work on a kibbutz unless you have already arranged a place before you leave and you are strongly advised to make arrangements beforehand. However, largely because of the political climate in Israel there are not so many volunteers as there used to be and many kibbutzim and moshavim are only too glad to accept people on arrival. It is certainly cheaper to get to Israel under your own steam than with an organisation.

It is quite easy to arrange a place on a Kibbutz on arrival by visiting the offices of one of the main movements (there are several) to see what places are available within their own movement. There are some 250 kibbutzim throughout Israel, so that there is a fair choice of location, objectives, age groups etc. The Kibbutz is not, as many people presume, a blanket organisation: it is made up of main movements each with many Kibbutz, all which vary in one way or another and it is possible for you to select the one most suitable to your own needs and views. Make sure you have enough money to cover the cost of accommodation in Tel Aviv while a place is being found for you – Israel is a very expensive country.

If you go through an agency in the UK, you are given the opportunity to travel as a group or independently. Group tickets are arranged for you and participants meet up at the airport, travel together, are met on arrival and transported directly to the Kibbutz. If you go as an individual you make your own travel arrangements (the organisation will want you to do this through their own Travel departments), and are allocated and directed to the Kibbutz when you arrive in Israel, which may take more than one day. If you go as an individual with an agency you are guaranteed a place but not to a particular Kibbutz.

As a working visitor on a Kibbutz, you work for 8 hours per day, 6 days per week alongside members of the Kibbutz, either in agriculture, services (dining room, laundry, clothes store, kitchen) or industry. The Kibbutz provide all your basic needs and in addition to board and lodging (2-4 in a room) a small personal allowance is given to cover basic toilet requisites, stationery etc. There is usually a minimum commitment of five weeks for individuals and three months for groups. If you want to move to a different kibbutz before your time is up, though, it is possible to do so but make sure you have a letter of reference from the kibbutz to testify to your character.

Work on a moshav can be much tougher and more demanding than on a kibbutz. The moshav is a collective settlement of families (as small as ten or as large as 100 families together) who have undertaken to work and develop an area of land for themselves but who share the capital costs of equipment, marketing and services necessary to make the settlement a success.

On a moshav you will be working with a family and, though you live in separate accommodation, you are expected to spend leisure time with the family and share in the social and cultural activities of the village.

Those who have had experience of both Kibbutz and Moshav seem to overwhelmingly prefer life on a Kibbutz, though if you are flat broke the small wage on the Moshav will enable you to travel elsewhere.

'Kibbutz Volunteer' from Vacation Work Publications lists all the kibbutzim and moshavim and gives information on the facilities.

Takam (United Kibbutz Movement), 82 Hayarkon St, POB 26131, Tel Aviv. Tel: (03) 655207/651710
Ha'kibbutz Ha'artzi, 13 Leonardo da Vinci St, Tel Aviv. Tel: (03) 435262/253905
Workers' Moshav Movement, 18-19 Leonardo da Vinci St, Tel Aviv. Tel: (03) 258473
Kibbutz Representatives, 1A Accommodation Rd, London NW11 8ED.
Tel: 01 458 9235
Project 67 Ltd, 10 Hatton Garden, London EC1N 8AH. Tel: 01 831 7626
Worldwide Student Travel Ltd, 36/38 Store St, London WC1E 7BZ
WST Charters, Priory House, 6 Wrights Lane, London W8 6TA.
Tel: 01 938 4362
'Kibbutz Volunteer', available from Vacation Work, 9 Park End St, Oxford

Au Pair
There are good opportunities in Israel for au pairs and mothers' helps. Applicants must be over 18 years of age and willing to work for a minimum of 3 months, although 6 months is preferable – longer term positions are available for mothers' helps.

Students Abroad, Elm House, 21B The Avenue, Hatch End, Middx HA5 4EN.
Tel: 01 428 5823
Anglia Agency, 15 Easter Ave, Southend-on-Sea, Essex SS2 5QX.
Tel: 0702 613888
Universal Care, Chester House, 9 Windsor End, Beaconsfield, Bucks HP9 2JJ. Tel: 0494 678811

Teaching

It is possible to get work teaching English in Israel though the competition is fierce from fellow travellers. Try the local newspapers, youth hostels and the University notice board.

Voluntary Work

Workcamps
The Christian Movement for Peace need volunteers in the summer to work with the League of Arabs who are involved in improving conditions in the fields of social security, education and housing in Palestine. Work involves clearing streets and public places, working in a public garden and reconstruction work. Volunteers should be over 18 with previous workcamp experience.

GAP Activity Projects offers school-leavers the chance to spend at least six months in Israel, living with host families and working with the sick/handicapped, teaching English, assisting in schools, farming and helping with conservation or working in an office.

Tear Fund also organise projects in Israel from time to time.

CMP, Bethnal Green URC, Pott St, London E2 OEF. Tel: 01 729 1877

GAP Activity Projects (GAP) Ltd, 7 King's Rd, Reading RG1 3AA.
Tel: 0734 594914
Tear Fund, 100 Church Rd, Teddington, Middx TW11 8QE

Archaeology
There are hundreds of digs in Israel for those wishing to volunteer. Most of the work is simply digging and sifting sand, but it is a wonderful way to spend a few weeks in Israel. You might even manage to get a tan. Most of the digs and other projects are organised by the universities in Israel, between June and September and you can get a complete list of them from the Department of Antiquities.

The Archaeological Institute of America publishes details of digs in Israel in its Fieldwork Opportunities Bulletin.

Project 67 organises archaeological tours to Israel. The cost includes insurance for four weeks, transfer on arrival, accommodation while on site, and return charter air travel (the maximum stay allowed is four weeks). If you want to stay longer you can get an open ticket which is valid for one year.

Department of Antiquities, Ministry of Education and Culture, PO Box 586, Jerusalem 91004.
Archaeological Institute of America, 675 Commonwealth Ave, Boston MA 02215.
Project 67 Ltd, 10 Hatton Garden, London EC1N 8AH. Tel: 01 831 7626

ITALY
Main Language: Italian
Currency: Italian Lira
Capital: Rome
Exports: Machinery, Vehicles, Textiles, Clothing, Petroleum products, Shoes, Iron and steel, Fruit.
Climate: Summer - Warm and dry in north, hot and arid in south
Winter - Heavy rain and snowfall in mountains.

Entry Requirements
Italian Consulate General, 38 Eaton Place, London SW1X 8AN. Tel: 01-235 9371

Italian State Tourist Office, 1 Princes Street, London W1R 8AY.
Tel: 01-408 1254

Visas
British nationals require either a Passport or a Visitors Card to enter Italy, but do not require a visa. British tourists are allowed to stay in Italy for a period of up to 3 months. For a longer period the tourist has to apply to the Police before the first 3 months have expired.

Work Permits
UK nationals may enter and stay in Italy for periods of up to three months in order to find employment without work permits. You must report, within 3 days of entering Italy, to the local Police Station informing them that you are seeking employment, and they will give you a 'Ricevuta di segnalazione di soggiorno', without which you cannot obtain a work permit. If you enter employment during this period you should apply to the Police for a residence permit, which is normally valid for five years and the holder is not subject to any restrictions in taking up

or changing employment. You are also required to contact the Town Hall to obtain the 'Libretto di Lavoro' (Work Permit).

Permanent Residence

EEC nationals may live in Italy for an indefinite period. No application for immigration is required by the Consulate General. The relevant residence permit (Permesso di Soggiorno) is issued directly from the Police Authorities in the locality in which you wish to reside. You are normally asked to show documented proof of your financial means, or where applicable, proof of your intended occupation (ie contract/letter of employment). If you purchase or rent a property in Italy, you would normally be entitled to a certificate of residence from the Town Hall.

Travel

Many of the discount travel companies offer low cost flights to Italy, including the Air Courier companies (see Chapter 4). The Centro Turistico Studentesco offers low cost rail travel and charter flights for students and young people, and also gives them reductions on Mediterranean shipping lines. Eurotrain has cheap rail fares to Italy and special passes for those under 26.

Sealink operate a service with connections at Venice for special Pullman trains (London-Folkestone-Boulogne-Venice).

Buses are also a cheap way of getting to Italy.

For covering distances between the major cities, the rail network is extensive but not renowned for its efficiency. Those under 26 can get from 20%-30% discount on inland railways with a special card, the 'Carta Verde'. For shorter journeys the buses offer a better deal; you can buy bus tickets at tobacconists'. Hitching is legal in Italy and relatively easy.

CIT offer a kilometric ticket valid for 3000 km (maximum 20 journeys) which can be used by up to 5 people at the same time and is valid for 2 months. They also issue a Travel at Will ticket which entitles you to unlimited travel on the entire Italian railway network.

Centro Turistico Studentesco UK Ltd, 33 Windmill St, London WIP IHH.
Tel: 01 580 4554
CTS (Head Office), Via Nazionale 66, 00184 Rome. Tel: (06) 46791
CIT (England) Ltd, 50-51 Conduit St, London WIR 9FB. Tel: 01 434 3844
Sealink, British Ferries Orient Express, 8th floor, Sea Containers House,
20 Upper Ground, London SE1. Tel: 01 928 6000
National Express, Victoria Coach Station, London SW1. Tel: 01 730 0202

Accommodation

The Italian State Tourist Office produces a Traveller's Handbook of Italy with useful information on travel, accommodation, places of interest, currency, climate etc.

Hotels must display an official price chart; the really cheap ones may rent by the bed. The area by the station in Rome is full of clean, budget hotels but the streets can be dangerous at night. There are good hostels in Rome, though some are quite a distance from the city centre. University Housing has rooms in the summer which can be booked through the tourist office.

As well as Youth Hostels for YHA members only, there are also students' hostels in many Italian towns available for students visiting the country. Ask for 'Caso dello Studente'.

There are excellent campsites in Italy, both in the cities and in the country, although in Venice camping is more expensive than staying in hotels. You can obtain an abridged list of sites with location maps by writing to the Centro Internazionale Prenotazione, Federcampeggio or from the Italian State Tourist Office.

Italian State Tourist Office, 1 Princes Street, London W1R 8AY. Tel: 01 408 1254
Associazione Italiana Alberghi per la Gioventu (Youth Hostels), Palazzo della Civilta del Lavoro, Quadrato della Concordia, 00144 EUR, Rome.
Tel: (06) 462342
Centro Internazionale Prenotazioni, Federcampeggio, Casella Postale 23, 50041 Calenzano, Florence. Tel: (055) 88 2391

Working Holidays

Job Advertising
Publicitas Ltd, 525 Fulham Rd, London Sw6 1HF (can place advertisements in 'Corriere della Sera' and 'Messaggero' (Rome daily)
AF International Advertising Services Ltd, 7 Ludgate Broadway, London EC4 (represents several Italian papers including the Milan, Florence, and Palermo dailies).

If you want to find work before you leave the UK, you can contact your local Job Centre in order to be registered as 'Job Seeker in Italy'. Your request will be forwarded through the EEC channels to the Italian Employment Office and if there are vacancies suitable to your specified trade or profession you will be informed.

The easiest jobs to find in Italy are usually teaching English in private language schools or in the catering and hotel business, though there is usually a plentiful supply of local staff for the latter.

Agricultural
There is little opportunity for farmwork in Italy as local labour is plentiful and cheap. However, it might be worth asking in villages for grape picking work as early as July/August although the harvest usually starts in September. Fruit is grown in the Alto Adige near Trento in Northern Italy (start looking in August/September for the October harvest), and in the Valtellina region, near the Swiss border.

The Agriturist organisation primarily rents cottages or farmhouses for holidays, but occasionally has places which offer free board and lodging in exchange for help with the harvests.
The Traveller's Handbook of Italy from the Tourist Office has addresses of the regional offices in charge of the various areas.

The International Farm Experience Programme offers language courses in French or German in France, followed by 4 1/2months of practical training in any of the EEC countries, including Italy. Courses begin in February and July and pocket money and board is provided during all courses. During the practical training you get wages and free board and lodging.

Agriturist, Corso V Emanuele, 101 Roma. Tel: (06) 651 2342
IFEP,YFC Centre, National Agricultural Centre, Stoneleigh, Warwickshire, CV8 2LG

Au Pair
Italy is probably one of the easiest and best countries for au pair and domestic work. Applicants must be at least 18 years of age and generally prepared to work for 6 months, although in the summer positions for as short as 4 weeks are available.

You can advertise for an Au Pair job in Italy, without charge, in the following women's magazines:
Amica, Sezione Annunci Gratuiti, Via Scarsellini 17, 20161 Milan
Gioia, Sez Annunci Gratuiti, Via Vitruvio 43, 20124 Milan
Grazia, Sez Annunci Gratuiti, 20090 Segrate, Milan

Au Pairs-Italy, 46 The Rise, Sevenoaks, Kent TN13 1RJ. Tel: 0732 451522
The Italian Bureau, 63 Cunningham Rd, London W12
Universal Aunts Ltd, 36 Walpole St, London SW3
Universal Care, Chester House, 9 Windsor End, Beaconsfield, Bucks HP9 2JJ. Tel: 0494 678811
Anglia Agency, 15 Eastern Ave, Southend-on-Sea, Essex SS2 5QX.
Tel: 0702 613888
Students Abroad, Elm House, 21b The Avenue, Hatch End, Middx HA5 4EN.
Tel: 01 428 5823
Firenze alla Pari-Babysitter, Via Pellicceria 6, Florence.
Tel: (055) 26 33 82

Secretarial Work
International Secretaries can place well qualified secretaries in all major Italian cities for a minimum period of one year. A knowledge of Italian is useful.

International Secretaries, 174 New Bond St, London W1Y 9PB

Tourism

Couriers/Campsites
Camping is very popular in Italy and it might be possible to find work in the bars, restaurants, shops or even cleaning on the sites, especially in the big cities and if you apply at the beginning of the season in March. If you speak Italian you are obviously in a better position.

Many tour operators in the UK organise camping holidays in Italy and you can write to them for jobs as couriers, camp site attendants, children's couriers, watersports instructors etc.

Other tour operators need reps to meet clients at the airport and sort out any problems. Get the addresses of these from any travel agent and write to them. EF Educational Tours need Tour Directors to lead American and Canadian school children on tours of Europe, including Italy. World Wine Tours need couriers with a knowledge of the wine regions to lead wine tours from March to October. For all these types of jobs, a knowledge of Italian and/or French is essential.

Club Cantabrica, 146 London Rd, St Albans, Herts AL1 1PQ. Tel: 0727 33141
Canvas Holidays, Bull Plain, Hertford, Herts SG14 1DY. Tel: 0992 553535
Eurocamp, Edmundson House, Tatton St, Knutsford, Cheshire WA16 6BG.
Thomson Holidays Ltd, Greater London House, Hampstead Rd, London NW1 7SD. Tel: 01 387 9321
Portland Holidays, 218 Great Portland St, London W1N 5HG. Tel: 01 380 0281
EF Educational Tours, EF House, 1 Farman St, Hove, Brighton BN3 1AL.
Tel: 0273 723651
World Wine Tours Ltd, 4 Dorchester Rd, Drayton St Leonard, Oxon OX9 8BH.
Tel: 0865 891919

Winter Resorts
You may be able to get work in the Italian Alps at ski resorts. Ski Europe have opportunities for part-time ski instructors in Piemonte and companies such as Snow World need chalet girls and

couriers for their winter holidays. If you can ski, then it might be worth contacting ski holiday companies.

Ski Europe, Northumberland House, 2 King Street, Twickenham, Middx TW1 3RZ. Tel: 01 891 4400
Snow World, 34-36 South Street, Lancing, West Sussex BN15 8AG
Tel: Lancing 750310

Teaching
There are a great many language schools in Italy, though because of the competition both from teachers and fellow travellers the standard of teaching tends to be high and TEFL qualifications are essential. In smaller towns you may be able to find teaching work, especially private tuition if you advertise yourself in the local papers or put notices up in shops etc. Newspapers often advertise for native speakers of English and university towns are a good source of employment for English speakers.

International House has a branch in Rome where jobs are advertised on the notice board. You can also enrol on a TEFL training course to get your necessary qualifications. The British Council has two centres in Italy, but if you don't have an RSA diploma in TEFL, a Post-Graduate Certificate of Education and at least two years' relevant experience there is no point in approaching them.

International House, 106 Piccadilly, London W1V 9FL. Tel: 01 491 2598
Accademia Britannica, International House, Viale Manzoni 57, 00185 Rome
British Council, Overseas Educational Appointments Dept, 65 Davies St, London W1Y 2AA. Tel: 01 499 8011

Voluntary Work

Workcamps
International Voluntary Service operate a number of camps in Italy, mostly for outdoor work, though there are also peace and study camps. Applicants must be over 18 years of age and have previous workcamp experience. Most projects last for 2-3 weeks during July/August.

Christian Movement for Peace organise a large number of camps in Italy. Recently they have been in the regions of Rome, Milan, Reggio Emilia and Sicily. Projects last for 2-4 weeks during July/August. Work is mostly manual and social. Volunteers must be over 18 and a knowledge of Italian is helpful.

Quaker International Social Projects run workcamps in Italy mainly concerned with environmental or ecological schemes, building playgrounds, or working with children and people in disadvantaged areas.

IVS, 162 Upper New Walk, Leicester LE1 7QA. Tel: 0533 549430
CMP, Bethnal Green URC, Pott St, London E2 OEF. Tel: 01 729 1877
QISP, Friends House, Euston Rd, London NW1 2BJ. Tel: 01 387 3601

Archaeology
The Italian Institute produces an information sheet listing all the archaeological groups/institutions in Italy. The Gruppo Archaeologico d'Italia requires volunteers for excavation and restoration.

The Archaeological Institute of America gives details of digs in Italy; the ones that aren't organised from America seem to be organised through the Gruppo Archaelogico d'Italia.

The Italian Institute, 39 Belgrave Square, London SW1X 8NX
Gruppo Archaeologico D'Italia, Via Tacito 41, 00193 Rome
Archaeology Abroad, 31-34 Gordon Square, London WC1H OPY
Archaeological Institute of America, 675 Commonwealth Ave, Boston, MA 02215

Conservation
The Italian Institute also produces an information sheet listing all the Conservation Societies in Italy as well as the National Parks. Write to various organisations directly for any volunteer work.

The British Trust for Conservation Volunteers organises holidays in Italy. Recently they have taken place at Maremma Regional park on the Mediterranean coast and the work has been concerned with habitat management. Accommodation is in dormitories.

The Italian Institute, 39 Belgrave Square, London SW1X 8NX
BTCV, 36 St Mary's Street, Wallingford, Oxon OX10 0EU. Tel: 0491 39766

IVORY COAST
Main Language: French
Currency: CFA Franc
Capital: Abidjan
Exports: Cocoa, Coffee
Climate: Dry season: Dec-May
Wet Season: Jun-Jul
Dry season: Aug-Sep
Wet Season: Oct-Nov
Equatorial in the south, tropical in the north

Entry Requirements
Ivory Coast Embassy, 2 Upper Belgrave Street, London SW1X 8BJ.
Tel: 01 235 6991

Visas
Information on visas can be obtained from the Embassy or from: Ministere des Affaires Etrangeres, BP V 109 Abidjan, Ivory Coast.

Work Permits
Write for information on work permits to:
Ministere du Travail, BP V 119 Abidjan, Ivory Coast

Voluntary Work
For information on workcamps write to:
Ministere de la Jeunesse et des Sports, BP V 136 Abidjan, Ivory Coast.

JAPAN
Main Language: Japanese
Currency: Jananese Yen
Capital: Tokyo
Exports: Iron and steel, Electrical machinery, Textiles, Other
machinery, Vehicles, Ships and boats.
Climate: Winter: snow and rain in western parts in north, 4°C
Warm in south
Summer: Warm in north, south subtropical, typhoons in late summer

Entry Requirements
Japanese Embassy, 46 Grosvenor Street, London W1X 0BA
Tel: 01-493 6030

Japan National Tourist Organisation, 167 Regent Street, London W1R 7FD
Tel: 01-734 9638

Visas
Full British passport holders may remain in Japan for a total period of six months as tourists, without visas. They are issued with leave to remain for an initial period of three months on entry, which may be extended for a further three months if required at the local Immigration Office in Japan.

Work Permits
Persons wishing to work in Japan must apply for an Employment visa which is only issued outside Japan and once the applicant has a firm offer of work. This takes between two to three months to process.

Travel
Most people arrive in Japan by air. See Chapter 4 for cheap discount travel companies that offer low cost fares. The other alternative is to buy a round-the-world ticket that stops in Japan.

Trailfinders has details of the Trans-Siberian Rover which lets you fly to Moscow then travel on the Trans-Siberian Railway and then by ship to Yokohama.

The best way to get around the country is by train with a rented fold-up bike ready for when you get off. Buy a Japan Rail Pass through your student travel shop or from the Japan National Tourist Organisation for budget travel on trains, boats and buses as you can't buy one there. Local buses radiate out from rail stations and the subway is fast, simple and has English-version diagrams. If you're leaving Tokyo straight away, take an overnight Dream Bus, specially designed for budget travellers. If you have an ISIC you can get up to 25% disocunt of principal domestic ferry routes and a 35% discount on domestic air fares on a standby basis if you're under 21.

The Japan Travel Phone is manned by English-speaking travel experts ready to assist every day from 9am to 5pm.

Trailfinders, 194 Kensington High St, London W8 7RG. Tel: 01 938 3939
Japan National Tourist Organisation, 167 Regent St, London W1R 7FD.
Tel: 01 734 9638
NFUCA (University Co-op), Sanshin-Hokusei Bldg, 2nd floor,2-4-9 Yoyogi, Shibuya-ku, Tokyo 151. Tel: (03) 379 6311
Japan Travel Phone, Tokyo 502 1461. Kyoto 371 5649.

Accommodation
Even cheap hotels in Japan are expensive; Youth Hostels are cheaper especially if you are a member. ISIC holders are entitled to special rates in over 400 Co-op Associated hotels

throughout Japan. ISTC publish the Sleep Cheap Guide to Asia/Australia/New Zealand and the Japan National Tourist Organisation produce Your Guide to Japan which contains useful information, including accommodation. Don't mistake motels for ordinary drive-in hotels; in Japan they are rented by the hour for couples. The Tokyo Journal and the Japan Times are English language papers that carry advertisements for cheap hostels or "gaijin houses".

Working Holidays

Job Advertising
Joshua B Powers, 46 Keyes House, Dolphin Sq, London SW1V 3NA (represents Asahi Evening News, English language daily.)

It is possible to get a work permit without leaving Japan, especially if you have a degree, and it usually takes about a month. You can just try to renew your tourist visa and work illegally or get a cultural visa which will enable you to stay in Japan. You have to prove that you are studying for at least 20 hours a week. Many people go to Seoul in Korea temporarily to renew or apply for visas.

Agriculture
The International Agricultural Exchange Association operate exchange programmes to Japan for people between the ages of 19 and 28 years who have good practical experience in their chosen trainee category (agriculture, home management, agri-mix, horticulture, hort-mix). You will stay with a host family and receive an allowance while you are training as well as three weeks unpaid holiday. In Japan the exchange lasts for 8 or 12 months leaving in April and you can choose to work with pigs, dairy cows, beef or vegetables.

IAEA, YFC Centre, National Agricultural Centre, Kenilworth, Warwickshire CV8 2LG. Tel: 0203 22890

Teaching
Japan is one of the best countries in which to teach English – the Japanese are very keen students and the pay is very high. Like Hong Kong, though, it takes a long time to save in Japan because of the high cost of living. There are a great many English language schools in Tokyo and in the other big cities and there are countless opportunities for private language teaching, either by looking at the paper, hostel notice boards or by advertising yourself. Business English is very popular both with businessmen and secretaries and is also very lucrative, as is 'English conversation'.

The British Council has a centre in Japan, but unless you have an RSA Diploma in TEFL, a Post Graduate Certificate in Education and at least one or two years' relevant experience, they will not accept you. They might have lists of language schools.

British Council, Overseas Educational Appointments Dept, 65 Davies St, London W1Y 2AA. Tel: 01 499 8011

Voluntary Work
Voluntary work is hard to obtain, but once obtained, the applicant requires an Employment visa. If you are interested in voluntary work in Japan you are advised to apply to the Consulate General of Japan directly.

KENYA
Main language: Swahili, English
Capital: Nairobi

Exports: Coffee, tea, pyrethrum, sisal, soda ash
Climate: Dry in north, monsoon rains in south, hot

Entry Requirements
Office of the High Commissioner, Kenya House, 45 Portland Place, London W1N 4AS.

Kenya Tourist Office, 13 Burlington St, London W1.

Visas
Holders of valid full British passports do not require a visa unless they are of Asian origin. Anyone with a South African stamp in their passport also needs a visa.

Work Permits
In order to take paid employment in Kenya a work permit must be obtained. These should be applied for by the prospective employer who must satisfy the
authorities as to the need to employ non-resident labour. Such permits are only available, generally, for skilled and professional jobs where there is a shortage of qualified residents.

Travel
Many of the discount travel companies offer cheap flights to Kenya (see Chapter 4). You can go overland independently but the route is subject to sudden closure through fluctuating no-go areas, or you can enter by train from Tanzania or Uganda.

There are many expedition travel companies that operate overland trips that include Kenya on their itineraries.

Buses are cheap and hitching is a good way to get around, although it is not wise to travel alone in the bush without seeking advice.

Guerba Expeditions Ltd, Dept TF, 101 Eden Vale Rd, Westbury, Wilts BA13 3YB. Tel: 0373 826611
Encounter Overland, 267 Old Brompton Rd, London SW5 9JA. Tel: 01 370 6845
Transglobal, 64 Kenway Rd, Earls Court, London SW5 ORD. Tel: 01 244 8571
Hann Overland, 201-203 Vauxhall Bridge Rd, London SW1V 1ER. Tel: 01 834 7337
Exodus Expeditions, 9 Weir Rd, London SW12 OLT. Tel: 01 675 7996
Trailfinders, 194 Kensington High St, London W8 7RG. Tel: 01 938 3939

Accommodation
There are a number of youth hostels in Nairobi and in Mombasa, both in the city and up and down the coast. The River Road area in Nairobi has the cheapest hotels and restaurants but it is also notorious for muggings and you are advised not to walk to and from the town after dark. Many of the cheap hotels rent rooms by the hour to couples - it's better to stick to the youth hostels or more expensive hotels. Contact the Kenya Tourist Office for details of accommodation and youth hostels.

Working Holidays
There are a few opportunities in Kenya for the intrepid traveller but it is up to you to find and make your own opportunities. In the expatriate community you may be able to get work translating documents, proof reading, doing office work at one of the Embassies, working in a playgroup etc. You might even get work at one of the tourist bars or clubs. The Thorn Tree Cafe in New Stanley Hotel, Kimathi St (opposite Woolworth's) is an outdoor bar which is popular with travellers and has a notice board for messages - a good place to go to pick up information and

advice. Kenya is famous for its Game Reserves and National Parks – if you have a particular skill or interest that might be useful, eg ornithology or zoology, you might be able to persuade someone to give you a job leading tours, giving lectures etc.

There are a number of film companies who work regularly in Kenya and there is usually an epic of one kind or another being shot out in the bush. You might find work as a gofer or even as an extra – ask on location.

Teaching
There is a great demand for secondary school teachers in Kenya and you may be able to get some work teaching in a school in a village, though the pay is very low. Several organisations in the UK recruit or help to recruit teachers for posts in Kenya.

The League for the Exchange of Commonwealth Teachers, Commonwealth House, 7 Lion Yard, Tremadoc Rd, Clapham, London SW4 7NF. Tel: 01 498 1101
Catholic Institute for International Relations, 22 Coleman Fields, London N1 7AF, Tel: 01 354 0883
Christians Abroad, Livingstone House, 11 Carteret St, London SW1H 9DL.
Tel: 01 222 2165
European Council of International Schools, 21b Lavant St, Petersfield, Hants GU32 3EL. Tel: 0730 68244
Gabbitas-Thring Service Ltd, 6-8 Sackville St, Piccadilly, London W1X 2BR.
Tel: 01 439 2071
IVS-DEEP, 109 Pilgrim St, Newcastle-upon-Tyne NE1 6QF.
British Council, Overseas Educational Appointments Dept, 65 Davies St, London W1Y 2AA.
Tel: 01 499 8011
Committee for International Cooperation in Higher Education, 10 Spring Gardens, London SW1A 2BN. Tel: 01 930 8466

Voluntary Work
VSO currently has 66 volunteers in Kenya involved in secondary education, youth training programmes, health work, special education and environmental projects.

VSO, Enquiries Unit, 317 Putney Bridge Rd, London SW15 2PN. Tel: 01 780 1331

Workcamps
The Kenya Voluntary Development Association has various camps in rural and under-developed areas. Projects include building schools and roads, renovating buildings, providing water supplies etc.

Kenya Voluntary Development Association, PO Box 48902, Nairobi, Kenya

Archaeology
The Archaeological Institute of America gives details of digs in Kenya in its Fieldwork Bulletin. East of Lake Turkana, the Koobi Fora Palaeoanthropological Field School introduces students firsthand to multi- disciplinary approaches of modern human origins research. The course provides classroom and field instruction and emphasises practical instruction in excavation techniques, field mapping etc.

Earthwatch sponsors expeditions to Kenya.

Archaeological Institute of America, 675 Commonwealth Ave, Boston, MA 02215
Earthwatch Expeditions Inc, 680 Mount Auburn St, PO Box 403, Watertown, MA 02272

KOREA
Main Language: Korean
Currency: Won
Capital: North – Pyongyang, South – Seoul
Exports: Minerals, Metal products, Clothing, Plywood, Textiles.
Climate: Similar to central USA. 4 distinct seasons.
Spring – Mar-May (warm, windy)
Summer – Jun-Aug (hot, rain)
Autumn – Sep-Nov (warm)
Winter – Dec-Feb (cold)

Entry Requirements
Korean Embassy, 4 Palace Gate, London W8 5NF. Tel: 01 581 0247
Korea National Tourism Corporation, 2nd floor, Vogue House, 1 Hanover Square, London W1R 9RD. Tel: 01 409 2100

Visas
Visitors with confirmed outbound tickets and a valid passport may stay up to 15 days without a visa. Anyone planning to stay in Korea longer than 15 days must obtain a visa before coming to Korea. UK nationals can enter Korea as a tourist or for commercial business purposes without a visa for 2 months. This can be extended for a further 30 days by applying to the District Immigration Office at least 1 day before the expiration of the visa.

A visitor who plans to stay in Korea for more than 91 days is required to apply for a residence certificate at the local District Immigration Office within 90 days of arrival.

Work Permits
Those who visit Korea for the purpose of employment should have a work permit before entering Korea.

Travel
See Chapter 4 for information on discount travel companies that offer cheap flights. Holders of ISICs can get reduced airfares to Korea. Ask about round-the-world tickets that include Korea on the itinerary.

If you are coming from Japan, there are two ferries to Pusan: the Pukwan ferry between Shimonoseki (Japan) and Pusan, and the Kuk Jae ferry from Osaka. The Pukwan ferry crossing is shorter and therefore cheaper and students can get a 20% discount.

Students can also get a 20% discount on domestic flights in Korea. The train network is extensive and well organised and has three types of train – ordinary express, express and super-express. Stations have special ticket counters where English is spoken and there is a Korail Pac tour programme for foreigners for 1-4 nights available from the main stations. Express buses operate from all the principal cities and resorts and it is a good idea to purchase tickets in advance on holidays or weekends. A free national student discount scheme booklet is available from the student office in Seoul.

KIYSES (Student Travel), Room 505, YMCA Building, 9 Chongro 2-ka, Seoul, Korea. Tel: 732 6646

Accommodation
Most people who live in Korea for any length of time and travel about the countryside stay in Korean inns or 'Yogwans', where you sleep on mattresses on the floor. There are also about 20 youth hostels in Korea, of which only 12 are members of the Korea Youth Hostel Association.

Students can get a 10%-30% discount in tourist hotels, hostels and inns in Seoul, Taegu, Pusan and Naksan and a 10% discount is available if booked through the KIYSES. The Korean Tourist Corporation produces a glossy brochure with a lot of useful information on travel, accommodation etc, and the Sleep Cheap Guide to Asia/Australia/New Zealand by the ISTC is available from student travel offices.

Korea Youth Hostel Association, 27 Sup'yo-dong, Chung-gu, Seoul.
Tel: (02) 266 2896
KIYSES, Room 505, YMCA Building, 9 Chongro 2-ka, Seoul. Tel: 732 6646

Working Holidays

Teaching
There are good opportunities for teaching English in Seoul and Pusan, though the wages are not as high as in Japan. Business English in particular is popular as is 'conversation'. It is against the law for foreigners to teach high school students and this is quite strictly enforced so make sure you teach only adults. Hostels (as usual) and hostel notice boards are good places for making contacts. Avoid being in the cities from mid-July to mid-August as Koreans head for the beaches and mountains and there will be little chance of work.

LESOTHO
Currency:
Capital: Maseru
Climate: Winter – 10°C-15°C
Summer- 24°C

Entry Requirements
Lesotho High Commission, 10 Collingham Rd, London SW5 ONR.
Tel: 01 373 8581/2

Visas
UK nationals do not require a visa to enter Lesotho.

Work Permits
Work permits can be obtained from the Department of Labour in Lesotho.

Permanent Residence
Those who wish to emigrate to Lesotho would, on arrival, report to the Department of Immigration where they would be issued with a temporary residence permit at intervals of 6 months, then one year. At the end of five years' continuous residence they could then apply for citizenship.

Travel
Trailfinders and STA travel have comprehensive information on travel throughout the world. Some of the overland tour companies might have details on how to get to Lesotho overland.

Trailfinders Travel Centre, 194 Kensington High St, London W8 7RG. Tel: 01 938 3939
STA Travel, 86 Old Brompton Rd, London SW7. 01 937 9962
Encounter Overland, 267 Brompton Rd, London SW5 9JA. Tel: 01 370 6845
Guerba Expeditions Ltd, Dept TF, 101 Eden Vale Rd, Westbury, Wilts BA13 3YB. Tel: 0373 826611
Hann Overland, 201-203 Vauxhall Bridge Rd, London SW1V 1ER. Tel: 01 834 7337

Accommodation
For information on Youth Hostel accommodation, contact the Lesotho Youth Hostels Association, Box 970, Maseru 100, Lesotho

Working Holidays
Lesotho is a very poor country surrounded by South Africa – indeed many of its inhabitants go to South Africa to find work,and the ones that remain engage mostly in subsistence farming.

Finding any work depends on individual luck according to the High Commission. The best bet is in the capital and by finding the places where the English-speaking community hang out. You could get work translating documents, doing secretarial work etc for one of the embassies.

Teaching
There are no opportunities for casual teaching work, but if you want a long-term teaching job in Africa the Association of Commonwealth Universities provides member universities and other institutions with facilities for announcing vacancies and assessing candidates. These facilities are most frequently used by Lesotho, among others.

Association of Commonwealth Universities, 36 Gordon Sq, London WC1H OPF. Tel: 01 387 8572

Voluntary Work
You may find voluntary work opportunities with non-governmental organisations such as Save the Children Fund, CARE etc, depending on the length of time you wish to spend in Lesotho.

Workcamps
International Voluntary Service recruits skilled and experienced personnel for work in Lesotho.

IVS, 162 Upper New Walk, Leicester LE1 7QA. Tel: 0533 549430

For more information on workcamps, contact:

Lesotho Workcamps Association, Box 6, Maseru 100, Lesotho

LUXEMBOURG
Main Language: Luxembourgeois, French, German
Currency: Luxembourg Franc
Capital: Luxembourg
Exports: Iron and steel, Vehicles, Machinery, Non-ferrous metals, Textiles.
Climate: Temperate: Summer – 67°F, Winter – 28°F

Entry Requirements
Luxembourg Embassy, 27 Wilton Crescent, London SW1X 8SD. Tel: 01-235 6961
Luxembourg National Tourist and Trade Office, 36/37 Piccadilly, London W1V 9PA Tel: 01-434 2800

Visas
British citizens need only a valid passport to enter the country for a stay of not more than 3 months. To stay longer than 3 months, it is necessary to obtain a resident permit by applying to the local police in Luxembourg.

Work Permits

EEC nationals can freely enter the Grand Duchy of Luxembourg and seek employment. A work permit is not required by the nationals of the member countries of the EEC.

Permanent Residence

All persons intending to reside in the Grand Duchy must produce the following documents to the 'Police des Etrangers':
1) Proof of identity.
2) Proof of sufficient means of subsistence or a Declaration Patronale.
3) A medical certificate
4) Declaration de Depart – ie references from the previous place of residence. If all the formalities are completed, an Identity Card for Foreign Nationals will be issued by the Police which is valid for five years and is renewable.

Police des Etrangers, Ministere de la Justice, 16 boulevard Royal, Luxembourg. Tel: 4794 450

Travel

Luxembourg shares its borders with France, Germany and Belgium, so is an easily accessible country by rail or road. Eurotrain offer cheap rail passes which are valid for two months to students and youth under 26. You can also get to Luxembourg by air.

Luxembourg has an extensive rail and bus network. '5-day Network' tickets are valid for unlimited journeys on any lines of the Luxembourg railway and bus system within a period of one month. For further information on cheap rail tickets within Luxembourg ask at the main station.

The Tourist offices in Luxembourg, Kiekirch and Mersch produce a leaflet with suggestions of cycling tours on cycling tracks and roads with minor car traffic. You can take bicycles with you on the trains if there is room for a flat rate of 18 francs.

Accommodation

There are youth hostels throughout Luxembourg which are open to anyone with a valid membership card. The travel department of the Luxembourg Youth Hostels Association combine accommodation in youth hostels with reduced train fares for young people under 26, such as Interrail-Junior and BIJ tickets. Send an IRC for more information to the Luxembourg Youth Hostels Association.

A list of camp sites is published free from the National Tourist Office and rest houses and holiday homes can be rented from Gites d'Etape Luxembourgeois.

Luxembourg Youth Hostels Association, 18 place d'Armes, Luxembourg City.
Tel: 2 55 88
Luxembourg National Tourist Office, 36/37 Piccadilly, London W1V 9PA.
Tel: 01 434 2800
Gites d'Etape Luxembourgeois, 23 boulevard Prince Henri, 1724 Luxembourg. Tel: 2 36 98
Bureau des Scouts de Wiltz, Chateau de Wiltz, Wiltz. Tel: 96199 (Camping).

Working Holidays

Job Advertising

Luxemburger Wort, 2 rue Christophe-Plantin, PO Box 1908, Luxembourg (largest daily newspaper). Letzeburger Journal, 123 rue Adolphe Fischer, Box 2101, Luxembourg

It can be difficult to find employment in Luxembourg without good French and German, which are both very commonly used in business and industry. There are a number of British and American firms established in Luxembourg and the Luxembourg Embassy produces an information sheet listing their names, addresses and products. Try placing an advertisement in any of the papers or English-language magazines.

International Secretaries have vacancies from time to time for well qualified secretaries with good French or German for one year contracts.
International Secretaries, 174 New Bond Street, London W1Y 9PB.

You could contact the following agencies in Luxembourg for work:

Administration de l'Emploi, 34 Avenue de la Porte-Neuve, Luxembourg.
Tel: 476855-1
Manpower-Aide Temporaire, 19 rue Glesener, Luxembourg.
Tel: 48 23 23 (Temporary jobs – all professions)
Bureau-Service, Sarl, 2 allee Leopold Goebel, Luxembourg.
Tel: 44 45 04 (Temporary office jobs)

For students:
Service National de la Jeunesse, 1 rue del la Poste, Luxembourg.
Tel: 46 80 2-331 (Dept of the Ministry of Education)
Officenter, 25 bld Royal, Luxembourg. Tel: 47 25 62 (Temporary office jobs)

Agriculture
Grapes are grown along the Moselle in the south east of Luxembourg and the harvest usually begins in late September and finishes in late October. Your best bet is to visit the vineyards directly and ask for work.

Au Pair
There are no special agencies in Luxembourg which deal with au pairs, but the Government Employment Office deals with all employment enquiries.

Administration de l'Emploi, 34 Avenue de la Porte-Neuve, Luxembourg.

Tourism
The Luxembourg Embassy produces a booklet containing the names and addresses of all the restaurants and hotels in Luxembourg and advises people to apply directly to them for seasonal jobs.

Teaching
Only Luxembourg nationals may teach in State schools, but there are two English speaking schools which may need teachers.
Contact also the Ministry of National Education.

Ecole Europeene, Plateau de Kirchberg, Luxembourg. Tel: 43 20 82

American School of Luxembourg, 188 avenue de la Faiencerie,
Luxembourg-Limpertsberg. Tel: 47 00 20

Ministere de l'Education Nationale, 29 rue Aldringen, 2926 Luxembourg.
Tel: 46 80 2

Voluntary Work
Information on voluntary work can be obtained from:
Cercle de Cooperation et d'Aide au Developpement du Tiers Monde, 5 avenue Marie-Therese, 2132 Luxembourg.

For youth exchanges contact:
Service National de la Jeunesse, 1 rue de la Poste, Place d'Armes, 2346 Luxembourg. Tel: 46802-335

MADAGASCAR
Main Language: Malagasy, French
Currency: Malagasy Franc
Capital: Antananarivo
Exports: Coffee, Spices
Climate: Summer - Hot and dry
Winter - Temperatures 10° to 15°C

Entry Requirements
Democratic Republic of Madagascar, Honorary Consulate, 16 Lanark Mansions, Pennard Road, London W12 8DT. Tel: 01-746 0133

Visas
Visas are required by all nationalities. For this you need your passport, 5 photographs, your return ticket, completed and signed application form and the fee of £30.

Work Permits
You need to have an employer in Madagascar willing to give you a contract of employment. As soon as you are in possession of such a document, you can apply for your work permit through the Honorary Consulate.

You will need the same items as you do for visas which are sent to the Ministry in Madagascar. A delay of at least 2 months is to be expected before an answer can be given to the application.

Travel
Madagascar is a huge island lying some 250 miles off the coast of Africa and the main way to get there is by air. Check the discount travel companies mentioned in Chapter 4 for flights there. Exodus Expeditions and Hann Overland do Adventure trips to Madagascar lasting 22-24 days.

Exodus Expeditions, 9 Weir Road, London SW12 OLT. Tel: 01 675 7996
Hann Overland, 201-203 Vauxhall Bridge Rd, London SW1V 1ER. Tel: 01 834 7337

Accommodation
Hotels and guest houses offer accommodation, some of which is very basic. You should allow about £12 per day.

Working Holidays
Madagascar is more of a place to travel to and around rather than a place in which to find work.If you have a good knowledge of French you may be able to find casual work helping out at embassies or offices, but local people are taken on in preference to outsiders.

Teaching
The British Council organises the Key English Language Teaching project in support of English language teaching in developing countries, including Madagascar. The project is aimed at increasing the potential of local teaching centres and at improving the English proficiency of students and trainees in developmental sectors of the economy. KELT projects normally extend over a five year period and a knowledge of French is desirable. Applicants should have a degree or

equivalent, inluding a substantial TEFL component, or a general teaching qualification in TEFL or Applied Linguistics and at least three years' teaching experience of which two years or more will have been spent in an appropriate overseas country.

British Council, Overseas Educational Appointments Dept, 65 Davies St, London W1Y 2AA. Tel: 01 499 8011

Voluntary Work
There are schools and hospitals that might take on volunteers, but you do need a work permit which takes 2 or 3 months to issue.

Contact the Embassy in Paris for more information:

Ambassade de Madagascar, 4 Avenue Raphael, 75016 Paris, France.
Tel: 145 04 62 11

MALAWI
Main Language: Bantu, English
Currency: Kwacha
Capital: Lilongwe
Exports: Tobacco, Tea, Groundnuts
Climate: Dry season (winter): May-Oct 21°C
Wet season (summer): Dec-Mar 26°C
Highlands – cold at night

Entry Requirements
Malawi High Commission, 33 Grosvenor Street, London W1X OHS.
Tel: 01-491 4172/7

Visas
UK nationals with a valid passport do not require a visa to enter Malawi.

Work Permits
If you secure a job in Malawi, your prospective employer will apply for a work permit for you.

Travel
Malawi is in central Africa, bordered by Zambia, Tanzania and Mozambique and is dominated by its huge Lake Malawi. You can fly to Malawi or go overland through one of the countries already mentioned. Exodus Expeditions organise a Malawi Safari, staying in hotels, lodges and safari cottages and occasionally camping. Try also the other travel companies mentioned in Chapter 4.

Exodus Expeditions, 9 Weir Rd, London SW12 OLT. Tel: 01 675 7996
Hann Overland, 201-203 Vauxhall Bridge Rd, London SW1V 1ER.
Tel: 01 834 7337
Guerba Expeditions Ltd, Dept TF, 101 Eden Vale Rd, Westbury, Wilts BA13 3YB.
Tel: 0373 826611
Encounter Overland, 267 Old Brompton Rd, London SW5 9JA. Tel: 01 370 6845

Accommodation
Malawi is a peaceful, relatively prosperous country with a good tourist industry, therefore tends to be expensive for Africa. There are several Game Reserves and National Parks which have safari

huts and lodges and there are camping sites by the Lake.You should allow about £15 per day for food and accommodation.

Working Holidays
There are few opportunities for casual work in Malawi. As in many places, you may well find some work by being on the spot and seizing your opportunity when one presents itself. As tourism is the main industry, you might be able to find work as a water sport instructor on the Lake for example.

Teaching
There are no opportunities for casual teaching in Africa generally, but there are some organisations that recruit staff in the UK. The Committee for International Cooperation in Higher Education assists in the recruitment of academic, technical, library and administrative staff to universities and colleges in Malawi. The British Council has a centre in Malawi for the KELT project which aims to increase the potential of local teaching centres and at improving the English proficiency of students and trainees in developmental sectors of the economy. Christians Abroad recruits graduate teachers for service abroad in church related schools and colleges in the developing countries of Africa. Gabbitas-Thring recruits well qualified and experienced staff at all levels for English medium schools in Africa.

The Committee for International Cooperation in Higher Education,
Higher Education Division, 10 Spring Gardens, London SW1A 2BN.
Tel: 01 930 8466
The British Council, Overseas Educational Appointments Dept, 65 Davies St, London W1Y 2AA.
Tel: 01 499 8011
Christians Abroad, Livingstone House, 11 Carteret St, London SW1H 9DL.
Tel: 01 222 2165
Gabbitas-Thring Service Ltd, 6-8 Sackville St, Piccadilly, London W1X 2BR. Tel: 01 439 2071

Voluntary Work
VSO currently have 62 volunteers in Malawi, working in the health field, training nurses and paramedical staff or helping to improve primary health care. Support to secondary education, especially in maths and science, is a priority as is providing specialist skills to small-holder agriculture by supplying economists and computer programmers.

VSO, Enquiries Unit, 317 Putney Bridge Rd, London SW15 2PN. Tel: 01 780 1331

MALAYSIA
Main Language: Malay, Chinese, English and others
Currency: Ringgit
Capital: Kuala Lumpur
Exports: Rubber, Tin, Sawn wood, Fish, Palm oil.
Climate: Hot and rainy throughout the year: 20°C-30°C
Oct-Mar: heaviest rainfall

Entry Requirements
Information Division, Malaysian High Commission, 45 Belgrave Square,
London SW1X 8QT. Tel: 01-235 8033

Work Permits
Work permits are issued only when the employer can satisfy the authorities that no Malaysian citizen is available for the post. When they are issued they are for fixed contract periods. No

person should leave their home country to take up employment in Malaysia without holding the appropriate work permit.

Permanent Residence
"The question of permanent residence does not arise," according to the Malaysian Embassy.

Travel
There are flights to Kuala Lumpur from many parts of the world (see Chapter 4 for details of travel companies). Polo Express book couriers to Kuala Lumpur for £275 for a 2 week return trip. Hann Overland organise trips to Sarawak and Kalimantan. You can also get to Malaysia from Thailand or Singapore by train or bus. Only Malaysian students studying in Malaya are able to get discounts on trains, though there is a 10-day and 30-day Malaysian Rail Pass. Ferries go from Kuantan on the East coast of Malaysia to Kuching in Sarawak, or Kota Kinabalu in Sabah, both of which are Malaysian states in Northern Borneo. Ferries also go from Penang on the West coast and to Medan in Sumatra. Holders of ISICs are entitled to discounts on the ferries.

In Sarawak, the main form of transport is by boat on one of the many rivers or by bus. Sabah is a much richer country and has an excellent system of buses but is more expensive.

Hann Overland, 201-203 Vauxhall Bridge Rd, London SW1V 1ER. Tel: 01 834 7337
MSL Travel SDN BHD, 1st floor, South East Asia Hotel, 69 Jin Hj Hussin,
50300 Kuala Lumpur. Tel: 03 2989722
MSL Travel SDN BHD, Ming Court Hotel Lobby, Macalister Rd, 10400 Penang.
Tel: 04 24748

Accommodation
Malaysia is quite a wealthy country and the cost of living there is comparatively high for South East Asia. There are many youth hostels and guest houses and students can get discounts at hotels in Kuala Lumpur, Penang and most major towns and resorts. The Sleep Cheap Guide to Asia/Australia/New Zealand has details on accommodation in Malaysia. In Penang, accommodation is not as expensive as the mainland and North Borneo is cheaper still.

Working Holidays
The authorities in Malaysia are very strict about work permits and virtually all appointments for the public and private sectors are made in Malaysia itself.

Teaching
There are, from time to time, employment opportunities in posts calling for high academic or professional qualifications in universities etc. The Economist and leading daily newspapers or professional journals carry advertisements for such jobs.

The Association of Commonwealth Universities provides member universities with facilities for announcing vacancies and assessing candidates, and these are used frequently by the University of Malaya. The Committee for International Cooperation in Higher Education assists in the recruitment of academic, technical, library and administrative staff to universities and colleges in Malaysia. The European Council of International Schools assists international English-medium schools throughout the world with staff recruitments.

Association of Commonwealth Universities, 36 Gordon Square, London WC1H OPF.
Tel: 01 387 8572
Committee for International Cooperation in Higher Education, Higher Education Division, 10 Spring Gardens, London SW1A 2BN. Tel: 01 930 8466
European Council of International Schools, 21b Lavant House, Petersfield, Hants GU32 3EL.
Tel: 0730 68244

Centre for British Teachers (GM2), Quality House, Quality Court, Chancery Lane, London WC2A IHP. Tel: 01 242 2982

Voluntary Work
VSO is involved in welfare (community-based rehabilitation, mental health and probation, education (teacher training, libraries, refugees and conservation) and fisheries in Malaysia. It is currently in the process of constructively winding down its involvement before a phased withdrawal in September 1991.

VSO, Enquiries Unit, 317 Putney Bridge Rd, London SW15 2PN. Tel: 01 780 1331

Workcamps
The World Council of Churches organises workcamps in Malaysia. The age limit is 18 to 30 years and volunteers must make their own travel arrangements and pay for insurance. In Malaysia a recent project has been in Sarawak constructing a concrete dam and connecting pipes to provide water to a longhouse. Write to the WCC for details of workcamps or write directly to the contact person in Sarawak.

World Council of Churches, Sub Unit on Youth, 150 route de Ferney, 1211 Geneva 20, Switzerland
Rev Wong Meng Chuo, Institute Pengajarn Komuniti, PO Box 8, Sibu/Sarawak, Malaysia.
Tel: (084) 322795

MALTA
Main Language: Maltese, English
Currency: Maltese pound
Capital: Valetta
Exports: Clothing, Textiles
Climate: Summer – Hot and dry, temperatures exceeding 24°C
Winter – Cool

Entry Requirements
Malta High Commission, 16 Kensington Square, London W8 5HH
Tel: 01-938 1712

Malta National Tourist Organisation, Suite 207, College House, Wrights Lane, London W8 5SH.
Tel: 01-938 2668

Visas
British nationals do not need a visa to visit Malta and may stay for up to 3 months.

Work Permits
Work permits are issued only in very rare circumstance, such as when a vacancy exists requiring special skills and qualifications which are not available on the Island. They must be applied for by the prospective employer on behalf of the foreign national. The employer must show sufficient proof that the employee will fill a position which no skilled Maltese national is presently available.

Permanent Residence
As an alternative to the permanent residency scheme, an individual may obtain an extended tourist permit to enable him to stay in Malta for a longer period than the three months allowed.

This permit is renewable at fixed intervals by the Principal Immigration Officer. Individuals with a temporary residence permit are subject to local tax conditions on income brought into the country only.

Travel
See Chapter 4 for information on cheap flights. In the winter special offers are often advertised by travel companies, aimed primarily at the elderly, but nevertheless they are a good way to get out there. Students can get a 20% discount on Gozo Channel Co Ltd's ferry to Catania in Sicily.

NSTS (Student and Youth Travel Office), 220 St Paul ST, Valletta. Tel: 624983

Accommodation
Students can get special reduced rates in various accommodation centres in Malta and Gozo. From the middle of October to Mid-December and from January to the end of March, students get a 50% discount at the NSTS Student Centre. The NSTS also has details of family accommodation programmes in Malta. The Malta National Tourist Organisation produces an information sheet 'Malta and its Islands' with information on accommodation, places of interest, climate etc.

NSTS, 220 St Paul Street, Valletta. Tel: 624983

Working Holidays
The NSTS organises activity holidays in the summer for anyone aged 15-29, and they need a variety of staff, eg kitchen porters, domestic staff, watersports instructors etc. Send applications before April to the NSTS.

PGL Adventure Ltd need reps to co-ordinate water sports at their hotel-based holiday in Gozo. Liaison with local windsurf and diving schools is important, plus the ability to instruct in snorkelling, windsurfing and canoeing.

NSTS, 220 St Paul St, Valletta. Tel: 624983
PGL Adventure Ltd, Station St, Ross-on-Wye, HR9 7Ah. Tel: 0989 767833

Voluntary Work
The Valletta Youth Hostels Association need volunteers to help with office work, renovation and construction work. In return for 21 hours' work a week, you receive hostel accommodation and breakfast. You have to pay insurance and travel costs and a £15 deposit. You should state whether you want to work the first or last two weeks of the month, and when applying send your details, 3 passport photos, and 2 IRCs at least 3 months in advance. The YHA will help you obtain your work permit.

Valletta Youth Hostels Association, 17 Triq Tal-Borg, Pawla, Malta. Tel: 229361

MAURITIUS
Main language: English

164

Capital: Port Louis
Exports: Cane sugar
Climate: Winter (July): cool, heavy rainfall 20°C
Summer (Jan) : calm, very hot 26°C

Entry Requirements
Mauritius High Commission, 32/33 Elvaston Place, London SW7.
Tel: 01 581 0294/5

Visas
UK nationals do not require visas to visit Mauritius.

Work Permits
Work permits are required by UK nationals and are rarely issued except for highly skilled or professional jobs where there is an acute need that cannot be met from within the country. They must be obtained from the Ministry of Employment, New Government Centre, Port Louis by the prospective employer.

Permanent Residence
Information on permanent residence and emigration can be obtained from the Prime Minister's Office, New Government Centre, Port Louis.

Travel
See Chapter 4 for discount travel companies that offer cheap flights. Polo Express book air couriers to Mauritius for £350 for a 2 week return trip.

Working Holidays
There is a large European population on Mauritius and you might find work in offices or at the embassies through personal contacts by frequenting the places where Europeans socialise.

Information on working holidays/student exchanges can be obtained from:
The Ministry of Education, Arts and Culture, New Government Centre,
Port Louis.

Voluntary Work
The Service Civil International organises workcamps in Mauritius. British residents should contact IVS for details and information on these workcamps. Also contact the Ministry of Youth and Sports.
IVS, 162 Upper New Walk, Leicester LE1 7QA. Tel: 0533 549430
Ministry of Youth and Sports, Level 3, Emmanuel Anquetil Building, Port Louis.

MEXICO
Main Language: Spanish

Currency: Mexican Peso
Capital: Mexico
Exports: Cotton, Sugar, Tomatoes, Coffee, Cattle, Machinery
Climate: Summer – Temperatures exceeding 25°C, heavy rain in South,
dry in central, western & norther areas
Winter – Warm (January 20°C)

Entry Requirements
Mexican Embassy, 8 Halkin Street, London SW1X 7DW. Tel: 01-235 6393

Mexican Tourist Office, 7 Cork Street, London W1X 1PB. Tel: 01-734 1058

Visas
Tourist cards are required for people entering Mexico as tourists. They are free of charge and
issued over the counter and must be obtained before departure from any Mexican consulate or
authorised airline flying Mexican routes. To obtain a Tourist Card from the Mexican Consulate
in London, the following documents must be submitted:

1. Passport which must be valid for at least six months;
2. International certificates against smallpox and cholera (only when infected areas have been
visited within the two weeks prior to entry into Mexico);

Work Permits
Foreigners are only allowed to work in Mexico if a company firm (Mexican) requires the service
of a certain qualified person, in which case the firm must apply to the Immigration authorities
in Mexico City for a work visa. They are only issued to skilled and professional personnel where
there is a definite need for their services which cannot be met from within the country.

Permanent Residence
Immigration, either temporary or permanent, is closed to foreigners wishing to start a private
business or take up employment in Mexico. Exceptions to this are made when Mexican firms
require the services of certain qualified executives, professionals, technicians or other specialists.

Travel
There are a great many cheap flights to Mexico from the UK and the USA (see Chapter 4 for
discount travel companies), and students can get reduced airfares from many destinations in
Europe. You can also get there by land, either by bus or train from the USA and other countries
in Central America.
Buses are cheap in Mexico and go to most places. Hitching is easy but you may have to pay (guard
your money belt as robbery is rife).

Journey Latin America, 16 Devonshire Road, London W4 2HD. Tel: 01 747 3108
Steamond Ltd, 23 Eccleson St, London SW1 9LX. Tel: 01 730 8646
Trailfinders Ltd, 194 Kensington High St, London W8 7RG. Tel: 01 938 3939
Wexas, 45 Brompton Rd, Knightsbridge, London SW3 1BR. Tel: 01 589 3315
Aero Mexico, 38 Morley House, Regent St, London W1. Tel: 01 637 4107
Explore Worldwide Ltd, 7 High Street, Aldershot, Hants GU11 1BH.
Tel: 0252 319448

Exodus Expeditions, 9 Weir Rd, London SW12 OLT. Tel: 01 675 5550
Ace Study Tours, Babraham, Cambridge CB2 4AP. Tel: 0223 835055
Swan Hellenic, 77 New Oxford St, London WC1A 1PP. Tel: 01 831 1616
Learn at Leisure, Dept of Adult Education, University of Nottingham,
14 Shakespeare St, Nottingham NG1 4FJ. Tel: 0602 483838

Accommodation
The area between Monumento a la Revolucion and Alameda Park have the best selection of
very cheap hotels in Mexico City. There are also youth hostels run by SETEJ (Student Travel
bureau) and a YMCA in Mexico City. Ask for a listing of hotels, campsites and discounts for
students throughout Mexico at SETEJ offices. Camping is free on almost any beach or you can
rent a hammock to get off the sand. The SETEJ office in Mexico City can assist in arranging
Homestay Programmes. Trailfinders produce 'Mexico – a Travel Survival Kit' which contains
detailed information on accommodation, food, places of interest and travel.

SETEJ Mexico AC, Hamburgo No 273, Col Juarez, 06600 Mexico DF. Tel: 5144213

Working Holidays
Joshua B Powers Ltd, 46 Keyes House, Dolphin Square, London SW1V 3NA (agents for Mexico
City News, an English language daily in Mexico City, and 'Novedades', a leading Mexican daily)

In Mexico you need to produce a Registro Federal de Contribuyentes for employers. If you find
work and wish to stay longer than the expiry date on your tourist card you can apply locally for
an extension or cross the border and get another stamp. The Mexican Embassy states that it is
strictly forbidden for tourists to engage in paid employment, and the authorities in Mexico might
well get suspicious if you keep applying for an extension.

You could try fixing yourself up with a job before you go as a driver/tour leader with one of the
expediton groups mentioned in the travel section.

Club Mediterranee operates holiday villages on the Pacific Coast of Mexico and need a wide
variety of staff from computer operators and musicians to electricians and water sports
instructors. All applicants must speak French, be aged between 21 and 30 and be available for
work from May to October. Applications for the following year can only be made in November
and December.

Club Mediterranee, 106-108 Brompton Rd, London SW3 1JJ.

Teaching English
There are plenty of opportunities to teach English in Mexico, though competition in Mexico City
is greater than in the large resorts. It is important to look the part of a teacher as appearance
carries more weight than qualifications or experience. Look in the English language paper for
tuition wanted and on youth hostel notice boards as well as the telephone directory. If you have
some training and experience the Berlitz Language Centre has a branch in Mexico as does the
British Council.

SETEJ run summer courses and need teachers for these but you must have some knowledge of
Spanish. English-media schools may also require teachers – look at Chapter 5 for addresses.

Berlitz Language Centre, Ejercito Nacional No 530 1er piso, Col Polanco, 11550 Mexico DF.

British Council, Overseas Educational Appointments Dept, 65 Davies Street, London W1Y 2AA.
Tel: 01 930 8466
SETEJ, Hamburgo NO 273, Col Juarez, 06600 Mexico DF

Voluntary Work
GAP Activity Projects offers school-leavers the chance to spend at least six months in another country, including Mexico, living and working with its people. At present GAP volunteers are doing various types of work including helping with the sick and handicapped, teaching English, assisting in schools, farming and helping with conservation, and office work. Volunteers live with a host family who provide board, accommodation and in most cases, pocket money.

SETEJ organise workcamps in small communities which include construction work, health and social work. Applicants must be aged 18 and over and have a basic knowledge of Spanish. Food and accommodation is provided by local families and facilities are often very primitive. Volunteers must pay their own travel and insurance costs as well as an administration fee, and should apply at least 3 months in advance.

Amigos de las Americas sends volunteers to Mexico for one or two months. Volunteers must have several months of training, which can be done by correspondence, and pay around US$2000-2400 which includes travel from the US.

The American Friends Service Committee organises workcamps in Mexico. It is necessary to apply by March and be fluent in Spanish, although vacancies are generally very limited.

GAP Activity Projects (GAP) Ltd, 7 King's Rd, Reading RG1 3AA.
Tel: 0734 594914
SETEJ, Hamburgo No 273, Col Juarez, 06600 Mexico DF. Tel: 5144213
Amigos de las Americas, 5618 Star Lane, Houston, Texas 77057, USA
American Friends Service Committee Inc, 1501 Cherry St, Philadelphia,
Pennsylvania 19102-1479, USA

Archaeology
From time to time The Archaeological Institute of America has details of digs in Mexico in its Fieldwork Opportunities Bulletin.

Earthwatch sponsors several projects in Mexico. Recent projects have been concerned not only with archaeology, but with architecture and marine ecology.

Archaeological Institute of America, 675 Commonwealth Ave, Boston, MA 02215.
Earthwatch Expeditions Inc, 680 Mt Auburn St, PO Box 403, Watertown, MA 02272

MONGOLIA
Main Language: Mongol
Currency: Tugrik
Capital: Ulan-Bator
Exports: Livestock, Wool, Meat.
Climate: Summer – 32°C +; Winter – Nov-Mar (-46°C), dry

Entry Requirements
Embassy of the Mongolian People's Republic, 7 Kensington Court, London W8.
Tel: 01-937 0180

Visas
An ordinary (tourist) visa is issued to those who are travelling to Mongolia and have booked a tour through the Mongolian National Travel Agency. Visas are issued by the Embassy's Consular Section with authorization from Zhuulchin (Mongolian National Travel Agency) and cost £14. It is necessary to state clearly the exact date of entry into Mongolia and the period of stay. The normal time for a visa to be processed is one week – transit visas take 48 hours. You must produce a valid passport and one recent passport size photograph. A group visa in the name of the tour leader is valid for all tourists in the group (for groups of more than 5 people), so names and passport details must be attached with the application. If you wish to apply for a visa by post you should enclose a large self-addressed and stamped envelope.

Zhuulchin, Travel Agency, Ulan Bator, Mongolian People's Republic

Travel/Accommodation
Travel routes in the country and special services for booking air/train tickets as well as accommodation are organised by Zhuulchin. You must let them know well in advance your arrival and departure dates, type of transportation, your chosen itinerary and the place where you will obtain your visa.

Unofficially, it used to be possible to get into Mongolia through China relatively easily. Check with other travellers to find out if this is still the case.

Working Holidays
There are no opportunities for the working traveller in Mongolia.

MOROCCO
Main Language: Arabic, French, Spanish
Currency: Dirham
Capital: Rabat
Exports: Phosphates, Oranges, Vegetables.
Climate: Summer temperatures exceeding 24°C, cool winters

Entry Requirements
Moroccan Embassy, 49 Queen's Gate Gardens, London SW7 5NE. Tel: 01-581 5001

Moroccan Tourist Office, 174 Regent Street, London W1R 6HB. Tel: 01-437 0073

Visas
British passport holders with a passport valid for 6 months can stay in Morocco without a visa for up to 3 months. If you wish to stay over three months you must register with the Police in the city where you are staying and must justify your stay by holding a valid work permit or by importing income from outside.

Work Permits
It is difficult for foreigners to obtain employment in Morocco, including part time jobs. Anyone wishing to take up employment must have a work permit issued by the Ministry of Labour in

Morocco on request of the prospective employer. No-one is allowed to enter paid or unpaid employment without the authorisation of the Ministry of Labour. Application should be sent to the following address:

Ministere du travail et de la Formation Professionnelle, Shellah, Rabat, Morocco

Permanent Residence
A British person wishing to emigrate to Morocco must register with the Police of their residing city. He should justify his stay with a valid work permit or by importing income from outside.

Travel
There are many cheap flights to Morocco from the UK (see Chapter 4). Students can get a 30% discount on Air Maroc flights from Paris. Eurotrain offer discount train fares for people under 26. Many people also get to Morocco by boat from Malaga in Southern Spain. From Spain or Gibraltar you could try getting a passage on a yacht either as crew or as a cook.

Many of the expedition travel companies include Morocco on the itinerary.
For example, Explore Worldwide organise a 2 week desert truck adventure to Morocco from Malaga.

STA Travel, 74 Old Brompton Rd, London SW7 3LQ. Tel: 01 937 9962
Trailfinders, 194 Kensington High St, London W8 7RG. Tel: 01 938 3939
Explore Worldwide, 7 High Street, Aldershot, Hants GU11 1BH. Tel: 0252 319448
Guerba Expeditions, Dept TF, 101 Eden Vale Rd, Westbury, Wilts BA13 2YB
Tel: 0373 826611
Encounter Overland, 267 Old Brompton Rd, London SW5 9JA. Tel: 01 370 6845
Hann Overland, 201-203 Vauxhall Bridge Rd, London SW1V 1ER. Tel: 01 834 7337

Accommodation
University residences are open to travellers from July 15 to September 15 in Rabat, Marrakech and Fes. Contact the UGEM (Student Travel Bureau) in Rabat. The UGEM can also arrange for a limited number of foreign students to live with a Moroccan family for 15-30 days in Safi, Marrakech, Rabat, Fes or Casablanca. You should apply at least 2 months in advance. The Union Marocaine and the Federation Royale Marocaine des Auberges de Jeunesse can give you information on youth hostels.

UGEM, 78 rue Sebou Agdal, Rabat, Morocco. Tel: 70024
Union Marocaine des Auberges de Jeunesse, 6 Place Amiral Philibert, Casablanca.
Federation Royale Marocaine des Auberges de Jeunesse, avenue Oqba Ibn Nafii, Meknes.

Working Holidays
It is very difficult for foreigners to obtain casual employment in Morocco. The needs at the present time are for qualified teachers, nurses and medical doctors, skilled technicians and experts who also speak Arabic and/or French. There are several British firms and institutions, however, and you may be able to fix up some employment by contacting one of the British missions in Morocco.

Several tour companies operate package holidays in Morocco and you could contact them before you go to enquire about jobs as couriers, reps, water sports instructors etc. Write to any of the expedition travel companies listed in the travel section for jobs as drivers/tour leaders.

The British Embassy, 17 Boulevard de la Tour, Hassan, Rabat

The British Consulate General, 60 Boulevard d'Anfa, Casablanca
The British Consulate General, 52 rue d'Angleterre, Tangier
The British Council, Overseas Educational Appointments Dept, 65 Davies St, London W1Y 2AA.
Tel: 01 499 8011

Voluntary Work

Christian Movement for Peace and the United Nations Association organise placements on workcamps in Morocco. You must be aged 18 years and over and be prepared to work a 35 hour week for two to three weeks in July and August. Accommodation is in colleges, schools or rural community centres and volunteers should take their own sleeping bags. Volunteers help with construction, renovation and conservation on community projects as well as being involved in discussions.

Quaker International Social Projects also place volunteers in Morocco. You can also write directly to Chantier de la jeunesse Maroc.

CMP, Bethnal Green URC, Pott St, London E2 OEF. Tel: 01 729 1877
United Nations Association, International Youth Service, Welsh Centre for International Affairs, Temple of Peace, Cathays Park, Cardiff CF1 3AP.
Tel: Cardiff 223088
QISP, Friends House, Euston Rd, London NW1 2BJ. Tel: 01 387 3601
Chantier de la jeunesse Maroc, 24 Av Madagascar, Rabat

NETHERLANDS

Main Language: Dutch
Currency: Gilder
Capital: Amsterdam
Exports: Machinery, Textiles, Chemical products,Petroleum, Meat, Iron and steel, Vegetables.
Climate: Summer – Cool, with frequent rain
Winter – Mild

Entry Requirements

Netherlands Embassy, 38 Hyde Park Gate, London SW7 5DP. Tel: 01-584 5040

Netherlands Board of Tourism, 25-28 Buckingham Gate, London SW1E 6LD.
Tel: 01-630 0451

Visas

UK citizens with a valid passport can stay in the Netherlands for up to 3 months without a visa. Those wishing to stay longer should contact the local police within 8 days of arrival in order to apply for a residence permit.

Work Permits

EEC nationals do not need an employment permit if they are intending to stay less than 3 months. If you intend to stay longer than 3 months you should contact the local police within eight days of arrival in order to apply for a Residence Permit. This may be refused unless you can prove you have sufficient means to cover your stay and unless you have sufficient funds for a return ticket.

Permanent Residence

In view of considerable unemployment, a shortage of accommodation and the increasing population, immigration is not encouraged and permanent residence is only rarely granted.

Travel
Amsterdam is very cheap to get to either by plane, train or bus. ISIC holders are entitled to up to 40% off trans-Euro rail and bus fares, as well as discounts on air fares depending on the route and the season (see Chapter 4). Netherlands Railways offer several rail passes for travel within the Netherlands: a Rail Rover entitles you to unlimited travel on trains for 3-7 days; a Public Transport Link Rover (used with a Rail Rover) entitles you to unlimited travel on Amsterdam and Rotterdam metro systems and on buses and trams throughout the Netherlands; a Benelux Tourrail Card entitles you to unlimited travel on the national railways of the Netherlands, Luxembourg and Belgium for 5 days.

Amsterdam has an extensive system of canals so it is easy to get around the city by boat. Buses in the city are less convenient than trains. As Holland is so flat it is an ideal country for cycling – many stations offer bicycles for hire at reduced rates for ticket holders. Hitch-hiking is easy in the Netherlands.

Topdeck Travel, 131 Earls Court Rd, London. Tel: 01 373 8406
Miracle Bus Company, 408 The Strand, London WC2. Tel: 01 836 3201
Eurotrain, 52 Grosvenor Gardens, London SW1. Tel: 01 730 3402
Netherlands Railways, 25-28 Buckingham Gate, London SW1E 6LD. Tel: 01 630 1735
NBBS (Student Travel Bureau), Dam 17, Dam Square, Amsterdam. Tel: (020) 205071
NBBS (Head Office), Schipholweg 101, 2316 XC Leiden. Tel: (071) 226475

Accommodation
The NBBS Incoming Department can make accommodation bookings and the Tourist office (look for sign VVV) in Amsterdam has a list of cheap accommodation. The Netherlands Board of Tourism also has details on different types of accommodation. The NJHC (Dutch Youth Hostel Federation) produces a free hostels list and basic language guide.

Through the NBSS Incoming Department you can book a cycling package which includes 8 days (2 in Amsterdam, 5 days touring) of accommodation on campsites while touring. The package includes the rental of bikes and camping equipment. Holders of ISICs can get a 10% discount. For really basic camping in Amsterdam try the Sleep-In in Gravesandestr.

Steer clear of hotel touts at the station who may take you miles out of town to share a dorm with hundreds of others and then rip you off. Beware of offers of houseboats too as they are actually illegal.

NBBS Incoming Department, Schipholweg 101, 2316 XC Leiden. Tel: (071) 253372
NJHC (Youth Hostels). Tel: 26 44 33
Netherlands Board of Tourism, 25-28 Buckingham Gate, London SW1E 6LD. Tel: 01 630 0451

Working Holidays

Job Advertising
Joshua B Powers Ltd, 46 Keyes House, Dolphin Sq, London SW1V 3NA
Publicitas Ltd, 525 Fulham Rd, London SW6 1HF.

Skilled workers over 21 (18 in some instances) who wish to find work for some length of time, may apply to the local employment exchange in the Netherlands in order to be recommended for employment under the scheme for International Clearance of Vacancies and Applications for Employment.

Seasonal work is available in hotels, canning factories, breweries etc for unskilled young persons of 18 years and over. Apply to the Director General for Manpower for short-term employment (at least six weeks) in summertime.

Ministry of Social Affairs and Employment, The Director General for Manpower, Visseringlaan 26, 2288 ER Rijswijk, The Netherlands. Tel: (70) 130911

Agriculture

Work can be obtained in the 'bulb' industry where large numbers of workers are required in the fields and factories between May and October (particularly late August to early September). The main areas are on the north and west coasts: try the area between Haarlem and Leiden. You need to be on the spot for hiring.

Young people of 18 years and over with at least two years' training or practical experience in agriculture or horticulture seeking similar employment in the Netherlands for a period of six months can apply to the International Farm Experience Programme.

International Farm Experience Programme, Young Farmers' Centre, National Agricultural Centre, Kenilworth, Warwickshire CV8 2LJ. Tel: 0203 29645

Au Pair

Universal Care, Anglia Agency and Students Abroad have vacancies in Holland for Au Pairs and Mother's Helps. Applicants must be between 18 and 30 years of age. Most Dutch families speak good English but a basic knowledge of Dutch is useful.

Universal Care, Chester House, 9 Windsor End, Beaconsfield, Bucks HP9 2JJ.
Tel: 0494 678811
Anglia Agency, 15 Eastern Ave, Southen-on-Sea, Essex SS2 5QX.
Tel: 0702 613888
Students Abroad, Elm House, 21b The Avenue, Hatch End, Middx HA5 4EN.
Tel: 01 428 5823

Tourism

Tourism in Holland is very healthy and there are over 400 local offices of the Dutch Tourist Board scattered around Holland. From these you can obtain the names and addresses of local hotels, restaurants, resorts etc who often employ foreign workers during the summer season. The wages are not especially good but quite a few working travellers find short term employment in Dutch hotels.

Many of the camping holiday companies organise camping holidays in Holland and need couriers/reps, watersports instructors etc in the summer season.

PGL Adventure Ltd operate holidays for young people in Holland. Couriers are required to take charge of groups of up to 34 youngsters (2 per group) for barge holidays, travelling and returning with the group for one or two trips during the summer months. Applicants must be over 21 years of age and be able to look after and communicate with children.

PGL Adventure Ltd, Station St, Ross-on-Wye, Herefordshire HR9 7AH. Tel: 0989 767833
Eurocamp, Edmundson House, Tatton St, Knutsford, Cheshire WA16 6BG

Other Employment

Technical students wishing to do practical work during their holidays should contact:
The International Association for the Exchange of Students for Technical
Experience, (IAESTE), Seymour Mews House, Seymour Mews, London W1H 9PE.
Tel: 01 486 5101

Under the ICN Exchange Programme, nurses (Registered nurses only) having a basic knowledge of the Dutch language, can apply to:

The Royal College of Nursing, Cavendish Square, London W1M OAB. Tel: 01 409 3333

International Secretaries recruits secretaries to work in the Netherlands for periods of about one year, although shorter contracts are sometimes available.

International Secretaries, 174 New Bond Street, London W1Y 9PB.

Voluntary Work
International Voluntary Service requires volunteers for several conservation and workcamps each year in various parts of the Netherlands. Volunteers must be over 18 year of age. Workcamps last for 2-3 weeks during July and August.

Christian Movemement for Peace places volunteers in workcamps in conjunction with ICVD. The work is mainly involved with community, social, horticultural and renovation projects.

The United Nations Association has both conservation and workcamps in a number of areas. Volunteers are involved in manual, conservation, community development projects as well as working with the handicapped and children.

For a list of workcamps in the Netherlands write to:

Central Bureau for Educational Visits and Exchanges, Seymour Mews House, Seymour Mews, London S1H 9PE (enclose large sae)

IVS, 162 Upper New Walk, Leicester LE1 7QA. Tel: 0533 549430
CMP, Bethnal Green URC, Pott Street, London E2 OEF. Tel: 01 729 1877
United Nations Association, Welsh Centre for International Affairs, Temple of Peace, Cathays Park, Cardiff CF1 3AP. Tel: Cardiff: 223088

NEW ZEALAND
Main Language: English
Currency: New Zealand Dollar
Capital: Wellington
Exports: Meat, Wool, Butter, Cheese.
Climate: North Island – warm in summer, subtropical in far north
(16°C-26°C Jan); winter (8°C-26°C Jul)
South Island – heavy round the year rainfall in SW, E drier,
summer cool (16°C Jan); winter cold (5°C Jul)

Entry Requirements
New Zealand High Commission, New Zealand House, 80 Haymarket, London SW1Y 4TQ. Tel: 01-930 8422

New Zealand Tourist Office, New Zealand House, 80 Haymarket, London SW1Y 4TQ

Visas
You do not need a visa if you are a tourist, on business, want to see friends or relatives or involved in cultural events. A British citizen may stay in New Zealand for up to 6 months with a British passort which is valid for at least three months past the date you intend leaving New Zealand.

On arrival you must apply for a permit and you will need to have:
- a passport valid for 3 months after your intended date of departure;
- enough money to support yourself while you are in New Zealand – NZ$1000 for each person for each month or NZ$400 for each person for each month if your accommodation is already paid.

If you do not have enough money you will need a guarantee of accommodation and maintenance from a friend or relative who lives in New Zealand – ask your friend/relative to complete the form Sponsoring a Visa and send it to you.
- a return or onward ticket.

If you want to stay in New Zealand for longer than the visa free period, you can apply for a further permit while in New Zealand. Your application must be made while the permit you hold is current. It is unusual for anyone to be granted a further permit which would allow a visit or working holiday of more than 12 months.

Work Permits

It is a condition of every vistor's permit that the holder does not work, study or undertake medical treatment while in New Zealand.

(a) Pre-arranged Employment: If you wish to take up pre-arranged work, your application for a work visa must be supported by an offer of employment from a New Zealand employer. In general only those people who are qualified in an occupation included on the Occupational Priority List (OPL) can be considered. Those who have been accepted under an approved exchange scheme or whose prospective employer has permission to recruit from the New Zealand Immigration Service may also be considered. You will need to apply at least four weeks before your intended date of departure from the UK. If you are a doctor, nurse, or other health professional, or a teacher with employment arranged, special conditions relating to registration authorities in New Zealand apply. You need to apply well in advance of your proposed travel date.

(b) Casual work: Work opportunities offered to visitors are likely to be of a short term nature such as seasonal work or employment calling for skills not readily available. You may apply for a work permit when you are in New Zealand. Particular consideration will be given to your application if you are young and on a genuine holiday, especially if employment is offered to you by a relative or a sponsor. You should approach the nearest regional/branch office of the Immigration Service with your written offer of employment if you want a permit to work. A fee of NZ$88 will be charged for the application. The Immigration Service will check that the employment offered to you cannot be undertaken by local job seekers and will not restrict employment opportunities for residents in New Zealand.

Permanent Residence

There are three main ways you can qualify for permanent residence in New Zealand. They are through your occupational skills, business skills or family relationship. The New Zealand High Commission produces an information sheet detailing these categories.

If you are overseas, you apply on an Application for Residence form, which you can get from a New Zealand diplomatic or consular office. Your application should be made at the office in your country of residence.

If you are already in New Zealand, you apply on the same form, which you can get from a District Office of the Department of Labour. Your application should be lodged at that office no later than 7 days before your temporary permit expires.

A 300-page guide for new settlers has been published by the Immigration Service. It aims to provide realistic and factual information about many of the day-to-day aspects of New Zealand life. Copies are obtainable from the New Zealand High Commission at a cost of £5.

Travel

Many of the discount travel companies mentioned in Chapter 4 offer low cost air fares to New Zealand, and students are eligible for discounts depending on the route and the season. Round-the-world tickets incorporating New Zealand on the itinerary are usually good value for money, though it depends on how long you intend travelling and working (they are usually valid for only a year).

Students are also eligible for a standby fare (a reduction of 50%) on almost all scheduled domestic airlines, and can get major fare concessions on the ARA weekly bus pass on regional bus services operated by the Auckland Regional Authority. There are student standby fares on Delata Coachline services and Newmans Coachlines. New Zealand Railways offer a Travelpass for unlimted travel on trains, buses and ferry for 8 days (details from Compass Travel).

Contiki, FREEPOST, Bromley, Kent BR1 1UW. Tel: 01 290 6777
Trailfinders, 194 Kensington High St, London W8 7RG. Tel: 01 938 3939
Travelbag, Dept TA, 12 High Street, Alton, Hants GU34 IBN. Tel: 0420 82456
Jetset, 74 New Oxford St, London WC1A 1EU. Tel: 01 636 7315
AAT King's, 2nd floor, William House, 14 Worple Rd, Wimbledon, London SW19 4DD
Tel: 01 879 7322
STA Travel, 74 Old Brompton Rd, London SW7 3LQ. Tel: 01 937 9962
Student Travel, 1st floor, 10 High Street, Auckland, New Zealand.
Tel: (09) 399 723
Compass Travel, 46 Albemarle St, London W1X 4EP. Tel: 01 408 4141

Accommodation
Student Travel offices in New Zealand have information on accommodation. There are also Youth Hostels and the ISTC produce a booklet 'Sleep Cheap Guide to Asia/Australia/New Zealand'.

Student Travel, 1st floor, 10 High Street, Auckland. Tel: (09) 399 723
YHA of New Zealand Inc, PO Box 436, Christchurch 1

Working Holidays

Job Advertising
There are two agencies in London which sell specimen copies of New Zealand papers and will arrange subscriptions if required.

New Zealand Associated Press, Ludgate House, 107 Fleet St, London EC4A 2AN.
Tel: 01 353 1814
Overseas Media Ltd, 40 Rosebury Avenue, London EC1R 4RN. Tel: 01 278 4165

New Zealand News UK is an independent weekly newspaper printed in the UK.
New Zealand News UK, PO Box 10, Berwick-upon-Tweed, Northumberland TD15 1BW

Copies of the Saturday editions of the principal New Zealand papers are set out for inspection at New Zealand House, 1st floor.

Agriculture
New Zealand is well known for its fruit production which takes place on both the North and South Islands, though mainly in the North. The main fruits are: kiwi fruit, peaches, plums, apricots, apples, strawberries, grapes, cherries and pears. The harvesting dates vary greatly depending on the location but fruit picking takes place almost continuously in one location or another from October through to May. The best way to locate orchard work is the same no matter where you are – simply visit the fruit growing areas and ask around in either the small towns or at the farms themselves. You may even see notices for 'Pickers Wanted'; watch for fruit stands by the side of the road, ask other pickers where you see them working in the orchards, watch notice boards etc. Farmers are generally more concerned with getting their crops picked than they are in work permits. We have not heard of anyone experiencing difficulty fruit picking in New Zealand.

New Zealand also has a tobacco industry in the northern part of the South Island (Marlborough County). Harvesting takes place in February/March. Conditions for tobacco pickers are reported to be good and this work can be combined with fruit picking.

There is a very large logging industry in New Zealand, and several large pulp and paper mills. Casual work is generally worth seeking out in these locations.

If you are interested in short term farm work, you can contact the Federated Farmers of New Zealand and enquire about placing a job seeker advertisement in their journal 'Straight Furrow'. There are a small number of officially approved schemes whereby successful applicants might be granted permission to engage in agricultural employment. Only those persons accepted by one of the organisations concerned would be eligible to apply for the necessary visa to work in New Zealand. Berkshire, Brooksy and the Welsh Agricultural Colleges operate student exchange schemes in co-operation with New Zealand institutes. If you have some experience in farming, especially dairy farming, enquire directly to the organisations listed below:

Federated Farmers of New Zealand, PO Box 715, Wellington.
The Worshipful Company of Farmers, Brooklyn, Park St, Princes Risborough, Bucks HP20 1BX.
National Federation of Young Farmers' Clubs, England and Wales, 6 Bells, The Paddocks, Parkhall Rd, Somersham, Cambs.
International Agricultural Exchange Association, YFC Centre, National Agricultural Centre, Kenilworth, Warwickshire CV8 2LG.
Marvin Relief Farm Services, PO Box 248, Matamata, New Zealand.

Fishing
New Zealand has a fair fishing industry and the waterfront is another good location for seeking casual work. You might well be able to find work unloading boats, packing, or even get a chance to go to sea. It doesn't matter in what country you are in – always spend time on the waterfront (and in waterfront bars). It is an excellent way of locating opportunities.

Teaching
There are a number of organisations in the UK that recruit or assist in recruiting staff for schools, colleges or universities in New Zealand. Contact the following for information on teaching opportunities in New Zealand.

Association of Commonwealth Universities, 36 Gordon Square, London WC1H OPF. Tel: 01 387 8572
League for the Exchange of Commonwealth Teachers, Commonwealth House, 7 Lion Yard, Tremadoc Rd, Clapham, London SW4 7NF. Tel: 01 498 1101

Tourism
There is a growing tourism industry and there are a number of popular resorts both in summer and winter. Try Mount Hutt, Mount Ruapehu, Mount Dobson, Lake Ohau for jobs during the skiing season. Summer resorts are scattered around on both islands. Try the area north of Auckland, Marlborough County and around Christchurch.

Other Employment
The Careers Research and Advisory Centre (CRAC) operates a vocational exchange scheme for under-graduates who can work and travel in New Zealand for three months (July, August, September). Work relates, wherever possible, to the student's studies. Although participants have to pay their own fares, they do earn money at reasonable rates whilst working in New Zealand which will cover their expenses there and contribute to their air fare.

Careers Research and Advisory Centre, 2nd floor, Sheraton House, Castle Park, Cambridge CB3 0AX. Tel: Cambridge 460277

Voluntary Work
GAP Activity Projects offers school-leavers the chance to spend at least six months in New Zealand assisting in schools. Volunteers stay with host families and are provided with accommodation, board and in most cases pocket money.

GAP Activity Projects (GAP) Ltd, 7 King's Rd, Reading RG1 3AA.
Tel: 0734 594914

Conservation
The Department of Conservation includes the National Parks and Reserves Authority, New Zealand Walkway Commission, Nature Conservation Council, regional national parks and reserves boards, the New Zealand Wildlife Service and the New Zealand Historic Places Trust. If you would like to volunteer your services, it might be worth contacting the Department. For a list of all conservation organisations in New Zealand, write to New Zealand House.

Department of Conservation, PO Box 10 420, Wellington

NIGERIA
Main Language: English, Hausa, Ibo, Yoruba
Currency: Naira
Capital: Abuja (Lagos the major city)
Exports: Petroleum, Cocoa, Groundnuts, Tin.
Climate: Dry season: Nov-Mar (Dec coolest)
Wet Season: Apr-Oct
Temperatures on coast up to 32°C, humidity up to 95%
North much drier: 12°C-36°C

Entry Requirements
Nigeria High Commission, 9 Northumberland Avenue, London, WC2

Visas
An application for visa must be accompanied by a Letter of Invitation from a Nigerian Sponsor who must take full immigration and financial responsibility on behalf of the applicant. All visitors must be in possession of return tickets. Evidence of means of financial support in the form of travellers' cheques will be required in the absence of a letter of invitation and should be at the rate of £40 per day.

Work Permits
Applications for temporary work will not be entertained if there is no approval from the Director of Immigration Services in Nigeria.

Permanent Residence
For full Immigration and Financial Responsibility of the applicant, you need a letter of invitation from a Nigerian Sponsor. For Permament Employment applicants must produce a Contract of Employment from the employer in Nigeria, and the original and four photocopies of each of all Credentials.

Travel
There are regular flights to Nigeria. Check the discount travel companies for low cost fares (see Chapter 4). Many of the travel companies offering overland expeditions include Nigeria on their itineraries. The north of the country around Kano and Kaduna are more interesting for the

traveller than the south, with the exception of Benin City which is the traditional centre for tribal art.

Hann Overland, 201-203 Vauxhall Bridge Rd, London SW1V 1ER. Tel: 01 834 7337
Exodus Expeditions, 9 Weir Rd, London SW12 OLT. Tel: 01 675 7996
Encounter Overland, 267 Old Brompton Rd, London SW5 9JA. Tel: 01 370 6845
Guerba Expeditions Ltd, Dept TF, 101 Eden Vale Rd, Westbury, Wilts BA13 3YB. Tel: 0373 826611
Trailfinders, 194 Kensington High St, London W8 7RG. Tel: 01 938 3939

Working Holidays
Nigeria is not a country for the working traveller. It is extremely difficult to enter Nigeria without a sponsor and, unless you have contacts there, virtually impossible to find any form of casual work. If you do have contacts there, you might be able to find office work at one of the Embassies.

Teaching
A number of agencies assist in the recruitment or recruit well-qualified teachers for the developing countries of Africa. Contact the following organisations for possible teaching opportunities in Nigeria.

Christians Abroad, Livingstone House, 11 Carteret St, London SW1H 9DL. Tel: 01 222 2165
Gabbitas-Thring Service Ltd, 6-8 Sackville St, Piccadilly, London W1X 2BR. Tel: 01 439 2071

Voluntary Work
At present VSO have 85 volunteers, most of whom are introductory technology teachers in junior secondary schools, whilst some are in other technical posts. There is also significant involvement in special education, and some posts in agriculture.

VSO, 317 Putney Bridge Rd, London SW15 2PN. Tel: 01 780 2266

NORWAY
Main Language: Norwegian
Currency: Norwegian Krone
Capital: Oslo
Exports: Non-ferrous metals, Ships and boats, Machinery, paper and cardboard, Fish, Iron and steel.
Climate: Summer – 10°C-18°C
Winter – -4.9°C (Jan)

Entry Requirements
Royal Norwegian Embassy, 25 Belgrave Square, London SW1X 8QD. Tel: 01-235 7151

Norwegian National Tourist Office, 20 Pall Mall, London SW1Y 5NE Tel: 01-839 6255

Visas
There are no visa requirements for British passport holders and they may reside in Norway as tourists for a maximum period of 3 months.

Work Permits
A work permit is required for all types of employment. British citizens who intend to undertake summer employment do not need to obtain a work permit in advance. Once a job has been found a work permit will be issued by the local police authorities after arrival in Norway.

Permanent Residence
There has been a halt in immigration to Norway since 1975. An exemption is most unlikely to be granted unless you have special skills which an applicant in Norway would not possess. In order to be granted exemption from the restrictions on immigration, the applicant must, in addition, meet the ordinary conditions for obtaining an initial work permit, ie he/she must have a concrete offer of employment for at least one year. Your application will be sent to the appropriate authorities in Norway who will normally require between 3 and 6 months for investigations and considerations. According to the Norwegian Aliens Regulations applicants should in their own interest, not enter Norway during the period in which the application for a work permit is under consideration.

Travel
ISIC holders can get discounts on scheduled flights or charter flights during the summer season. See Chapter 4 for discount travel companies that offer low-cost fares. Eurotrain offer a discount off rail fares to Norway for people under 26. The tickets are valid for two months and the journey can be broken. The Nordtourist Rail Rambler ticket gives you unlimited travel on trains in Norway, Sweden, Finland and Denmark and is valid for 21 days. You can also get connecting rail/ship tickets from Oslo-Copenhagen.

Norwegian State Railways, 21-24 Cockspur Street, London SW1Y 5DA.
Tel: 01 930 6666

Accommodation
Contact the Univers Reiser (Student Travel office) in Oslo for information on accommodation. Students are entitled to a 25% discount on certain hotel accommodation in Oslo, Bergen, Stavanger and Tromso. The ISTC publication 'Sleep Cheap Guide to Europe' contains details of other accommodation in Norway. The Norwegian Youth Council has information on youth hostels.

Univers Reiser, Universitetssentret, Blindern, Boks 55, 0313 Oslo 3.
Tel: (02) 453200
Norwegian Youth Council (LNU), Rolf Hofmostgt 18, 0655 Oslo 6, Norway.

Working Holidays

Job Advertising
Frank L Crane Ltd, 8 Salisbury Sq, London EC4Y 8HR (agents for 'Dagbladet') Joshua B Powers Ltd, 46 Keyes House, Dolphin Sq, London SW1V 3NA (represents a number of leading newspapers)

You can try and find employment either by contacting Norwegian employers direct or by registering with the official employment service, though it is a condition that the position in question must be reported vacant and that efforts to fill it with a Norwegian application have failed. You are advised to bring sufficient money for daily living. Once you have found a job you have to have a chest X-ray and fill out a form at the tax office which you then take to the city hall. It is worth doing as you can then claim a tax rebate at the end of your job (you should do this in good time before you leave Norway).

The best opportunities of obtaining jobs are normally between 5th May and 15th June and between 15th July and 30th September as many young Norwegians seek summer employment themselves in the intervening periods. Norway is an expensive place to live in but the Norwegians are very hospitable and you might be able to work in exchange for your board and lodging. Try farms, youth hostels, or even offer to teach English in exchange for your keep.

The fish processing plants along Norway's coast employ additional workers during the summer months. Many working travellers have obtained work by personally visiting the plants – try Trondheim and Bergen.

Agriculture
The Norwegian Youth Council (LNU) arranges individual stays for young people aged between 18 and 30, as working guests on Norwegian farms. You get free board and lodging and some pocket money (min NOK 300 per week) in exchange for taking part in the daily work and life of the farm. Farming experience is desirable but not essential. Work includes haymaking, weeding, milking, picking fruit, berries and vegetables, tractor-driving, painting, feeding cattle etc. You may also have to do some housework, and/or take care of children as well. The period of stay is 4-12 weeks and you should work for a maximum of 35 hours a week with 1.5 days off per week. You pay all travelling expenses to the farm.

The International Farm Experience Programme organises placements on farms and nurseries in Norway in the Spring and Summer months for three months. You receive £30 per week plus board and lodging and pay your own travel costs plus registration fee and insurance. You must have at least two years' experience of farming or horticulture and be aged between 18 and 26.

Norwegian Youth Council (LNU), Rolf Hofmosgt 18, 0655 Oslo 6.
Tel: 02 67 00 43
IFEP, YFC Centre, National Agricultural Centre, Stoneleigh, Warwickshire
CV8 2LG

Au Pair
The following agencies occasionally have vacancies for au pairs in Norway.
Universal Care, Chester House, 9 Windsor End, Beaconsfield, Bucks HP9 2JJ. Tel: 0494 678811
Students Abroad, Elm House, 21b The Avenue, Hatch End, Middx HA5 4EN.
Tel: 01 428 5823

Tourism
Hotel work is available during the summer months. You can either write to the hotels early in the year (the addresses can be obtained from the Tourist Office) or simply in the normal way whilst you are out there. The best area to try is the south of the country. Wages are quite good, but the cost of living is very high in Norway.

Voluntary Work

Workcamps
International Voluntary Service organises placements at a number of international workcamps in Norway from the end of June to the end of September. You must be aged 18 or over and have some previous workcamp experience. Projects in Norway are invariably interesting and involve reconstruction, landscaping, tree planting etc.

IVS, 162 Upper New Walk, Leicester LE1 7QA. Tel: 0533 549430

PAKISTAN
Main Language: Urdu, English
Currency: Pakistan Rupee
Capital: Islamabad

Exports: Textiles, Cotton, Leather, Rice.
Climate: Nov-Mar: Generally dry to arid, Cool in the hills at night May-Aug: Hot, misses the heavy rains

Entry Requirements
Embassy of Pakistan, 34 Lowndes Square, London SW1X 9JN
Pakistan Tourism Development Corporation, M/s Marketing Services, (Tourism and Travel), Suite 433, High Holborn House, 52-54 High Holborn, London WC1V 6RL
Tel: 01 242 3131

Visas
All British citizens require a visa to gain entry into Pakistan. A single journey entry visa is valid for a stay up to 3 months. Multiple journey visas are valid for up to 5 months. Foreigners entering any province of Pakistan do not have to obtain a fresh visa; however specific permission for visiting restricted areas is necessary.

Work Permits
Work permits are not issued to foreigners.

Travel
Some of the discount travel companies offer low-cost flights to Pakistan. The cheapest airlines are the Eastern European and Middle Eastern airlines, eg Tarom (Roumania) and Syrian Airways. Many of the expedition travel companies such as Exodus Expeditions and Dragoman, include Pakistan on their itinerary on overland trips. You can also get to Pakistan via India.

There is a good rail system in Pakistan, including an airconditioned express train from Karachi to Lahore (expensive, comparatively, but worth it!) Students travelling individually or in parties are allowed up to a 50% concession in rail fares on production of passports and a certificate from the Head of the Educational Institution to which they belong. Other tourists travelling individually or in parties are allowed a 25% concession in rail fares in all classes. Apply for the discounts to the superintendents or railway managers at the principal stations.

Exodus Expeditions, 9 Weir Rd, London SW12 OLT. Tel: 01 675 7966
Dragoman, 10 Riverside, Framlingham, Suffolk IP13 9AG. Tel: 0728 724184
Encounter Overland, 267 Old Brompton Rd, London SW5 9JA. Tel: 01 370 6845

Accommodation
Hotels are cheap in Pakistan. You can also stay in cottages, dak bungalows and rest houses at all principal hill stations and health resorts. There are also a number of Youth Hostels throughout Pakistan.

Pakistan Youth Hostels Association, 110-B 3, Gulberg-III, Lahore

Working Holidays
There are no opportunities for the working traveller in Pakistan. It is worth going there, though, for mountaineering in the Himalayas and white water sports on five rivers in northern Pakistan. All peaks/routes in the mountains are divided into open and restricted zones. Permits for climbing peaks are issued when you have paid the required 'royalty' at the Embassy and you must take a Liaison Officer with you. Contact the Embassy for more information.

Teaching
The British Council has established a KELT (Key English Language Teaching) project in Pakistan to increase the potential of local teaching centres and improve the English proficiency of students

and trainees in developmental sectors of the economy. Applicants must have a degree or equivalent, or a general teaching qualification in TEFL or Applied Linguistics, and at least three years' teaching experience.

British Council, Overseas Educational Appointments Dept, 65 Davies Street, London W1Y 2AA. Tel: 01 499 8011

Voluntary Work
You could contact the various relief agencies, Oxfam, Save the Children, etc for voluntary work in Pakistan. VSO currently has about 24 volunteers in Pakistan mainly working in special education and health, although they are hoping to diversify into other sectors, particularly natural resources.

GAP Activity Projects offer school-leavers the chance to spend at least six months in Pakistan, living with a host family who provide board, accommodation and in most cases pocket money.

VSO, Enquiries Unit, 317 Putney Bridge Rd, London SW15 2PN. Tel: 01 780 1331
GAP Activity Projects Ltd, 7 King's Rd, Reading RG1 3AA. Tel: 0734 594914

Workcamps
The World Council of Churches organises workcamps in Pakistan. Recently the participants helped to repair and renovate a Christian conference centre in the Murree Hills and modernise its sanitation. The aim of the camp is to promote ecumenical vision through collected efforts. Volunteers must be 18 to 30 years and pay their own travel expenses to the camp.

World Council of Churches, Sub-Unit on Youth, PO Box 66, 150 route de Ferney, 1211 Geneva 20, Switzerland

PAPUA NEW GUINEA

Main Language: Pidgin (English)
Capital: Port Moresby
Climate: Tropical – hot and wet

Entry Requirements
Papua New Guinea High Commission, 14 Waterloo Place, London SW1R 4AR.
Tel: 01-930 0922/6

Visas
Visitors to Papua New Guinea need to apply for a visa at least 48 hours in advance of departure. You need to enclose your travel itinerary from an authorised travel agency, a letter of invitation from friends with whom you will be staying or proof of funds, ie a letter from your bank confirming that you will be able to maintain yourself financially during your stay in Papua New Guinea. Passports must be valid for one year from your proposed date of entry.

Work Permits
The Immigration Policies do not permit foreigners to seek employment whilst travelling on tourist or visitors visas. The individual who is applying for a work permit, must remain outside Papua New Guinea while the application is under consideration.

Permanent Residence
There is no policy regarding persons wishing to enter the country as an immigrant. A Temporary Residence permit (over 2 months) is issued only if you have obtained employment in Papua New Guinea. Your employer in Papua New Guinea must request a visa on your behalf to the Immigration Athorities in Port Moresby.

Travel
You can get to Papua New Guinea via Australia. Contact a travel company such as Trailfinders or STA Travel for the best and most economical route.

Trailfinders, 194 Kensington High St, London W8 01 938 3939
STA Travel, 86 Old Brompton Rd, London SW7. Tel: 01 937 9962

Working Holidays
There are no opportunities for the working traveller in Papua New Guinea. A 'Nationalisation Scheme' has recently been implemented to protect jobs for citizens of Papua New Guinea. However there are certain jobs that require specialised skills and experience from abroad (see the Voluntary Work section for the types of skills needed). Vacancies for these jobs are often advertised in major newspapers and specialised publications. The High Commission advises that you call at the office and consult the Public Telephone Directory of Papua New Guinea for addresses of Government departments, firms and private businesses in Papua New Guinea whom you may like to contact directly concerning job vacancies.

Voluntary Work
VSO currently has 70 volunteers in Papua New Guinea, promoting health care, teaching in Provincial High Schools, working as High School farm managers, as instructors in vocational centres, in vegetable farming extension and marketing and as managers and advisers assisting business development initiatives. There are also several special education teachers. New posts include road construction engineers, volunteers in small scale agriculture, nutrition and business projects and maintenance co-ordinators with Provincial High Schools.

VSO, Enquiries Unit, 317 Putney Bridge Rd, London SW15 2PN. Tel: 01 780 1331

PARAGUAY
Main Language: Spanish, Guarani
Currency: Guarani GUA
Capital: Asuncion
Exports: Cotton, soya beans, manioc, maize
Climate: Winter (Jul) Temperate, seasonal, dry. Summer – 20°C + (Jan),

Entry Requirements
Consulado General Del Paraguay, Braemar Lodge, Cornwall Gardens, London SW7.
Tel: 01-937 6629

Visas
British nationals holding a valid passport do not require a visa and can stay for up to 90 days. However they must obtain a Tourist Card on arrival at Asuncion Airport which costs US$3 or the equivalent in Paraguayan currency.

Work Permits
There are no guidelines as to work permits in Paraguay.

Permanent Residence
A foreigner who enters the country with the intention of residing, providing for his upkeep by his own resources, or under the employment of another person, enterprise or company, can become an immigrant. All immigrants must have a passport or an identification card, a certificate giving evidence of occupation, degree or diplomas, a doctor's certificate of good health, and a police certificate of good conduct. Immigrants must obtain a certificate of residence while in Paraguay.

Travel
Paraguay has borders with Argentina, Brazil and Bolivia and so it is possible to enter Paraguay through one of these countries. Many discount travel companies offer flights to Asuncion via connections in Europe. The following companies specialise in overland tours, expeditions and trekking holidays in Latin America, including Paraguay:

Journey Latin America, 16 Devonshire Rd, London W4 2HD. Tel: 01 747 3108
Trailfinders, 194 Kensington High St, London W8 7RG. Tel: 01 938 3939
Wexas, 45 Brompton Rd, Knightsbridge, London SW3 1DE. Tel: 01 589 3315
Encounter Overland, 267 Old Brompton Rd, London SW5. Tel: 01 370 6845
Exodus Expeditions, 9 Weir Rd, London SW12 OLT. Tel: 01 675 5550
Explore Worldwide Ltd, 7 High St, Aldershot, Hants GU11 1BH.
Tel: 0252 319448

Working Holidays
Paraguay is a poor, underdeveloped country and does not seem to have caught up with the twentieth century. Because of this, any work you might get there will be very poorly paid, but might be enough to live on while you are there. Try the university for English teaching – private tuition to students or helping out with translation (if you speak Spanish). You could set yourself up as a guide at the Iguacu falls, arguably the most spectacular waterfalls in South America.

Before you go contact one of the expedition travel companies for work as trek leader/driver.

Voluntary Work
Amigos de las Americas sends volunteers to Paraguay every year. You must pay a fee which includes travel from the US. All volunteers must participate in several months of training either in the US or by correspondence.

Amigos de las Americas, 5618 Star Lane, Houston, Texas 77057, USA

PERU
Main Language: Spanish
Currency: Inti (I/.)
Capital: Lima
Exports: Copper, Fish meal, Iron ore, Cotton.
Climate: Summer: Dec-Apr 22°C-30°C (Lima), rainy season in mountains and jungle
Winter: May-Nov 11°C-18°C (Lima)

Variety of temps – hot, humid in jungle 25°C-30°C temperate, dry in desert 12°C-30°C cool, changeable in mountains 11°C-22°C

Entry Requirements
Peruvian Embassy, 52 Sloane Street, London SW1X 9SP. Tel: 01 235 6867
FOPTUR, Peru Tourist Office, 10 Grosvenor Gardens, London SW1W OBD.
Tel: 01 824 8693

Visas
UK visitors do not require visas to enter Peru. Upon arrival an entry permit valid for 90 days is issued which is renewable if necessary. To prolong your stay, before your permit has expired, contact the:
Direccion General de Migraciones, Paseo de la Republica 585, Lima

Work Permits
It is illegal to obtain work in Peru whether paid or unpaid, without authorisation from the Peruvian Immigration Service.

Travel
The Peruvian airlines office, Faucett, offer a 'Visit Peru' Air Pass valid for 30 or 60 days for unlimited travel within Peru when you buy an international ticket. See Chapter 4 for discount travel companies that offer low cost fares to Peru. As Peru shares its borders with Ecuador, Colombia, Brazil, Bolivia and Chile getting there overland is no problem either as an individual traveller or with an expedition travel company. The Peru Tourist Office produces a tourist information leaflet which contains useful information on entry requirements, climate, transport etc, as well as a detailed list of travel companies which specialise in trips to Peru.

Within Peru all major cities and tourist attractions are linked by air, railway or bus lines. Students can get a 7% discount off domestic flights and 10% reduction on domestic buses plus discounts on student tours.

If you intend travelling around a bit it might be worth paying out US$25 to join the South American Explorers Club. Membership will allow you free access to the club premises, a meeting place for travellers which can provide information and advice as well as a refuge in the city.

Faucett, Suite 163, 4th floor, 27 Cockspur St, London SW1 5BN.
Tel: 01 930 1136
Journey Latin America, 16 Devonshire Rd, London W4 2HD. Tel: 01 747 3108
South American Explorers Club, Casilla 3714, Lima 100.
INTEJ (Student Travel Bureau), Av San Martin 240, Barranco, Lima.
Tel: 77 4105

Accommodation
There are many cheap hotels in downtown Lima close to the Plaza de Armas. There is also an Asociacion Amistad Peruano/Europeo hostel on the 7th floor, Camana 280 and a youth hostel at Miraflores, a seaside suburb. Students can get discounts in 39 hotels, including all Entur-Peru hotels as well as a 10% discount at the Youth Hostel in Cuzco. The Peru Tourist Office can provide information on accommodation.

INTEJ, Av San Martin 240, Barranco, Lima. Tel: 774105
FOPTUR, Peru Tourist Office, 10 Grosvenor Gardens, London SW1W OBD.
Tel: 01 824 8693

Working Holidays

Job Advertising
Media Universal Services, 34-35 Skylines, Lime Harbour, Docklands, London E14 9TA. Tel: 01 538 5505

Peru is probably the most visited country in Latin America because of its Inca civilisation and the architecture and culture that is associated with it. Who for example, has not heard of Machu Picchu? Because of this it is possible to find work at one of the main tourist centres, Cuzco for example, as a guide though you must of course know what you are talking about (some local tour operators employ foreign workers at these places). The South American Explorers Club would be a good place to pick up advice on casual work from fellow travellers.

Try contacting one of the many expedition travel companies that organise tours in Peru and Latin America for work as a tour leader/driver. For a comprehensive list of these companies write to the Peru Tourist Office.

Teaching
There are a number of English language schools in Peru, mostly in Lima or Miraflores. The wages are not very high but are excellent when compared to wages earned by the average local worker and especially when compared to the low cost of living. The Consulate General produces a list of English language schools in Peru together with phone numbers.

Voluntary Work
Operation Raleigh has strong links with Latin America and has sent expeditions to Peru in the last 4 years. The expeditions are based on community work, scientific research and conservation and consist of young people aged 17-25 who are split into groups of 5-15 to tackle individual projects normally lasting 10-12 weeks. Anyone can apply provided that they can swim 500 metres and understand basic English.

The Catholic Institute for International Relations (CIIR) recruits professionally qualified people with a minimum of 1-2 years' work experience in the fields of health and agriculture. At present it has volunteers in Peru who provide technical support for community projects which tackle the causes of poverty.

The Co-ordinating Committe for International Voluntary Service has over 100 member organisations engaged in volunteer work, some of which are involved in Latin America. 'Workcamp Organisers', published by CCIVS contains the addresses of several short-term voluntary service organisations in Latin America. The committee will reply to requests for information and, on receipt of 4 IRCs will send information sheets on long and medium-term voluntary service.

Operation Raleigh, Alpha Place, Flood St, Chelsea, London SW3 5SZ.
Tel: 01 351 7541
Catholic Institute for International Relations, Recruitment Coordinator,
22 Coleman Fields, London N1 7AF. Tel: 01 354 0883

Co-ordinating Committee for International Voluntary Service, UNESCO, 1 rue Miollis, 75015 Paris, France

Archaeology
As you would expect, there are numerous digs in Peru. The Archaeological Institute of America publishes details of digs in its Fieldwork Bulletin. Generally experience is not necessary, though in some cases it is desirable and volunteers will receive field training.

Earthwatch also has details of many archaeological expeditions in Peru as well as research into other fields, such as entomology.

Archaeological Institute of America, 675 Commonwealth Avenue, Boston, MA 02215
Earthwatch Expeditions Inc, 680 Mount Auburn St, PO Box 403, Watertown, MA 02272

PHILIPPINES
Main Language: Tagalog, English
Currency: Philippine Peso
Capital: Manila
Exports: Wood, Sugar, Copra, Copper.
Climate: Hot throughout the year, typhoons in late summer
Dry season: Mar-Jun

Entry Requirements
Embassy of the Philippines, 9a Palace Green, London W8. Tel: 01-937 3646/7/8

Visas
Visas are issued on regular passports. No visa is required for transit and bona fide tourists whose stay does not exceed 21 days, provided their passports are valid for at least one year and they have return or onward tickets. A temporary single entry visa is valid for 59 days and must be used within 3 months from the date of issue (£9.70). A temporary visitor entering the Philippines without a visa and desiring to remain in the country beyond 21 days may apply for an extension of stay with the Philippine Commission on Immigration and Deportation in Manila. A temporary visitor, entering the Philippines on a 59-day visa who wishes to remain in the country for longer, may likewise apply for an extension of stay with the Commission on Immigration and Deportation. If you apply for an extension be prepared to give up at least one whole day to get it.

Work Permits
A temporary visitor's visa does not entitle an alien to take up employment, practice his/her profession or study in the Philippines. A pre-arranged work permit is authorized only on approval of the petition for your entry under a pre-arranged employment visa which must be filed by your prospective employer who should state fully the nature of the job, the duration, the salary and allowances being offered. This should also be accompanied by a certified copy of a written contract between you and your employer.

Permanent Residence
Individuals who meet all requirements and have been given a quota number are admitted into the Phillipines, preference being given to fathers and mothers of Philippine citizens as well as

spouses and married children under 21 of aliens lawfully admitted for permanent residence. Those who are willing to invest not less than US $75,000.00 are also accorded immigrant status.

Travel

See Chapter 4 for the discount travel companies that offer low-cost fares from the UK. You can also get bargain fares to the Philippines from Hong Kong or Bangkok. Within the Philippines students can get a 10% discount on Philippine National Railways and on some bus routes and up to 10% off domestic ferry routes. For information on trains go direct to the railway stations. In Manila the best way to get around is by 'jeepney', which as the name implies are converted jeeps, highly decorated, colourful and cheap.

Buses are the cheapest way of travelling around the rest of the country. The Philippines is made up of thousands of islands and there are regular ferry services between them, cheaper than flying.

The only way out of the Philippines is by air from Manila. At one time it was possible to go by boat to Northern Borneo, but it is now illegal to go by boat from the south and piracy is rife. You can fly to Sabah, N Borneo from Manila but it is very expensive (comparatively).

YSTAPHIL (Student Travel Bureau), 4227 Tomas Claudio St (Next to Excelsior Hotel, Roxas Blvd), corner R Custodio St, Paranaque, Metro Manila.
Tel: 01 832 0680

Accommodation

Accommodation is fairly cheap in the Philippines and there is a variety to choose from. In the cities there are hotels (ISIC holders can get discounts – enquire at the YSTAPHIL office), hostels, guest houses, lodges, pensions and on the islands there are huts/beach huts. The 'Sleep Cheap Guide to Asia/Australia/New Zealand' published by ISTC has information on accommodation throughout the Philippines.

Working Holidays

Compared to other countries in South East Asia, Japan, Hong Kong and Singapore for example, the Philippines is very much a third world country and poverty is widespread. We would also strongly advise that you take the political situation into consideration before you plan your journey. Having said that, as long as you stay away from the capital and some of the more turbulent islands, such as Mindanao in the extreme south, then you should find the Philippines a wonderful place to visit.

There are few opportunities for the working traveller in the Philippines apart from the occasional job teaching English. The British Council have at present one KELT (Key English Language Teaching) post in the Philippines. You could contact the British Council for any information on language schools. The standard of English in the Philippines is generally very high, thanks largely to the American presence there, and there are not so many language schools as elsewhere in South East Asia. There is also such a high population and labour is so cheap that casual work, for example in bars, is reserved exclusively for the local people. Manila is notorious as sin city throughout South East Asia, so you would want to beware of any work you might be offered in a 'bar'.

Travel writing or freelance journalism are good ways to earn a bit of extra money, especially if you have fixed up beforehand, in Hong Kong for example, somewhere to sell your stories, If not, then you could always try and sell them to any magazine directly, in the UK or abroad.

The Philippines are best for just travelling around in; if you manage to pick up any work on your travels, it is a bonus.

Voluntary Work
At present VSO has 17 volunteers in the Philippines. The programme provides skills support for farmers trying to reduce the effects of soil erosion and indebtedness. In addition, volunteers work in health care support, education, marine ecology and research.

VSO, Enquiries Unit, 317 Putney Bridge Rd, London SW15 2PN. Tel: 01 780 1331

POLAND
Main Language: Polish
Currency: Zloty
Capital: Warsaw
Exports: Coal, Ships and boats, Meat, Dairy products, Machinery, Clothing.
Climate: Summer – Warm with temperatures of 15°C-20°C Winter – Long and cold, sub-zero temperatures

Entry Requirements
Polish Embassy, 47 Portland Place, London W1N 3AG. Tel: 01-580 0476
Consulate General of the Polish People's Republic, 73 New Cavendish St, London W1N 7RB. 01 636 6032

Polarbis Travel Ltd, 82 Mortimer St, London W1N 7DE. Tel: 01 636 2217

Visas
Entry Visas are granted for a period of up to 90 days. Visas are granted for a definite number of days, so when applying for a visa, you should indicate the length of stay in Poland. Visas should be used within 6 months from the date of issue. To apply for a visa you need your passport, two recent photographs, supporting documents, form and the fee. Visa extensions can be arranged in Poland through the District Militia Office or through ORBIS offices or your hotel reception before the original visa expires.

Transit Visas are issued to persons travelling through Poland to neighbouring countries and are valid for up to 48 hours only. Those applying for a transit visa should submit a visa of the country of their destination.

Work Permits
There are no opportunities for foreigners to work in Poland (unless sponsored by a Polish business organisation) and so the question of work permits does not arise.

Those intending to work as volunteers on language and work camps will be informed how to obtain the necessary work permit by the sponsoring organisation.

Travel
You can fly, take the train or go by bus to Poland from the UK. Fregata Travel offers an express rail ticket from London-Poznan-Warsaw which includes couchettes and luggage service from £151 return. They also operate a coach service from Manchester, Nottingham or Birmingham to Poznan or Warsaw from £129 return. Polorbis Travel can issue you with a Polrailpass which entitles you to unlimited travel on local and express trains and is valid for 8,15, 21 or 30 days. Eurotrain offer up to 50% off full rail fares to Poland for those under 26. Journeys can be broken and tickets are valid for 2 months.

Holders of an International Union of Students (IUS) card, available from most student travel offices on production of a valid ISIC, can get a 25% discount for rail travel within Socialist European countries. Students can also get a discount on ferry routes from Poland to Copenhagen and Helsinki. Ask for more details at Polorbis Travel.

The Cyclists Touring Club has quite recently-revised information sheets on Poland which explain general travel procedures as well as covering problems specific to bicycle travel. Poland is rapidly improving its minor road network and cycling offers the chance to get to see much of rural Poland.

When travelling to Poland on your own (ie independently, and not as part of an organised tour), with no services prearranged, you are expected to spend a minimum amount of money per day of your stay in the country. This is done by purchasing Money Vouchers from Polorbis which can be converted into Polish currency at several exchange counters. Money Vouchers are not refundable if you do not use or exchange them. A refund can only be given if you cancel your trip altogether (full refund), or when you shorten your stay (part refund according to the number of days cancelled). Money Vouchers can be used when settling hotel and other bills. Adults over 21 are expected to spend £10 per day, holders of ISICs £4.40. If you are over 21 and hold an ISIC you are expected to spend £2.20 per day after 30 days in Poland.

Do not be tempted to change your currency on the black market unless you intend to spend it all within Poland, as funds are checked when you enter and leave the country and you have to produce official receipts to cover the difference.

Fregata Travel Ltd, 100 Dean St, London W1V 6AQ. Tel: 01 734 5101
Polorbis Travel Ltd, 82 Mortimer St, London W1N 7DE. Tel: 01 636 2217
ALMATUR (Student Travel Bureau), ul Ordynacka 9, 00-364 Warsaw, Poland.
Tel: 262356
CTC, Cotterell House, 69 Meadrow, Godalming, Surrey GU7 3HS. Tel: 04868 7217

Accommodation
During the summer months it is possible to buy special student price 'open' vouchers for overnight accommodation on a bed and breakfast basis in 19 cities in Poland. No advance booking is required before 2pm and unused vouchers are refundable in Polish currency. Ask at Polorbis or ALMATUR for more details. Polorbis have information on accommodation as well as special offers.

Working Holidays
There are no opportunities for working in Poland, except on an exchange basis.

Agriculture
The International Farm Experience Programme organises work-experience exchanges for young farmers and horticulturists in Poland from 3 months. Trainees get paid £30 per week plus board and lodging and pay their own travel costs plus registration fee and insurance. You must have at least two years' experience and be aged from 18 to 26. Applications should be made at least four months before your intended starting date.

IFEP, YFC Centre, National Agricultural Centre, Stoneleigh, Warwickshire CV8 2LG.

Voluntary Work

Workcamps
Previous experience is essential for workcamps in Poland.

The United Nations Association have a number of workcamps throughout Poland, mostly for manual, construction and renovation work for 2 weeks during July and August. You must be aged between 18 and 30.

International Voluntary Service organise placements in Poland on projects involving archaeological excavations, conservation etc.

CMP can place volunteers on workcamps in Poland to work on projects concerned with archaeology, peacework and ecology. As volunteers coming from Poland can bring very little currency with them volunteers going to Poland are asked to send in an extra £30 with their application to finance the Polish volunteer. In return you receive a few days' guided tour free of charge at the end of the camp.

EYCE organise workcamps in Poland. Recently the workcamp has involved 5 days of working in a publishing house for approximately 12 hours per day. The remainder of the time is free for excursions, hiking and discussions.

United Nations Association, Welsh Centre for International Affairs, Temple of Peace, Cathays Park, Cardiff CF1 3AP.
IVS,162 Upper New Walk, Leicester LE1 7QA. Tel: 0533 549430
CMP, Bethnal Green URC, Pott St, London E2 OEF. Tel: 01 729 1877
EYCE Secretariat, 217 Holywood Rd, Belfast BT4 2DH, N Ireland.
Tel: 44 232 651134

Archaeology
The Archaeological Institute of America publishes details of digs in Poland. The Polish Archaeological Field School offers training in all aspects of archaeological survey and excavation. Volunteers must be over 18 and do not need experience; students of anthropology or archaeology are especially welcome.

The Atelier for Conservation of Cultural Property, Batuty Str 76 ∦703, Warsaw, Poland. Tel: 439100
Archaeological Institute of America, 675 Commonwealth Ave, Boston, MA 02215

PORTUGAL
Main Language: Portuguese
Currency: Escudo
Capital: Lisbon
Exports: Textiles, Clothing, Wine, Diamonds, Machinery, Fish, Cork.
Climate: Summer – Very warm, July temperatures exceed 20°C
Winter – Mild and damp
South East coasts are generally hotter and dryer

Entry Requirements
Portuguese Embassy, 11 Belgrave Square, London SW1X 8PP. Tel: 01-235 5331
Portuguese Consulate General, "Silver City House", 62 Brompton Rd, London SW3 1BJ. Tel: 01 581 8722

Portuguese National Tourist Office, New Bond House, 1/5 New Bond Street, London W1Y 0NP. Tel: 01-493 3873

Visas
Full British citizens may enter Portugal without a visa and remain there for tourism/business purposes for an initial period of sixty days. If you wish to extend your stay you may apply to the 'Servico de Estrangeiros' (Alien Registration Office) in Portugal for up to two extensions of 60 days each, giving a total stay of 180 days (6 months), well before your initial 60 days expires.

Work Permits
Even though Portugal is now a member of the EEC, the reciprocal arrangements governing the employment of EC nationals do not come into force until 1993. A work permit is required for

all types of employment and will be applied for by the prospective employer from the local authorities. (Residents who are self-employed do not require a work permit).

Permanent Residence
Applications for permanent residence should be made at a Portuguese Consulate before going to Portugal. These may take at least 3 months to be issued. Once the residence visa has been endorsed in the passport, the applicant gains permission to reside in Portugal but he will still be required to fully legalise his residence status within 90 days of his arrival in Portugal. The residence visa has a validity of 120 days.

Travel
See Chapter 4 for discount travel companies offering low cost air fares. CTS Courier Club offer an open return flight to Portugal for £80 return. Eurotrain offers up to 50% off full rail fares to destinations in Portugal for those under 26. You can also enter Portugal through Spain. Discounts for students are available on buses from Portugal to various destinations in Europe and tickets are valid for 6 months.

Within Portugal students can get discounts on buses from Braga-Porto-Lisbon-Algarve, and from Braganca-Lisbon-Algarve. If you are under 26 you can get a Youth Card on CP Railways which gives you a 50% discount off the normal fare through Portugal for one year.

The Portuguese National Tourist Office produces a brochure "Portugal, Enjoy It" which contains information on the different regions, food, festivals, travel and accommodation.

ATEJ (Student Travel Bureau), Rua Miguel Bombarda 425, 4000 Porto.
Tel: (02) 698149
TAGUS-TJ (Student Travel Bureau), Praca de Londres 9 B, 1000 Lisbon.
Tel: 884957

Accommodation
The Portuguese National Tourist Office has lists of hotels, pousadas (Government hote', often in historic houses, castles, palaces) and campsites. There is an acute housing shortage particularly in and around Lisbon, Porto and Funchal. Long term rentals in the Algarve are virtually impossibile, or if available very expensive.

Working Holidays

Job Advertising
Publicitas Ltd, 525/527 Fulham Rd, London SW6 1HF. Tel: 01 385 7723
(agents for Diario de Noticias, Lisbon daily; Journal de Noticias, Oporto)

Anglo-Portuguese News, Apartado 113, 2765 Estoril, Lisbon. Tel: 244 3115/3950.
(published weekly, wide circulation among British community, small ads can be placed, especially good for work in families as au pairs and domestics)

Algarve News, PO Box 13, 8400 Lagos, Algarve. (published monthly, specialises in information of interest to British community, has small ads section)

Temporary employment will require a work visa endorsed in the passport by the Servicos de Estrangeiros.

Opportunities for casual work in Portugal are very limited. Although it is a comparatively expensive country to live in (£10 per day, excluding accommodation, is considered the minimum amount you can live on), Portugal is a very poor country and local labour is cheap and abundant. There are also strict laws protecting the rights of employment for Portuguese nationals and even work in tourism is hard to come by.

Gardeners, apparently are in short supply. You could try offering your services among the local British community (of which there are a number, especially in the Algarve), although the British tend to prefer to give work to the locals.

Au Pair
The Anglo Portuguese News and Algarve News have advertisements for domestic and au pair work. Try also Turicoop and the Centro de Intercambio e Turismo Universitario.

Turicoop, rua Pascoal de Melo, 15-1 Dto, 110 Lisbon.
Centro de Intercambio e Turismo Universitario, avenida Defensores de Chaves, 67-6 Dto, Lisbon
Universal Care, Chester House, 9 Windsor End, Beaconsfield, Bucks HP9 2JJ.
Tel: 0494 678811

Medical Work
There is a small British 'cottage' hospital (23 beds) in Lisbon. The nursing staff are British or British-trained. If you are a doctor or have any nursing qualifications it might be worth contacting them for any temporary work especially during the holiday periods.

British Hospital, rua Saraiva de Carvalho 49, 1200 Lisbon. Tel: 602020

Teaching
It is not so easy in Portugal for find casual teaching work. Most of the language schools are 'bona fide' and hire well qualified and experienced staff. The Hispanic and Luso Brazilian Council produces an information sheet on working and living in Portugal and it contains a list of British schools in Lisbon, Porto, the Algarve and Funchal which may be worth contacting. The British Council has an office at the British Institute.

Tourism
It is difficult to find casual work in hotels, restaurants etc in Portugal. You may find some work on the Algarve as a water sports instructor or in the entertainment business (casino, theatre etc). Many British travel companies organise holidays in Portugal and you could apply for a job as a courier/rep, water sports instructor before you go. Get brochures with addresses of companies to write to from any travel agent. Golf is popular on the Algarve, so if you have any aptitude/experience you could try contacting one of the many golf clubs.

Voluntary Work

Workcamps
ATEJ (the Student and Youth Association) organises a number of international workcamps. Previous experience is not necessary. Volunteers must be aged between 16 and 30 and have a knowledge of French, English, Spanish or Portuguese.

ATEJ, rua Miguel Bombarda 425, 4000 Porto. Tel: (02) 698149

The Instituto da Juventud organises 46 international workcamps which begin in July and end in September. Workcamp projects are concerned with protection of the natural environment, protection of cultural patrimony, construction of social equipment and agriculture. Each camp lasts about two weeks and volunteers must be between 18 and 25. Food and accommodation are provided and social and cultural activities will be organised in each camp. Volunteers are normally required to work 5-6 hours a day for 6 days a week and have to pay their own travel expenses to the camp.

Volunteers must apply for the workcamps through their own country's organisations:

International Voluntary Service, 162 Upper New Walk, Leicester LE1 7QA. Tel: 0533 549430
CMP, Bethnal Green URC, Pott St, London E2 OEF. Tel: 01 729 1877
Quaker International Social Projects, Friends House, Euston Rd, London NW1 2BJ.
Tel: 01 387 3601
Concordia, Youth Service Volunteers, 8 Brunswick Place, Hove, E Sussex BN3 1ET
Tel: Brighton 772086
United Nations Association, International Youth Service, Welsh Centre for International Affairs,
Temple of Peace, Cathays Park, Cardiff CF1 3AP.
Tel: Cardiff 223088

Conservation
The British Trust for Conservation Volunteers organise conservation projects in Portugal.
Recently they have been involved in working with Portuguese volunteers undertaking revetment
and bridge construction at the foot of the Cousa Mountains.

BTCV, 36 St Mary's St, Wallingford, Oxon OX10 0EU. Tel: 0491 39766

Archaeology
The American Archaeological Institute publishes details of digs in Portugal in its Fieldwork
Bulletin. Volunteers should be at least 18 years of age and have previous experience.

Earthwatch also sponsors digs in Portugal from time to time. Recently volunteers with an interest
in construction, photography, drawing, botany or pre-history have been needed to excavate an
Iron Age hill fort.

Archaeological Institute of America, 675 Commonwealth Ave, Boston,
MA 02215
Earthwatch Expeditions Inc, 680 Mount Auburn St, PO Box 403, Watertowtown,
MA 02272

ROMANIA
Main Language: Romanian
Currency: Leu
Capital: Bucharest
Exports: Machinery, Consumer goods, Petroleum products, Cereals.
Climate: Hot summers 20°C +, Cold winters – below freezing

Entry Requirements
Embassy of the Socialist Republic of Romania, 4 Palace Green, Kensington, London W8. Tel:
01-937 9667

Romanian Tourist Office, 17 Nottingham St, London W1. Tel: 01 224 3692

Romanian Airlines Office, (Tarom) Tel: 01 224 3693

Visas
UK nationals require a visa to enter Romania. The tourist visa is valid for 3 months from the
date of issue and cost £20. You can obtain a visa from any Romanian Embassy or on arrival in
Romania at any of the border checkpoints or the airport. Visas are granted on arrival to tourists
having prepaid accommodation.

Work Permits
Tourists are not allowed to engage in any paid or unpaid employment.

Travel
Romanian Airlines (Tarom) is one of the cheapest airlines and you could perhaps combine a trip to Romania with a trip to India by stopping over en route for example. Eurotrain offer a 50% discount on the full fare throughout Europe to those under 26. Contact the Romanian Tourist Office for information on bus and train travel.

The Cycling Touring Club has quite recently-revised information sheets on Romania which explain general travel procedures as well as covering problems specific to bicycle travel.

CTC, Cotterell House, 69 Meadrow, Godalming, Surrey GU7 3HS. Tel: 04868 7217
BTTR (Student Travel Bureau), Onesti St, 6-8, Bucharest 1. Tel: 140566

Accommodation
Contact the Romanian Tourist Office for details of accommodation in Romania. Tourists not having pre-paid accommodation have to change the equivalent of US$10 for each expected day of stay in Romania.

Working Holidays
There are no opportunities for employment in Romania and we do not know of any workcamps. There are ski resorts in the country and it is just possible that you might find some (badly paid) casual work in one of them should you, for some unknown reason, wish to work in a country that is still (early 1990) one of the last bastions of Stalinist communism.

SAUDI ARABIA
Main Language: Arabic
Currency: Rial
Capital: Ar Riyad
Exports: Crude petroleum, Petroleum products.
Climate: Summer – Intensely hot, Jun-Aug – 30°C +
Winter – Cool

Entry Requirements
The Saudi Arabian Information Centre, Cavendish House, 18 Cavendish Square, London W1M 0AQ. Tel: 01-629 8803

Visas
All UK citizens need a visa. You will be unable to obtain this if you have an Israeli visa stamped in your passport or any indication of a visit to Israel. Passengers proceeding to a third country do not need a transit visa, but they must have a confirmed onward ticket and are forbidden to leave the airport.

Work Permits
A work visa is required by all foreigners working in Saudi Arabia and is obtained by the sponsor or employer, who applies to the relevant department at the Interior Ministry. The permit is valid for 3 months. A residence permit should be applied for by the employer within 3 days of arriving, on behalf of the employee.

Anybody working in Saudi Arabia must have a sponsor. Imprisonment is now the penalty for employing a non-sponsored worker – one week to one month plus a fine of SR 2000-10,000.

Permanent Residence
All foreigners working in the kingdom need a residence permit, which can be obtained on submission of a work visa and application form to the passport office. A residence permit is

available for one or two years, and is renewable. Employees usually surrender their passport to their employer in exchange for the Iqama (white card with employee's photograph), which must be carried at all times as evidence of the residence permit's issue. People not carrying identity cards are liable to serious penalties if stopped by the police.

Travel
Contact the Saudi Arabian Information Centre for information on travel to Saudi Arabia as well as Trailfinders and STA Travel.

Trailfinders, 194 Kensington High St, London W8 7RG. Tel: 01 938 3939
STA Travel, 86 Old Brompton Rd, London SW7. Tel: 01 937 9921

Working Holidays
There are no opportunities for casual work in Saudi Arabia and, as previously mentioned, the penalties for working without a permit are severe in Saudi Arabia. The only way you can work there is with a company who must employ you before you go. Doctors, engineers, lawyers, teachers, and senior and general managers are in demand. Look in the appropriate journals, the Times Educational Supplement, the Guardian etc for job vacancies. Jobsearch Bulletin also advertises vacancies for engineers etc in Saudi Arabia.

The only advantage of working in Saudi Arabia is that you can earn vast amounts of money usually tax free, enough, in fact, to subsidise your travels for a great many years!

Voluntary Work
There are no opportunities for voluntary work, workcamps or student exchanges in Saudi Arabia.

SEYCHELLES
Capital: Victoria, Mahe Island
Exports: Copra, cinnamon and tea
Climate: Tropical, dry at sea-level, wet in mountains, tropical storms
Jan – 26.4°C
Jul – 25.6°C

Entry Requirements
Director General, Ministry of Planning and External Relations, PO Box 656, National House, Victoria, Republic of Seychelles. Tel: 24041

Visas
A visa is not required if the visitor is in possession of a return or onward ticket, confirmed accommodation, valid travel documents and enough funds to support himself during his stay.

Work Permits
A 'Gainful Occupation Permit' must be applied for by the prospective employer. If a person wishes to be self-employed, he applies for the permit on his own behalf. The Ministry in the Seychelles advises that anyone interested in working in the Seychelles should pay a visit first.

Permanent Residence
A person who wishes to stay in the Seychelles for longer than 3 months can apply for a residence permit if he has a family connection in the Seychelles. Application by a person who has made or

will make a special contribution to the economic/social or cultural life of the Seychelles will also be favourably considered.

Travel
Contact the discount travel companies listed in Chapter 4 for air travel to the Seychelles. Many travel companies now operate package holidays in the Seychelles.

Working Holidays
Tourism and fishing are the main industries. There are four main islands, Mahe (where the capital is), Praslin, Silhouette and La Digue and numerous smaller islands, 14 of them inhabited. Aldabra Island houses a scientific base for the study of giant tortoises and other unique fauna and flora. If you have a science degree and/or any experience in conservation/ecology it might be worth writing to the Ministry of Planning and External Relations about possible voluntary, short-term or long-term work on the island.

Many travel companies now organise package holidays in the Seychelles and you could contact any of these for a job as a courier/rep, watersport instructor etc. As in many places, word of mouth is the best way to find work. Try the waterfront for jobs related to the fishing industry, packing, sorting etc.
You might be able to get some work on FEBA Christian Radio either as a technician, producer or radio journalist.

Dragon Yachts Ltd operate luxury charter yachts in East Africa and the Seychelles and the company employs many young people who want to work and travel to new parts of the world.

Dragon Yachts Ltd, 788 Bath Rd, Cranford, Middx TW5 9UL. Tel: 01 897 9995
FEBA Christian Radio, Ivy Arch Rd, Worthing, W Sussex BN14 8BX.

Voluntary Work
There are no workcamps in the Seychelles. You could, however, offer your services at local schools, hospitals etc.

SIERRA LEONE
Main Language: English, Krio
Currency: Leone
Capital: Freetown
Exports: Root and staple crops, Fish, Iron ore, Gemstones.
Climate: Dry season: Nov-Apr 24°C-27°C
Wet season: Jul-Sep
Harmattan : Dec-Feb 22°C-24°C (cool breeze from Sahara)

Entry Requirements
Sierra Leone High Commission, 33 Portland Place, London W1N 3AG

Visas
British citizens require a visa (£20) which is valid for up to 30 days. Applicants are requested to complete an application form and submit this with one passport-size photograph and passport.

Work Permits
A work permit is requested in the same way as for a visa. In addition a letter of undertaking/guarantee from the company the applicant is representing is also to accommpany it.

Permanent Residence
If a person wishes to stay longer than 30 days, approval has to be obtained from the authorities. The applicant should ask his/her contact in Sierra Leone to apply to the Principal Immigration Officer to request him to cable approval to the High Commission. Once the authority is received, the passport can be stamped.

Travel
Travel companies, such as STA Travel and Trailfinders offer low-cost fares to Freetown (see Chapter 4 for information on air travel). Sierra Leone is bounded on the north and northwest by Guinea and on the southeast by Liberia and it is possible to enter Sierra Leone overland.

STA Travel, 86 Old Brompton Rd, London SW7. Tel: 01 937 9921
Trailfinders, 194 Kensington High St, London W8 7RG. Tel: 01 938 3939

Working Holidays
There are few opportunities for casual work in Sierra Leone, and as in many parts of Africa, any work you may find is a bonus and of your own making. There is a small European community – it might be worth locating where they socialise and keep your ears open for any work you might be able to do.

Teaching
Many organisations in the UK recruit or help in the recruitment of teaching staff to schools, colleges and universities in Sierra Leone. You generally have to be well qualified and experienced. The following organisations might be able to help:

European Council of International Schools, 21b Lavant St, Petersfield, Hants GU32 3EL.
Tel: 0730 68244
Gabbitas-Thring Service Ltd, 6-8 Sackville St, Piccadilly, London W1X 2BR.
Tel: 01 439 2071
Christians Abroad, Livingstone House, 11 Carteret St, London SW1H 9DL.
Tel: 01 222 2165
League for the Exchange of Commonwealth Teachers, Commonwealth House, 7 Lion Yard, Tremadoc Rd, Clapham, London SW4 7NF. Tel: 01 498 1101
Committee for International Cooperation in Higher Education, Higher Education Division, 10 Spring Gardens, London SW1A 2BN. Tel: 01 930 8466

Voluntary Work
VSO currently has 34 volunteers in Sierra Leone. Projects include introducing improved farming or fishing techniques, teaching nutrition, tackling primary health needs, midwifery, teaching and administration and keeping mobile immunisation units on the road with the help of motor mechanics.

VSO, Enquiries Unit, 317 Putney Bridge Rd, London SW15 2PN. Tel: 01 780 1331

Workcamps
Sierra Leone has a number of workcamps and the High Commission in London sometimes recruits volunteers directly. Voluntary services in the UK who recruit volunteers for workcamps in Africa insist that you have experience before you go. IVS can give you information on how to qualify. Usually you have to apply to join a workcamp through a coordinating agency in the UK.

IVS, 28-30 Mosley St, Newcastle-upon-Tyne NE1 1DF

The following are workcamp organisations in Sierra Leone:

Voluntary Workcamps Association of Sierra Leone, PO Box 1205, Freetown, Sierra Leone.
GADO (Gormogor Agricultural Development Organisation), c/o Njala University College, Private Mail Bag, Freetown, Sierra Leone.
PASACOFAAS, 5a City Rd, Wellington, PMB 686, Freetown, Sierra Leone.
Community Service Association (COSA), PO Box 220, Koidu Town, Kono District, Sierra Leone.

SINGAPORE
Main Language(s): English, Chinese, Malay, Tamil
Currency: Singapore Dollar
Capital: Singapore
Exports: Rubber, Petroleum products, Machinery.
Climate: Hot and sunny throughout the year
Monsoons: Nov-Jan

Entry Requirements
Singapore High Commission, 5 Chesham Street, London SW1. Tel: 01-235 9067/8/9

Visas
Holders of a full British passport do not require a visa for a three month visit, but you must have an onward ticket or proof of sufficient funds for your stay.

Work Permits
For all matters relating to work permits you must contact the Controller of Immigration in Singapore.

The Controller of Immigration, Immigration Dept, 95 South Bridge Rd, 7 & 8 Storeys, South Bridge Centre, Singapore 0105

Permanent Residence
For information on immigration you must contact the Controller of Immigration in Singapore.

Travel
Many of the discount travel companies mentioned in Chapter 4 offer low-cost flights to Singapore either direct or as part of a round-the-world trip. CPJ Travel who organise couriers from the UK offer 13 nights in Singapore for £300 return. STA Travel have an office in Singapore and can give useful information on travel within and from Singapore. If you plan to go on to Bangkok, get an Asian Overland Travel Pass for approximately £120 which is valid for three months and provides coach or train transport, the ferry to Penang and six nights' accommodation at hotels en route.

Catch the No 390 bus from the airport to Bencoolen St, Beach Rd, Middle Rd where the cheapest accommodation is. You must have the exact fare on the buses so make sure you get some coins when you change money.

CPJ Travel, Orbital Park, 178-188 Great South West Rd, Hounslow, Middx TW4 6JS
Tel: 01 890 9393 Ext 3407
STA Travel, 86 Old Brompton Rd, London Sw7. Tel: 01 937 9921
STA Travel, 02-17 Ming Court Road, 1 Tanglin Rd, Singapore 1024.
Tel: 734 5681

Accommodation
Hotels in Singapore are expensive by Asian standards; the YMCAs are cheaper though not as cheap as you would expect. Bencoolen St, Beach Rd, and Middle Rd are the cheapest areas for

accommodation. The New Seventh Storey Hotel allows travellers to sleep up on the roof for a reasonable fee.

'Homestays', referred to as crash-pads were once flats which have been turned into dormitories. Few have ground floor signs and they are quite hard to find. If you want your own room and can afford to pay a bit more try the Nam Hai, the Soon Seng Long and the Palace.

Students can get special rates in some tourist class hotels. The STA Travel office can give you more information on accommodation as can the ISTC publication 'Sleep Cheap Guide to Asia/Australia/New Zealand'.

YMCA, Tanlin Centre, 60 Stevens Rd
YMCA International Centre, 70 Palmer Rd
YMCA, 1 Orchard Rd
New Seventh Storey Hotel, 229 Rochor Rd
Peony Mansions, 5th floor, No 50e, Bencoolen St
Bencoolen Home Stay, 7th and 8th floor, No 27, Bencoolen St
Goh's Homestay, 5th and 6th floor, Hong Guan Building, No 173/5, Bencoolen St
Philip Choo's, 3rd floor, Hong Guan Building, No 173/5, Bencoolen St
Airmaster Travel Centre, 369 Prinsep St
Sim's Rest House, 114a Mackenzie Rd
Nam Hai, 166 Bencoolen St
Soon Seng Long, 26 Middle Rd
Palace, Jalan Besar

Working Holidays
Singapore is similar to Hong Kong with regard to its work opportunities and the high cost of living. Many people who have worked in both places say they prefer Hong Kong as Singapore has a more sterile environment (there are very strict laws for many day-to-day things, such as crossing the road in the right place, washing taxis daily, painting houses yearly, and of course heavy fines for dropping litter, strictly enforced). However, Singapore has a charm of its own, and is more cosmopolitan than Hong Kong.

There is a large European community in Singapore, and therefore a number of night clubs and hotels where Europeans socialise – you are more likely to find work in these establishments than in those that are frequented mainly by the local people. Many people set themselves up as freelance journalists, either working for a paper or magazine or selling their stories where they can. Television can offer work doing voice-overs for commercials; you could try radio journalism. If you are a photographer you could offer your services on a freelance basis to magazines. There are a number of opportunities, the way to take advantage of them is to keep your eyes and ears open. Look at YMCA notice boards, the Yellow Pages and the Straits Times for job vacancies.

Teaching
The standard of English teaching in Singapore is very high, and generally the standard of English among the Singaporeans is higher than in Hong Kong. The British Council have an office there. Look up addresses of Language schools in the Yellow Pages.

British Council, Singapore Rubber House, Collyer Quay, Singapore
British Council, Overseas Educational Appointments Dept, 65 Davies St, London W1Y 2AA.
Tel: 01 499 8011

If you are well-qualified and have teaching experience, try contacting one of the organisations mentioned below:

Committee for International Cooperation in Higher Education, Higher Education Division, 10 Spring Gardens, London SW1A 2BN. Tel: 01 930 8466

European Council of International Schools, 21b Lavant St, Petersfield, Hants GU32 3EL. Tel: 0730 68244

Voluntary Work
The Singapore Council of Social Service can give information on voluntary work. Try contacting the Red Cross and branches of Christian organisations, such as the Salvation Army. There is no programme of work/conservation camps in Singapore.

Singapore Council of Social Service (SCSS), 11 Penang Lane, #02-02 SCSS Building, Singapore 0923.

SPAIN
Main Language: Spanish
Currency: Spanish Peseta
Capital: Madrid
Exports: Machinery, Fruits, Vegetables, Footwear, Petroleum products, Textiles, Ships and boats, Olive oil.
Climate: North & North West – Mild, damp, humid South and East - Hot, dry in summer

Entry Requirements
Spanish Embassy, 24 Belgrave Square, London SW1X 8QA. Tel: 01 235 1484

Spanish Consulate General, 20 Draycott Place, London SW3 2RZ. Tel: 01 581 5921

Spanish Labour Office, 20 Peel Street, London W8 7PD

Spanish National Tourist Office, 57/58 St James's St, London SW1. Tel: 01 499 0901

Visas
Nationals of EEC countries do not need a visa for visits to Spain up to 90 days. If you wish to prolong your stay once you are in Spain, it is necessary to obtain an extension form from the local Spanish Police department dealing with aliens. This permit, the 'permanencia' is normally valid for a further 3 months, after which a residence permit, 'residencia' should be obtained.

If a British passport holder knows before leaving the UK that he/she will be staying in Spain for more than 90 days an application for a special visa should be made well in advance to the Spanish Consulate General.

Work Permits
Although Spain is now a member of the EEC, the free movement of workers will not become effective until 1st January 1993. Work permits are, therefore, still required for those wishing to take up paid employment. A permit is normally granted only when the work to be performed cannot be done equally well by a Spanish employee, or when the vacancy has been advertised for at least a month by the government employment office without being filled by a Spanish national. If and when employment is found the employer must generally apply for the work permit on behalf of the prospective employee, once the employee has applied personally for the appropriate visa at the Spanish Consulate. The employee must present proof of the offer

of employment and complete 4 application forms before the employer can apply to the Spanish Employment Authorities.

Permanent Residence
Contact the Spanish Consulate General for information on permanent residence.

Travel
You can travel to Spain by ferry – either to one of the French Channel ports and then by road or rail to Spain, or by ferry to Santander from Plymouth by Britanny Ferries. For information on rail travel to Spain contact British Rail Continental Section; they can make bookings by train from Victoria Station to Madrid via Irun. BIGE tickets are available to everyone under 26 and offer savings of up to 50% off the normal rail fares to Europe. These can be obtained at student travel centres at universities and polytechnics as well as at student travel offices. Spanish railway timetables are published twice a year and are available from BAS Overseas Publications.

There are several coach companies that run services to various destinations in Spain and students are often entitled to discounts on these. Many of the discount travel companies offer low-cost air fares to Spain and Polo Express Air Couriers, offer a 1 or 2 week return to Barcelona for £39. Look in the national press small ads section for latest details of budget flights available.

Brittany Ferries (Plymouth-Santander) Tel: 0752 221321
Brittany Ferries (England-France) Tel: 0705 827701
British Rail Continental Section, Victoria Station, London SW1.
Tel: 01 834 2345
Eurotrain, 52 Grosvenor Gardens, London SW1. Tel: 01 730 3402
BAS Overseas Publications Ltd, 48/50 Sheen Lane, London SW14 8LQ.
Tel: 01 876 2131
Worldwide Student Travel, 37 Store St, London WC1. Tel: 01 581 8233
Student Travel, 234 Earls Court Rd, London SW5. Tel: 01 373 0495
STA Travel, 74 & 86 Old Brompton Rd, London SW7. Tel: 01 937 9921
Atlantida Travel Ltd, 21 Garrick St, London WC2E. Tel: 01 240 2888 (specialists in charter flights & travel to Spain)
Euroways Express Coaches Ltd, 52 Grosvenor Gardens, London SW1W.
Tel: 01 730 3643
Victoria Coach Station, 164 Buckingham Palace Rd, London SW1.
Tel: 01 730 0202
SSS International, 138 Eversholt St, London NW1 1BL. Tel: 01 388 1732

Accommodation
Cheap and reasonable accommodation can be found in 'pensiones', 'hostales' and 1 and 2 star hotels, details of which can be obtained from the Spanish Tourist Office.

The Dept of North America and Europe at the Instituto de Cooperacion Iberoamericana assists foreign students with information concerning accommodation. Upon their arrival in Madrid, foreign students may request names and address of Spanish families (in the Madrid area only) who wish to have boarders in their homes on full/half board or just to rent a room. Ask at the tourist offices throughout Spain about accommodation at the university halls of residence in the summer as well as camping.

It is best to try and book ahead if you want to stay at a Youth Hostel, especially in the summer.

If you are planning on staying in one place for a while, notice boards in the various faculties of the university usually have notices about flat-sharing as do the local newspapers under the heading 'alguileres'. Apartment buildings often post signs announcing apartments for rent; usually you have to rent for a minimum of one year.

Spanish National Tourist Office, 57/58 St James's St, London SW1.
The Dept of North America and Europe, Instituto de Cooperacion Iberoamericana, Avenida Reyes Catolicos 4, Ciudad Universitaria, 28040 Madrid.
Red Espanola de Albergues Juveniles (Youth Hostels), Jose Ortega y Gasset 71, Madrid 6.

Working Holidays

Job Advertising
Publicitas Ltd, 525 Fulham Rd, London SW6 1HF (represents Vanguardia)

AF International Advertising Services ltd, AF House, 283 Cricklewood Broadway, London NW2 6NZ (agents for a number of Spanish papers including ABC Seville and El Pais)

We would recommend using the Spanish newspapers in order to look up jobs advertised rather than for placing your own advertisements in them.

The Spanish Embassy can provide a useful booklet 'Spain for young visitors', produced by the Insituto de la Juventud which gives information on work regulations, youth organisations and services, what to do when things go wrong, etc.

At present it is very difficult for foreigners to find employment in Spain: unemployment is high and the labour laws are very strictly enforced. You are likely to be arrested, imprisoned, deported and possibly banned from Spain for a couple of years if you are found working illegally. The only types of employment which are acceptable (only because Spaniards cannot do the work themselves) are teaching and acting as a courier/tourist guide. For these jobs a work permit is usually given on production of a contract of employment.

However, many people do manage to find work in Spain. The safest places are those on the South Coast which are full of British tourists - you are not as likely to stand out in the crowd as you would elsewhere in Spain - and if possible, try to get work indoors. Try the modern bars and clubs which cater for tourists as they are often under foreign ownership.

Fruit picking, the mainstay of the working traveller, offers few opportunties in Spain. There is a very high unemployment rate amongst young people and the local labour force in any given location is more than sufficient to handle the crop and it is not worth seeking such work out.

Instituto de la Juventud, Centro Nacional de Informacion y Documentacion de Juventud, c/Marques de Riscal 16, 28010 Madrid.

Au Pair
There are plenty of opportunities for au pairs and mother's helps in Spain although wages are lower than in most other countries. The following agencies can make the necessary arrangements:

Students Abroad, Elm House, 21b the Avenue, Hatch End, Middx 4EN. Tel: 01 428 5823

Helping Hands Au Pair & Domestic Agency, 10 Hertford Rd, Newbury Park, Ilford Essex 1G2 7HQ. Tel: 01 597 3138

Anglia Agency, 15 Eastern Ave, Southend-on-Sea, Essex SS2 5QX. Tel: 0702 613888

Universal Care, Chester House, 9 Windsor End, Beaconsfield, Bucks HP9 2JJ. Tel: 0494 678811

Relaciones Culturales Internationales, Calle de Miguel Angel 13-3, Madrid 28010. Tel: 419 3216

Couriers/Reps

As might be expected with a country receiving over 40 million tourists a year there are plenty of campgrounds, holiday villages, etc run by British tour operators. Opportunities for those interested in working as couriers, site attendants are very good. The season is from April to October and you have to be over 18 (21 for some companies). You are usually provided with self-catering accommodation in tents or caravans and wages of £50 to £75 a week. Some companies offer bonuses and commission in addition.

Companies such as Thomson and Portland Holidays need reps to meet clients at the airport, transfer them by coach to their hotel and generally give them advice and assistance on their holiday. A knowledge of Spanish is required and applicants should be aged between 21 and 30 and be single.

If you have a knowledge of the wine regions of Europe you could try getting a job as a courier with World Wine Tours. Applicants must speak French, and a knowledge of Italian, Spanish or Portuguese is an advantage. Tours operate from March to October and accommodation is provided.

EF Educational Tours need tour directors to lead groups of visiting American and Canadian school students on tours of Euorpe, ranging from 9-35 days in length. You have to handle hotel check-ins, reconfirm bookings, give group briefings etc and you must have a working knowledge of the major European cities as well as some skill in a second language or two.

Eurocamp, Edmundson House, Tatton St, Knutsford, Cheshire WA16 6BG.

Club Cantabrica, Holiday House, 146-148 London Rd, St Albans, Herts AL1 1PQ Tel: 0727 33141/66177

Canvas Holidays Ltd, Bull Plain, Hertford, Herts SG14 1DY. Tel: 0992 553535

Thomson Holidays Ltd, Greater London House, Hampstead Rd, London NW1 7SD. Tel: 01 387 9321

Portland Holidays Ltd, Overseas Personnel Dept, 218 Great Portland St, London W1N 5HG. Tel: 01 387 3685

World Wine Tours Ltd, 4 Dorchester Rd, Drayton St Leonard, Oxon OX9 8BH. Tel: 0865 891919

EF Educational Tours, EF House, 1 Farman St, Hove, Brighton BN3 1AL. Tel: 0273 723651

Haven Abroad Ltd, PO Box 9, Hayling Island, Hants PO11 ONL.

Club 18-30 Holidays Ltd, Overseas Dept, Greater London House, 24-28 Oval Rd, London NW1 7DE.

Art Specialist Travel, 17 Chorley Old Rd, Bolton BL1 3AD.

Ibiza Club, Apartado Correos 73, Es Cana/Santa Eulalia de Rio, Ibiza, Balearic Islands, Spain. Tel: 971 33 06 50

Relaciones Culturales Internationales, Calle de Miguel Angel 13-3, Madrid 28010. Tel: 419 3216

Teaching

There are many private language schools in Spain, which offer English classes to adults and children. The British Council in Spain has lists of English teaching schools both in Madrid and in the rest of Spain. The Spanish Institute has a similar list. Applications for teaching posts should be made direct to the language institutes concerned. Advertisements for such posts also occasionally appear in the Times Educational Supplement or the Guardian. In some cases the work is hard and poorly paid, and contracts (usually 9-12 months) should be carefully examined before any commitment is made. Most of the more reputable language institutes demand a TEFL qualification but some of the smaller ones will usually accept a BA degree.

International House has a branch in Barcelona where you can enrol on a TEFL course which is cheaper than it is in London. You need to apply well in advance, though.

There is a fair demand for private tuition in Spain but experienced, well-established teachers already on the spot are more likely to obtain this type of work. A notice in local schools, universities and shops often brings results, however, and once you have a few pupils, recommendations are made by word of mouth. During the summer months (July, August and September) the demand for private lessons is not so high as many people take their vacations.

If you are a full-time serving teacher of Modern Languages, the Central Bureau operates an exchange scheme whereby teachers can spend a year, a term 6 or 3 weeks teaching English abroad while their foreign partners teach their own language in a British school. Participants are seconded on a full salary with incremental rights safeguarded as is the right to return to their own posts after the exchange. The Central Bureau also operate a Language Assistant scheme which enables graduates and undergraduates in Modern Languages to spend a year working in Spain if Spanish is their chosen language. The Central Bureau can place a certain number of students aged 18-20 with an A level in Spanish as Junior Assistants in secondary schools in Spain between January and June.

The British Council, Overseas Educational Appointments Dept, 65 Davies St, London W1 2AA.
Tel: 01 499 8011
Director of Studies, British Council, Calle Almagro 5, 28001 Madrid.
Tel: 4191250
The Spanish Institute, 102 Eaton Square, London W1. Tel: 01 235 1484/5
International House, Teacher Selection Dept, 106 Piccadilly, London W1V 9FL.
Tel: 01 491 2598
International House, Trafalgar, 14-Entlo, 08010 Barcelona.
Central Bureau for Educational Visits and Exchanges, Seymour Mews House, Seymour Mews, London W1. Tel: 01 486 5101
Relaciones Culturales Internationales, Calle de Migue Angel 13-3,
Madrid 28010. Tel: 419 3216 (language assistants)

Other Employment/Exchanges
You could try getting a job as crew/bosun mechanic/cook etc on a yacht that is going to Spain and the Mediterranean. Dragon Yachts operate luxury charter yachts in the Mediterranean and employ many young people for varying periods. Crewitt Services can arrange contacts between private boat owners and delivery companies, as well as delivering boats themselves and cater for novices as well as experienced sailors.

Posts in overseas branches of British companies are occasionally advertised in the national press or through employment agencies. The agencies listed below specialise in placing people with language skills and sometimes have details of posts in Spain.

The Central Bureau operate the European Community Young Worker Exchange Programme to enable young people aged between 18 and 28 to gain vocational experience in another European country through a work placement with a host employer. Applicants, who must have already received some basic vocational training, normally spend between 3 weeks and 6 months abroad and receive general living expenses and up to 75% of their return travel costs.

The International Association for the Exchange of Students for Technical Experience (IASTE) operate an exchange scheme which provides undergraduates with course-related industrial, technical or commerical experience in any of the 50 EC countries. Minimum length of stay is 8-12 weeks during the summer vacation and the maximum length of stay is one year. Lodgings are arranged. Students should apply to their own university/college which should normally be affiliated to the national IASTE office.

Dragon Yachts (Worldwide) Ltd, 788 Bath Rd, Cranford, Middx TW5 9UL.
Tel: 01 897 9995
Crewitt Services, Cobbs Quay, Hamworthy, Poole, Dorset BH15 4EL.
Tel: 0202 678847
CLC Language Services, Buckingham House, 6 Buckingham St, London WC2N.
Tel: 01 839 3365
International Secretaries Ltd, 174 New Bond St, London W1Y 9PB.
Tel: 01 491 7100
Multilingual Services, 22 Charing Cross Rd, London Wc2H OHR.
Tel: 01 836 3794
Polyglot Agency, Bank Chambers, 214 Bishopsgate, London EC2
Central Bureau, Seymour Mews House, Seymour Mews, London W1.
Tel: 01 486 5101

Voluntary Work
The following organisations arrange workcamps in Spain. It is advisable to apply, enclosing a stamped addressed envelope, before April for camps held in the summer. In return for 6 to 8 hours daily, generally doing manual or social work, such as building, decorating, working in community centres, being involved in conservation or archaeological projects etc, volunteers receive board and lodging. Strong religious beliefs are not a prerequisite to joining a workcamp; a desire to work hard to benefit the community is more important.

Quaker Work Camps, Friends House, Euston Rd, London NW1 2BJ.
Tel: 01 387 3601
CMP, Bethnal Green URC, Potts St, London E2 OEF. Tel: 01 729 1877
Concordia Youth Service Volunteers, 8 Brunswick Place, Hove, East Sussex
BN3 1ET
United Nations Association, Welsh Centre for International Affairs, Temple of Peace, Cathays Park, Cardiff CF1 3AP. Tel: 0222 38549
IVS, 162 Upper New Walk, Leicester LE1 7QA. Tel: 0533 549430
Companeros Constructores, San Miguel 51-3, Zaragoza, Spain

Archaeology
Excavations abroad requiring volunteers are published in a booklet called 'Archaeology Abroad'. Contact also the Catalan Archaeological Society in Barcelona for information on digs in Spain.

Archaeology Abroad, 31-34 Gordon Square, London Wc1H OPY.
Societad Catalana d'Arqueologia, Bailen 125, e-08009 Barcelona.

SRI LANKA
Main Language: Sinhalese, English, Tamil
Currency: Sri Lanka Rupee
Capital: Colombo
Exports: Tea, Rubber, Copra, Coconuts, Coconut fibre.
Climate: May-Jul – south-west monsoon (in West, South, Central regions)

Dec-Jan – north-east monsoon (in North, East)
Lowlands 27°C, Highlands 16°C

Entry Requirements
Sri Lanka High Commission, 13 Hyde Park Gardens, London W2 2LU. Tel: 01 262 1841

Ceyon (Sri Lanka) Tourist Board, London House, 53-54 Haymarket, London SW1Y 4RP. Tel: 01 925 0177 or 01 321 0034

Visas
British nationals do not require entry visas for a period of thirty days. All visitors require a valid passport, sufficient funds for their stay and an onward or return ticket, or foreign exchange to purchase an outward ticket. If you wish to stay longer than thirty days you must apply to the Controller of Immigration and Emigration in Colombo, and if successful, must then go to the Aliens Bureau for registration.

Dept of Immigration and Emigration, Chaitiya Rd, Colombo 1, Unit 06. Tel: 21509
Aliens Bureau, Ground Floor, New Secretariat Building, Colombo 1

Work Permits
Non-nationals are not normally issued work permits by the Sri Lanka authorities. However, in exceptional circumstances work permits are issued to non-nationals after specific job offers have been made and duly authorised by both the foreign company/UN organisation and Government authorities.

The same applies for temporary work permits issued for work with charitable, voluntary and other recognised social and welfare bodies.

Permanent Residence
Purchase of residential property is allowed subject to a 100% tax surcharge (stamp duties). Contact the Controller of Immigration and Emigration in Colombo.

Travel
We would strongly advise that you take into account the current political situation in Sri Lanka before you decide when to travel there.

The following airlines fly to Sri Lanka at a reasonable fare: Air Lanka, Emirates, Gulf Air, Kuwait Air, UTA, Aeroflot and Pakistan International Airlines. Students should get discounts off the full fare. Many people also get to Sri Lanka via India. See Chapter 4 for information on discount travel companies and look also in the national papers' small ads section for latest travel bargains.

The Railway network is fairly extensive and an inter-city express service is available from Colombo to Kandy/Banadarawela. Special tours by restored vintage steam train are also operated (details from the Railway Tourist Office). Buses are cheap and express services are available to principal towns every half hour (every fifteen minutes for regular buses) from the Central Bus Stand, Pettah.

Railway Tourist Office, Fort Railway Station, Colombo. Tel: 35838
Central Bus Stand, Olcott Mawatha, Colombo 11. Tel: 28081

Accommodation
The Ceylon Tourist Board publishes a comprehensive Accommodation Guide which is supplied free of charge by the Tourist Information desk at the Airport and at 321 Galle Rd, Colombo 3. There is a wide range of accommodation from international chain hotels to informal guest houses and 'rest houses'. Rooms are also available in homes if you fancy becoming acquainted with the Sri Lankan way of life. You can also stay at park bungalows run by the Wild Life Conservation Dept and on tea plantations in 'estate' bungalows.

Working Holidays
There are few opportunities for work in Sri Lanka - the population is high and there is an abundance of cheap labour. It is a country to travel around and enjoy rather than get frustrated in looking for work.

As one would expect on an island, sailing and deep-sea fishing are popular sports and you can contact the Royal Colombo Yacht Club in advance for information. You might get lucky and get taken on as crew/cook.

You could try contacting the main tour operators to Sri Lanka for a job as courier/rep, watersport instructor etc. These are: Thomson, Kuoni, Speedbird, Hayes and Jarvis, Saga, Panorama Holiday Group, Thomas Cook, Keith Prowse and Sovereign (addresses from local travel agent).

Royal Colombo Yacht Club, Colombo Harbour, Colombo 1. Tel: 34926

Voluntary Work
Despite the civil unreset, VSO has managed to maintain a programme of 26 volunteers mainly concerned with English language teaching and working with handicapped and disadvantaged children. VSO is hoping to increase its contribution to forestry development and conservation.

VSO, Enquiries Unit, 317 Putney Bridge Rd, London SW15 2PN.
Tel: 01 780 1331

The following addresses have been recommended by the High Commission who suggest you write directly to them:

Sarvodaya Research Institute, 41 Lumbini Mawatha, Moratuwa, Sri Lanka
Secretary, Ministry of Social Services, 14 Barnes Place, Colombo 7, Sri Lanka
Dept of Social Services, 136 Vauxhall St, Colombo 2, Sri Lanka
Secretary, Ministry of Youth Affairs and Employment, 4th Floor, Inland Revenue Building, Colombo 2, Sri Lanka.

SWAZILAND
Main Language: Siswati, English
Currency: Lilangeni
Capital: Mbabane

Climate: Summer: Sept-Feb (Oct-Feb v hot 32°C), rain
Winter: June-Jul (cold, zero temperatures at times)
Apr -Jun (crisp, sunny, mild, cold nights)

Entry Requirements

Kingdom of Swaziland High Commission, 58 Pont St, London SW1X OAE.
Tel: 01 581 4976

Swaziland Tourist Office, PO Box 451, Mbabane. Tel: 42531

Visas

British passport holders do not need visas to visit Swaziland. All visitors require valid passports or travel documents. They are required by law to report to an immigration office or to any police station within 48 hours of their arrival unless they obtain accommodation on the night of their arrival at a hotel where they must fill in the appropriate forms. Visitors wishing to stay for more than 60 days must apply for a temporary residence permit from the Chief Immigration Officer in Mbabane.

Chief Immigration Officer, PO Box 372, Mbanane, Swaziland

Work Permits

Work permits are required by all except Swaziland citizens and are obtainable from the Chief Immigration Office, Mbanane.

Permanent Residence

Permanent residence permits are obtainable from the Chief Immigration Officer.

Travel

Swaziland (roughly the size of Wales) is bordered on three sides by South Africa and by Mozambique on its eastern side. There are no direct flights to Swaziland from the UK, but there are scheduled services from Botswana, Kenya, Zambia, Lesotho, Malawi, Mauritius, Tanzania and Mozambique. Most of these countries have connecting flights to Europe, the US, the Middle East, some South American countries as well as Australia. Royal Swazi Air and Comair operate regular services between Matsapha and Johannesburg in South Africa.

Excellent roads connect Swaziland with South Africa and Mozambique but you are advised to check on the closing times of border posts (most visitors arrive by road).

Accommodation

Apart from international hotels there are less formal, family style hotels and motels. Contact the Tourist Office in Mbanane for more information. Camping is encouraged; you should ask the Chief or Headman if you are going to camp in a village, they are generally very helpful. You can camp or sleep in rough huts at some of the Wildlife Sanctuaries.

National Trust Commission, PO Box 100, Lobamba Tel: 61151

Working Holidays

There are few opportunities for the working traveller in Swaziland – as usual it is a question of keeping your eyes and ears open for vacancies. There are two local English daily papers which you can scan for work.

Unlike many other African countries, Swaziland has managed to preserve her culture and there

are many traditional dances and ceremonies. At the end of August is the annual Swaziland Trade Fair when dance competitions are held.
If you are in the area it is definitely worth taking a trip to Swaziland for its mountains and game parks.

Voluntary Work
Information on voluntary work opportunities can be obtained from:
Ministry of the Interior & Immigration, PO Box 432, Mbabane, Swaziland

International Voluntary Service recruits skilled and experienced personnel for work in Swaziland as part of the British Volunteer Programme.

IVS, 162 Upper New Walk, Leicester LE1 7QA. Tel: 0533 549430

SWEDEN
Main Language: Swedish
Currency: Krona
Capital: Stockholm
Exports: Machinery, Iron and steel, Paper and cardboard, Wood pulp, Vehicles, Sawnwood, Ships and boats, Iron ore.
Climate: Summer – 15°C-20°C
Winter – Nov-Apr (long, dark, cold winters in north, milder in south)

Entry Requirements
Swedish Embassy, Consular Section, 11 Montagu Place, London W1H 2AL.
Tel: 01 724 6782

Swedish National Tourist Office, 3 Cork St, London W1X 1HA. Tel: 01 437 5816

Visas
Anyone entering Sweden needs a valid passport or a recognised travel document. Visas are required for nationals of certain foreign countries – contact the Swedish Embassy for information on this.

Persons who may enter Sweden without a visa are allowed to stay in Sweden for three months. If you have stayed in Denmark, Norway, Finland or Iceland during the six months preceding your entry into Sweden, your stay in these countries will be included in the three months mentioned above.

If you wish to stay longer than three months a residence permit is required and it must be issued before entering Sweden. Applications for residence permits are not usually accepted by the Immigration Board from foreign visitors already in Sweden. Residence permits are initially issued for a limited period of time but extensions can be applied for at the local police station in Sweden.

Work Permits
Foreign nationals entering Sweden for the purpose of employment, including au pair work, are required to hold work permits which are issued for a specific job and period once an offer of employment has been obtained. Application for work permits are, as a general rule, not accepted by the Immigration Board from foreign visitors already in Sweden. Furthermore, an applicant who has entered Sweden before the permit has been granted will, as a rule, be refused such a permit.

You may apply for a vacation work permit for work between 15th May and 15th October.

Your work permit application must be filed through a Swedish embassy in your country of origin or domicile at least 6 weeks before your intended date of arrival in Sweden. You must be at least 18 but under 30 years old on 15th May of the year of your application. When applying for a permit you need: - a written offer of work from your prospective employer in Sweden;
- firm housing arrangements;
- a certificate showing that you are enrolled at a foreign educational establishment;
- a valid passport.

Permanent Residence
For information on permanent residence in Sweden, contact the Swedish Embassy.

Travel
See Chapter 4 for discount travel companies that offer low-cost fares. You can get a Nordic Tourist Ticket from Norwegian State Railways - it entitles you to unlimited travel on trains in Sweden and the rest of Scandinavia for 21 days. It is also valid on some inter-Scandinavian ferry services and you can get a discount if you are under 26. Eurotrain offer special rail passes throughout Europe for those under 26. The Swedish National Tourist Office produce a free magazine giving general information on travel, accommodation, maps, eating, medical care etc.

STA Travel, 86 Old Brompton Rd, London SW7. Tel: 01 937 9921
Norwegian State Railways, 21/24 Cockspur St, London SW1Y 5DA.
Tel: 01 930 6666
Eurotrain, 52 Grosvenor Gardens, London SW1. Tel: 01 730 3402

Accommodation
Sweden is a very expensive country and it is hard to find cheap accommodation. Contact the Swedish Student Travel Bureau, SFS-Resor and the STS (Youth Hostel Association). The ISTC publication 'Sleep Cheap Guide to Europe, available from student travel offices, has details of places to stay. Try also the Ostermahus Fritidsgard in Stockholm which has accommodation for young people who are members from mid-June to the end of July.

SFS-Resor, Kungsgatan 4, 103 87 Stockholm. Tel: (08) 234515
STS, Vasagatan 48, 101 20 Stockholm
Ostermahus Fritidsgard, Valhallavagen 142, 115 24 Stockholm

Working Holidays
Work permits for vacation employment in Sweden are very difficult to obtain as Sweden accepts very few foreign nationals for employment at present and there is a great deal of competition for the available job opportunities. Swedish and foreign nationals living in Sweden have priority over applicants from other countries.

If you are not deterred, the Swedish Embassy advises enquiring at the local Job Centre as government employment agencies in Sweden and the UK co-operate to a certain extent.

Try the hotels for kitchen work, fruit and vegetable picking in the Southern part of Sweden, the docks in Goteborg for general maintenance work or the timber industry for tree felling/planting.

Agriculture
Young people aged between 18 and 30 can obtain temporary work permits in Sweden for employment in the market gardening sector. The conditions are exactly the same as for vacation work permits, (ie you need a written offer of work from your prospective employer in Sweden

and a valid passport), except that these permits are not restricted to students. Write to the Swedish Embassy for addresses or try contacting the:
Arbetsmarknadsstyrelsen, 17199 Solna, Sweden

The International Farm Experience Programme organises practical work experience on farms and nurseries. If you have obtained your own placement they are able to help with work permits. The placements are from 3 to 12 months and you live with a host family. You receive about £30 per week plus board and lodging and pay your own travel costs plus registration fee and insurance. Applicants must be aged from 18 to 26 and have at least two year' experience. You must apply at least 4 months in advance.

IFEP, YFC Centre, National Agricultural Centre, Stoneleigh,
Warwickshire CV8 2LG

Au Pair
The following agencies can occasionally place au pairs or mother's helps in Sweden. You usually have to stay a minimum of 6 months and must be aged between 17 and 27. Apply at least two months before your intended departure date.

Students Abroad, Elm House, 21b The Avenue, Hatch End, Middx HA5 4EN
Tel: 01 428 5823
Universal Care, Chester House, 9 Windsor End, Beaconsfield, Bucks HP9 2JJ
Tel: 0494 678811
Anglia Agency, 15 Eastern Ave, Southend-on-Sea, Essex SS2 5QX.
Tel: 0702 613888

Teaching
Most English teachers who work in Sweden are recruited in Britain. The Folk University recruit English teachers for the British Centre where general English is taught at all levels to adults. There is also some teaching in schools. You must be aged between 22 and 40 and have a degree and/or a certificate in education or TEFL qualification. Most teachers stay for at least two years. Interviews are held in spring, early summer and November.

Folk University of Sweden, The British Centre, c/o International Language Services (Scandinavia), 14 Rollestone St, Salisbury, Wilts SP1 1ED.
Tel: Salisbury 331011

Voluntary Work

Workcamps
IVS arranges placements for volunteers at international workcamps in Sweden. Volunteers should be 18 years of age and over and should preferably have previous workcamp experience. Food, accommodation and insurance is provided but not travel.

IVS, 162 Upper New Walk, Leicester LE1 7QA. Tel: 0533 549430

SWITZERLAND
Main Language: German, French, Italian
Currency: Swiss Franc
Capital: Bern
Exports: Machinery, Watches & Clocks, Pharmaceuticals, Food & Confectionery, Textiles & Clothing
Climate: South of Alps – mild Mediterranean climate
North of Alps – hot summers, v cold winters

Entry Requirements
Swiss Embassy, 16-18 Montagu Place, London W1H 2BQ. Tel: 01 723 0701
Swiss National Tourist Office, Swiss Centre, 1 New Coventry St, London W1V 3HG Tel: 01 734 1921

Visas
British passport holders do not need a visa for a stay of up to three months. If you want to stay longer than this, then you have to apply to the police for an extension.

Work Permits (Residence Permits)
The residence permit is a combination of both a residence and work permit, entitling the holder to live in a particular canton and work for a specified employer. The prospective employer in Switzerland has to apply to the Cantonal Aliens Police for a work permit for a foreign national. If this is granted than an 'Assurance of a Residence Permit' is sent to the employee outside Switzerland. The prospective employee must make a personal application for the work visa at the same time as the employer applies, and an authorisation to issue the visa is sent to the Swiss Embassy after the work permit has been granted. (This procedure also applies to 'Au Pair' girls and trainees).

The Swiss Government's very restrictive immigration policy has made it extremely difficult to obtain a residence permit with a view to taking up employment. As a rule only persons who have been offered a job (usually only in a highly specialised field) which cannot be filled by Swiss nationals or by those who already have a residence permit, have a chance of obtaining residence permits.

There are two types of permit of interest to the working traveller:

(a) Seasonal Permit: For seasonal employment in the building, hotel and (A-Permit) holiday industry. The maximimum period allowed is 9 months, but the usual period is 4-5 months.
(b) Standard 1-Year Designated to a person for a specific employment. Permit : It is valid for a limited period, usually one year (B-Permit) and is renewable.

These permits are issued after arrival in Switzerland, but only to persons holding an 'Assurance of a residence permit'. After arrival in Switzerland, every prospective employee must undergo a medical examination and must register with the Aliens Police within 8 days of arrival, before starting work.

Permanent Residence
Only those aged 60 and over and retired from all employment and gainful activity, or those who have close ties with Switzerland may apply for permanent residence. Once you have been issued with a 'Assurance of a residence permit', valid for 6 months, you will be granted a permanent residence permit once you have taken up residence and registered with the aliens office of the canton of domicile.

Travel
Many of the discount travel companies mentioned in Chapter 4 offer low cost fares to Geneva and/or Zurich. The Swiss Student Travel Bureau (SSR-Reisen) offers reduced air and train fares and Eurotrain offers discounts to those under 26 .

A good rail network covers the country and for more out of the way places, there are postal buses usually found next to rail stations. There are several joint-transport deals: the Swiss Rail Pass which offers eight days unlimited travel on all federal railways, all lake steamers, most private railways and postal buses, and discounts on the most expensive mountain railways and cable-cars; the Half-Fare Travel Card which gives 50% reductions of federal and private railways, postal buses and steamers. A Day Card is available for free travel of State and some private rail lines and a Regional Holiday Season Ticket gives you five free days travel or ten half-fare journeys. You can rent bikes from any station and return them to any station. If you are intending to climb consider joining the Swiss Alpine Club.

For details of these passes ask at the main rail stations (you must produce an ISIC or passport) or the Swiss National Tourist Office who also produce a booklet called 'Travel Tips for Switzerland'.

SSR-Reisen (Student Travel Bureau), Backerstrasse 52, 8004 Zurich.
Tel: (01) 2423000
Swiss Alpine Club, Obergrundstr 42, 6003 Lucern

Accommodation

The tourist offices in the main railway stations and airports have free maps, accommodation addresses, diary of events etc. In Geneva the tourist office at the station will book accommodation for you, or just outside the station you can try the CAR (Centre d'Accueil et de Renseignements) for help in finding cheap rooms.

The Swiss Student Travel Bureau (SSR-Reisen) has information on cheap places to stay as well as general tourist information. The Swiss National Tourist Office's booklet 'Travel Tips for Switzerland' also has information on accommodation.

Youth Hostels in Switzerland are clean and cheap. You can get a list of them from the YHA in England.

Jugendherberge Zurich, Mutscellenstr 114, Zurich. Tel: 482 35 44
Glockenhof YMCA (men only), Sihlstr 33, Zurich. Tel: 221 36 73
Foyer Hottingen (women only), Hottingerstr 31, Zurich. Tel: 261 93 15
Hotel Martahaus, Zahringer 36, Zurich. Tel: 251 45 50
Hotel Splendid, Rosengasse 5, Zurich. Tel: 252 58 50
Auberge de Jeunesse (IYHF hostel), 28-30 rue Rothschild, Geneva.
Tel: 732 62 60
Cite Universitaire, 26 Av Miremnont, Geneva. Tel: 46 23 55
Hotel International & Terminus, 20 rue des Alpes, Geneva. Tel: 32 80 95
Hotel Luserna, 12 Av Luserna, Geneva. Tel: 44 16 00

Working Holidays

Job Advertising

Publicitas Ltd, 525 Fulham Rd, London SW6 1HF (represents a number of Swiss papers – Basler-Zeitung, La Suisse, Tribune de Geneve)
International Graphic Press, 6 Welbeck St, London W1M 7PB (represents the German language weekly 'Die Weltwoche')

Despite the bureaucracy and difficulties in getting a work permit, it is not too hard to find employment of some sort in Switzerland. There are advantages, however, in getting a work/residence permit: you become eligible for the state insurance scheme; if you have paid contributions for at least 150 days you are eligible for unemployment benefit whatever your nationality (Australians and New Zealanders are no longer allowed to obtain a work permit); and you are entitled to a 'Red Card' from the Aliens Police which enables you to travel on public transport at a subsidised local rate and to buy a cheap seasonal ski pass.

The Swiss Student Travel Bureau (SSR-Reisen) can give you information on finding employment, as well as possibly giving you work themselves at one of their student hostels.

Agriculture
There are many small farms in Switzerland that rely on manual labour to get crops sown, picked or harvested especially in the Spring and in August-September when Swiss students are back at University/College. The Rhone Valley from Montreux to Sion is where most fruit and vegetables are grown. Grape picking begins at the beginning of October, mainly in the area north of Lake Geneva and in Valais near Sion. It might be worth hiring a bicycle to cover the distance between farms and improve your chances of finding work.

Vacation Work International arrange working holidays on farms or grape picking in the summer for single participants. Farm work includes cleaning out cow stalls, hay making, grass cutting, manure spreading, vegetable and fruit picking etc as well as housework, childcare (if you are female). You can work from 3 to 8 weeks. Hours are long and the work hard, but you should get at least one free day. Board and lodging are free and you will live as one of the family. You get paid by the farmer – the minimum is about £48 per week, though many farmers pay more than this, for a maximum 50 hour week. Farms and villages are mostly in the German-speaking sector and may be remote and a bit lonely; there are also a few places in the French and Italian cantons. You must be between 17 and 30, and have GCSE German (or French/Italian for the French and Italian cantons).

The grape picking holidays last for approximately 10 days (depending on the vendage) anytime between 30th September and 20th October, so it is essential that only those with flexible plans should apply. Harvesters work alongside Swiss and people from many other countries from 7am-12 noon and 1pm-6pm for 6 days a week and receive about £21 per day, though many proprietors pay more. Food and lodging are provided by the farmer. Accommodation is generally good but can be in a barn or outhouse – a sleeping bag is essential. You should apply not later than 1st September.

The International Farm Experience Programme organises work experience exchanges in Switzerland on farms and nurseries in the Spring and summer. You receive about £30 per week plus board and lodging, and have to pay travel costs plus registration fee and insurance. You must have at least two years' experience and be aged from 18 to 26.

Vacation Work International, 9 Park End St, Oxford, Oxon OX1 1HJ.
Tel: Oxford 241978
IFEP, YFC Centre, National Agricultural Centre, Stoneleigh, Warwickshire CV8 2LG

Au Pair
The following agencies can help to arrange au pair and mother's helps in Switzerland. You usually have to work for a minimum of one year and be aged between 17 and 29. Board and lodging is provided in return for a maximum of 30 hours per week, plus babysitting once or twice per week. You should get between £175 and £215 per month and get a 4 or 5 week paid holiday. You might also find advertisements for nannies and au pairs in ski resorts – look at notice boards in hotels, tourist offices, etc.

Universal Care, Chester House, 9 Windsor End, Beaconsfield, Bucks HP9 2JJ.
Tel: 0494 678811
Anglia Agency, 15 Eastern Avenue, Southend-on-Sea, Essex SS2 5QX.
Tel: 0702 613888
Pro Filia, 14B avenue du Mail, 1205 Geneva. Tel: 022 29 84 62

Teaching
Most English teachers who work in Switzerland are recruited in Britain, partly because of the work permit problem and partly because the standard of English is high and teachers are expected to be well qualified and experienced.

The Swiss National Tourist Office can provide a booklet 'Switzerland – Country for Children' which contains a list of schools to which teachers can apply. The Swiss Federation of Private

Schools produces a booklet 'Private Schools in Switzerland' which gives details of international, elementary/secondary, and 'finishing schools' to which teachers can apply direct.

The Central Bureau administers a scheme for the interchange of qualified, experienced teachers of Modern Languages and related subjects for 3 weeks, 6 weeks, one term or one year with Switzerland.

Swiss National Tourist Office, Swiss Centre, 1 New Coventry St, London W1V 8EE. Tel: 01 734 1921
Swiss Federation of Private Schools, 40 ru des Vollandes, PO Box 171, 1211 Geneva 6
Central Bureau, Seymour Mews House, Seymour Mews, London W1H 9PE. Tel: 01 486 5101

Tourism

There are many opportunities for casual hotel work in Switzerland in the ski resorts and by the lakes in both summer and winter if you go at the right time. The summer season is from July to September, the winter season from December to April, so if you get there before the season starts you stand a better chance of getting a job. January is also a good time to look for casual hotel work as the permitted one month trial period has come to an end and those who want to leave can do so.

'Jobs in the Alps' is an agency which places British workers in mountain resorts for the whole winter season and for the summer. In the national hotels the standards are high and the work is hard with long hours. Most winter jobs start in early to mid December and last until mid-April; summer jobs are from mid-end of June to mid-end of September. You are on probation for two weeks – after that time if you wish to leave you may, but if you decide to stay on you must undertake to work for the whole season. There are jobs for waiters, kitchen staff, hall porters/night porters, chambermaids, receptionists, barmaids, swimming pool attendants. There are also jobs in mountain restaurants, village pubs and occasionally jobs for baby sitters or au pairs. All employees get full board and lodging and you are entitled to cheap lift passes and cheap travel. The hours of work are approximately 48 hours a week and pay varies from £90 to £120 per week. Some jobs require fluent French or German.

Alpotels, part of 'Jobs in the Alps' produce lists (50p) of the main resorts in Switzerland as well as a booklet 'Work in the Alps' (£5). You can write to the hotels or visit them directly in search of work.

Many of the ski tour operators and camping holiday companies require couriers/reps, chalet maids or qualified ski instructors. You can get the addresses of these companies from a travel agent and write to them for vacancies.

'Jobs in the Alps', PO Box 388, London SW1X 8LX. Tel: 01 235 8205
Snow World, 34-36 South St, Lancing, W Sussex BN15 8AG. Tel: Lancing 750310
Ski Europe, 6 Kew Green, Richmond, Surrey
Eurocamp, Courier Dept, Edmundson House, Tatton St, Knutsford, Cheshire WA16 6BG.
Canvas Holidays Ltd, Bull Plain, Hertford, Herts SG14 1DY. Tel: 0992 553535

Voluntary Work

Workcamps

International Voluntary Service arranges placements in workcamps in Switzerland for 2-3 weeks between July and September. Volunteers must be 18 and over and the work includes farming, clearing land, reconstruction of village houses, forestry, gardening, fruit picking or being involved in social projects.

United Nations Association organises some 30 camps in Switzerland with Aktion 7, an umbrella organisation covering a number of voluntary and community organisations in the French speaking area of Switzerland. A knowledge of French is therefore useful. 12-20 volunteers attend each camp and engage in manual, conservation and social work.

EYCE organise camps jointly with Belgium, West Germany and Switzerland. Volunteers work for 2 weeks for 4 days a week. Recently the work involved renovating the basement and bathroom equipment and building a meditation room in the Catholic Students' Home. No special skills are required and the third week of the camp is spent travelling around Switzerland visiting congregations, a monastery and hiking in the mountains.

IVS, 162 Upper New Walk, Leicester LE1 7QA. Tel: 0533 549430
United Nations Association, Welsh Centre for International Affairs,
Temple of Peace, Cathays Park, Cardiff CF1 3AP. Tel: Cardiff 223088
EYCE, Christoph Schuler, Belchenstr 11, 4310 Rheinfelden, Switzerland

THAILAND
Main Language: Thai
Currency: Baht
Capital: Bangkok
Exports: Rice, Maize, Rubber, Fruit and vegetables, Tin.
Climate: Mar-Jun – hot, mainly dry (28°C-40°C)
Jul-Oct – monsoon, heavy rain, valleys drier than hills
Nov-Feb – less hot, dry (21°C-27°C), best time to go

Entry Requirements
Royal Thai Embassy, 30 Queens Gate, London SW7 5JB

Visas
Citizens of the UK do not require a visa for a stay not exceeding 15 days, if they enter Thailand through the Thai/Malaysian border or by air if they hold confirmed air tickets, and hold a valid passport. Visitors who want to stay more than 15 days must apply for a visa. You can apply for a transit visa which is valid for a stay of 30 days from the date of entry or a tourist visa which is valid for a stay of 60 days from the date of entry. All visas are valid for entry into Thailand within 90 days from the date of issue.

Work Permits
If there is a remaining quota of non-restricted jobs to offer, work permits can be obtained through a prospective employer. Persons with a tourist visa are not permitted to engage in any profession whilst in Thailand.

Permanent Residence
Thailand does not have an immigration policy.

Travel
Many of the discount travel companies offer cheap air fares to Thailand. Look also at the small ads section of the national papers and London evening papers for latest bargain fares. You can also include Bangkok on a round-the-world ticket which usually lasts one year. Bangkok is renowned for its cheap air fares to other destinations so it might be worth waiting to buy your ticket there. STA Travel have an office there.

You can also get to Thailand by train from Penang; the train service is excellent, clean, comfortable and very spacious. There are no special discounts for students but train fares are reasonable. Buses also go from Penanag – again remarkably comfortable.

The airport is about 14 miles from the city. Airport minibuses run every half hour or outside the airport buses go to the city for a fraction of the cost.

The ETC (Educational Travel Centre) and STA Travel can give you information on trains to Chiang Mai and other destinations and well as information on buses. They can also arrange various tours (and discounts for students) eg – the River Kwai, jungle tour in Chiang Mai, river rafting and the River Kwai, Thailand trekking, and central and Northern Thailand overland.

'Life Tours' of Bangkok offer the chance to spend several days in a Thai village sharing the lives of the villagers. The price includes accommodation, meals, inland transport, guides etc. Write to the Life Travel Service Co office in Bangkok for more information.

STA Travel, Thai Hotel, 78 Prachatipatai Rd, Bangkok 10200. Tel: 2815314
ETC, Room 318, Royal Hotel, 2 Rajdamnoen Ave, Bangkok 10200. Tel: 2244623
Life Travel Service Co Ltd, 15 Soi Soonvijai, 8 New Petchburi Rd, Bangkok 10310. Tel: 318 1287

Accommodation
The cheapest area for accommodation is Kao San Road and Tannao Road, Banglampu. (PB Guest House, US1 and US2, UP, UIP, Apple Guest House, 160 (Marco Polo) Guest House). If you are prepared to pay a bit more, try the Crown Hotel in Sukumuit Rd. Special student rates are offered at many hotels in Bangkok, Chiang Mai, Pattaya and Phuket.

The Trailfinders Travel Pass booklet has details of hotels giving discounts and the ISTC publication 'Sleep Cheap Guide to Asia/Australia/New Zealand' has useful information on accommodation in Thailand. The Tourist Office at Ratcadainnoen Nok Road is open daily from 9am-4pm and has a selection of useful handouts.

Working Holidays
Although you need a work permit in Thailand, it is possible to get casual work without one, mainly teaching and occasionally in the tourist industry. Most people renew their visas by going across to Penang every 3 months.

Teaching
There are plenty of opportunities to teach English without any qualifications in Thailand although the pay is poor. Bangkok is a sprawling, noisy, very dirty city and getting around is a headache so it's best to get a map and concentrate your efforts in small areas. Look in the papers for advertisements for English Teachers, or look up the addresses of language schools in the Yellow Pages. American University Alumni Centres are established through Thailand and are worth contacting. The most productive times for looking for teaching work are June and November.

If you are qualified the British Council has two centres in Thailand, but they generally want some long-term commitment. The European Council of International Schools assists international English-medium schools with staff recruitment and operates a year-round placement service for teachers/administrators with a minimum of 2 years' teaching experience. There are a few International Schools in Thailand that may be worth contacting directly or through the ECIS.

Outside Bangkok, Hat Yai in southern Thailand has opportunities for teaching as well as Chiang Mai in the North where there are language schools.

British Council, Overseas Educational Appointments Dept, 65 Davies St, London W1Y 2AA. Tel: 01 499 8011
European Council of International Schools, 21b Lavant St, Petersfield, Hants GU32 3EL. Tel: 0730 68244

Tourism
The Beach resorts of Pattaya and the island of Phuket might offer opportunties in the tourist industry, teaching watersports, as a guide etc. Contact STA travel at the Thai Hotel for any work as possible couriers/guides on the tours they organise.

Voluntary Work
There are opportunities for voluntary work in the refugee camps which is coordinated by Oxfam. Write directly to them for information.

VSO currently has 28 volunteers working in agriculture, fisheries, animal husbandry, youth work, English language teaching, dentistry and rehabilitation or education for handicapped people in Thailand.

VSO, Enquiries Unit, 317 Putney Bridge Rd, London SW15 2PN.
Tel: 01 780 1331

TONGA
Main Language: English
Capital: Nuku'alofa
Exports: Copra, bananas
Climate: Warm, moist

Entry Requirements
Tonga High Commission, New Zealand House, Haymarket, London SW1.
Tel: 01 839 3287

Visas
British nationals do not need a visa to enter Tonga.

Work Permits
A work permit is needed from the Ministry of Labour in Nuku'alofa to work in Tonga. This applies to working holidays also.

Travel
Contact the discount travel agencies for the cheapest way to get to Tonga. Trailfinders and STA travel have comprehensive information on travel worldwide.

Trailfinders, 194 Kensignton High St, London W8 7RG. Tel: 01 938 3939
STA Travel, 74 & 86 Old Brompton Rd, London SW7. Tel: 01 937 9962

Working Holidays
There are no opportunities for casual work in Tonga. Tourism is a rapidly growing industry, though, and it might be possible to find work as a watersports instructor or crewing on a yacht. Try writing about your travels and sell your stories to magazines/papers in New Zealand or the UK.

Voluntary Work
There are various voluntary work opportunities. For more information on these contact:

Director of Education, Nuku'alofa, Tonga Islands, South West Pacific

TUNISIA
Main Language: Arabic, French
Currency: Dinar
Capital: Tunis
Exports: Petroleum, Olive oil, Phosphates, Fertilizer.
Climate: Summer – Hot, 24°C +
Winter – Cool, 10°C +

Entry Requirements
Tunisian Embassy, 29 Princes Gate, London SW7. Tel: 01 584 8117
Tunisian Tourist Office, 7a Stafford St, London W1. Tel: 01 499 2234

Visas
United Kingdom passport holders do not require a visa to enter Tunisia for up to three months. You must have a valid passport and be able to provide evidence of being able to support yourself while in Tunisia.

Work Permits
Employment for foreigners is subject to obtaining a work permit. The work permit is applied for by the prospective employer and is granted by the Ministry of Social Affairs. This permit, however, is only delivered in rare cases when the local employment market cannot meet the demands of the job applied for.

Permanent Residence
A residence permit can be applied for to the Ministry of the Interior once the applicant is in Tunisia. Consideration is then given to this application after presentation of both the applicant's personal file and work permit.

Travel
Some of the discount travel companies offer cheap flights to Tunis (see Chapter 4 for details). You can also get there by ferry from Marseilles- the journey takes takes 2 days. Many of the expedition companies include Tunis on their itineraries.

Sotutour/Stav (Student Travel Bureau) in Tunis organises many tours in Tunisia, eg travel by bus visiting Sousse and many other destinations for a week between April and October; Les Oasis, Tour in the Sahara for 1 week, (staying overnight in bedouin tents in Ksar Ghilane); and camel trekking for 1 week. Some of these tours are open to individuals (as opposed to groups of students).

Trailfinders, 194 Kensington High St, London W8 7RG. Tel: 01 938 3939
STA Travel, 74 & 86 Old Brompton Rd, London SW7. Tel: 01 937 9921
Dragoman, 10 Riverside, Framlinghm, Suffolk IP13 9AG. Tel: 0728 724184
Exodus Expeditions, 9 Weir Rd, London SW12 OLT. Tel: 01 675 7996
Guerba Expeditions Ltd, Dept TF, 101 Eden Vale Rd, Westbury, Wilts BA13 3YB. Tel: 0373 826611
Encounter Overland, 267 Old Brompton Rd, London SW5 9JA. Tel: 01 370 6845
Hann Overland, 201-203 Vauxhall Bridge Rd, London SW1V 1ER. Tel: 01 834 7337
Sotutour/Stav (Student Travel Bureau), 2 rue de Sparte, Tunis. Tel: 348011

Accommodation
For information on accommodation contact the Tunisian Tourist Office and the Association Tunisienne Tourisme et Jeunesse.

Association Tunisienne Tourisme et Jeunesse, 1 avenue de Carthage, Tunis

Working Holidays

Many of the tour operators organise holidays in Tunisia and need couriers/reps to meet clients at the airport and give them advice and assistance during their stay. Write to companies such as Thomson and Portland about such work.

Thomson Holidays Ltd, Overseas Personnel Dept, Greater London House, Hampstead Rd, London NW1 7SD. Tel: 01 387 9321
Portland Holidays, Overseas Personnel Dept, 218 Great Portland St, London W1N 5HG. Tel: 01 387 3685

Voluntary Work

Workcamps

IVS organises camps for 2-3 weeks in July and August throughout Tunisia concerned with conservation, restoration and construction projects. Applicants should be between 18 and 35 and have a knowledge of French.

Quaker International Social Projects organises camps in North Africa. You should have previous workcamp experience; projects include environmental or ecological schemes, building playgrounds, and working with children and people in disadvantaged areas.

Contact the Tunisian Youth Organisation about workcamps that they organise.

IVS, 162 Upper New Walk, Leicester LE1 7QA. Tel: 0533 549430
QISP, Friends House, Euston Rd, London NW1 2BJ. Tel: 01 387 3601
Union Tunisienne des Organisations de Jeunesse, s/c de Rassemblement Constitutionnel Democratique, boulevard du 9 Avril, Tunis, Tunisia.

TURKEY

Main Language: Turkish
Currency: Lira
Capital: Ankara
Exports: Cotton, Nuts, Tobacco, Raisins.
Climate: Summer – Hot 22°C + (on coasts 32°C)
Winter – V cold in the interior, rainy on coasts esp Black Sea

Entry Requirements

Turkish Embassy, 43 Belgrave Sq, London SW1X 8PA.
Turkish Consulate General, Rutland Lodge, Rutland Gardens, Knightsbridge, London SW7 1BW. Tel: 01 589 0360

Turkish Tourist Office, 1st floor, 170-173 Piccadilly, London W1V 9DD. Tel: 01 734 8681

Visas

Citizens of the United Kingdom do not require visas to enter Turkey as tourists for stays for up to 3 months.

Work Permits

All foreign nationals who are going to Turkey to take up employment must have a working visa, issued by a Turkish consulate before arriving in Turkey. A working agreement must first be concluded with an employer in Turkey. An application must then be made to the Turkish

Consulate and a visa application form obtained, completed and returned, which will then be submitted to the appropriate Turkish Authority. The applicant will be contacted by the Consulate once a reply has been obtained.

Persons who enter Turkey as tourists (with or without tourist visas) are not permitted to take up employment there.

Students (citizens of Western European countries) who obtain temporary working positions in Turkey through the Students' Training Exchange Scheme do not require work visas.

Permanent Residence
If you wish to obtain a residence visa in Turkey you are required to submit: a passport, one passport-sized photograph, visa application form, banker's statement of your current finances, and the reasons for your intended settlement in Turkey. All enquiries on the subjects of the purchase of property or business investment should be addressed to the Turkish Embassy, Financial Section.

Travel
Many discount travel companies offer cheap fares to Turkey. WST (World Student Travel) Charters operate low cost flights to Istanbul or Dalaman on the south coast between May 1st and October 31st. You can also see two countries for the price of one – flying first to Istanbul, making your own way to Tel Aviv and flying back to London from Tel Aviv (from £168) or vice versa (from £217). STA Travel have details of these flights and information on other flights to Turkey.

Some expedition travel companies travel through Turkey as part of an overland expedition to Asia or the Middle East. Exodus organise walking explorer trips to Turkey.

Eurotrain give up to 40% off full rail fares to anyone under 26 – you can break the journey and tickets are valid for 2 months. You can also get to Turkey by bus/coach from the UK or other places in Europe, and by ship from Kos or Rhodes in Greece.

There are plenty of buses that connect the airport and coach station with the city of Istanbul. Buy bus tickets from kiosks, not from the driver. If you travel by taxi, make sure you agree a price before you start your journey – meters are rarely used. Dolmus, which have a yellow band below the windows, are collective taxis and set off only when they are full. They follow a fixed route and you pay a set charge. Travel is cheap, especially the buses. Boats go up the Bospherus to the Black Sea.

WST Charters, Priory House, 6 Wrights Lane, London W8 6TA. Tel: 01 938 4362
STA Travel, 86 Old Brompton Rd, London SW7. Tel: 01 937 9921
Trailfinders, 194 Kensington High St, London W8 7RG. Tel: 01 938 3939
Exodus Expeditions, 9 Weir Rd, London SW12 OLT. Tel: 01 675 7996
Dragoman, 10 Riverside, Framlingham, Suffolk 1PI3 9AG. Tel: 0728 724184
Hann Overland, 201-203 Vauxhall Bridge Rd, London SW1V 1ER.
Tel: 01 834 7337
Transglobal, 64 Kenway Rd, Earls Court, London SW5 ORD. Tel: 01 244 8571

Accommodation
Accommodation in Turkey is cheap – in Istanbul the cheapest area is the Sultanahmet quarter. Students can get discounts of between 10% and 30% at many hotels, motels and university residences. Student travel offices in Turkey can give you a comprehensive list and will make reservations for travelling students. There are also youth hostels and pension-type accommodation. The Turkish Tourist Office in London produce 'Turkey Travel Guide' which contains information on accommodation, travel and general information.

Turkish Tourist Office, 1st floor, 170-173 Piccadilly, London W1V 9DD. Tel: 01 734 8681

7 Tur Tourism Ltd, Travel Shop, Inonu Cad 37/2, Gumussuyu-Taksim-Istanbul.
Tel: (1) 1494090
Genctur (Student Travel Bureau), Yerebatan Cad 15/3, 34410 Sultanahmet-Istanbul. Tel: (1)
5120457
Yucelt Youth Hostel, 6 Caferiye Sokagi, Istanbul. Tel: 513 61 50
Topkapi Hostel, (at junction of Ishak Passa Caddesi and Kutlugum Sokagi), Istanbul. Tel: 513
61 50

Working Holidays
There are few opportunities for casual work in Turkey – most has to be fixed up before you go.
The recent boom in the tourist industry, though, has meant that in the south it is possible to get
some work in the southern resorts. Be prepared for a few hassles if you are a blond male with
blue eyes!

Teaching
The British Council in Istanbul can provide a list of English schools. Many of the language
schools may offer you work provided you are willing to stay for the whole academic year, though
this causes problems with your visa limit of 3 months. You may be able to get private tuition work
through notices on youth hostel boards or by being approached directly.

Christians Abroad recruit TEFL teachers for Turkey. The Youth Exchange Centre run an English
language summer school at a Turkish college on the Mediterranean coast which requires EFL
teachers.

The British Council, Overseas Educational Appointments Dept, 65 Davies St, London W1Y 2AA.
Tel: 01 499 8011
Christians Abroad, Livingstone House, 11 Carteret St, London SW1H 9DL.
Tel: 01 222 2165
The Youth Exchange Centre, Central Bureau, Seymour Mews House, Seymour Mews,
London W1H 9PE. Tel: 01 486 5101

Tourism
In the resorts on the Mediterranean and Aegean Seas, many private yachts put in to port. Visit
bars/eating places where the 'yachties' socialise, as well as the harbours and keep your ears open
for work as crew or cooks or even cleaners.

Many of the tour operators organise holidays in Turkey. Find the addresses of these companies
from brochures at your local travel agent and write to them for information on jobs as
couriers/reps.

Sunsail operate flotilla sailing holidays in Turkey and need skippers, hostesses and mechanic
bosuns (£80 pw). For their Sunsail Clubs they require a wide range of staff, including dinghy
sailing/windsurfing instructors, cruising instructors, bar staff, nannies, cooks and catering
assistants. Pay is from £50 per week depending on position, and you also get accommodation,
half board and flights to and from the UK.

Thomson Holidays, Greater London House, Hampstead Rd, London NW1.
Tel: 01 387 9321
Portland Holidays, Overseas Personnel Dept, 218 Great Portland St, London W1N 5HG. Tel: 01
387 3685
Sunsail, The Port House, Port Solent, Portsmouth, Hants PO6 4TH. Tel: 0705 219847

Voluntary Work
There are many opportunities in Turkey for participation at international workcamps. Generally
these take place in small villages and conditions can be very primitive. Volunteers must be

224

between 18 and 35 and have previous workcamp experience. Work is hard and involves heavy manual work in construction, renovation, repairing of traditional old houses, ecological work in the forest, irrigation, etc. Volunteers work a 6-8 hour day with one free day per week and camps last for 2 weeks between June and September. Accommodation and half board is provided (approx £35 pw). Accommodation may be provided in schools or village centres and volunteers may have to sleep on the floor. Genctur (Student Travel Bureau) who organises the workcamps have to offer a 5-day beach holiday at the end of the camp as part of the programme, though many volunteers prefer to go travelling on their own. Volunteers pay their own travel costs to Turkey.

CMP, Bethnal Green URC, Pott St, London E2 OEF. Tel: 01 729 1877
IVS, 162 Upper New Walk, Leicester LE1 7QA. Tel: 0533 549430
Concordia (Youth Service Volunteers), Recruitment Secretary, 8 Brunswick Place, Hove, Sussex BN3 1ET. Tel: Brighton 772086
Quaker International Social Projects, Friends House, Euston Rd, London NW1 2BJ. Tel: 01 387 3601
United Nations Association, Welsh Centre for International Affairs, Temple of Peace, Cathays Park, Cardiff CF1 3AP. Tel: Cardiff 223088

Archaeology
The Archaeological Institute of America provides details of digs in Turkey in its Fieldwork Bulletin. Volunteers, who must be at least 18, should apply as early as possible. For Turkey, in general, students who are serious about wanting to be apprentices in Turkey should write two years in advance to the Director of the excavation they would like to join.

Archaeology Abroad give details of excavations abroad requiring volunteers.

The Archaeological Institute of America, 675 Commonwealth Ave, Boston, MA 02215
Archaeology Abroad, 31-34 Gordon Sq, London WC1H OPY.

UNITED KINGDOM
Main language: English
Currency: English pound
Capital: London
Climate: Mild winters, cool summers; cloud, rain, clear spells; colder in north.

Entry Requirements
Foreigners coming to the UK should apply to the British Embassy in their own country for entry requirements. Commonwealth citizens with UK ancestry can contact the Home Office for general immigration requirements.

Home Office, Lunar House, Wellesley Rd, Croydon, Surrey CR9 2BY. Tel: 01 686 0688

British Tourist Authority, Thames Tower, Black's Rd, Hammersmith, London W6 9BL. Tel: 01 846 9000
Scottish Tourist Board, 23 Ravelston Terrace, Edinburgh EH4 3EU. Tel: 031 332
Wales Tourist Board, Brunel House, 2 Fitzalan Rd, Cardiff CF2 1UY. Tel: Cardiff 499909

Work permits
EC nationals, except for nationals of Spain and Portugal, do not need a work permit to look for or take up employment in the UK. Non-EC nationals who are subject to immigration control need a work permit and will be refused entry if they cannot produce one when the enter the UK. A

work permit is not required for au pair posts or temporary employment at approved farmcamps, but you must produce a letter of invitation from the family or farmcamp. Permits are not usually required for temporary employment on international workcamps or for voluntary organisations (check with the workcamp/voluntary organisation in your country or with the British consulate). Overseas students studying in Britain who wish to work in their free time or during vacations do not need a work permit, but must obtain the consent of the Department of Employment through the local Jobcentre and must provide written assurance from their college that employment will not interfere with their studies.

Leaflets OW5 and OW21, from Department of Employment
Overseas Labour Section, Department of Employment, Caxton House, Tothill St, London SW1H 9NF. Tel: 01 213 3332

Permanent Residence
Information concerning permanent residence should be obtained from the Home Office.

Travel
Contact your own discount travel shops for cheap flights to the UK. Many European countries operate their own Interrail Passes for cheap train travel to the UK and there are bus/coach companies that offer low cost fares to the UK. Students can also get a discount of 15%-50% on Cross Channel Ferries and Irish Sea crossings, depending on the ferry company.

A National Express Coach Card (£3.90), valid for one year, entitles students to special fares to most major towns and cities in the UK. Coach travel is generally the cheapest way to travel over long distances and is often not much slower than the train. Cycling, of course, is cheaper still.

Full-time students of any age or those under 24 can get a 33% discount on a range of rail tickets with a Young Person's Railcard (UK£15) which is valid for a year. Rail travel is very expensive in the UK. There are a variety of special fares and you should always ask for the cheapest way of getting from A to B. If you're prepared to be flexible you should not have to pay the very expensive standard fare. Ask at any British rail station for information.
A BritRail 'Silver' Pass offers unlimited travel by all scheduled British Rail services for people from overseas (the validity varies slightly according to the country of purchase). The Flexible BritRail Pass is available in all countries and allows for between 4 and 15 days' travel within a month, depending on the country of issue. In most countries outside Europe an alternative BritRail Pass is available for consecutive days' travel for up to a month. Young people aged between 16 and 25 can buy a BritRail Youth Pass. All these passes are available only for overseas visitors and must be bought before you leave. Contact your travel agent for information on these passes
or British Rail offices in your own country.

National Express, Victoria Coach Station, 164 Buckingham Palace Rd, London SW1
Tel: 01 730 0202
Cyclists' Touring Club, Cotterell House, 69 Meadrow, Godalming, Surrey
GU7 3HS. Tel: 04868 7217
BritRail International: 630, Third Ave, New York 10017. Tel: 212 599 5400
94 Cumberland St, Toronto M5R 1A3
BritRail Sales Agent Thomas Cook, 44 Market St, PO Box C354, Sydney,
NSW 2000. Tel: 234 4000

Accommodation
International Travellers' Aid can give advice on accommodation as well as giving advice and help to overseas travellers who have just arrived in the UK and may be having a few problems.

Accommodation in London is expensive, though student-type hotels and hostels are plentiful. In all parts of the country, there are Youth Hostels as well as B & Bs (Bed and Breakfast) which are generally reasonable. Details of Bed and Breakfast accommodation can usually be obtained from local Tourist Information offices in most large towns. They also have information on places of interest, travel etc. During the summer period most universities and the larger colleges have student residences which are open for vacation accommodation. The local Students' Union can provide you with details. Camping is popular, though the unpredictable weather can dampen your spirits somewhat.

International Travellers' Aid, The Kiosk, Platform 14, Victoria Station, London SW1V 1JT.
Youth Hostels Association, Trevelyan House, 8 St Stephen's Hill, St Albans
Herts AL1 2DY. Tel: 0727 55215
National Union of Students, 461 Holloway Road, London N7 6LJ. Tel: 01 272 8900
International Students House, 229 Great Portland St, London W1N 5HD. Tel: 01 631 3223

Working Holidays
This section is aimed primarily at travellers from overseas who want to earn some money. Unlike in many countries abroad that British people travel to and manage to find work in without necessarily speaking the language, it is pretty well essential that in Britain, if you want to work, you must have a fairly good knowledge of English.

In the UK new employees (paid by cheque) are automatically put on the emergency tax code (X) which means that a quarter of your earnings are paid in tax. If you have been resident in the UK for at least six months, you can apply to the Department of Social Security for a National Insurance Number which entitles single people to a tax free allowance of £2,600 a year. To get a rebate before you leave the UK , get form P86 from your local tax office. When you leave your job, you will be given a P45 which has details of your earnings – send this and form P86 to your local Inland Revenue Office (address from phone book) for a tax rebate. The process can sometimes take months and it would be wise to ask someone to send the money on to you. If you take a series of jobs, between travelling around, remember to take your P45 with you to the next employer.

Nationals of Belgium, Denmark, France, the Federal Republic of Germany, Gibraltar, Greece, Republic of Ireland, Italy, Luxembourg and the Netherlands can apply at the local JobCentres under reciprocal work agreements with the EEC. Look in the newspapers – papers like the London Evening Standard and local papers offer more in the way of casual work than national papers like the Guardian. Throughout London, especially outside travel agencies, there are distribution boxes containing free copies of 'The News and Travel International' (TNT) and 'New Zealand News', aimed mainly at Australians and New Zealanders. Both papers contain advertisements for jobs in pubs, restaurants, domestic work etc. Look in newsagents' windows – many have a notice board advertising jobs for nannies, cleaners, gardeners etc and for a small sum you can place your own advertisement. Try employment agencies for temporary office work (addresses from the Yellow Pages, newspaper ads) – you have to perform a speed test (typing/shorthand) which determines what kind of work you will be allowed to do. 'The Directory of Summer Jobs in Britain' (£6.90) lists 30,000 vacancies in the UK and gives full details of wages, hours, qualifications, and general conditions of work etc. Word of mouth is still an excellent way of locating work – ask around if you see something that that needs doing.

'The Directory of Summer Jobs in Britain, Vacation Work International, 9 Park End St, Oxford OX1 1HJ.

Agriculture
Apples, cherries, pears, plums and many different kinds of soft fruit (strawberries, raspberries etc) are grown in the UK, mainly in the Wye and Usk valleys, Kent, Lincolnshire, East Anglia (Wisbech) and North of the Tay Estuary (Blairgowrie, Forfar) in Scotland. Vegetables are also grown in these areas and throughout the UK. Hops for making beer are grown in Kent, Hereford and Worcester. Guernsey in the Channel Islands produces a large quantity of vegetables (especially tomatoes), and flowers under glass the whole year round. Work in the greenhouses can be claustrophobic and very hot, but pickers as well as packers are in short supply.

Harvest dates vary widely from Scotland to the South of England but generally soft fruit is picked from mid-June to mid-October; apples, cherries etc from July to October. Many vegetables, such as cabbage, lettuce and cauliflower are grown all year, but in general the best time for harvesting vegetables is from May to October. Hops are picked in September.

In many of the growing areas in the UK, gypsies traditionally move in to pick the fruit and vegetables at harvest time, and outsiders are not well received. Some of the smaller farms might offer better prospects away from the main growing areas, although many of these now are 'Pick Your Own' establishments and do not employ pickers as such. If the farm supplies local hotels, restaurants or the local market/shops etc they might be glad of extra help in the harvest season. Check the notice boards at the Job Centre or contact the Farmer's Union in the area you would like to work, or look up addresses of farms in the Yellow Pages.

International Farm Camps are an excellent way of meeting fellow travellers who are a good source of travel advice and tips. Workers come from all over Europe, both from EEC countries and from North Africa, the Eastern bloc etc as well as the UK, and the camps give them a chance to work, live and, in some cases, study together and improve their English.

EEC nationals are normally admitted to the UK for up to 6 months on production of either a valid national passport or an identity card. No work permit is required (this does not apply to Spanish or Portuguese nationals as their countries are not yet full members of the EEC). Nationals of all other countries must a have a valid national passport (endorsed where necessary with a UK visa), and an entry authorisation from the camp you will attend. Polish citizens who require an official letter of invitation must send a further £10 to cover the fee charged by the Polish Consul in the UK.

Visas issued to holders of camp entrance authorisation cards are only valid for the period of the camp and a holiday afterwards. Holders of these visas are not allowed to take up other employment in the UK. The camps are obliged to notify the immigration authorities of the names of any persons not arriving at the camp or leaving early. If these people are then found to be in the UK they are liable to be treated as illegal immigrants and deported.

The farmcamps usually provide accommodation, either in huts or on a campsite. Some camps charge for accommodation which usually also includes meals, some camps provide free accommodation and you have to provide and cook your own meals. The work generally consists of fruit picking, market gardening, vegetable/apple/hop picking, cereals or nursery gardening. There is no fixed wage and you are paid for every pound of fruit etc picked (approx 10 pence for every pound of fruit, 22 pence per kg). Your total earnings will depend on how hard you work, the weather (it may not be possible to pick every day or all day), and whether there is a good or bad crop, which varies from year to year. Usually the camps operate only for the harvest period eg July and August. Sometimes you must book for a minimum period eg 3 weeks, although if places are available you may be able to extend your stay. You won't earn enough to cover the cost of air fares to and from the UK but you should earn enough to be able to spend time touring round or for pocket money.

For information and addresses about volunteer agricultural camps, send a stamped addressed envelope or IRC to:

The Recruitment Secretary, Concordia, 8 Brunswick Place, Hove, East Sussex BN3 1ET

The following camps offer farm work on privately owned and run farms. Applications for them should be addressed direct to the camp, enclosing a stamped addressed envelope, and for overseas enquiries, an IRC.

The Manager, Hickman & Co, International Farm Camp, Leverington, Wisbech, Cambs PE13 5DR. (British & foreign students 16-30, soft-fruit picking)
The Organiser, International Farm Camp, Tiptree, Essex CO5 0QS (British & Foreign students, 18-25, soft-fruit picking)

The Organiser, R & JM Place Ltd, International Farm Camp, Church Farm, Tunstead, Norfolk NR12 8RQ. (volunteers from British and EEC countries, 17+, soft fruit picking)

Camp Organiser, Vacation Work Ltd, 9 Park End St, Oxford OX1 1HJ (for Lentran Fruit Farm, Lentran, Inverness-shire, volunteers from Britain and foreign countries, 17-25, soft fruit picking)

Mr PMS Barron, Tinkletop Farm, Blairgowrie, Perthshire PH10 6TB (volunteers from Britain and foreign countries, 17-30, soft fruit picking)

Fridaybridge Camp, March Rd, Fridaybridge, Wisbech, Cambridgeshire (British volunteers must apply direct to this camp; Concordia recruits foreign volunteers)

WWOOF (Working Weekends on Organic Farms) publishes a newsletter which is sent to members every two months. Details of organic farms, gardens and smallholdings which need help are listed in the newsletter. Members can then make bookings for the weekends, or days of their choice and if a place is available will receive full details including travel information. A detailed 'Fix-It-Yourself' list of WWOOF places in the UK, Ireland and overseas is also available to members who have satisfactorily completed at least two scheduled weekends, so that they can make their own arrangements to work, possibly for longer periods. Special arrangements can normally be made for overseas visitors and others unable to complete two scheduled weekends.

WWOOF is an exchange: in return for your work on the farms you receive meals, accommodation and, if necessary, transport to and from the local station. To become a member, and receive further information, send an sae to:

The Membership Secretary, WWOOF, 19 Bradford Rd, Lewes, Sussex BN7 1RB

Au Pair

There will be agencies in your own country that can organise au pair positions for you. In the UK au pairs do not need a work permit as long as they have a letter of invitation from the family giving details of accommodation, pocket money, work required etc. The minimum length of service is 6 months, the maximum is a total of two years as an au pair. Posts for nannies, au pairs, mother's helps, housekeepers etc are available for British citizens, EEC Nationals and Comonwealth citizens in possession of a 'Working Holidaymaker's' Permit. EC nationals wishing to stay longer than 6 months must obtain a residence permit by filling in form EEC1 from the Home Office, Department of Employment or police stations. Other western European nationals from Cyprus, Malta, Turkey and Yugoslavia can be placed only as au pairs. Normally au pairs work a maximum of 30 hours a week plus 2/3 evenings babysitting and should have one day free each week. Pocket money in the UK is usually about £25 per week.

The following agencies arrange au pair positions in the UK.

Anglia Agency, 15 Eastern Ave, Southend-on-Sea, Essex SS2 5QX.
Tel: 0702 613 888
Helping Hands Au Pair and Domestic Agency, 10 Hertford Rd, Newbury Park, Ilford, Essex IG2 7HQ. Tel: 01 597 3138
Students Abroad, Elm House, 21b The Avenue, Hatch End, Middx HA5 4EN.
Tel: 01 428 5823

Teaching

For English-speakers there are many opportunities for teaching English as a Foreign Language in the UK, especially in London and resorts on the south coast such as Brighton, Bournemouth etc. The Association of Recognised English Language Schools (ARELS) produces an annual guide, listing all private schools in the UK which have been recognised by the British Council for the Teaching of English as a Foreign Language, and are members of the Association. There is also a monthly Bulletin to all members in which qualified EFL teachers can place an advertisement for a minimal fee.

If you have no qualifications, you could approach the many language schools in London or other big cities that are not members of ARELS and offer your services to teach 'conversation'. In the smaller centres such as Brighton, there are generally fewer opportunities – there are not so many schools, and the ones there are tend to demand high qualifications, experience etc because of the competition. They are also popular places to work in, so competition from other teachers is likely to be greater.

Foreign visitors can make use of their native language by placing advertisements in shop windows, launderettes, newspapers etc (an expensive option) for private tuition – in London you could charge anything from £5 to £10+ depending on your confidence, ability, and the popularity of the language you speak. With 1992 looming, many British people will want to learn or improve their knowledge of a European language. Languages such as Japanese are also popular. If you have a permanent/semi permanent base, students could come to you. Many private students like to learn in their own environment, and as long as you charge them for your travelling expenses and you don't waste too much time getting there, it is worth going to them in their own homes. The local Adult Education Authority might be interested in putting on a course in the language you speak, if they do not already run one (find the address in the phone book). Contact your country's Institute in London (if they have one), for example the Instituto de Espana, or the Italian Institute and ask them for advice.

Association of Recognised English Schools, 2 Pontypool Place, Valentine Place, London SE1 8QF. Tel: 01 242 3136

Tourism
In spite of the high rate of unemployment in the UK there are still many opportunities for seasonal and temporary work, depending on which part of the country you are in. Head for the tourist spots – the coastal resorts especially in the south, Cornwall (where unemployment is high the rest of the year), The Lake District, Scotland, Wales, Channel Islands, and of course London. Towns like Bath, Oxford, Chester, York are also on the tourist trail and are worth a visit for work purposes. Get lists of hotels from the English Tourist Board and write giving details of past experience, type of work you are looking for etc. Wages are low in the hotel and catering trade (£1.85-£3) and in London hotels do not generally provide accommodation for staff. In other parts of the country accommodation may be provided and if it isn't will not be as expensive as in London. Pubs in bigger towns/cities might hire you - in smaller communities, locals tend to get preference over outsiders. Fast food chains, such as Wimpy, MacDonalds, etc are always worth a try and if you can get a reference, you are more likely to be taken on at the next place you visit.

Youth Hostels often need extra help in the tourist season from Easter to October to do general domestic work, cooking, working in the hostel shop etc. You should apply in the winter (if possible) to the regional headquarters of the YHA, whose addresses are in the YHA handbook. Shops in seaside resorts such as Torquay, Newquay, Blackpool etc all need extra staff in the tourist season.

Activity Holidays/Couriers/Guides
Many holiday companies offer activity holidays in Britain for both children and adults and require a large number of staff in the summer season. Many holiday companies also organise tours of historic sites etc for groups of foreign tourists; if you have a sound knowledge or interest in a historical site/building/town you could try offering your services as a guide/interpreter. Find the addresses from travel agents' brochures and write directly to the companies.

PGL Young Adventure organise children, family and adventure holidays at centres in England, Scotland, Wales, Guernsey (as well as France, Austria, Sweden and Holland). During the summer PGL open up many centres for six weeks, and outside of the school holidays, school groups go on adventure courses so that some centres are open from February to November. If you want to work for just a short time, lots of extra staff are needed for the Easter fortnight and late May holiday week.

The centres in the UK require: Group Leaders (over 20 years); instructors for specific activities such as pony trekking, sailing, canoeing, mountain activities etc; instructors for watersports, abseiling, judo, tennis, drama, archery, hockey, American football etc; senior staff (group leaders, instructors, stores, site and administration); mini-motorsports organiser (go-karts, mini-bikes etc); nurses; and support staff (kitchen assistants, drivers, administration assistants etc). Staff who start work before July 1st are paid £35-£40 per week, (after July 1st £25-£30), senior staff anything between £50 per week (nurse) and £200 per week (manager). All positions provide free accommodation and three meals a day. You need to be at least 18 and over 20 to be a group leader or to apply for positions abroad, and must enjoy working as a team and work hard.

Quest Adventure organise adventure holidays for schools and young people in the Lake District, North Devonshire coast, and require a variety of staff: They need: managers (£100/£180 pw), Admin/nurse (£65-/£100 pw), instructors at all levels (£30-£180), chefs (£85/£150), assistant cooks (£55/£75 pw), bar staff, housekeepers, domestics, drivers, group leaders, entertainments officers, and nurses.

PGL Young Adventure Ltd, Personnel Dept, Station St, Ross-on-Wye, HR9 7AH.
Tel: 0989 767833
Quest Adventure, Grosvenor Hall Leisure, Bolnore Rd, Haywards Heath, W Sussex, RH16 4BX. Tel: (0444) 441300

Voluntary Work

GAP Activity Projects arranges for overseas students to work in the UK on an exchange basis (countries involved include: Australia, Canada, Falklands, France, India, Israel, Mexico, Nepal, New Zealand, Pakistan and W Germany – soon to be included the USA, Eastern Europe, Japan and China). School-leavers can spend at least six months in the UK and work in various fields: helping with the sick, handicapped; assisting in schools; farming and helping with conservation; or office work in banks and businesses. They live with a host family who provides board, accommodation and in most cases pocket money.

The closing date for applications is the end of March, interviews begin in December and applicants are recommended to send in their applications during the first term of their final school year.

GAP Activity Projects (GAP) Ltd, 7 King's Rd, Reading, Berks RG1 3AA.
Tel: 0734 594914

Organisations such as The Shaftesbury Society, Mencap, Help the Aged etc often need extra helpers each year for a fortnight to take care of elderly or disabled people when they go on holiday.

The Shaftesbury Society, 2A Amity Grove, Raynes Park, London SW20 OLH.
Tel: 01 946 6635

Workcamps

Most workcamps require that volunteers have had previous experience of workcamps in their own country, and if you want to volunteer abroad it is essential that you gain experience in Britain first. They are also an excellent way of making contacts with people from overseas who may be able to offer you help, support or even accommodation in their own country, apart, of course, being worthwhile projects in their own right.

Most of the agencies that organise workcamps abroad also recruit volunteers for camps throughout the UK from Devon to Fair Isle in the far north of Scotland. British volunteers must be aged 17 and over, overseas volunteers must be 18 and over. Workcamps usually run from 2-3 weeks from May to September and volunteers work a 30 to 36 hour week. Board, lodging and insurance are provided but volunteers pay their own travel costs. Work is often manual – decorating, reconstruction, etc as well as social – helping at playschemes, working with handicapped, the elderly etc. Most workcamps require at least a working knowledge of English.

CMP, Bethnal Green, URC, Pott St, London E2 OEF. Tel: 01 729 1877
Quaker International Social Projects, Friends House, Euston Rd, London NW1 2BJ.
Tel: 01 387 3601
IVS (Scotland), St Johns Church, Princes St, Edinburgh EH2 4BJ. Tel: 031 229 7318
IVS (North), 188 Roundhay Rd, Leeds LS8 5PL. Tel: 0532 406 787
IVS (South), Old Hall, East Bergholt, Nr Colchester, Essex CO7 6TQ. Tel: 0206 298 215
ATD Fourth World Movement, 48 Addington Sq, London SE5 7LB. Tel: 01 703 3231

Conservation

There are many opportunities for voluntary conservation work in the UK. In some parts of the country there are steam railways that need volunteers to help maintain the engines and tracks, canals that need clearing and maintaining etc. Offices of the Citizens Advice Bureau may be able to help you get in touch with such organisations.

The National Trust organise week-long Acorn projects, camps and special working holidays throughout England, Wales and N Ireland. Volunteers can work for longer, though the Trust warns against this. Tasks range from dry stone walling in the Peak District to vegetation mapping in Surrey. Volunteers should be reasonably fit and are encouraged to attend independently although two people coming on a project together are accepted. Most Acorn Projects consist of about 14 volunteers ranging in age from about 18 to mid 20s. Facilities can be fairly basic although accommodation is always in buildings such as volunteer hostels, farm houses or village halls. Food is provided, though not on the half day off that all volunteers get each week and volunteers must pay for their own travel expenses and £19 per week to cover board and lodging.

The British Trust for Conservation Volunteers train and equip volunteers to tackle environmental projects ranging from tree planting and woodland management, repairing drystone walls, clearing polluted ponds and choked canals and improving access to the countryside throughout England, Wales and N Ireland. Accommodation and food is provided. They also run a programme of 'Natural Break' conservation working holidays which cost from £27 per week.

Cathedral Camps recruit volunteers to work on projects to preserve, conserve, restore and repair Cathedrals and buildings of great architectural significance. Work involves maintenance, cleaning roof voids, spiral staircases, wall memorials, painting iron railings etc. Volunteers work a 36 hour week, with Saturday afternoon, Sunday and evenings free. Food and self-catering accommodation is provided in Cathedral halls or similar buildings.

You must be aged 16-30 and be willing to do a fairly hard day's work. Camps are held at different Cathedrals for one week from mid-July to early September and cost £25.

National Trust, Volunteer Unit, PO Box 12, Westbury, Wilts BA13 4NA.
Tel: 0373 826302
BTCV, 36 St Mary's St, Wallingford, Oxfordshire OX10 0EU.
Tel: 0491 39766
Cathedral Camps, Manor House, High Birstwith, Harrogate, N Yorkshire HG3 2LG.
Tel: 0423 770385

Archaeology

The Council for British Archaeology publishes the 'British Archaeological News' for members six times a year which carries advance information about sites in Britain where volunteers are needed, with brief details of the location and nature of the site, accommodation, dates etc. The majority of digs occur in the summer months, and there is usually a minimum age limit of 16 years.

The Archaeological Insitute of America gives details of digs in Britain in its Fieldwork Bulletin and Earthwatch have details of their expeditions in Britain, particularly in Scotland and Ireland in their magazine 'Earthwatch'.

Council for British Archaeology, The King's Manor, York YOI 2EP. Tel: 0904 433925

Archaeological Institute of America, 675 Commonwealth Ave, Boston, MA 02215. Tel: 617 353 9361
Earthwatch Expeditions Inc, 680 Mount Auburn St, PO Box 403, Watertown, MA 02272

UNITED STATES
Main Language: American
Currency: U.S Dollar
Capital: Washington
Exports: Machinery, Vehicles, Aircraft, Cereals, Chemical products, Iron and steel, Non-ferrous metals, Soya, Metals, Coal, Textiles.
Climate South – Subtropical, hot, humid summers; mild winters
Central – Hot summers; shorter winters,
North – Long, severe winters; short late Springs; warm, humid summers; long warm autumn until October

Entry Requirements
United States Embassy, 24 Grosvenor Square, London W1A 1AE. Tel: 01 499 7010
US Embassy, Visa Branch, 5 Upper Grosvenor St, W1A 2JB. Tel: 01 499 3443

United States Travel & Tourism Administration, 22 Sackville St, London W1X 2EA.

Visas

Most British, French, West German, Italian, Dutch, Swedish, Swiss and Japanese travellers to the US no longer need visas. In order to meet the requirements for visa-free travel the traveller must be:

- a citizen of one of the countries named above, travelling on an unexpired national (or EC) passport;
- travelling for business, pleasure or transit only;
- staying in the US for 90 days or less;
- holding a return or onward ticket;
- in possession of a completed visa waiver form 1-791, obtainable from your travel agent or airline;
- entering the US aboard an air or sea carrier that has agreed to participate in the programme. This precludes initial entry by land from Canada or Mexico without a visa, although travellers who have entered the US visa-free may, within the 90 day admission period, make side trips to Mexico, Canada, the Caribbean Islands and Bermuda and return visa-free by any mode of transport.

Travellers without visas must meet the same entry requirements as travellers with visas. All travellers may be asked for evidence of their ability to finance their planned stay in the US and of their intent to depart the US after that stay. Travellers without visas may be asked to show their return or onward tickets which may not terminate in Mexico, Canada, Bermuda or the Caribbean Islands unless the travellers are residents of these areas.

(The Visa Branch at the US Embassy has a list of participating carriers for travel without a visa).

Work Permits
Anyone who is not a US citizen wishing to work in the US must first obtain an immigrant visa, whether you wish to find temporary or part-time jobs or whether you wish to work and/or live there permanently. Persons entering the US as a tourist or business visitor are not permitted to work while there.

An exception is made to the immigration visa requirement for anyone who:

- is being transferred by his current employer to a specific technical or executive job with the same firm or subsidiary;
- is to perform a prearranged professional or highly skilled job for a temporary period, provided such employment has been approved in advance by the US immigration authorities;
- is taking up a prearranged appointment under an officially approved programme sponsored by an educational or other non-profit institution as a teacher, professor, researcher, lecturer etc for a temporary period.

If you are going to the US on an exchange programme you should obtain an exchange visitor visa. This will permit you to carry out the work, training or research that you have in mind.

However, in spite of this formal requirement many people do successfully work and travel in the USA taking 'unofficial' work, and provided that you exercise reasonable discretion there is no reason why you should not have a very enjoyable and rewarding time, as thousands of others do.

If you enter the USA without a visa you will be permitted to stay for a maximum of 90 days. With a visa (class B-2 Visitor for Pleasure) you may be permitted to stay for up to 6 months. The period of time you are allowed to stay will depend on the examining immigration office, what his impression is of you, and what you say to him. For example, one recent traveller had a 6-month date stamped in his passport without even being asked how long he wanted to stay, another was given a quizzing when he requested 3 weeks and had a return ticket.

Remember that a visa is only a permit to present yourself at a port of entry and it is up to the examining immigration officer at that time to decide how long you can enter for, depending on his or her assessment (which will depend on the mood they are in that day). A lot of confusion surrounds visas and from past experience we know that a lot of people do not understand the difference between 'single' and 'multiple' entry, one of which will appear on the visa stamped in your passport.

A visa valid for a single entry can, obviously, be used once only, and another visa has to be obtained for further visits: one valid for multiple entry can be used as many times as the holder wishes within the period of validity. A visa may have a date stamped on it by which time it must be used, or it may have the word 'indefinitely' on it. This simply means that it is valid for the length of the passport and NOT as some people seem to think, valid for an indefinite stay IN the USA.

Having obtained your visa you are past stage one, the preliminary examination to make sure that you have not, basically, given some daft answers to a few basic questions. The second examination comes at the port of entry when you will be asked the purpose of your trip and how long you wish to remain in the States. Now normally this takes but a minute or so, provided that you have a return ticket and will be staying for what if considered a normal holiday period, ie 2-4 weeks or so. If you have no return ticket, limited funds, and request a stay of six months don't be surprised if you are given something of a quizzing. The examining officer will naturally have good reason to be suspicious of your motives of entering the USA, and how you intend supporting yourself.

It really is simply a matter of common sense. Regarding what is considered adequate funds for the duration of your stay, there is no set figure because a person can live on $5 a day if he is camping or staying with friends and has simple needs and desires, like hiking and fishing. On the other hand, someone staying in NYC with no friends or relatives there, and who likes wining and dining can hardly live on 10 or 20 times that. A basic figure for a budget stay would be not less that $20 a day.

Some people are, of course, refused entry or allowed to stay for a shorter period than requested, but these are generally the people who are outwardly stupid in their approach, and represent the tiniest fraction of one per cent.

One last point, don't take a copy of a book that implies you may be going to do something you shouldn't, or any documents or letters (or newspaper advertisements of jobs) that may give this impression.

Consider the example in Chapter 8.

Permanent Residence

Anyone who is not a US citizen and who wishes to live and/or work in the US indefinitely or permanently must obtain an immigrant visa. Once the holder of an immigrant visa has been admitted into the US he may remain there for as long or short a period as he wishes and may take up employment without obtaining an additional permit from the immigration authorities. After residing in the US for five years, he may apply for naturalisation as a citizen of the US.

While the number of immigrant visas issued each year in most categories is limited by United States immigration law, the law exempts certain categories of persons from the numerical limitation on immigrants entering the US. The following immigrants do not need a visa number before a visa may be issued:

- the husband or wife of a United States citizen;
- the children (under 21) of a United States citizen, includig stepchildren, legally adopted children and orphans to be adopted legally in the US;
- the parent of a United States citizen child if that child is 21 years of age or over;
- certain aliens who previously immigrated to the US and are returning to resume their unrelinquished permanent residence there;
- certain former United States citizens;
- certain ministers of religion;
- certain employees and former employees of the US government who have had 15 years or more of US government service.

The following immigrants need a visa number but are eligible for preference status in the allotment of a number:

- first preference – the unmarried son or daughter (over 21) of a US citizen;
- second preference – the spouse or unmarried son or daughter (over 21) of a permanent resident alien of the United States;
- third preference – persons who are members of a profession or have an exceptional ability in the sciences or arts and who have a prearranged job to take up in the US;
- fourth preference – the married son or daughter (over 21) of a US citizen;
- fifth preference – the brother or sister of a US citizen provided that citizen is at least 21 years of age;
- sixth preference – persons with a prearranged job in the US who are not qualified for third preference status.

Anyone not eligible for immigrant classification in a category exempt from the numerical limitation on immigrants entering the US or for a preference status must be considered as a nonpreference immigrant. Nonpreference immigrants intending to seek gainful employment in the US must have a prearranged job and a Labor Certification, ie work permit, to be registered on the waiting list of intending immigrants in the nonpreference category. The law grants certain exemptions to this Labor Certification requirement to persons such as the elderly and retired, and immigrants investing substantially in a business in the US, etc.

Under US law anyone born in the US may, with a very few exceptions, have a claim to US citizenship regardless of how short a time he/she may have spent in the US or of any other nationality he/she may possess. Moreover, anyone born outside the US to a father or mother who was born in the US or otherwise held US citizenship may also have a claim to US citizenship even though he/she may have never lived in the US. A US citizen does not need a visa for travel to the US. If you believe you have a claim to US citizenship you should write to the Passport and Citizenship Branch of the Embassy, giving your full name, date and place of birth, and the grounds on which you believe you may have a claim to citizenship and requesting that a determination concerning your citizenship status be made before you apply for a visa.

For those interested in making their home in the USA and finding the easiest, and cheapest, way through the 'red tape' there is an excellent book on the market, wirtten by a US Immigration Lawyer.

'Getting into America', by Howard Deutch, published by Coronet Books, £6.95 (ISBN 0 340 36935 3)

Travel
There are many cheap fares to the US offered by the discount travel agencies and airlines such as Virgin Atlantic and the Eastern European and Middle Eastern airlines. (See Chapter 4 for addresses of these agencies). Look at the small ads section of the national papers and London Evening Standard for latest bargain prices. If you are not pressed for time, try going 'stand-by'. Students are entitled to reduced airfares on many flights.

For long distance travel getting around by bus and even by air (along east and west coasts and from coast to coast) is generally cheaper than train travel. You can get special passes on bus and trains. Greyhound offer a 7, 15 or 30 day Ameripass which entitles you to unlimited travel in the US. You can break your journey for as long as you wish and continue your trip, provided you complete your travel during the time for which your ticket is valid. You can buy the tickets either through your UK travel shop, Greyhound offices, or from CIEE Travel Centres. Amtrak also issue 45 day rail passes which you have to purchase before you go (information from the US Travel & Tourist Administration).

Some travel companies such as 'Goway' offer active adventure holidays in the US and Canada. They organise overland camping tours, activity holidays, for example wilderness canoe trips or you can combine the two. Some trips are restricted to those aged between 18 and 35, other trips are open to anybody. Trips last from 7-70 days.

Green Tortoise offer an excellent way of crossing the USA and seeing some of the sights on the way at a realistic cost. East and West bound 14 day trips cost $279. If you took a cheap fare to New York and travelled to San Francisco with Green Tortoise it would cost little more than the direct flight. They also offer trips round the southern national parks, tours of northern California, trips to the Grand Canyon and Yosemite National Park as well as expeditions to Alaska and Mexico. In the winter there are trips to the Mardi Gras in New Orleans, sailing and windsurfing trips to Baja, and expeditions to mainland Mexico and Belize. As well as the fare, you have to pay a food fund ($71-$81) which includes the cookouts and Park entrance fees. Rafting is optional and costs about $10-$20.

Greyhound International, 14-16 Cockspur St, London SW1. Tel: 01 839 5591
Greyhound Lines Inc, 901 Main St, Suite 2500, Dallas, Texas 75202
Greyhound Lines Inc, New York, 625 Eight Ave. Tel: 212 971 0492
US Travel & Tourist Administration, 22 Sackville St, London W1X 2EA.
Tel: 01 439 7433
Amtrak, reservations and information, USA. Tel: 1-800 872 7245 (toll-free)
Goway Adventure, c/oTravel Cuts, 295a Regent St, London W1R 7YA.
Tel: 01 637 3161
Green Tortoise Adventure Travel, PO Box 24459, San Francisco, CA 94124
CIEE/Council Travel Services, 205 East 42nd St, New York, NY 10017. Tel: (212) 661 1414

Accommodation
American Youth Hostels Inc is the US affiliate of the International Youth Hostel Federation. Members of any hostelling association affiliated with the IYHF are welcomed at AYH hostels in the US. Listings for US hostels are available from the YHA in the UK. If you are not a youth hostel member in the UK you can purchase an International Guest Membership upon arrival in

the US. Although most hostels have dormitory-style accommodation with separate facilities for men and women, some hostels also have special family accommodation which can be reserved in advance.

There are also plenty of YMCAs (the Ys). The CIEE education council has offices throughout the US and can give you information on cheap student accommodation. They publish 'Where to Stay USA (From $3 to $30 a night)' which is available from any CIEE/Council Travel office. Students can get discounts on accommodation in New York, Los Angeles and San Francisco. In New York students can stay at the International Student Centre and sometimes at New York University. Other cities, too, often have accommodation in the student residences of the universities.

The American Camping Association publishes a booklet 'Guide to Accredited Camps' which lists all the accredited campsites in America, Canada and Puerto Rico, with information on the activities, fees, facilities, and operating season of each camp.

American Youth Hostels Inc, PO Box 37613, Washington DC 20013-7613
Tel: (202) 783 6161
YHA, Trevelyan House, 8 St Stephen's Hill, St Albans, Herts AL1 2DY.
YMCA, 356 West 34th St, 3rd floor, New York, NY 10001
International Student Centre, 500 Riverside Drive, New York City
CIEE/Council Travel Services, 205 East 42nd St, New York, NY 10017
Tel: (212) 661 1414
New York University, 54 Washington Sq, New York City
American Camping Association, Bradford Woods, 5000 State Road 67 North, Martinsville, IN 46151-7902. Tel: 317/342-8456

Working Holidays

Job Advertising
Joshua B Powers, 46 Keyes House, Dolphine Sq, London SW1V 3NA (agents for New York Times and can place advertisements)

The 'Ayer Directory of Publications' contains a complete list of all US and Canadian newspapers and magazines together with circulation figures, advertising rates etc. Copies are available in the reference section of some main public libraries.

Exchange Visitor Programmes
The Exchange Visitor Programme (EVP) offers one way of being able to work in America. Some AYH Hostels offer work/exchange programmes. Those interested should contact the hostel manager directly. The YMCA sponsors international exchanges of camp counsellors. The Camp America Summer Programme sends many young people to work and teach sports and outdoor pursuits on American children's summer camps each year. By far the largest organisation dealing with EVPs is BUNAC and all applications for a work visa (J-1 visa) have to go through them.

BUNAC (British Universities North America Club)

BUNAC's work/travel programme is jointly administered by its US sponsors, the Council on International Educational Exchange (CIEE), and you must become a member to participate on one of its programmes (£3). Once you have been accepted on one of its three programmes, you then apply through BUNAC for acceptance on the Exchange Visitor Programme and the J-1 work visa. Attendance at an orientation is another compulsory part of the visa application. Once accepted on the EVP, you will be issued with an 1AP 66 form, without which you are not eligible for the work visa J-1. You will then only need to complete it and send it to BUNAC so that your final visa application can be lodged with the American Embassy.

BUNAC offer 3 kinds of programme: Work America; Bunacamp; and KAMP (Kitchen and

Maintenance Programme). Applications to more than one BUNAC programme will not be considered.

Work America: If you are enrolled on a HND or degree level course, are a member of BUNAC and know someone in the USA who can sponsor you or else have arranged a job for yourself before departure (either with a definite offer of a job for the summer or with an indefinite offer of private sponsorship or job, backed up with a substantial amount of funds) you can qualify for a place on this programme. You must also attend a Work America orientation course, prior to applying to the programme as well as on arrival in New York and must produce a certificate saying you have attended. You can take any job, anywhere in the USA (apart from au pair work, camp counselling or medical interning), for as long or short as you like.

The most flexible and independent way of going about it is to apply for Work America on the basis of private sponsorship. All you need is a letter from someone living in the US offering to sponsor you and look after you in an emergency. You also need proof that you have bought at least $500 worth of travellers cheques. Job-hunting in person often results in a more interesting and better paid job than if you obtained a written job offer whilst in the UK.

If you want to arrange your job before you go, you can make use of the Work America Job Directory which is a free listing of employers who have been recommended by previous Work America participants (see para 4 in Working Holidays section for other ways of finding a job).

Preference is given to those with definite offers of employment or sponsorship.

BUNACAMP: This involves working on a children's summer camp as a camp counsellor for at least 9 weeks between mid-June and the end of August. It is open to anyone between the ages of 19.5 and 35 who likes working with children and does not object to hard work and long hours. You must have one or more skills to offer ranging from sports, watersports, music, arts and crafts, science, secretarial, pioneering, entertainments, dance etc. At the end of your work period, you can have time off to go travelling or have a holiday.

You pay a registration fee of £48 which covers: your flight and transport from airport (fare is advanced by BUNAC and recouped by them from your salary at the camp); orientation and training; J-visa; night in hotel/hostel upon arrival in the US; free food and accommodation for 8-9 weeks; and a 520 page BUNAC Moneywise Guide to North America. After the cost of your flight has been deducted you should end up with an in-hand salary of between $360-$420.

KAMP: People working on KAMP (Kitchen and Maintenance Programme) will be employed in the utility areas of a children's summer camp in the USA. This normally involves work in the kitchens, but work in the laundry and outside, on general maintenance is also possible. The jobs include cooking, maintenance both indoors and out (mowing, weeding, building, repairing, plumbing, electrical etc), porter (general cleaning etc), cleaning (toilets and shower areas, mopping floors, kitchen etc), or driving.

Applicants must be current members of BUNAC; be full-time students at a British educational institution studying at HND or degree level; attend a KAMP/BUNACAMP orientation and be available to work at camp as early as possible in June until the last week in August.

You pay a registration fee of £58 and the BUNAC insurance premium (about £70). The camp pays for your air fare (it recoups it directly from your salary), all your board and lodging and a salary. Travel to camp from New York or other port of entry arranged by BUNAC (one way only) will be provided by the camp – you either catch a camp staff bus or they will reimburse your bus fare. Leaving camp at the end of your job is at your own expense and for you to arrange.

BUNAC, 16 Bowling Green Lane, London EC1R OBD. Tel: 01 251 3472
BUNAC, C/O USIT, 19 Aston Quay, Dublin 2. Tel: 778117

YMCA, Fairthorne Manor, Curdridge, Southampton SO3 2GH
Camp America Summer Programme, Dept UT, 37A Queens Gate, London SW7 5HR.

Au Pairs
There are a number of organisations that operate Government approved schemes to recruit and select qualified young people to travel to the USA on an Au Pair Homestay programme for 1 year. Applicants must be aged between 18 and 25, be non-smokers, hold a current GB driving licence, and have relevant child-care experience. You work for a maximum of 45 hours per week, receive free accommodation and food and receive $100 per week as pocket money. In addition, each au pair receives $300 over the 12 month period of the programme, to help with a course of study at a local night school or college. A 13th month can be added to enable Au Pairs to travel and see more of the USA.

Each au pair also receives free medicare and insurance, a free return flight and the back-up of a professional counselling staff in the USA. A 2-4 day orientation session is provided soon after arrival during which time successful applicants will receive detailed training and advice on how to adapt to and get the most out of the programme.

In addition to the year long Au Pair programme there is the Family Companion Summer Programme that operates only during the summer months. You must be at least 18 and available between late June and early September. The Family Companion Summer Programme offers the same type of positions as the au pair programme but the placement is only for ten weeks, and the total pocket money paid will be $300. The ability to drive is not essential but is desirable.

Au Pair in America, 37 Queens Gate, London SW7 5HR. Tel: 01 581 2730
EIL Au Pair, Otesage, Upper Wyche, Malvern, Worcs WR14 4EN. Tel: 0684 562577
Family Companion Summer Programme, Dept UT, 37A Queens Gate, London SW7 5HR

Agriculture
The mainstay of the working traveller is, as in many other places, fruit picking. Fruits of one type or another are grown in almost every state of the USA although major commercial production is confined to mainly California and Florida. Because of the great variation in climatic conditions, harvesting dates vary from one state to another and with quite wide variations sometimes within the same state. In addition to this the actual weather conditions of each year can make for an early or late harvest.

In southern California and throughout Florida, citrus fruit - lemons, limes, oranges etc - are harvested in late October/early November until the middle of the following year. Cherries, peaches, pears, prunes, and apricots tend to be ready for harvesting from late June to August. Apple picking commences in late September and continues through to November in some places. Grapes are harvested in late July/early August. Cherries are grown in Michigan, in particular around The Old Mission Peninsula area around Traverse City where the annual cherry festival is held during July each year. Michigan is also a good state for apple picking. The Okanagan Valley extends south into Washington State where there are plenty of apple orchards.

Many areas have Farm Labour Contractors providing a service to farmers and orchard owners. For some fruits where 'spot' picking is necessary, such contractors tour the orchards and farms each day with a crew working a couple of hours or so in each. In this case, a seven day week might be worked with 10-12 hours in the orchards each day. Pay will tend to be less in this instance. It is better to work directly for the farmer as some of these contractors can be unscrupulous, particularly if they know that any worker does not have the necessary permit. Hourly rates for this type of work are not good if done for any length of time, unless of course there are other benefits to be derived from staying in that particular area.

Many of the smaller orchards provide 'pickers' cabins which are often simple but adequate. These are usually free of charge and with cooking facilities. Some of the larger orchards which provide accommodation can deduct around $50 a week for accommodation and another $50 a week for food. The food is fair at that rate, but simple accommodation should be free. Suspect any orchard where it is not. Smaller orchards are generally the best bet.

The following table gives the principal fruit and and vegetable picking seasons in different parts of the USA.

	(Mar/Apr/May)	(Jun/Jul/Aug)	(Sep/Oct/Nov)	(Dec/Jan/Feb)
West Coast –	Strawberries	Peaches	Apples	
California	Cherries	Peppers	Walnuts	
Oregon		Grapes	Olives	
			Oranges	
Mid West –	Asparagus	Cherries	Potatoes	
Wyoming, Idaho		Tomatoes	Apples	
Nebraska, Iowa			Beetroot	
Kansas, Illinois				
Indiana, Colorado				
New England –		Strawberries	Apples	
New York		Blueberries	Tomatoes	
Massachusetts		Leaf veg		
New Jersey		Aubergines		
Pennsylvania		Zuchinni		
South –	Potatoes	Melons		Oranges
Florida		Tomatoes		Grapefruit
Georgia				Lemons
Alabama				Beans
S Carolina				Cabbage
Tennessee				Celery
				Sweetcorn etc

Tobacco is grown mainly in the areas east of the Mississippi River, as well as in western Missouri. The most active harvesting dates are as follows:

Georgia Jun 20-Aug 15
Kentucky Aug 25-Sep 25 Christian, Todd, Trigg, Calloway
Missouri Aug 25-Sep 15 Platte, Buchanan
North Carolina Jul 10-Sep 15
South Carolina Jul 10-Aug 15 Clarendon, Sumter, Lee
Tennessee Aug 20-Sep 20 Obion, Henry, Weakley
Virginia Aug 10-Sep 25

The International Agricultural Exchange Association operates exchange study tours on farms in Montana, North Dakota, Minnesota or Texas. Applicants should be over 19 and have at least one year's experience in agriculture. They can choose the type of farming they wish to work with (agricultural, agricultural/home management, horticultural or home management) and are placed with selected host families. The IAEA make the travel arrangements on a group basis, and are responsible for obtaining work permits. Trainees are paid realistic wages – take home pay, after deductions for board and lodging and income tax, should be around £80 per week. Participants have to pay their own travel costs and the IAEA administration fee. You should apply at least four months in advance. There are two programmes to the USA – a direct programme lasting 7 months from April to November, and an Around the World Programme which combines Australia and the USA or New Zealand and the USA for 13 months from October to November.

The International Farm Experience Programme organises exchange programmes at Ohio State University and the Univeristy of Minnesota. You must have at least two years' experience and be aged from 18 to 26.

Ohio State University offers three schemes: Scheme A involves a 12 month programme for horticulture and begins in March or June. You will be working in Ohio while attending the University part-time and studying courses of your choice; Scheme B offers twelve months of practical work in agriculture and horticulture anywhere in the US. All trainees begin with an orientaion at Ohio State University. The University also offers a combining scheme whereby you work for six months on one of the large combining crews from Texas to Canada. You spend the winter months working on arable holdings.

The University of Minnesota offers two schemes: the MAST scheme involves an 8-21 month programme of work experience and university tuition for agriculture and horticulture. Programmes start in March, July and November; the PART scheme offers 5-8 months of practical training on farms and is similar to the Ohio State 'B' Scheme.

On all schemes you will be paid a minimum of $3.35 an hour. Board and lodging may be deducted. Costs for tuition on Ohio State 'A' Scheme and Minnesota MAST scheme ar deducted monthly. All participants have to pay a registration fee, travel costs and medical and personal insurance.

If you have your own placement in the US the IFEP are able to obtain your work permit for you. You need to apply at least four months before you want to travel and for a placement on the combining crews apply well in advance of the April start-date.

IAEA, YFC Centre, National Agricultural Centre, Kenilworth, Warwickshire CV8 2LG
IFEP, YFC Centre, National Agricultural Centre, Kenilworth, Warwickshire CV8 2LG

National Parks/Forests and Reserves
Virtually all of the National Parks and Forests employ seasonal workers of one sort or another. A number of the vacancies are available to overseas personnel through the Student Conservation Association. The name is something of a misnomer because you certainly don't have to be a student, nor necessarily young as all applications are viewed on their own merit.

The SCA provides a wonderful opportunity to experience life in the Great American Outdoors for a period of three months (sometimes longer), generally in the summer although some autumn (fall) positions are available. You will work a 40 hour week with accommodation provided in an apartment, trailer (caravan in the Park) or ranger station. Assistance with visas is provided, as well as return travel from port of entry in the USA to place of work, and daily travelling expenses. An allowance is provided in the region of $50 to $100 a week (more in Alaska), together with a uniform allowance if required.

Some tremendously interesting jobs are available, from assisting with the relocation of black bears in the Great Smokey Mountains to mapping and photographing caves along the Buffalo River in over 200 national parks, forests and wildlife refuges throughout the US, including Alaska, Hawaii and the Virgin Islands.

Some examples of the listings in the SCAs programme for 1989 are given over:

"Alaska, Glacier Bay National Park. Glacier bay is a 5,000 square mile wilderness in Southeast Alaska accessible only by boat or aircraft. Duties include: serving as a member of the park structural fire brigade and maintaining fire suppression equipment, 20%; staffing visitor centre and showing park movies on request, 20%; performing resource management duties such as resource monitoring, helping to census seals, otters, and nesting birds and entering bear and wildlife sightings on a computer, 25%; trail and campground clearing and improvement, 15%; serving as a boathand on cruiseship transfers during inclement weather and performing miscellaneous maintenance projects around Bartlett Cove, 20% Require: ability to deal effectively with the public, to work outdoors during inclement weather, and to perform duties with minimal direct supervision. Desire: background in natural sciences."

"Washington, North Cascades National Park. Duties include interpretation of park resources including evening campfire programs, nature walks, informal public contacts, information desk, 30%; campground operation including helping visitors register, answering questions and using the back country permit system, back country patrol, river/lake patrol by whitewater raft, resource management and firefighting. Require: ability to travel and do strenuous work in steep terrain, backpacking skills, ability to work with minimum supervision, good speaking skills. Desire: background in natural science, personal transportation desirable."

"Hawaii, Volcanoes National Park. Duties include assisting ranger with trail maintenance, maintenance of six cabins and shelters and identifying resource deterioration and visitor impacts. Assisting staff with mapping fuels for wildland fire suppression, exotic plant removal, providing logistical support on fire suppression expeditions. Require: Good physical condition, ability to perform duties at altitude, valid driver's license, ability to work with minimal supervision. Desire: Experience with horses, plant identification skills."

The Student Conservation Association Inc., PO box 550, Charlestown, NH 03603.

Other Employment
Fast food restaurants and the like are good places to pick up casual work. Most American cities and towns have 'chains' of these on the roads in and out, mixed in with gas stations, motels etc. There's always the chance of some work even if it is only washing-up for a day or two – there is a very fast turnover of labour at these establishments so your chances are good of picking something up whenever you arrive at a medium size town.

The waterfront is another good place for locating work, whether it be painting on a private yacht or commercial fishing. Wages are highest on the highliners operating out of Alaska (Kodiak, Ketchikan, Petersburg, Chignik) but these jobs are well sought after and you must be in the area at the start of the season. Tuna fishing also offers opportunities out of ports such as San Diego in California, and many ports on the east coast offer fishing opportunities provided that you are persistent enough to get taken on.

At the waterfront, try to make the rounds of all the boats two or even three times a day. Once in the early morning is a good practice, since it shows how sincere you are. As a rule, the professionals are suspicious of outsiders, and the more you show your face around the harbour the more willing they will be to help you. In a smaller town especially, let as many people as possible know you are looking for work on a fishing boat. A hotel clerk, a waitress, a supermarket cashier – any of these may prove valuable contacts. In the evening go to the local bars patronised by fishermen and strike up conversations with those around you. Get to know the harbourmaster – some harbourmaster offices have bulletin boards where you can put up a placard offering your services. Have your most important belongings in a semi-packed state so that you will be ready to leave at almost any time.

The Dude Rancher magazine lists all the 'dude' ranches in Arizona, Arkansas, California,

Colorado, Idaho, Oregon, South Dakota, Texas, Montana, and Wyoming. A Dude Ranch invites guests to live and share the life of the ranch. Some of the ranches are working dude ranches (Type A) and guests may participate in ranch work; some are resort dude ranches (Type C) and offer a variety of activities; and some are just plain dude ranches (Type B) in scenic surroundings. Here is an example of one listing:

"Hunewill Circle H Ranch, California, Type A: A real cattle ranch founded in 1861. Cattle raising always the main industry. 4400 acres – more than 2000 cattle. Horse-back riding, cattle work and all regular ranch activities. Alt. 6500'. Breakfast rides, cookouts, picnics, hiking, swimming, square dancing, good trout fishing, day trip with lunch, auto trips to deserted mining towns, interesting Nevada less than an hour. Yosemite Park near-by – Lake Tahoe near. Appetizing food, with our own aged beef. 40 guest capacity. Guest season May 1 to Sept 20. Reached by major airlines to Reno, then rental car or bus. Greyhound daily from either Los Angeles or San Francisco. Airfield at Bridgeport for private places where ranch car meets you. Call or write ...."

Some of the ranches take on extra workers in the holiday season. If working on a ranch appeals contact some dude ranches and offer your services.

The Dude Ranchers' Assn, Box 471, LaPorte, Colorado 80535. Tel: (303) 493 7623

Interesting jobs will crop up no matter where you are – this is one of the great things about working and travelling in the USA. Jobs can be anything from being a film extra in Hollywood (simply ask around as to where films are being made and hang about where you can be seen) to helping with a rattlesnake round-up. If you see building work along the roadside, then stop and ask if they need help for a day; if you see trucks being hand-loaded with lumber or whatever, then see if you can get an hour's work there. If you travel the simple and cheap way it is surprising how far you can go on just the money from a day's work here and there.

Voluntary Work

There are a great many opportunities for voluntary work in the United States. Volunteers are needed to help with community work, building, conservation etc. Applicants should be between 18 and 35 and should have previous workcamp experience, be fit and prepared to work hard. Workcamps generally last from 2-3 weeks from June to August. Food and accommodation is provided but volunteers have to pay their own travel costs.

British citizens who wish to do voluntary work in the US should contact one of the following organisations:

Christian Movement for Peace, Bethnal Green URC, Pott St, London E2 2EF.
Tel: 01 729 7985
United Nations Association, International Youth Service, Welsh Centre for International Affairs, Temple of Peace, Cathays Park, Cardiff CF1 3AP.
Tel: Cardiff 223088
International Voluntary Service, 162 Upper New Walk, Leicester LE1 7QA.

There are also many organisations in America that recruit volunteers both from America and internationally for work in underdeveloped/developing countries. Some organisations only recruit US citizens for such volunteer work.

US Citizens Only

The Peace Corps need men and women with three to five years of work experience and/or a college degree. You must be at least 18 although few applicants under 21 have the skills and experience to qualify. Specifically, the Peace Corps needs the following kinds of volunteers: agriculturalists, natural resource managers, teacher trainers, liberal arts generalists, fishery specialists, engineers, business people, nurses and other health professions, home economists, skilled trades people, and teachers. Volunteers are at present serving in 57 different countries throughout the world from the Eastern Caribbean to Central and South America, Africa, the Pacific Islands, South East Asia and the Middle East. Most Peace Corps assignments are for two years and begin after the successful completion of training (8-14 weeks in host country). Volunteers are expected to speak the language of the people with whom they live and work, so language instruction is intense during this period. A living allowance in the local currency is issued to cover housing, food, essentials and a little spending money. When service is completed, volunteers receive a $200 readjustment allowance for every month served.

Volunteers in Service to America (VISTA) is a full-time volunteer programme for people of all ages and backgrounds who are assigned to local sponsors and who work and live among the poor. VISTA is a programme of ACTION, the US Government umbrella organisation for voluntary service.

Under the umbrella of ACTION there are several part-time volunteer programmes for example, Foster Grandparent Programme, Young Volunteers in ACTION, Senior Companion Programme and the National Center for Service Learning which promotes student participation in projects that provide assistance in the areas of housing, food and nutrition, literacy and drug abuse.

Internships in the US, although primarily a career training programme, can also take place in voluntary organisations concerned with civil liberties, education, nutrition and health. 'Internships' published by Writer's Digest Books concentrates on the possibilities in the US. Los Ninos Internship Programme, for example, involves direct contact with third world poverty through direct assistance, development and education projects in orphanages, communities and schools in Mexico. (Los Ninos also organise volunteer programmes and work/study programmes).

For a full list, as well as detailed information, of voluntary organisations in the USA together with information on international workcamps for US citizens to apply to, contact CIEE in New York.

Peace Corps, Recruitment Office, 806 Connecticut Ave, NW, Washington DC 20526
Tel: (800) 424 8580 (Toll-free)
VISTA, c/o ACTION, 806 Connecticut Ave NW, Washington DC 20525.
Tel: (202) 634 9135
'Internships', Writer's Digest Books, 1507 Dana Ave, Cincinnati, Ohio
Los Ninos, 1330 Continental St, San Ysidro, California 92073.
Tel: (619) 690 1437
CIEE, 205 East 42nd St, New York, NY 10017
Benedictine Lay Volunteer Program, Mother of God Priory, RR #3, Box 254,
Watertown, South Dakota 57201. Tel: (605) 886 6777

For UK citizens
VFP International Workcamps produce an International Workcamp Directory with details of workcamps throughout the world. Annual membership is $10. It is a very useful booklet for UK citizens as well as US citizens as it contains information on many American workcamps.

Peace Brigades International have an office in the Netherlands. PBI volunteers provide protective accompaniment for union leaders, human rights and peasant organisations and a watchful presence at demonstrations and in workplaces in Guatemala and El Salvador. They are also involved with peace and human rights education. They are involved in Sri Lanka, South Africa, Costa Rica and Europe.

Amigos de las Americas recruits volunteers each year for one or two months in Mexico, Costa Rica, the Dominican Republic, Brazil, Ecuador and Paraguay. All volunteers must undergo several months of training, either in the US or by correspondence.

The Sioux indian YMCAs organise community work projects in small, remote reservation communities for periods of four to ten weeks in the winter, spring and summer. They also organise summer camps and day camps and need camp counsellors who come from both the USA and overseas.

VFP International Workcamps, 43 Tiffany Rd, Belmont, Vermont 05730.
Tel: (802) 259 2759
Peace Brigades International, 4722 Baltimore Avenue, Philadelphia,
PA 19143. Tel: (215) 724 1464 or 727 0989
Amigos de las Americas, 5618 Star Lane, Houston, Texas 77057
Sioux Indian YMCAs, Box 218, Dupree, South Dakota 57623.
Tel: (605) 365 5232

Conservation

Many of the National Parks recruit volunteers in the summer to maintain and improve the beauty and resources within the state park system. Trail workers are needed for trail construction and maintenance, clerical assistants are needed to provide secretarial services, grounds assistants assist in the care and maintenance of the parks etc. Generally anyone who is in good physical condition (ie able to hike 10/20 miles with a heavy pack), is at least 16 years of age and willing to work hard can be accepted as a volunteer. You should contact individual parks to offer your services or put forward an idea for a project. Generally, some form of housing is provided, either in tents or trailers, as well as tools and camping equipment. Volunteers need to bring boots, a sleeping bag and rain gear. Some of the projects are for US citizens only. Contact the organisations listed below for details of volunteer programmes and lists of individual parks to which you may apply.

Send a couple of 1RCs if outside the US or a couple of stamps to cover postage within the US.

United States Youth Conservation Corps (YCC), US Dept of the Interior, Fish and Wildlife Service, National Park Service, Washington DC 20240
YCC, US Dept of Agriculture, Forest Service, Washington DC 20256
Volunteers for Outdoor Colorado, 1410 Grant St B105, Denver, Colorado 80203,
Tel: (303) 830 7792
Colorado Trail Foundation, PO Box 260876, Lakewood, Colorado 80226-0876
Nevada Division of State Parks, 201 South Fall St, Room 119, Carson City,
Nevada 89710. Tel: (702) 885 4384
Forest Service Volunteer or Wilderness Volunteer, Rocky Mountain Region,
11177 W 8th Ave, PO Box 25127, Lakewood, Colorado 80225. Tel: (303) 236 9624
Student Conservation Association Inc, PO Box 550, Charlestown, NH 03603.
Tel: (603) 826 5741
Dept of Natural Resources, 500 Lafayette Rd, St Paul, Minnesota 55155-40
Tel: (612) 296 6157
Coastal Resources Centre, Graduate School of Oceanography, The Univeristy of Rhode Island,
Narrangansett, RI 02882. Tel (401) 792 6224
Foundation for Field Research, 787 South Grade Rd, PO Box 2010, Alpine,
California 92001. Tel: (619) 445 9264
Human Resource Programs, Personnel Management, USDA – Forest Service,
Federal Building, PO Box 7669, Missoula, MT 59807. Tel: (406) 329 3194
Volunteer Program, DNR (Dept of Natural Resources) Personnel Division,
Box 30028, Lansing, MI 48909
New Mexico State Parks Volunteer Program, New Mexico Energy, Minerals & Natural Resources
Dept, PO Box 1147, Santa Fe, New Mexico 87504.
Tel: 827 7465
Appalachian Trail Conference, PO Box 738, Blacksburg, Virginia 24060. Tel: (703) 552 1784
Appalachian Mountain Club Program, Pinkham Notch Camp, Box 298, Gorham,
NH 03581
Green Mountain Club Inc, PO Box 889, 43 State St, Montpelier, Vermont 05602.
Tel: (802) 223 3463
Volunteer Coordinator, Division of Parks & Recreation, Fountain Sq C-1,
Columbus, OH 43224. Tel: (614) 265 6549

California Conservation Corps, 1530 Capitol Ave, Sacramento, CA 95814-9990
Tel: (916) 445 8183
SERVE/Maine Program, Dept of Conservation, State House Station #22, Augusta,
Maine 04333. Tel: (207) 289 4945
National Audubon Society, 950 Third Ave, New York, NY 10022
Sierra Club Hawaii Chapter, 1100 Alakea St, Rm 330, Honolulu, Hawaii 96813.
Tel: (808) 538 6616
Earthwatch Expeditions Inc, 680 Mount Auburn Stm PO Box 403, Watertown,
MA 02272. Tel: (617) 926 8200

Archaeology

The Archaeological Institute of America in its Fieldwork Bulletin publishes details of digs from
Alaska to New Mexico that require volunteers. Earthwatch Magazine also contains information
of expeditions throughout the USA, not only concerned with archaeology but also with ecology,
biology, botany, geology, marine ecology, ornithology etc.

Archaeological Institute of America, 675 Commonwealth Ave, Boston,
MA 02215. Tel: (617) 353 9361
Earthwatch Expeditions Inc, 680 Mount Auburn St, PO Box 403, Watertown,
MA 02272. Tel: (617) 926 8200

USSR

Main Language: Russian
Currency: Rouble
Capital: Moscow
Exports: Machinery, Iron and steel, Crude petroleum, Non-ferrous metals, Petroleum products,
Sawnwood, Cotton, Vehicles.
Climate: Winter: V cold, -15°C to -45°C
Summer: warm/hot 15°C-26°C

Entry Requirements

USSR Consulate, 5 Kensington Palace Gardens, London W8 4QS. Tel: 01 229 3215
Intourist Moscow, 292 Regent St, London W1R 6QL. Tel: 01 631 1252

Visas

Visitors to the USSR need a visa and a full British passport. You also need evidence that your
tourist itinerary has been approved by one of the State travel agencies, Intourist or Sputnik.

Work Permits

You can only be given a work permit when you have been accepted by a Soviet school, university
or company on an exchange basis.

Permanent Residence

To emigrate to the Soviet Union it is necessary to apply through the consular department at the
Soviet Embassy in London.

Travel

All travel arrangements must be organised through one of the two state travel agencies, Sputnik
or Intourist. In any case, travelling independently to the USSR is very expensive. Accommodation
is also much more expensive as foreigners have to stay in 3 or 4 star hotels and pay extra for
meals. Booking a tour lets you stay in much cheaper places and you don't have to stay with the
tour group. You can wander around on your own within a 25 kilometre radius of the city you're
visiting and perhaps join the tours that interest you and eat the occasional official meal.

Exodus organise a Trans Mongolian Railway trip which flies to Peking and then goes to London by train through China, Mongolia and Russia. It takes 19 days and costs approximately £1790.

Intourist Moscow Ltd, 292 Regent St, London W1. Tel: 01 631 1252
Sputnik (Student Travel Bureau), 15 Kosygin St, 117946 Moscow.
Tel: 9398201
Exodus Expeditions, 9 Weir Rd, London SW12 OLT. Tel: 01 675 7996

Accommodation
Accommodation is included in the price of a tour. As soon as you arrive in the Soviet Union, either independently or as a group, by train or by plane, you are met by a representative from Sputnik or Intourist who will escort you to your hotel and give you a programme of your meals and the tours planned.

Working Holidays
Apart from arranging an exchange scheme through your university/college or company (contact the British Council for information), there are no opportunities for casual work in Russia. On arrival you must fill in a money and valuables declaration form, and on the way out account for everything you have spent (remember to keep receipts of goods bought and money changed). Customs can be quite thorough especially at the smaller departure points. If you try and leave the country with more money than you brought in, it will be confiscated.

If you want to augment your travelling money while you are there, audio and video cassettes are popular, but make sure you spend all the money you make in the Soviet Union before you leave.

Teaching
The Central Bureau administers a scheme for the interchange of qualified, experienced teachers of Modern Languages and related subjects for 3 weeks, 6 weeks, one term or one year with the Soviet Union.

Central Bureau, Seymour Mews House, Seymour Mews, London W1H 9PE.
Tel: 01 486 5101

Voluntary Work
IVS arranges placements on international workcamps in the Soviet Union. Recently work has involved conservation work at a nature reserve south of Moscow, and agricultural work at Kalinin. Volunteers work a 4 hour day for 1-2 weeks from June to August and attend study programmes in the afternoons as well as going on study visits to Moscow, Vilnius and Kiev. Volunteers must be 18 or over and have previous workcamp experience, preferably in an Eastern European country. Food, accommodation and insurance is provided, but volunteers must pay for their own travel.

IVS, 162 Upper New Walk, Leicester LE1 7QA. Tel: 0533 549430

VENEZUELA
Main Language: Spanish
Currency: Bolivar
Capital: Caracas
Exports: Crude petroleum, Petroleum products, Iron ore, Coffee.
Climate: Hot throughout year, 25°C , cooler in mountains
Wet season: May-Dec (Apr-Oct: heavy rains in llanos of
Orinoco
Dry season: Dec-Apr

Entry requirements
Venezuelan Embassy, Consular Section, 56 Grafton Way, London W1P 5LB.
Tel: 01 387 6727

Visas
British subjects and nationals of other countries can obtain an entry tourist card for a period of sixty days from authorised airlines the traveller is flying with to Venezuela.

British subjects and nationals of other countries can obtain a tourist visa for a period of up to one year if they are in possession of:
- a passport valid for a minimum period of six months;
- letter of introduction from the applicant's firm and bank;
- a return or onward ticket;
- one application form completed and signed;
- consular fee, approx £7

Work Permits
Before a working visa can be issued, authorisation from the Venezuelan Ministry of Internal Affairs is needed. This authorisation must be requested by the employer in Venezuela. Once granted and received at the Consular Section in London the visa can be issued.

Permanent Residence
For information on permanent residence, contact the Venezuelan Embassy.

Travel
Venezuela is one of the cheapest Latin American countries to fly to from the UK. Its national airline, Viasa, is used by many of the travel companies that offer tours of Latin America.

Venezuela is bordered to the north by the Caribbean, to the east by Guyana and the Atlantic Ocean, to the south by Brazil, and to the west and southwest by Colombia. Many travellers save up money in the US and come overland into Venezuela hitching or by bus.

There are no international rail links into Venezuela and only one railway link between Barquisimeto and Puerto Cabello. Road access is from Colombia (Barranquilla and Medellin) to Maracaibo and the Amazon territory of Brazie (Manaus) to Caracas. The principal Venezuelan ports are La Guaira, Puerto Cabello, Maracaibo, Guanta, Porlamar and Ciudad Bolivar. From the US there are ships that sail to Venezuela. Ships also sail from Amsterdam, France and Spain.

Within Venezuela, the Avensa Air Pass gives tourists 4,7 or 21 days unlimited air travel. Students can get discounts of between 30% (with reservations) and 50% (standby) on Aeropostal domestic flights. Caracas has an inexpensive metro system. Conventional bus services have deteriorated, and 'Por Puestos' (shared taxis) are common. These are operated by minibus companies and are the main form of public transport in Caracas and major cities. Students can get 50% reductions on long distance domestic buses.

If you are planning your own expedition, the Royal Geographical Society Expedition Advisory Centre will reply to requests from individuals as well as providing information and training for scientific expeditions. The centre offers regularly updated fact sheet for each of the Latin American countries which give addresses and contacts for further advice, and information on visas, climate etc. The centre keeps reports of past expeditions, a register of future expeditions and lists of suppliers.

There are a number of expeditions and overland tours that take in Venezuela on the itinerary. The following travel companies specialise in such holidays:

Journey Latin America, 16 Devonshire Road, London W4 2HD, Tel: 01 747 3108

Encounter Overland, 267 Old Brompton Road, London SW5, Tel: 01 370 6845
Explore Worldwide Ltd, 7 High Street, Aldershot, Hants GU11 1BH,
Tel: 0252 319448
Twickers World, 22 Church Street, Twickenham TW1 3NW, Tel: 01 892 7606/8164
Bales Tours Ltd, Bales House, Barrington Road, Dorking, Surrey RH4 3EJ,
Tel: 0306 885991
Dragoman, 10 Riverside, Framlingham, Suffolk IP13 9AG, Tel: 0728 724184
Exodus Expeditions, 9 Weir Road, London SW12 0LT, Tel: 01 675 7996
The Royal Geographical Society Expedition Advisory Centre, Information Officer, 1 Kensington
Gore, London SW7 2AR, Tel: 01 581 2057
ONTEJ (Student Travel Bureau), Parque Central, Av Lecuna, Edf Catuche,
Nivel Bolivar, Ofic 37, PO Box 17696, Caracas 1015-A. Tel: 5733722

Accommodation
Local tourist offices in Venezuela can provide a 'Guia Turistica de Caracas Litoral y Venezuela',
which contains useful information on accommodation, travel, etc. Hotels outside Caracas are
cheaper. Camping is possible on beaches, on the islands, in the Llanos or in the mountains though
there are no special campsites as such and no good facilities for campers.

Working Holidays

Job Advertising
Media Universal Services, 34-35 Skylines, Lime Harbour, Docklands,
London E14 9TA, Tel: 01 538 5505
Joshua Powers Ltd, 46 Keys House, Dolphin Square, London SW1. Tel: 01 834 5566

Teaching English
The British Council recruits a limited number of teachers, lecturers, administrators and
educationalists to work in Latin America for periods of 1-3 years. British Council branches
in Latin America may have addresses of other language schools where English is taught.

Some international language schools with bases in Britain also have branches in Venezuala, eg
Berlitz. You may also be able to find work as a private tutor especially in the large cities, although
well established teachers already on the spot will have a great advantage over newcomers.

British Council, Overseas Educational Appointment Dept, 65 Davis Street, London W1Y 2AA,
Tel: 01 930 8466
British Council, 10 Spring Gardens, London SW1 (for branches in Latin America)
Berlitz, Wells House, 79 Wells Street, London W1A 3BZ
Jose Alvarino, Latin American Division, Berlitz Language Centre, Ejercito Nacional No 530
1er Piso, Col Polanco 11550, Mexico DF (for full-time teaching posts available in some Latin
American countries)

Expedition Leaders/Drivers
Many overland tour companies require guides and drivers for their expeditions throughout South
America. Contact any of the companies listed in the travel section offering your services,
especially if you have a HGV or PSV licence.

Voluntary Work
There are no workcamps in Venezuala. The main demand is for long term volunteer work
(minimum of 2 years) in the fields of engineering and technical subjects as well as health and
agriculture.

The co-ordinating Committee for International Voluntary Service, UNESCO has over 100 member organisations engaged in volunteer work, some of which are involved in Latin America. 'Workcamp Organisers', published by CCIVS contains the addresses of several short-term voluntary service organisations in Latin America providing information on the activities, types of work and financial condition of the camps. The commitee will reply to requests for information, and on receipt of 4 IRCs will send information sheets on long and medium term voluntary service.

Co-ordinating Committee for International Voluntary Service, UNESCO, 1 rue Miollis, 75015 Paris, France

YUGOSLAVIA
Main Language: Croatian, Serbian
Currency: Yugoslavian Dinar
Capital: Belgrade
Exports: Machinery, Non-ferrous metals, Ships and boats, Clothing, Meat, Textile, Iron and steel, Shoes.
Climate: Summer – 25°C (on coasts), 15°C-25°C (uplands)
Winter – Rain and snow with sub-zero temperatures.

Entry Requirements
Yugoslav Embassy, Consular Section, 7 Lexham Gardens, London W8 5JU.
Tel: 01 370 6105

Yugoslav National Tourist Office, 143 Regent St, London W1R 8AE.
Tel: 01 734 5243

Visas
British subjects holding a valid full British passport or British Visitor's Passports can visit Yugoslavia without a visa for up to 90 days. If you intend to stay longer than 90 days, the necessary permission should be obtained from the local authorities within 7 days of arrival.

Work Permits
There appear to be no restrictions on finding temporary or seasonal work in Yugoslavia though the Embassy does point out that the lack of knowledge of any of the Yugoslav languages makes finding a job very difficult.

Permanent Residence
Yugoslavia is not a country of immigration. For information on permanent residence contact the Yugoslav Embassy.

Travel
Yugoslavia is rapidly developing its tourist industry and some of the discount travel companies offer cheap flights to Yugoslavia (see Chapter 4). Eurotrain offer up to 50% discount on full rail fares to Yugoslavia for those under 26. Contact Victoria Coach Station for information on bus travel.

Holders of International Union of Student cards (IUS) are entitled to special fares on train journeys originating in Belgrade to Eastern European countries.

The Yugoslav National Tourist Office produce a booklet 'Yugoslavia – Travel Information' which gives details of travel, accommodation, events, etc.

Eurotrain, 52 Grosvenor Gardens, London SW1. Tel: 01 730 3402

Victoria Coach Station, 164 Buckingham Palace Rd, London SW1. Tel: 01 730 0202
Yugoslav National Tourist Office, 143 Regent St, London W1R 8AE.
Tel: 01 734 5243
Yugotours-NAROM (Student Travel Bureau), Djure Djakovica 31, 11000 Belgrade.
Tel: (011) 764622

Accommodation
Students can get a 10% discount at Genex Hotels. The 'Sleep Cheap Guide to Europe' published by ISTC, available from student travel offices, contains information on accommodation in Yugoslavia. Contact also the Yugoslav Tourist Office.

Working Holidays
It is not easy to find employment in Yugoslavia; many Yugoslavians themselves work in other Western European countries to earn better wages, and the lack of knowledge of the language makes it even more difficult.

However, you may contact the local employment bureaus or tourist associations, which might be able to help you find temporary or seasonal work. The Adriatic coastline between Pula in the North West and Dubrovnik in the South East has many resorts where you may be able to find work in the tourist industry. You may be able to find work on private yachts as crew or cook.

Some camping holiday companies offer camping holidays in Yugoslavia and need couriers, children's couriers, watersports instructors and site supervisors to erect and dismantle tents at the beginning and end of the season. Wages are generally around £75 and transport and accommodation is provided.

Sunsail operates flotilla sailing holidays in Yugoslavia and need experienced skippers, hostesses to run the social side of the trips, and mechanic bosuns with previous diesel experience to service/maintain the engines on the flotilla yachts. Wages are from £80 per week, together with accommodation on their own pilot yacht and flights to and from the UK.

Canvas Holidays Ltd, Bull Plain, Hertford, Herts SG14 1DY. Tel: 0992 553535
Eurocamp, Edmundson House, Tatton St, Knutsford, Cheshire WA16 6BG.
Sunsail, The Port House, Port Solent, Portsmouth, Hants PO6 4TH.
Tel: 0705 219847

Voluntary Work

Workcamps
There are a number of international workcamps in Yugoslavia. Volunteers must be 18 and over and have previous workcamp experience. They generally work a 40 hour week for 3-4 weeks between July and September. Food, accommodation and medical insurance is provided, but volunteers must pay their own travel costs. The work is generally manual - construction, renovation, etc or concerned with social projects working with disadvantaged children etc.

IVS, 162 Upper New Walk, Leicester LE1 7QA. Tel: 0533 549430
United Nations Association, Welsh Centre for International Affairs, Temple of Peace, Cathays Park, Cardiff CF1 3AP. Tel: Cardiff 223088

ZAMBIA
Main language: English
Capital: Lusaka
Exports: Copper
Climate: Hot in summer - Jan - 21°C,
Cooler in winter - Jul 16°C

Entry Requirements
Zambia High Commission, Zambia House, 2 Palace Gate, London W8.
Tel: 01 589 6655

Visas
Holders of a British passport do not need a visa to enter Zambia for up to 3 months. If you wish to extend your stay you must apply to the Chief Immigration Officer in Lusaka. On entry you must show you have sufficient funds for your stay in Zambia and have a valid cholera, yellow fever and smallpox certificate.

Work Permits
An employer in Zambia must apply for a work permit on your behalf.
Tourists are not permitted to engage in employment in Zambia.

Travel
Many of the discount travel companies offer cheap fares to Lusaka. Zambia is a landlocked country in southern-central Africa and shares borders with Zaire, Angola, Botswana, Mali, Tanzania and Zimbabwe so entering Zambia overland is easy (except possibly from Angola). There are many expedition travel companies that organise overland trips that include Zambia on the itinerary.

Guerba Expeditions Ltd, Dept TF, 101 Eden Vale Rd, Westbury, Wilts BA13 3YB.
Tel: 0373 826611
Encounter Overland, 267 Old Brompton Rd, London SW5 9JA. Tel: 01 370 6845
Hann Overland, 201-203 Vauxhall Bridge Rd, London SW1V 1ER. Tel: 01 834 7337
Exodus Expeditions, 9 Weir Rd, London SW12 OLT. Tel: 01 675 7996
Trailfinders, 194 Kensington High St, London W8 7RG. Tel: 01 938 3939
STA Travel, 86 Old Brompton Rd, London SW7. Tel: 01 937 9962

Working Holidays
There are no opportunities for casual work in Zambia. It is an extremely poor country and labour is cheap.

Teaching
There are a number of organisations in the UK that recruit or assist in recruiting qualified teachers for employment in schools, colleges etc in the developing countries of Africa. Teachers of General Science, English, Maths, Agricultural/Rural Science, Technical Drawing, Metalwork, Woodwork and Building are in greatest demand.

The British Council help to organise the Key English Language Teaching Project in Zambia to increase the potential of local teaching centres and improve the English proficiency of students and trainees in developmental sectors of the economy. Applicants should have a degree or equivalent qualification with a substantial TEFL component, or a general teaching qualification in TEFL and at least three years' teaching experience, two years of which will have been spent in an appropriate overseas country.

International Voluntary Service organise a Development Education and Exchange Programme with some countries in Africa. This exchange takes place mostly in the period June to September.

Catholic Institute for International Relations, 22 Coleman Fields,
London N1 7AF. Tel: 01 354 0883
Christians Abroad, Livingstone House, 11 Carteret St,London SW1H 9DL.
Tel: 01 222 2165

European Council of International Schools, 21b Lavant St, Petersfield,
Hants GU32 3EL. Tel: 0730 68244
Gabbitas-Thring Service Ltd, 6-8 Sackville St, Piccadilly, London W1X 2BR.
Tel: 01 439 2071
Committee for International Cooperation in Higher Education, Higher Education
Division, 10 Spring Gardens, London SW1A 2BN. Tel: 01 930 8466
The British Council, Overseas Educational Appoitments Dept, 65 Davies St, London W1Y 2AA.
Tel: 01 499 8011
IVS-DEEP, 109 Pilgrim St, Newcastle-upon-Tyne, NE1 6QF.

Voluntary Work
VSO currently has 25 volunteers in Zambia working principally in health, higher education,
community development and the co-operative sector. They are also investigating new areas of
involvement including youth training and agriculture.

VSO, Enquiries Unit, 317 Putney Bridge Rd, London SW15 2PN. Tel: 01 780 1331

Workcamps
The World Council of Churches through its Ecumenical Youth Action programme sponsors
workcamps in many parts of Africa. They take place in the spring and summer. The leaflet giving
details of the workcamps for 1990 is printed in March.

Tear Fund sends volunteers to countries in the developing world usually for periods of between
four and nine weeks. Volunteers pay a realistic contribution towards fares and Tear Fund
arranges all international travel and covers board and lodging costs. Work ranges from basic
repair work to construction of buildings, provision of piped water and specialised installation or
repair of equipment.

WCC, Sub-Unit of Youth, PO Box 66, 150 route de Ferney, 1211 Geneva 20,
Switzerland
Tear Fund, 100 Church Rd, Teddington, Middx TW11 8QE. Tel: 01 977 9144

Chapter 7
Adventure

It's really a bit of a misnomer to have a separate chapter on this subject as adventure starts the moment you set foot outside your front door. When you are abroad, adventure will creep up on you when you least expect it and take the most surprising form.

You can't really go looking for adventure but you can put yourself in positions where it is more likely to happen. A journey through the Hindu Kush has slightly more adventurous potential than a trip to Skegness.

You can also expect to get measurably more excitement from your travels if you try some of the activities that every country has to offer. Snorkelling around the great barrier reef is going to give you more pleasure than sitting on Bondai beach. And climbing Mt Mckinley is always a better option than just taking photos of it.

This chapter gives you some idea of the range of activities you can partake in. To what level you progress is entirely up to you but do at least give some of them a try. If possible get some practice or take some lessons in the activities that most appeal to you before you leave. That way you'll have much more confidence. It's easy to find ways of doing a familiar activity in an unfamiliar setting.

We also include some advice on what to do if you get into difficulties whilst 'adventuring' overseas. The concept of adventure also implies the existence of risk and the well prepared traveller will try to minimise this beforehand and cope with it should the need arise.

Canoeing & Kayaking
There is a profound tranquillity in paddling a canoe or kayak down a gently flowing river. In your mind, you journey back to the days when natives travelled the waterways in this fashion; times when canoes were made of birch bark. But then the river's pace increases and you are nearing a waterfall or shooting rapids and the excitement of this activity takes over.

Canoeing and kayaking have become increasingly popular with people who seek adventure. Whitewater is found in a number of rivers, and in conditions that range from mild enough for a novice to those impossible for even the most experienced rapids runner. The degree of risk, of course, is up to you and depends on your abilities and experience. You can always portage around the rapids if they seem too difficult; that is just another part of canoeing and kayaking.

There is no other type of watercraft that offers the versatility of a canoe or kayak, enthusiasts of the sport will tell you. You can use most models of canoes or kayaks to paddle flatwater or whitewater. You can journey, race, hunt or fish from your canoe. You can paddle, pole, sail or even use a motor on some canoes. The boats are light enough to carry on the roof of a car or on your shoulders. You do not have to worry about fuel or engines, winds or masts. And there is a canoe or kayak for almost every budget.

There is no large initial outlay needed for equipment in this sport, because the boats are normally available on a rental basis. You can sample the pleasures before you sign up for a school or buy your own craft. But you should not, under any circumstances, attempt whitewater boating without experienced training, nor should you ever travel a river that you have not fully scouted unless you are with someone else who knows it well. Rivers can be dangerous and travelling on them requires skills that come only from guidance and practice.

People have taught themselves to canoe and kayak. Many have learned from friends. But there are also many schools and clubs that can teach and train the novice river runner in most areas of this country and also of course overseas, especially in Canada and the US. Courses can be as short as a day or two or as long as several weeks. They can be held indoors, at a swimming pool, for example; or they can be on the river expeditions that involve camping, portaging and actual whitewater running.

Once you have mastered the basics, you may be ready to canoe or kayak but you will still be learning. River running can be an endless learning experience. With practice, you should be able to navigate some very exciting rapids and know the great feeling of accomplishment that it provides.

Once you feel ready to take on a river, there are some basics that you must observe. Check the river first either on foot or at least from a map. Maps of the area you are to canoe can be a great help in pointing out falls and the like, and they are essential for any extended river trip. Your training should also provide you with an understanding of what you will need in the way of equipment and clothing for different kinds of river outings in different environments and climates. Expect to get and stay wet for a long time.

Like riding, you can canoe in most countries of the world. The best however tend to be Canada and the US, Nepal, Sweden and Norway, Iceland and New Zealand.

Climbing
Mountaineering, or mountain climbing, is among the most demanding, thrilling and romantic sports in the world; it is also one of the most dangerous. An error or miscalculation can bring disaster. Rock slides, avalanches, hidden crevasses, sudden storms and sleet-coated rock are among the hazards that can confront a climber. Yet the idea of pitting yourself against a mountain is a compelling one.

Mountain climbing can be broken down into four different types. In order of difficulty, they are: hiking / scrambling, vertical rock climbing, ice and snow climbing and expedition climbing. Any climb may involve several of these categories, and expedition climbing normally involves all of them.

Hiking/scrambling is little more than backpacking, except that the terrain is a hill or a mountain that you can walk up. The hill is not steep enough to require you to actually climb. This is a good way for beginners to get themselves into condition, to build up their mountain legs for more strenuous types of climbing and to get a feel for the mountain and the rigours of achievement.

Real climbing is just that: you make your ascent by climbing up vertical walls, with or without equipment to aid you. This can include anything from a relatively easy stepladder-like face that you move up with the aid of good footing and balance to the absolutely vertical faces of a mountain like El Capitan in the Rockies where you might ascend certain parts at a rate of only 60 feet an hour.

On an international level, mountaineering is governed and coordinated by the Union Internationale das Association d'Alphinisme, headquartered in Geneva, Switzerland.

If you want to get into mountain climbing, at least beyond the level of hiking/scrambling, you would be wise to obtain formal instruction on all the basics from an experienced mountaineer or mountaineering school. There are so many fundamentals you need to know, that it is just not practical or safe to try and pick up expertise on your own.

Among the sources for mountain climbing instruction and training are mountaineering clubs and outward bound centres. You can check with the large organisations for what they offer and if they can direct you to a similar club in an appropriate area. There are also organised schools of instruction that you can attend. They offer a variety of courses, for the beginner, intermediate and experienced climber. Most extended courses have good on-the-mountain training at a variety of levels and conditions.

There are many parts of the UK where you can learn climbing and mountaineering and in most big cities there are now sports centres that offer instruction indoors on climbing walls which are an excellent way to start.

If you do have the opportunity to climb whilst abroad, take it. But do remember, amongst all the other guidelines the one cardinal rule – never climb alone.

Hang Gliding

Hang gliding as a sport has been with us for only a short time, gaining popularity in the late 1960s and early 1970s. The desire to fly and attempt to do it by leaping from heights, however, goes back several hundred years. In those less enlightened days, adventurous souls equipped with an imaginary variety of homemade wings tried and routinely failed to fly by jumping off cliffs, rooftops and steeples. Then in 1853, George Cayley invented the glider, a man-carrying motorless aeroplane. It was the first major step in refining the principle of flight that would later govern hang gliders.

The only way to take up the sport, all experienced hang gliding pilots will tell you, is with proper equipment, after formal training from a good hang gliding school. Training usually begins with an orientation programme – a classroom-like presentation that tells what hang gliding is all about. This may be done with lectures, films or demonstrations, depending on the facilities of the particular school you attend. At the end of the orientation you should have a basic understanding of the hang glider you will pilot, its parts and functions. You should have a knowledge of the sport's safety requirements, what the limitations of the hang glider are as well as your own limitations, what the proper equipment is, what the local regulations are, if any, what wind and weather conditions are proper for gliding and how to judge and interpret those conditions.

From there you should progress to work on a hang glider simulator. This is a device that recreates on the ground what the experience of hang gliding is like. Here, you get the feel of being harnessed in, of what you must do to control the flight, and how to react to various situations that you may encounter in the air.

Then you will be taught how to set up a hang glider for flight. It is a procedure that you will have to learn yourself. After that, there is the very important process of flight inspection. Any good hang gliding school will thoroughly train you in the procedures of checking all equipment before you fly just as you would if parachuting.

First jumps will be closely supervised. They will be from mild heights, probably progressing from five or ten feet to fifty feet above the ground. Some schools provide radio-equipped helmets so the instructor can give you guidance and instructions while you are in the air. Some schools utilise the double-seat harness so the instructor can go along with you. When the instructor feels that you have mastered the basics and can handle yourself well in actual flight, you will be on your own.

Hang Gliding is most popular in the States, Western Europe and Australasia but you will be surprised where facilities for this popular sport turn up. We once looked up from a trek through the jungles of Borneo to see a hang glider soaring overhead.

Hiking/Trekking

The lure of a hike through the wilderness varies with each individual. For some it is the chance of finding secret places, exploring trails in parts of the world that perhaps only a few humans have ever seen. There are other hikers for whom the trek itself is the thrill: the mountains to be climbed, the rivers to be forded, the wilderness to be traversed. For others, the adventure is in living off the land, existing as a part of nature. Still others may stalk wildlife in remote regions, hunting with their eyes or cameras. Finally there are those who feel that the wild places of the world are fast disappearing and who want to experience the remote regions before they are gone for ever.

Neither climate nor environment deters true hikers. They walk through the bitter cold and deep in snow drifts of mountain ranges, through the desert's extremes of boiling days and bone-chilling nights, through the steamy leech infested rainforests or the vast pine woods of northern Europe the Soviet Union and Canada where wolves still prowl. The variations of climate and terrain encountered by the wilderness hiker can be boundless and that is what makes the sport one of continually changing challenges.

Once you feel that wilderness hiking is for you, it would be wise to sign on for a brief, professionally guided hike before committing a lot of money in tuition, equipment, and instruction fees. Formal schooling is not a necessity, but it is a definite help. You will, however, need guidance from those who know what they are doing. Once you have mastered the fundamentals, all you will need is continuing good health, common sense, an abiding respect for nature and a determination to help preserve and enjoy the wilderness.

Even in Britain it is possible to simulate some of the hardships and challenges of a long-distance trek and at least get used to carrying packs over long distances and sleeping under the stars – or rain clouds.

The type of equipment you need depends on how many people are going on the hike, where you are going, the climate and territory and how long you intend to be gone. The quality and sophistication of equipment varies as widely as does its cost. Personal preference aside, however, an improperly outfitted hiker is one who is taking risks with his health and safety.

Rafting
All the countries mentioned in the section on canoeing are also excellent for rafting. Rafting the rapids is a sport that has grown tremendously in popularity in recent years. There are many raftable rivers that cut across practically all areas of the United States and Canada, where it is particularly popular.

Rafting is a versatile sport. You can outfit yourself completely if you plan to do it on your own, or you can simply indulge yourself sporadically or on a whim with no investment other than the cost of a professionally guided and equipped trip. It is also a sport that can involve anything from an elaborate 21 day, 275 mile journey down the Colorado River through the Grand Canyon to a simple one-day outing. Whatever the duration, there is always the intense thrill of running the rapids.

Rafting the rapids as a sport, is a 20th century phenomenon. The development of rubber rafts, especially those used in Word War II, made it all possible. Today, thousands of people raft rivers and rapids throughout the world; some on their own, others as part of supervised tour groups.

Some instruction courses on the art of rafting are part of adventure tours, a kind of in-service training while you are actually taking a raft trip. Other courses are more formal, set up like schools with basic instruction and then on-the-site training. Courses can be as short as one day or last more than a month with their classroom being moved from river to more difficult river.

Riding
Horseback riding in all its forms is available to practically everyone. Riding schools exist throughout the country. More and more people are discovering that this sport is not only an enjoyable one but one that can be breathtaking in excitement as well.

Once you can ride you will find opportunities to see the country from the back of a horse (and there are few better ways) in many parts of the world. All through Western Europe, horse riding and pony trekking is widely available. In Spain and Portugal you can take trips of several weeks long if you choose and see parts of the country that few of the Costa del Yobbo tourists ever manage. In Asia you can ride in Russia on the steppes. in Mongolia (visa permitting) across the plains and in Kashmir up into the High Himalayas. In Australia you can ride into the wildest parts of the outback and of course in the US the horse is still widely used in many parts of the West.

Competent riders may even have the chance of using their skills to get work. There are a couple of Kibbutzim in Israel which use horses and in the States, South America and Australasia the ability to ride might get you a job on a cattle or sheep ranch.

Most stables in the UK offer basic riding instruction, usually in classes for beginners, intermediate and advanced students. You may have to search a bit to find a school that offers training in jumping and other more-advanced equestrian arts but these are not the skills you'll need when taking a horse safari into the Atlas Mountains. Look in the Yellow Pages for addresses of riding stables near you.

Sailing
The sport of sailing is a special one, yet contrary to many expectations the world of sailing is by no means restricted to men and women of great wealth. It includes the great tall ships, the many masted windjammers that sail the oceans and tiny Mirror dinghies, sunfish sailboats and wind surfers that ply the smallest of lakes. There are personal sailboats on the market costing more than £100,000 and as little as £100.

Both forms of sailing, cruising and racing, are exciting in their own ways. Each takes you out on the water with only the boat, its sails, the wind and your skill to get you where you're going. Sailing is a personal thing. Your skill harnesses the elements and controls the vessel. Perhaps that is why it is such a satisfying pastime.

No one, however, becomes an instant sailor. It takes training, practice and experience. You can learn the basics in a variety of ways. From there the thrills of sailing are many and varied, whether you go in for ocean cruising or organised racing.

If you want to get into sailing, there are many people and organisations who stand by ready to help you. Many clubs and schools throughout the country offer a great variety of courses. There are a number of things you need to learn before setting sail. These include: The parts of the sailboat and their function, how to handle a boat under various water and weather conditions, the necessary equipment to have on board, basic navigation, the kinds of weather conditions that are safe, the rules of the nautical road, boating laws and regulations, general safety precautions and what to do in emergencies. It is possible to pick up most of this knowledge on your own with the help of books and perhaps the advice of an experienced sailor but there is no substitute for first-hand experience.

Once you have mastered the rudiments of sailing, the possibilities for work, travel and adventure all rolled into one are endless. How about delivering boats from Cornwall to the Caribbean for example; or crewing on a yacht that is touring the Mediterranean or the South Seas?

Scuba Diving
Scuba diving is not just a matter of strapping on some gear and dropping into the water. It is a sport that requires qualified instruction, thorough training and frequent practice. The underwater world can be as treacherous as it is beautiful, and you must know what you are doing.

Scuba diving is an offshoot of the much older sport of skin diving; it differs in that skin divers do not utilise any form of underwater breathing equipment. Scuba, in fact, is an acronym for 'self-contained underwater breathing apparatus.' Skin diving has been around for ages and practised by people around the globe in search of pearls, sponges, or simply delicious seafood.

It developed as a sport in the 1930s when divers with nothing more than a mast, a pair of fins, and a spear or harpoon would go spearfishing.

A prerequisite for any scuba diver is that he or she be in good health – not bothered by any heart, respiratory, or other disorders that might be aggravated by this strenuous sport. Some schools, in fact, may require a physical examination before allowing you to enrol in their scuba courses. Whether they do or not, a pre-training physical makes good sense.

Proper training is essential. It begins with the basics: physical conditioning, basic swimming on and underwater, submerging and diving. All responsible scuba divers insist that you have formal training and certification by the national scuba diving organisation before they will take you diving. If you are not certified, you may not be able to get an air tank refilled at a dive shop or other diving installation, rent equipment, or be allowed on a scuba diving charter boat.

How do you go about getting certified? Very simply, you take a course offered by a number of schools under the auspices of the British Sub Aqua Club.

The training course itself will teach you the basics. You will learn snorkelling first, then familiarisation with equipment, water entries, techniques of diving, what to do in emergency and so forth. Air tank systems, air, and buoyancy compensators are usually provided. Often, however, a student must supply his or her own mask, fins or snorkel.

A training course may be as short as 18 hours, but more likely it will involve from 24 to 40 hours of instruction. Usually this time will be divided half and half between actual water-work in a swimming pool and lectures. The course will end with several real dives.

Advanced diving courses are also available. Although they can vary considerably in content and cost from one school to another, these advanced courses are generally more expensive than basic courses because most of the teaching takes place during actual on-location dives.

If you are planning to visit the Carribean, Australia or the Red Sea then do learn at least the rudiments of snorkelling and diving. It will be one of the best investments you have ever made.

Skiing

Both types of snow skiing, alpine and Nordic, are growing in popularity. Nordic skiing is actually a very different sport from alpine skiing; it is for those who enjoy trekking or touring across relatively flat stretches of land. It is an invigorating sport that requires its own specially designed equipment.

Alpine skiing is truly a sport for everyone; everyone, that is, who is in reasonably good health and is physically fit. Two-year olds and octogenarians alike have made their way down the slopes and have become hooked on the feeling. Beginners can have as much fun and experience the same sense of accomplishment as do the daredevil acrobats and Olympic racers.

Ski acrobatics, ski jumping and racing are the proprietary rights of experts and professionals, persons who have worked up to them over long years of arduous practice. But whether or not you are at home on the expert trails or just making your way down the easiest of the beginner's slopes, you can experience the basic thrill of what skiing is all about: the speed, the balance, the manoeuvring, the freshness of the winter air in your face and the special camaraderie that is so much a part of the sport.

Skiing really involves not much more than the desire to do it, snow, and an ability to get to the slopes. Once you are there, you can usually rent the necessary equipment, take lessons if you want them, and ride the lift up and ski down.

Skiers are classified by their abilities and experience, as beginners, intermediates and experts. A skier must begin with the basics: how to walk on skis, how to get up when you fall, how to stay up on them, how to stop and how to turn. It won't be long, however, until you are into manoeuvres: traversing, stem turns, schussing, christies, side-slipping, parallels, wedels and the like. In the process, you will find that you are learning another language as well. You will learn that a mambo is not always a dance, that a herringbone is not necessarily a tweed fabric, and that there are snowploughs that do not clean the roads.

Skiing need not be an expensive sport. It requires a good amount of basic equipment and proper clothing to combat harsh weather conditions. Products available in both categories cover a wide range of prices and styles. Most of the necessities are available for hire in the ski areas of the world.

This is one of the few adventure sports that it is difficult to do in Britain before you leave. However there are the Scottish centres such as Aviemore and an increasing number of dry-ski facilities where you can learn the basics.

Many jobs in Switzerland, France, Austria and Germany can be found in ski resorts and you can learn all you need there.

Surfing
"The quest may lead from the Eastern Seaboard to the California Coast, from South America to South Africa, from Indonesia to Australia to Hawaii to Europe. The search for the perfect wave can take a lifetime. The surfer who has become addicted to the sport will go almost anywhere to find that wave, the wave."

"If you really want to be a decent surfer, and to truly enjoy the sport, it takes two basic things: concentration and practice, and a lot of both. But that is a small price to pay for one of the most exciting experiences of your life."

The sport in fact began on the ocean long ago, somewhere in the South Pacific islands. Natives were fashioning surfboards out of wood or tightly woven grass mats and taking them to the sea to surf. The explorer and sea captain James Cook discovered surfing about the same time he discovered the island of Hawaii in 1778 and brought word of it back to the English-speaking world.

Today, surfing is both a leisure activity and a hotly contested sport. Surfing competitions are held throughout the world on regional, national and international levels. There are associations for the promotion of surfing and there are literally hundreds of clubs composed of many thousands of active and avid surfers. And for all the thousands of surfers, there are at least several hundred times as many observers who watch them with the same awe and astonishment as Captain Cook did 200 years ago.

There are no formal surfing schools or certified instructors, as such. There is, however, the need for certain elements of training and preparedness for any would-be surfer.

As a start, a surfer should be in reasonably good health and good physical condition. Surfing is a demanding sport that requires strength and endurance. Secondly, the surfer must be a good swimmer - most experienced surfers recommend that you be able to swim a minimum of half a mile in rough water and be able to stay afloat unaided, for at least half hour. The reason is that rip currents or tides can sweep a surfer a mile or more out to sea. In emergency situations it may take some time before someone sees that you are in trouble and then perhaps even more vital minutes to actually reach you in the water.

You can learn to surf in this country. South Wales and the West Country have beaches with surf good enough for the world championships to be held here.

Survival Techniques
If you are an adventurous person by nature (and if not you probably won't have got this far in this chapter) you will need to have a certain amount of knowledge of survival techniques.

Lost and Found

There are countless stories of lost persons who wander for hours in a circle, only to return after great struggle to where they originally started. It is possible that you or your party may someday be lost in unfamiliar terrain and in this section we will describe some measures that may help you with survival in such a situation.

First, do not panic or become excited. Sit down, relax, drink a hot beverage if you can, and calmly think over your problem. Try to establish a campsite or 'base' which searchers may locate and which can be seen from the air. If you leave this area, devise a note which identifies you and reveals the direction in which you have walked; blaze the trail you take with an axe or knife. Try to keep your feet clean and comfortable, as they may be your sole means of transport to safety. The most important thing is to keep a sane, collected attitude.

Shelter

There are two types of shelter: natural, such as caves, rock ledges and fallen trees and manmade, such as tents, lean-to's and cabins. Your shelter should give you enough room to move about freely, to dry your clothes, and to sleep comfortably. A bed may be made of spruce tips, dry grass, leaves, and many other soft natural materials. Try to keep your bed off the ground by building a raised framework of boughs or by insulating it with a plastic sheet or other material.

A lean-to is made by lashing poles to a stout frame which may consist of two trees or two forked uprights driven firmly into the ground. Cross-poles will hold the thatching, which can be made of any foliage that will pack closely together.

Start the thatching at the bottom of the lean-to and overlap each row on your frame in the same manner as shingles are laid. Where dead wood is plentiful, a roof can be made of split shakes or shingles. Live trees should not be used for this purpose unless the emergency demands their use and even then do not cut down the complete tree.

Establish your campsite in an area near protection and water and where there is plenty of shelter material and firewood. Do not camp in the bottom of a dry wash or drainage area during a rainy season, for you may find yourself caught in a flash flood. Part-way up a slope is a safer and warmer place to camp than in the bottom of a valley.

Heat-warmth

Before you go out on any expedition, always carry a large supply of matches in a waterproof container. If you become lost, do not panic and use them carelessly. Conserve them – they may prove to be your most valuable possession. Before lighting any matches, gather a supply of firewood and timber such as bark, and small dry twigs. Build your logs up in square levels or in a V-shape. Preparing the fuel beforehand saves time and matches.

A good method to waterproof your matches (before leaving civilisation) is to take 50 or 100 of them and roll them up in a thin cloth. Tie the roll with a rubber band, then dip in a can of melted paraffin wax. When you want a match, just tear off one with a bit of cloth attached. This more than doubles the 'fire power' of each match. Plastic film canisters are also good for carrying a supply of matches.

Proper clothing

Proper clothing is that which will provide sufficient protection against the worst possible weather you can expect to encounter. Any form of clothing protects against hot weather although it is no fallacy that pale-coloured clothes keep you cooler than dark ones. However it is selected clothing for cold weather that demands forethought. So far as shoes are concerned, wear any good quality boot – never just shoes or trainers. The boot should be large enough for you to wear two pairs of woollen socks without pinching or cramping. Keep your socks clean, for dirty or damp socks will not insulate feet properly.

On your body wear several layers of clothing – so that when you get warm from activity you can remove outer layers for convenience, but always maintain body warmth. If cold is severe, wear long woollen underwear, a good woollen shirt, and wool pants. If it is extremely cold, provide yourself with a second pair of pants – preferably of close-weave cotton twill – to serve as a wind break. A two-piece jacket, coat, or parka is the best outer garment. With such an arrangement, the outer garment serves as a wind break while the inner layer provides warmth when you are not active. All of your clothes should be loose fitting for comfort and warmth. Each day make any necessary repairs – this means you must carry a needle and thread. To dry clothes, hang them near a flame, but not over as they may drop into the fire. The important thing is to prepare yourself with clothes which will give you warmth, protection, and comfort in an emergency.

Signalling practices

Smoke, fire, sound, or reflection are your best bets for communicating and attracting the attention of search parties, aircraft, etc. Fire and smoke are usually the best and easiest to make. To make a signal fire, build three fires in a prominent place at night and let them smoke during the day. The smoke may be spotted by fire lookouts. You should take precautions to ensure that you do not start a serious fire. In open areas, you may write a message such as SOS with contrasting material on the ground – footprints in the snow, or pine boughs on light coloured ground. Sound signals to attract ground search parties can be used if you carry an air horn or whistle. A mirror's reflection may also be used for signalling, especially for attracting aircraft.

Food & Water

When travelling or hunting in remote areas with which you are not familiar, carry a minimum of one day's supply. This in an emergency can be stretched to last at least three days. How much you eat, your emotional attitude, and your conservation of energy are important factors for survival. Your food pack should contain high protein food such as cheese, dried beef jerky, bacon, malted milk tablets, chocolate bars, raisins, dried apricots or peaches, soup mix, tea bags, or other energy foods. You may be able to augment your diet by hunting, trapping and fishing, and finding berries and other edibles, but don't count on it. Preserve any fresh meat or fish by smoking it over a fire made of green wood. Wrap your food in brush or slabs of bark, tie it with a cord, and hang it from a safe tree limb, away from the trunk and the ground.

To find water if you run out, follow trails of animals and watch for the concerted flights of birds in morning and evening. When you find water, boil or purify it. A free-running stream with a sandy or gravel bottom is usually safe to drink from without taking precautions.

Roasting and boiling are the best food preparation methods, although spit cooking is also acceptable. You may make a stove or oven from natural materials – stones, clay, mud, etc. A spit may be made from forked sticks and a fire. To 'steam roast', build a fire in a rock-lined pit, cover the fire with green shrubs when the rocks are red hot, then place food in the pit and cover with additional greenery, add a small amount of water, and then top it off with a layer of sand or dirt.

Travelling

Before leaving camp, observe and establish in your mind certain characteristics of the area and try to take a bearing on a mountain, lake or range of mountains. Follow the line of least resistance, that is, follow the general pattern of the earth. Follow game trails if they go in the direction you desire. Follow watercourses downstream, for they usually lead to camps and people. Avoid taking unnecessary risks such as jumping from ledges, banks, or logs. Try to avoid slippery ground and scree. Always keep your eyes on the ground and scenery ahead of you for any danger or obstacles.

Recommended equipment

Here are some suggested items that you should take on any trip off the beaten track. Proper clothing (depending upon weather and terrain), matches in a waterproof container, one-day's supply of food, hatchet, belt or pocket knife (and small sharpening stone), 10-20 feet of rope, pencil and small notebook, compass, map, binoculars, fish hooks, line, lures, needle and thread, first-aid kit and dry clothes in a waterproof wrapping.

Survival First Aid

What is First Aid? According to the Red Cross, it is 'the immediate and temporary care given the victim of an accident or sudden illness until the services of a physician can be obtained'. The importance of knowing first aid cannot be overstressed. Learn and memorise the following basic rules. They may someday mean the difference between life and death.

General Rules:

1) Have a reason for what you do.
2) Keep an injured person in a prone position, head level with the body or
feet slightly higher than the head. This guards against shock. If the victim vomits, however, turn his head to one side to prevent choking. If his face is flushed, raise his head slightly.
3) Look for severe bleeding, breathing cessation, poisoning, wounds, burns, fractures, and dislocations. Be sure you locate all obvious injuries. If the injured person is conscious, ask him to describe the location of pain. When examining, remove enough clothing to determine the extent of the injury or wound but no more.
4) Breathing stoppage, serious bleeding and poisoning, in that order, must be treated immediately. When breathing has ceased, apply artificial respiration at once. When treating a group of persons, determine the worst injured and proceed from there. Symptoms of poisoning are burns or discolourations on the lips and in the mouth. Bloody froth on the victim's lips may indicate either epilepsy or a lung injury.
5) Never give stimulants in cases of severe bleeding, suspected internal bleeding, or head injury and be especially wary of giving alcohol.
6) Keep the injured person warm. Attempt to maintain normal body temperature. In cool weather, wrap the victim underneath as well as on top. This may prevent serious shock.
7) Send someone for a doctor or ambulance. The messenger should relate the location of the injured person, the cause and extent of injury, available supplies, and what first aid has been or is being given.
8) Keep calm – do not be hurried into moving the injured person unless it is absolutely necessary. Before moving the injured, first aid should be given and the nature and extent of the injuries determined.
9) Never give liquid to an unconscious person.
10) Make the victim comfortable and keep him cheerful.
11) Don't let the patient see his own injury (in severe cases) or relate the extent of the injuries.

Shock Treatment:

First aid for shock is as follows. Stop the flow of blood. Keep fractured bones immobile. Wrap the patient completely to prevent loss of body heat (keep him warm but not hot). Keep the victim horizontal or tilt his body by raising his feet. Always keep his head low and do not use a pillow except in chest injuries to help maintain breathing.

If the patient is able to drink, give him a small amount of water, hot tea, coffee, milk, or broth, but do not give fluids if there is evidence of abdominal injury, nausea, or vomiting. Do not give him/her alcohol.

Bleeding Controls:

Severe bleeding is usually controlled by applying direct pressure on the wound with gauze or cloth. For quick but partial control, apply pressure on the blood vessels and arteries feeding the bleeding area. This will diminish the bleeding, but will not stop it entirely. This is a secondary method and should be used in conjunction with the direct pressure method. Elevation of the bleeding portion of the body and keeping the patient absolutely still will help considerably.

Do not hesitate to use your bare hand to stop bleeding when quick action is necessary and no cloth is available.

Improvised bandages or compresses may be made from clean handkerchiefs, towels, and other clothing. When sterile bandages are not available, scorching the dressing with a match, or putting the bandage on top of a stove over a flame, will achieve a degree of sterilisation.

The Tourniquet:
The use of a tourniquet is justifiable only rarely. If a tourniquet is applied for much over two hours, its release may produce severe shock; leaving a tourniquet on for too long can also 'kill' a limb and result in amputation.

Treatment for Gunshot Wounds:
Three life saving methods are important for gunshot wounds:
1) Stop the bleeding. Use a pressure compress. If this cannot control the bleeding, use a tourniquet.
2) Treat for shock.
3) Protect the wound, but don't remove the bullet.

Snake Bite First Aid
Place a constricting band around the bitten limb, above the bite, always between the bite and the heart. The band can be improvised from a handkerchief, a necktie, or a strip cut from a shirt. It should be just tight enough to cut off the circulation under the skin, but not to cut off the underlying larger blood vessels. If it is properly adjusted, there will be some oozing from the wound.

After constricting, paint the vicinity of the bite with an antiseptic. A small cross-shaped cut should then be made in the skin over each fang puncture. To try to make the cuts over the venom deposit point, remember that the snake strikes downwards and the fangs curve under. If a surgical knife as furnished in most snake kits is not available, use a razor blade or sharp knife, making certain that the blade has been sterilised, either with an antiseptic or with a match flame. The cuts should not be too deep; generally an eight to a quarter of an inch will suffice, for this is the usual depth of penetration of the snake's fangs. Take caution not to cut the muscles and the nerves of the fingers, hands, or wrist for these lie immediately below the skin. Also beware of cutting a large blood vessel (those near the surface can usually be seen).

Suction should then be applied to the cuts, to encourage flow of blood and lymph, and consequent removal of venom. If no suction cup apparatus is at hand, the mouth may be used.

Mouth-to-Mouth Resuscitation:
Mouth-to-mouth resuscitation is the most practical treatment for breathing stoppage, and the easiest method to learn and apply. This method can be used anywhere with a good chance of success. The victim need not be prone, and space is not a critical factor. It should be administered as follows:

1) Clear the mouth of any foreign matter with the fingers and press the tongue forward.
2) If possible place the victim on his back, tilt his head back, and lift his lower jaw so it juts out. This will open his windpipe.
3) Hold the jaw in this position and place your mouth, opened wide, over the victim's mouth. If the victim's mouth is clenched shut, attempt to blow air between the teeth. Failing this, hold his mouth shut and blow into his nose instead. In mouth-to-mouth resuscitation, you must remember to hold the patient's nose shut so that the air will pass into the lungs and not directly out of the nostrils.
Remember to keep the victim's head tilted back and the jaw jutted out, thus keeping the windpipe open.

If the first blowing attempts indicate an obstruction is in the windpipe, attempt to clear this, using the fingers, or possibly by patting the victim's back in the case of a small child.

4) Remove your mouth after blowing. Listen for the air to rush back out. After a normal breathing interval, repeat the blowing effort.

How to Treat Bone and Joint Injuries

The objective of first aid for a broken bone is to keep the broken ends and the adjacent joints quiet.

One can detect a fracture by noting tenderness, swelling, deformity, and limitation of movement in the area of the fracture. These clues may not be obvious and the victim may think he is not seriously injured, especially when he remains still and feels no pain. The victim may be able to move his fingers or toes in spite of a serious broken bone. Keep him warm and go for help if possible.

If you must transport the victim, his broken limb should be splinted. Straightened limbs generally permit the compound fractured bones to slip back into place. Slight stretch induced by the splint will keep the broken ends from touching and prevent unnecessary damage and pain.

Splints should never be hard or sharp. Pad the splints with available materials. Be sure the splint extends beyond the joints above and below the break.

First Aid for Injuries from Excessive Heat and Cold

The objective is to relieve pain, prevent contamination, and treat for shock. Serious burns will need immediate hospital treatment.

Many people become victims of heat exhaustion and heat stroke. In heat exhaustion cases, the victim may become weak, nauseated, and have a headache. The skin may become clammy, the face pale, the temperature slightly above or below normal. The best treatment for heat exhaustion is rest and quiet, several half teaspoons of salt water, and such stimulants as coffee and tea. Give plenty of juice or water in small quantities.

Heat stroke can be detected if the victim's face is flushed, the skin dry, the pulse rapid, and the temperature high. Unconsciousness may occur. For treatment, place the victim on his back with his head slightly raised and reduce the body temperature by sponging with lukewarm water or alcohol. Do not give stimulants.

In extremely cold weather, parts of the body may freeze, resulting in frostbite. Rubbing the frozen part, either with the hand or with snow, is definitely harmful. This rubbing of injured tissue can cause gangrene.

Cover the frozen part with blankets or extra clothing or immerse it in water at body temperature, but not hot. Excessive heat, such as from a hot water bottle or heat lamps, may increase damage. Give the victim warm drinks.

Poisoning

If poison has been taken internally, the first objective is to dilute the poison as quickly as possible and, in most cases, to induce vomiting. Administer large amounts of fluids immediately. Use four or five glasses or more. Water or milk may be given. Milk lines the digestive tract and slows the absorption of the poison.

With any injury or illness seek medical aid as soon as possible.

Chapter 8

Personal experiences

We asked a selection of world travellers to write about their experiences of work and travel overseas. Here are some of the highlights (and lowlights) of their trips.

We've tidied up the grammar and spelling in some of them and had to shorten a couple but otherwise these experiences are just as they were sent to us – straight from the horses mouth. The views expressed are the authors' own and, while we agree with much of what they say, do not necessarily coincide with ours.

THE NEAR EAST by Robert Jeffery

The first time I decided to go to Israel was to experience the Kibbutz, avoid becoming another stereotype in society and because I was getting bored with the job I was doing in England. However I enjoyed myself on the kibbutz and liked that part of the world so much that I decided to return and to see Egypt too.

Fortunately I knew some people from my old kibbutz (via Project 67) when I was last in Israel who went on to a moshav. Having not known very much about moshavs I got in touch with one of the girls called Melanie who managed to set me up with a job when I got there.

All I knew about moshavim was they were made up of groups of farmers similar to a kibbutz who owned their own land but shared some of the tools on a commercial basis. They still have a community hall and schools etc, although the children live with their parents. The volunteers are paid about 600 shekels and given basic accommodation in return for six eight-hour days of hard work a week. We also did our own cooking.

As soon as I put the phone down that was it. I would leave this cold and boring town as soon as possible. I finally managed to get a flight leaving at 10pm on 1st April for Tel Aviv.

The next day I got all my stuff together making sure I didn't make the same mistakes as last time. Recorded as many tapes as possible and said goodbye.

After just managing to collect my bucket ticket by 10 minutes I made it to Heathrow and was airborne by 10.30pm.

On the seat next to me were a couple of Americans who were very helpful as to where I should go in Minneapolis and behind I had some Christian fanatics waving their bibles about and lecturing me on what religious things I ought to be doing when I got to Israel.

Finally we landed in Israel (Ben Gurion Airport 10 miles out of Tel Aviv). They didn't ask me any questions at the airport and my next task was to get to Beersheeva down south. So I caught the first bus to Tel-Aviv where I immediately ate a falafel (a vegetable delight of hot peppers, aubergines, tomatoes you name it, its in it) for about 75p or 2 shekels.

I didn't have to wait very long before I could get away from the slums around the bus station. I paid the bus driver and was off into the desert.

When I finally arrived at Beersheva I had to wait 4 hours in very hot temperatures but was amazed at all the Arabs in their Arabian Night outfits. Anyhow finally I made it to Moshav Talmei Yosef in the heart of the Negev desert (next to the Gaza strip). I looked around to see if I could recognise anybody, but all I could see was these hot houses everywhere (plastic greenhouses). When I did see someone they passed me on to another person and them onto another until finally I ended up after nearly being savaged by dogs at the volunteer leaders house. Here I was immediately welcomed by this loud Jewish American woman who let me in, offered me some spaghetti and warned it might be too hot, Heinz spaghetti would have been hotter.

She introduced me to my boss (we called them our farmers) and he showed me my accommodation.

My farmer, who was a South African Jew, was literally a slave driver. Previous volunteers had left yet the Arabs who worked for him were a good laugh. One was called Arafat and the others called him Yasser. Contrary to common belief all the volunteers got on well with the poulin (Arab workers). they even let us have breakfast with them, unless you were a woman who had to eat with the other women. The women all wore black and had to walk 2 metres behind the men. No girl would bend over to pick something up near an Arab nor be on her own with them. One Arab flashed his private parts at a girl. All she did was laugh, which killed his ego.

The best workers out there were the Bedouin. Although these people were nomadic travellers we could always be sure of some being around the corner. We would drive to a camp, beep the hooter and they would come running out of the tents just awakened and fully dressed. They'd go to the toilet and then jump in the van. However when they left the Moshav the women were usually twice as fat with stolen fruit hidden in their clothes.

After I finished working for the first farmer, I started working for yet another South African (a little better this time) a woman called Leana who let me use the tractor. However I never argued with her Arabs about this as they were always fighting to drive it.

The sort of work I did in the hot houses (which were hot) was to lay guide wires down and twist courgettes around them. Another job I spent a lot of time doing was to comb grapes. I know it sounds stupid, but we used this plastic dish scrubber to loosen off half the young grapes. Most of the work consisted of pruning grapes, courgettes and other hot house crops. We also boxed fruit like melons and went around in the tractor to fill the fertilizer tanks and turn the irrigation on. My favourite job there was spraying the fruit (from mangoes to peppers) with grow-fast hormones (sometimes dangerous). All the very laborious jobs like collecting the melons were done by the Arabs but jobs like pruning the roses (for sale in Europe) were done by us volunteers.

After work and in our lunch breaks, which often lasted up to 4 hours in hot weather, someone in the house where I lived would grab a tractor with a trailer and we'd go down to a neighbouring Moshav's swimming pool. However we were only able to do this from July onwards. Before this if we were hot we would probably have a water fight which put the water bill up and upset the farmers who paid for it.

Sometimes if there was a good film on at the local cinema we would be invited by our farmer or someone else to see it. The trouble with this was that if it was a comedy you didn't get to hear the funny part because the Israelis were ahead of you from the Hebrew subtitles. The only Hebrew I know means Happy birthday (pronounced yom holdet samech).

On a Friday evening shabat or sabbath, which means the day of rest, begins. To celebrate this event they have a special meal with all this religious fuss of lighting candles beforehand. Anyhow the meals were great, especially as it was the only proper meal I had in the whole week. That night after the meal you could guarantee a party somewhere. There were about 30 volunteers in 4 houses and each house had its name, like the Girls house, because a lot of girls once lived there, Then there was the Twilight zone – one with no electricity. The Boys house which is obvious and the Miserables which is obvious too. Anyhow at these parties one would bring some light refreshment like 95% alcohol vodka which incidentally came from the Israeli Marks & Spencer in BeerSheeva and was a good steriliser. Another popular drink was cheap vodka (wadka on the label) or Arack which was similar to pernod but very cheap and had strange effects on people. Especially in the morning. Maccabee beer or Gold Star were the runners up after the spirits.

On the Saturday we nearly always had nothing to do especially before the swimming pool opened. So most of us went for a walk/drive in the tractor into the desert or just watched telly.

The accommodation was bungalows with 4 bedrooms, a toilet, bathroom plus shower and kitchen with one fridge, sink, cooker and tables etc. All this kit was secondhand. As I was an electronics engineer I was always repairing something for someone somewhere.

After two months of this exciting living I and two sisters called Janice and Lisa decided to go to Egypt. So we left for Tel-Aviv to book up. However we left on a Sunday so we met some friends in town and booked into the Top Hostel (84, Ben Yehuda St.) with its lovely view over Tel-Aviv and in the area best for travellers for 10 shekels a night.

The next day we went to Galilee Tours (Hayarkon St somewhere) to book up but one of the girls visas was up so she couldn't get her Egyptian visa.

On Tuesday we went down to Shalom tower (the tallest building in Israel) to get her the Israeli visa for another 3 months that was only needed till Friday and a fine all costing 50 shekels. We then went to Galilee Tours to buy our tickets and pay for our Egyptian visa. The total cost of just the Egyptian visa, 3 nights 3 to a room in a 3* hotel (bed and breakfast) and return coach to Cairo and back cost about $120 which was quite good. (There are other companies and ways to get into Egypt).

After having to wait a day because of an Israeli holiday, we finally left on Friday morning. En route we stopped at a service area in Israel and drove right past our old Moshav until we finally came to the border.

My first impressions of the customs were good (all I heard was bad news from people) until we came to the Egyptian side where we had to pay for something else (forgotten). After ages of pushing and queuing we finally got through to our bus (not a bad bus) and realised we were now in a completely different world of poverty. To think this was right next door to rich and successful settlements was incredible. The following bus journey to Cairo was to be the best bus ride yet. We drove through territory that was once Israeli occupied but was now derelict, into a real saharan dune like desert with small oases here and there and the most beautiful empty beaches too.

After about 3 hours we came to the Suez canal. To get across this big wide canal we caught a ferry to a relatively fertile land. We drove and stopped at a restaurant where the humidity and flies made eating rather uncomfortable especially as you're also unsure of everything.

We drove on again into another desert before finally hitting Cairo. We didn't drive through any suburbs we literally went straight into a city. As we got closer into the heart our crackpot driver started showing us things of beauty like strange monuments, fascinating places and where their president lives etc. The centre of Cairo seemed to be one big traffic jam with horns blowing everywhere, taxis and old bangers for buses literally cramming the streets.

Fortunately the Windsor Hotel (19 Alfy Bey St. Tel 915277) was better than the one we were supposed to stay at. It was one of these old British Colonial hotels but now a bit run down compared to the Sheraton and Hilton.

That night we went to a local restaurant on Alfy Bey St. with an American girl we had met. The meal we ordered should have cost approximately £8-15 in a good European restaurant but only cost us LE95 Egyptian pounds or £3 to our astonishment plus the girls got the attention of the Arab waiters. We dared not go any further that night.

The following day after an early start we left for the Egyptian museum in the centre of Cairo (Tahir Sq.). It is situated to one side of a big space, about the size of 3 football pitches with five roads entering it and a real mess of traffic trying to get from one side to the other. The museum itself cost approximately £1 to enter; however we had purchased a scholar card in Tel-Aviv (ISSTA 109 Ben Yehuda) which was to give us on average 50% reduction on certain transport and entrance fees.

The museum itself was an incredible look into history of the land even for me and I wasn't too interested in history. It ranged from the Tutankhamen collection to all the Egyptian dynasties with monuments and articles (mummies too) going back four thousand years.

The rest of that day we spent looking for a good restaurant from a "Let's Go" book and got lost at night, only to be rescued by a local student who happened to be driving past. He was called Mohammed and was to be a great help in showing us the sights of Cairo.

On Sunday we were picked up by Mohammed who took us to the Pyramids where the view was incredible – even more so as all the tourists and sellers asking for baksheesh (money) had not arrived yet plus a smog was hiding the City. We had all the Pyramids to ourselves, until everyone arrived.

At one point we decided to hire some horses and ride about. After I finally got used to riding a horse and Lisa could sit straight we left, led by this boy of about 8 who constantly tried to kiss the girls. We even went inside the three main Pyramids down small narrow tunnels. We went into Cheops 137m tall, Chephren 136m and Mycerinus 66m, without the horses of course. The entrance fee was LE3 to see them all. Inside they were something else. Cramped small passageways led for miles to what seemed into a hot and smelly tomb (empty). In the middle you can see the exact centres of the Pyramid where strange gravitational forces are supposed to exist. After this tour and being asked to pay a bit more Baksheesh we finally left these incredible 4670 year-old time capsules.

The night that followed we all went out with our friend to see where he and his friends go out at night-fortunately not one of the many homosexual nightclubs but to a tea bar right in the heart of the old City. It was one of these very old establishments covered with mirrors everywhere. They are like British pubs but men go to drink lots of tea and smoke hashish. I enjoyed myself there but the girls must have felt like beauty queens because all the men, trying to look as inconspicuous as possible, crowded round. At one point they were arguing for seats. As we left the bar a local grabbed Janice where he really shouldn't have. In reply to this she hit him really hard then the other Arabs laid into the dirty old man.

The next day I stayed in bed with the notorious Egyptian diarrhoea (notorious to any tourist in Egypt) with its painful effects. Fortunately I managed to struggle off to the local Chemist (where all Egyptian pharmacists have to be trained doctors) and came up with the miracle cure of some funny tablets.

At night we left Ramsis station (for Luxor). We had to buy the tickets about 24 hours before departure which cost us about LE4 with a scholar card.

As we got on the train we managed to grab some seats which were not ours but as nobody sat in their correct allocated seat, who cared. The journey took 18 hours and involved one bloke asking me to come to his flat (I told him what to do with his flat in a few words). Another bloke who constantly stared at people and a crackpot Dutch girl who would not shut up, drove everybody crazy. The train carriage itself was like any English train (a lot cheaper though) except on the 3rd class carriage next door where 3 sat to a seat in noisy wooden smelly carriages with people sleeping on the racks. The toilets were the worst. The floor was smothered with excrement.

When I woke early in the morning the view from the train was over the Nile lined with palm trees and bright green fields on the other side. However if I looked out the other side of the train all I could see was dry rocks and desert.

We arrived in Luxor at 2pm to be mobbed by touts. It was very very hot and dirty with horse droppings from carriages everywhere. We booked into the Sphinx hotel. Our stay at the Sphinx wasn't to last very long as we found a pension on the more cleaner, better side of town. We made friends with the owners who fortunately gave us a reduced price and a fan. Because it was so hot, everywhere shut up during the day so we only did things in the morning. unless we went to the swimming pool at the Etap hotel. I was chased by this Arab who either fancied me or wanted me to buy some special carpets.

There are two main Temples in Luxor. Karnak and Luxor Temple. Karnak had a sound and light show at night like the Pyramids in Cairo. Both Temples are pretty impressive.

We cycled all the way via a ferry to the valley of Kings. This was a big mistake. We left at 8am but by 9am it was in the 90's and we were drinking Baraka (water) like fish. By 10am it was in the 100's, Lisa was cracking up with the pressure of pedalling up the hill through this continuous valley in very hot temperatures.

When we finally made it we went straight into the air conditioned cafe and drunk like we'd been lost in the desert for weeks. As the tourists left early we got to see all the tombs minus anyone except for the guards. One of these exposed my film to the light. Inside the hieroglyphics were impressive and gave an impression that we were trespassing over sacred places.

On 14th June we left Luxor to travel further South to Aswan, a much cleaner town and better people too. Aswan itself is the gateway to Egypt and to the Aswan dam and the end of the train line.

For a day trip a whole bunch of us hired a taxi and went even further South (about 300km) through alien desert with its mirages and no sign of life to the most southern point of Egypt. Abu Simbel being 3 hours drive costing LE10 for the taxi and LE4 entrance (scholar) was well worth it. The size of these two monuments was colossal, with its giant statues. These ancient people sure knew how to impress. The idea was to scare the Nubiens in this case. We couldn't stay too long because of the extreme temperature even at 9am.

We left Aswan by Felucca (a traditional fishing boat about 8 metres long) to sail for 3 nights until arriving at Esna. This was the peak of my travels - the scenery and the fact you were so far away from civilisation. Just two boats sailing down stream together made this paradise and there's even a couple of small Temples on route too. There were 8 in our boat and 10 in the other.

At one point the Captain (Pastawi) even took us to his home in a small village just off the Nile where his mother made us tea and a meal which tasted great.

Despite rumours the Nile is relatively clean until you come to Cairo so we were free to swim about as much as we liked. The trip cost us about LE20. All meals were prepared by the Captain and his assistant but we paid for all the food beforehand and it was extremely cheap.

When we got off we headed straight for Luxor by taxi. We had a quick shower at our friends pension before leaving by the night train for Cairo.

We didn't stay long in Cairo because we stayed in a dump called the Golden Hotel. When someone complained about a faulty shower the owner would replace it with someone else's. However we ate well at the Felfela restaurant off Talaat Harb St. somewhere, we also made a good American friend who was studying Arabic.

At exactly 12am on 25th June we left by coach for Dahab in the Sinai Peninsula. We arrived at about 10am at an ex Kibbutz (taken over by Egyptians and Bedouin) where I met a friend from Newcastle and we all got a taxi to the Bedouin Village. The village itself was a settlement of straw huts, some restaurants along the palm fringed sandy coast and some small accommodation blocks about 2m by 3m big for LE1 a day. They had nothing inside, not even locks so one of us always looked after our important possessions.

What made this place was the coral reef with its spectacular under water scenery, supposedly the best in the world. Fortunately we had the foresight to buy a snorkel and goggles in Cairo although you also need something to protect your feet from the sharp coral. The underwater scenery was so good that I was forever swimming about investigating different coloured fish etc. The reef was a sharp contrast to the mountainous desert behind us. One mountain being Mt Sinai where Moses received the 10 Commandments and is a monastery now. Unfortunately I never had the money to see this.

The restaurants were okay but everything was more expensive, probably because there wasn't any electricity, (generators only) or water or sewage. All the water we bought in bottles, and a toilet was a hole in the ground. You had to be careful of the scorpions and sand spiders.

Unfortunately I couldn't stay long at this paradise with its hot sun and cool breezes before I had to leave Janice and Lisa and other traveller friends for Israel again. I left by bus, which went by the coast road and only occasionally went inland into the mountainous interior. I finally made it through the border at Taba and caught the bus for Eilat (10 shekels).

On arriving in Eilat I couldn't believe how clean it was and the fact I was back in civilisation again. I put my watch forward, had a good meal at the bus station and caught the bus to BeerSheeva via the Jordan Valley while just catching a glimpse of the Dead Sea for the first time.

After BeerSheva I managed to make it back to my old Moshav with two Shekels to spare to be greeted by a proper bed and old friends.

On the following day we had a party for some reason and the next morning, while getting over a big hangover, I was offered work with yet another South African called Ivan who turned out to be really good. He'd give me a lift to the pool whenever I liked, a beer after work sometimes plus food for nothing. He even invited me to his wife's birthday party which gave me a chance to see other members get drunk and make fools of themselves.

The first job I did with Ivan was in the old hothouse pruning roses but this time I had a Scottish girl to work with. Another job which was quite different was to dismantle the electrics from one of his hothouses.

Unfortunately a lot of the other volunteers had left and all there was to do was swimming or the cinema. Even when Janice and Lisa returned Lisa left for England. I hung on at Talme Yosef for a month until I decided to leave and visit my old Kibbutz on the Lebanese border.

To my astonishment a lot of the old volunteers had returned but I couldn't stay as there weren't any places for volunteers. This didn't bother me because I was a bit bored with Israel by this time (& my visa was up).

On Tuesday 3rd August I purchased a standby ticket for $110 from ISSTA Travel Agents and left Israel and the best adventure of my life for boring Northampton the next day.

THE WILD FRONTIER

I can put my finger on two reasons for my decision to travel. The first was a simple curiosity, perhaps more a yearning, to discover the world outside my own existing and rather limited one; a trait, I think, you'll find in a lot of people. The second was the result of spending four years at university being groomed for a career in Town & Regional planning and realising that our glorious bureaucratic system wasn't going to allow me or my peers any real say or control in our area of competence for at least the first 20 years or so. I didn't feel like nine-to-fiving it to find out if I was right and having only regrets that I didn't take the opportunity, when I'd had it, to taste a little bit of adventure and see what the world in general had on offer. You'd be amazed at how many times I've been confronted with that last regret from people I've met along the road.

So much for the reasons to my venture, the planning was equally uncomplex. Obviously a persons' reqirements for any globe trotting trip will be tailored to his or her individual needs and good, basic check-lists you can find in a host of travel books invariably covering every coneivable area of interest so I won't bore you with a blow by blow account of mine. As far as baggage was concerned, weight was my prime concern. Again, you could make use of a travel book, liberal quantities of plain commonsense never go amiss. I'll guarantee you'll end up dumping half of your gear along the way as it is, so I wouldn't worry too much about it. I personally invested in a good tent, sleeping bag and backpack to stuff them all in. You get what you pay for in this world so before you start cutting corners to finance that last big drinking session prior to heading off into the wide blue yonder, take a moment to reflect on what that yonder's going to be like with a tent that's as waterproof as a brown paper bag and a backpack that decides to tear its straps half way up your first mountain trek.

Musts for the traveller as far as I'm concerned have to include a Walkman and a couple of tapes of your all-time favourites. I'm all in favour of absorbing oneself into a culture as much as possible but after a couple of weeks of good ol' Mexican bee-bop you'll be thankful for those tapes you brought along. You can always swap them when you're fed up with them. The same goes for a good book.

Get some heavy-duty bin-liners and masking tape for tears. They will protect your gear, and yourself at a pinch, from getting wet, and also your backpack from the ravages of public transportation systems. Bus baggage holds, even in the States, can be pretty filthy and a plastic bag also prevents baggage handlers from picking up your rucksack by the inevitable wrong strap.

Take a camera and keep a diary too for those memory making, earth shattering experiences. You might even be able to make a few bob out of writing the odd article.

Obviously, money is important. Take as much as you can legally get your hands on or better still, to aviod carring around wads of traveller's cheques, arrange access to a home account before leaving. Credit cards are also handy and help you negotiate that first obstacle, the dreaded Immigration Officer, if you're short on ready cash. I took about $1,000 U.S. in traveller's cheques, about $100 of it in dollar bills.

I never bothered with insurance of any kind for my travels. It's a good idea if you can afford it. I couldn't so I didn't bother. However, whilst in the States I found an organisation 'Youth International Educational Exchange' that for a £10 membership fee will provide a year's worldwide medical insurance that includes, amongst other things, $100 U.S./day to a maximum of 60 days for in-hospital sickness and $2,000 U.S. accident related medical reimbursement for each accident. To be eligible you don't have to be a student or under 26 or any other such nonsense. The only requirement is that you have to buy the card in the States. Great if you're going to America, not so great if you aren't.

My first destination was the U.S.A., primarily because of the language. Having a somewhat supercillious 'couldn't care less' attitude towards other languages in my younger years, English, I ashamedly admit, is the only one I know, so my choice of the States as a travelling first base was made out of caution.

As far as a more detailed plan of attack I didn't have one, except the goal of experiencing as many cultures and lands as I could. Plus, there was always that thought gnawing at the back of my mind that I'd fall flat on my face within the first two weeks or perhaps not even make it past immigration.

And with all those reassuring thoughts I set off on the 10 pm Newcastle to London Rapide bus wondering whether that 9 to 5 option wasn't such a bad idea after all!

Eight or so hours and one rotten movie later, I was at Heathrow boarding by budget necessity a Kuwait Airlines plane, every worst case scenario of general death, destruction and mayhem that could possibly be waiting for me on the other side of the Atlantic churning through my head.

Seven hours later, via another rotten movie and a lot of reading from the Koran, courtesy of Kuwait Airlines, I was in J.F.K. airport facing a rather stern looking gentleman spouting a nifty pair of polarised glasses and not too keen on letting me into his country. I'd heard a lot of horror stories about immigration, especially in the States. I took the precaution of bringing letters from home, a return ticket (I found no difficulty in selling the return portion once in New York, the hostels and Universities are good bets) and a £1,000 bundle of low denomination travellers cheques to impress our friendly immigration officer with. I didn't come up against any problems, however be warned, they can and will search you and your possessions including diary, letters etc. for incriminating evidence of intentions to work illegally. They're obsessed that everyone's going to steal their country away from them and suck their economy dry. Now, after traversing a few borders I've found that money ($100 U.S. a week) and a clean respectable appearance should get you in with little trouble.

The money end of it, if you don't have sufficient, can be solved with a simple dodge. First of all, you need to borrow a sizeable chunk of readies from a very, very trusting and generous friend. Buy your travellers cheques with them and then simply pretend to lose them. All you need is a simple convincing story and probably a police report. Thence to the nearest phone to report your tragic misfortune to your traveller cheque company. Make sure you do all of this in a city with a branch of your chosen travellers cheque company so you can get hold of your replacement cheques. Took me 3 days with American Express in Belize. So now you have your old invalid set and your new valid set. Cash your new set in and return your borrowed money to your trusting and generous friend. This leaves you with the old set, a nice wad of flash money, not to spend but to impress nasty immigration officials.

Cashing travellers cheques is no problem in the States or Canada, however, in Central America at least, you can find yourself being docked a few dollars worth on every cheque cashed. A few dollars might not sound much but when you realize that these few dollars will get you a bed for the night and a good meal in your belly, you may not be so inclined to pay. The only sure way not to have to pay a commission is to cash your cheque at the nearest travellers cheque representative office. American Express have, by far and away, the greatest coverage in Central America so that's the company I'd purchase my cheques from.

Regarding length of stay in a country, I found the States and Canada no real problem as long as you're not caught in possession of an expired entry permit whilst in the country. I found leaving Canada and Mexico didn't pose any difficulty. The only other countries I've had direct experience of immigration in are Mexico, Belize and Guatemala. Basically, expect to pay bribes entering and leaving Guatemala and you won't be disappointed 9 times out of 10. Their size usually depends on how bad a day the bloke on the other side of the counter's had. The biggest fine (bribe) I paid was $2 so it isn't that bad. Just think of the poor Aussies who forever seemed to be the butt of $10, $20 and even $50 bribes when I was down there. If you're hell bent against parting with your money I found that the officials usually stamped my passport before requesting a bribe and a simple excuse to get you outside i.e. my money's with my friend outside etc. and a quick jog over the border and you're away. Personally, for a couple of bucks I don't think its worth the hassle.

I had no problems with the slightly more official Mexican border crossings and that seems to be the rule, the same with Belizean crossing points. If you do get asked for a bribe and no way out of paying it my advice is to simply fork up. Blowing your top and arguing with them simply bounces off and only leads to more hassle, a vigorous bag search and probably an increased bribe to pay. One word on the Belizean/Guatemalan border crossing and a further indication not to treat as gospel what you read in travel guides: I found that contrary to what I'd read in so-called up to the minute guides, the Guatemalan/Belizean border was fully open to British subjects. I ended up crossing it several times, once during the attempted coup, and never encountered any problems except the usual petty bribe. This serves as an illustration of relying on second-hand information too much. It's an obvious point but the only way to find out about something is to see for yourself. I've kicked myself a few times for relying on the information of so-called experts on my travels and ended up missing out. With a little practice and a few hard lessons however, you soon learn to sort out, with reasonable accuracy, the good information from the bad. In the end, if in doubt, go and see for yourself.

So much for customs. Just one of the little irritations of travelling. For my first night in the good ol' US of A, I actually ended up getting lost on the New York subway and landed in Harlem at

11 pm. One naive, white honky, resplendent in backpack, subway map in hand. I stuck out in the crowd you might say. However, I was directed to a Hostel cum bedsit for illegal aliens and there I stayed in Harlem for the next month. My plans initially dictated that I pass straight through New York. So much for planning. To survive in the 'Big A', as you can imagine, requires money in copious amounts, so work soon became the order of the day for which I discovered you need a 9 digit social security number. The first 3 give you the State, the middle 2 have something to do with the year of issue and the last 4 don't matter.

Basically, you choose a state at the opposite end of the country to which you're working to prolong the bureaucratic processing system, anything from 90 days to forever. The second item, if you can't fake a Yankee accent, and I soon found on my first job hunt that I'm apparently hopeless, is a believable cover story to get around the necessity for a work visa. You know, mother was a Yank etc. etc. With these in hand I headed off for my first contact, a removal company, and landed a job on the spot. It sounded too easy and as it turned out it was. All I ended up being was a fill-in with all of the full-time work going to local people – I only made $38 for half a days work. However, I eventually turned up a job as a messenger, a bringer of gifts, an essential cog in the vast machine that is New York. I legged it around Manhattan Island as fast as I could delivering everything from "final demands" to the latest Yves St. Laurent creation. However, it turned out to be an excellent way of seeing New York and getting paid for it. It also turned out to be a lot easier after the purchase of a bike. You can imagine the sight, biking down 5th Avenue dressed in a baseball cap, shades, brown-ale T-shirt and bikers shorts screaming at the tourists to get out of the Goddamn way. It did take me a while to reach that state but reach it I did. The job literally took me to the four corners of Manhattan, from the Wall Street Stock market to the Harlem of Manhattan, from China Town to Greenwich Village. The transition between different areas is sudden and total with no more than a street to separate them. By the end of an average day I'd have criss-crossed through at least a third of them and was invariably suffering from multiple culture shock.

Cruising around the New York Subway System is quite an eye-opener. It's advisable to travel in pairs, though, on certain lines. Quite a few women carry knuckledusters in plain view on the uptown line and it's one of the few places you can see very quiet and meek looking Americans en masse. The beggars or 'panhandlers' are 10 a penny down there too. Everything from supposed Vietnam vets to drug victims. I got to know them by sight after a while especially when I was a foot messenger and using the subway a lot. There was a bloke down there who'd been lost and looking for a dollar to get him home for over 3 weeks. He's probably still down there. They're all fakes. There are some panhandlers who can earn upward of $100 a day. I could well believe it looking into some of their cups which are regularly emptied to look suitably bare, so I wouldn't feel any moral obligation to pay these people anything. I gave money according to performance of which I think the best was the black dude who must've walked down 3 flights of stairs to the subway covered in false blood to ask me for a dollar to get to the hospital. I had to give him a buck for the acting alone.

The other illegal jobs people got from the hostel included painters, waiters/waitresses, gallery assistants, night watchmen, all the way to nude models for art students – up to $9 -10 an hour for that. Later on this year I should, hopefully, be selling Xmas trees on the streets out there.

I bumped into one traveller who swore by a pair of Dr. Martin's and a stylish haircut as the essential items for any traveller waiting to pick up work on the way. When looking for work he would just pick out some conspicuous cafe and place himself open to public viewing. He claimed that it had gotten him a job twice in Toronto, as a barman and a hair stylist. He'd never cut hair in his life, which brings me neatly to a further point worth noting when looking for work on your travels. Don't be daunted by the fact that you haven't the slightest clue what the job on offer entails. I fell into that trap in New York and missed the opportunity of some interesting and well paid work. Nothing ventured nothing gained as they say and in any case most of the jobs travellers find themselves going for require only common sense. A few days following somebody's coat tails will find you at ease with it as if you were a veteran. Basically, the only way to get most jobs while you're travelling is to lie your head off.

My stay in New York was in April/May and I was due to be in Canada by June. I decided that hitching would be both the most economical and probably the most interesting means of travel. So it was that on a bright, crisp morning, I landed on the first of many, many on-ramps to the freeway system of the U.S., clutching my little Union Jack and smiling my biggest smile for all of the nice motorists. Needless to say I was slightly apprehensive of sticking my thumb out in violent America and had been pumped with the usual stories of mayhem and destruction that were bound to befall any unwary traveller. As usual, while having a basis of truth, they were mostly the result of over imaginative minds and armchair experts. It took me all of 10 minutes to procure my first lift, a lift which also ended in an offer of work in the construction industry when I returned to New Jersey, and 5 minutes for the next which took me 500 miles deep into Indiana and introduced me to the interstate system of the U.S. Basically similar to our dual carriageways, mostly a lot emptier, but with the usual truck stops. I discovered that hitching in the States is just as easy or difficult as in Europe. I must have covered around 15,000 miles by now in the States and have had some great experiences ranging from crawfish parties in Mississippi to side-trips in Mount St. Helen's and the bayous of Louisiana, and practically every lift ended in an offer of a meal and a bed for the night. At one stage I ended up behind the wheel of a 75 ton, 18 wheel, Kenworth semi hauling everything from bicycles and the finest Idaho potatoes to 200 barrels of solid cyanide capsules. Driving the semi lasted for about 3 weeks covering 2 loops of the U.S. and was just through hitching and a willingness to have a go. I can't even drive, but over the course of the 3 weeks I learnt to line-haul the freeways, just driving the inter-state system to avoid any complicated manoeuvres or gear-changes. It was a fantastic experience introducing me to the States from the perspective of the "Trucker" and again, by pure chance whilst hitching. Chasing a sunset into the Canyonlands of New Mexico or driving through an electrical storm on the Great Plains of Wyoming behind the wheel of a semi are just two of the sights I'll never forget.

Hitching tricks revolve simply around common sense. Look respectable and clean. The main reason, I was often told, for my lifts was the Union Jack I displayed. A sign telling where I was headed didn't go amiss either. As long as you look the clean, respectable tourist you shouldn't have too many problems. As far as best places to hitch from, you're supposed to stay off the freeways but, of course, that's where the traffic is. I just stand 100 yards or so down the freeway from the on-ramp where traffic can see me clearly yet I can still debate as to whether I'm on the freeway or ramp if some police officer turns up. I actually had no problems with the police, just laid the accent on thick and pleaded ignorance. It seemed to work for me, even to the extent of getting the odd lift off them to a better hitching spot. I've heard bad stories concerning Georgia, Louisiana and Mississippi where on-the-spot fines are common and so are free lifts into the back of beyond to be dumped. However, I've hitched around the States for many miles without so much as a police car even stopping. I also found truck-stops, unlike in Europe, to be a pain where back packers are illegal and considered to be social deviants, hell bent on killing every truck driver they see. After a few failed attempts I've given up on them but I've bumped into travellers who head straight for the nearest '76' truck-stop every time they're hitching somewhere. Apparently, the best places to ask around are the pumps or outside the restaurant/store.

I left the trucking business in July and after a rather expensive 4th July in Philadelphia I was left requiring employment again. This time I had no success and I ended up travelling north towards New York and managed to land a job on an apple/pumpkin orchard in New Hampshire, where I ended up working for the next 5 months pruning, spacing and picking and generally having the time of my life. The New England colours in Autumn have to be seen to be believed.

My target for the start of the New Year was Central and South America, a 6 month jaunt originally. However, as so often with plans, it didn't work out. I actually never managed to get past Guatemala. I hitched to Mexico in the late fall arriving in Mexico City via Xmas day in a mission in some hick town in Texas, temperatures in the 90's and not a soul to be seen. On the way down to Mexico I spent a couple of weeks trying out mission life in New Mexico and Texas. It was an illuminating experience. Also one of the most depressing times of my life as I witnessed the sad existence of some of the people living in these hostels. At a pinch missions are fine if you're in dire need of a free meal and a roof over your head. But realise that you'll certainly be the only back packer in these places and as such looked upon as a source of money, clothing etc. Make sure your back pack is securely locked away. Sleep in your clothes or they'll get nicked and put your shoes under your pillow or, likewise, they'll disappear. With these precautions taken you'll still be in for an eye-opening experience as to how the more unfortunate of U.S. society manage to survive. As a foot note, always go for the private church missions as they provide the best food and lodgings, the Salvation Army the worst and often the most dangerous. The only exception is apparently the Salvation Army mission in Seattle which according to my bed-fellows down in Las Cruces and Van Horn is the best Goddamn mission in the States.

Juarez, my first stop in Mexico, was quite a shock in spite of my expecting the worst. Everything was crumbling, filth everywhere, a planners worst nightmare. People with no shoes and soldiers all over the place. I eventually found the railway station and after 6 hours managed to get a train to Mexico city. I should've suspected something was up when I only had to pay $10 for the ticket. Mexico city was 1500 miles away. Sure enough, the fun started when I realised that the only way onto the train was through one of the windows. My first view of the inside was almost enough to send me back the way I had come. Every conceivable space had jammed or crushed into it some human or material object – I was fortunately spared the cattle and chickens on this trip. I caught up with my backpack down by the toilet, a hole in the wagon floor, where I spent the next 36 hours protecting myself and my belongings from spit, spilt food and drink and excrement, slowly making its way the length of the wagon. Not speaking a word of Spanish I amused myself with watching the ice form on the inside of the wagon windows. I spent 2 nights on the train with temperatures well below 0 c. There was this one bloke who hadn't paid for his ticket so they made him stand outside during the night. He was in a pretty bad state to begin with but by the time he managed to hobble back in his lips had turned blue and all he could do was dribble at the mouth and shake a lot. I didn't see him again. I woke up in Mexico City in the early hours with only myself left on the train and feeling like death warmed up. So if you think the 36 hour train rides through Yugoslavia, Greece and the East coast of Italy are bad wait until you try the Mexican version.

The above is just a sample of what the transportation system in Central America can be like. Taking all things into consideration bus travel is by far the most convenient and cheapest. Further, while learning of baggage being lost or stolen on trains I encountered no such problems with the buses there. Indeed, a lot of bus lines in Mexico are now being held responsible for any luggage stolen. Bus travel in Belize and Guatemala is still dominated by the wonderful combi' in which the traveller invariably shares seats with chickens, goats, etc.

It's in countries such as Mexico, Belize and Guatemala that you begin to reap the real rewards of travel. For me this is the direct experience of other cultures and a few memories to take home with me. Some of my more vivid experiences include watching a sunset from atop the pyramids at Tikal, 196 feet above the jungle canopy, being in the Guatemala capital at the time of the attempted coup there, finally being able to hold down a conversation in Spanish, spear-gun fishing for nurse sharks in the Belizean Caribbean, being arrested for drinking (I was walking home) by two Guatemalan cops drunk as skunks and hunting for gringo money, getting drunk on rum on a deserted island in the Caribbean in front of one of the most beautiful sunsets I've ever seen and then waking up with the hangover of hangovers in front of the most beautiful sunrise I've ever seen, walking into a little Mexican church and realising that I'm probably the first gringo some of the children in front of me have ever seen (their running, crying, to their mothers' skirts was pretty good confirmation), watching the rising sun slowly haul itself over the coastal ranges of Puerto Escondido, casting the sea an orange pink, and watching the locals and the pelicans fish in the lagoon opposite.

Hotels for the budget traveller can be quite a shock on first encounter – I lived comfortably in cities for around $10 a day more or less. Most of the £2 a night variety are basically places to wash and sleep in. I won't describe them as having a toilet, shower and sink, as in a lot of the places that would be stretching the bounds of imagination to the very limit. If you're really lucky you can manage to get water from two of the implements, and as far as hot water is concerned – get with it – this is Central America. Stick a bucketful in the sun for an hour or two, that'll do you. Used toilet paper is usually deposited in a bin by the side (the toilets can't handle it). Unfortunately, due to the rather sporadic cleaning of the rooms within most of the hotels this results in some rather strange and fantastic scenes when first entering the domain of your bathroom. The smells, well I don't think that they can be adequately translated into the written word, at least not by me.

A lot of the beds I wouldn't dare sleep on unless a clean sheet could be procured. There you lie, gazing around at your room, the fan above you, if you have one, humming away and the window slats, if you have a window that is, casting striped shadows across the room, wondering what movie the scene come from. All good fun.

One thing to remember in Central America is to haggle for everything, even the cold drinks sold on the corner stands. Local people see you mostly as a walking money machine and constantly try to squeeze it out of you. For this reason it's always important to ensure that you know the price of something before you consume it, otherwise you won't have a leg to stand on when you're charged quadruple its value. I was constantly confronted with idiots not realising the harm they were doing as they played the rich important tourist in poor little Central America. Firstly, for travellers like myself who immediately became subject to the prices they paid, but more importantly for the locals who have to live in the aftermath of the money spewing tourists. Tourist frequented stores steadily hike up prices driving away local custom to fewer and fewer stores, which naturally seeing the increasing demand hike up their prices also. However, the inability of the workforce to push through pay increases in line with the price rises, i.e. the same old too many people, not enough jobs syndrome, creates an even more tenuous financial position for the average family. And I mean just your average family which is invariably living on the bread line to begin with. If you want to see real poverty just hang out in places such as Acapulco or the more popular resorts in the Yucatan.

My experience with the diseases of Central America has thankfully been limited to a bout of advanced amoebic dysentry coupled with intestinal fever, for good measure. It's something I don't exactly recall with fondness and serves as a painful lesson not to mess around with the tap water down there. I caught it towards the end of my stay in Guatemala, entirely through my own stupidity thinking that 6-months was sufficient time for my antibodies to have adjusted to the local strains of bacteria. I learnt to my cost after drinking water around the Lake Atitlan area, a particularly notorious spot for bad water, that my immune system had a long, long way to go. It hit me halfway up a volcano, not the best place in the world to develop symptoms of amoebic dystentry, and I literally spent the next week on a toilet, with stomach cramps, unable to keep anything down and basically wanting to curl up and die, before I could get hold of some decent medication.

If you are ailing at any time, I advise a doctor as opposed to well-meaning advice from friends. The doctor might be more expensive but you're sure of a cure. I was eventually put on to Flagyll which did the job perfectly. It has, apparently, no side effects and, talking to a doctor from the States, is about the only safe drug that will kill off amoebic dysentry.

Innoculations against some of the more serious strains of diseases down there are, as any good travel book and as commonsense should dictate, strongly advisable. If our glorious leader Margaret Thatcher hasn't by now totally ruined the health service, you'll still be able to get all of the ones you need back home. If for some reason you can't or fail to complete a course never fear. You can get them done for no charge down Mexico way in Mexico City. I forget the place you go to now but any of the tourist information booths or the youth hostels will be able to direct you. As far as taking malarial pills, I found that quite a large proportion of the people don't bother, mostly on the grounds of assumed side-effects. As to the truth on side effects I don't know. I never actually met anyone going blind or losing hair through taking them, however, I did actually meet people who had caught malaria and believe me, it's not a pretty sight. I was able to get malarial tablets free of charge in Mexico City.

The language, or rather lack of it, was an obvious barrier on my travels in Central America. However, with the cost of living being so low in these countries, signing myself onto a language course in Guatemala for a few weeks cost me only $70 a week. That included full board and lodging and 4-hours tuition, 5 days a week.

I managed to live very well on $100 a week in the cities, eating out, getting drunk and living in hostels, and when out hiking or in small villages I was living on a lot less than that. It all depends on your lifestyle but I found few travellers who went over $100 a week.

I have only one regret about my Central American trip and that is my failure to venture off the well-worn 'gringo trail'. Sticking to what travel books tell you takes away some of the sense of discovery in travel. There's so much more to see and do if you only push yourself a little away from the relative security of the well beaten path. Hopefully I'll get to correct it next time around.

Whilst on my chilly wanderings north and then back south to Mexico I made use of the plasma centres, found in almost every town of any size, to earn myself a few bucks. Prices range from $8 to $16 for first timers. I don't know if you receive more cash for rarer blood. I've only got the boring ordinary type so I didn't enquire. You're supposed to give blood only every other day and to ensure this they coat your finger with a ultra-violet dye, but if you're particularly in need of money simply cover your hands in grease and dirt before you enter the plasma centre and Bob's your uncle. However, I really wouldn't recommend this practice and there are plenty of other less detrimental ways of making steady money. I never quite managed to get myself on to one of those weekend experimental test programs but they are out there and it's possible to get as much as $300 U.S. a weekend. However, there are obvious risks and if you have limited or no medical knowledge the safest bets are the psychological test programs. I'd recommend staying away from tests involving needles or brightly coloured little tablets.

The beginning of June saw me almost penniless again in Guatemala and in dire need of well-paid work. The only place to make money fast is in North America so with a cheap Greyhound ticket bought in Mexico City ($109 for 7-days unlimited travel in the U.S. and Canada) I headed north. Six or seven days later I ended up in Prince George, British Columbia and via a few chance meetings became involved in the world of tree-planting in which I worked for 3-months, June to August. It's hard work, 10-hours minimum a day but more often 12 and up and you're lucky to get out of the bush before the end of the contract, anything from a fortnight to a month. It's piece rate so if you don't work you don't get paid. When it rains it pours, often sleet. The sun raises temperatures into the 90's bringing the mosquitoes, blackflies, noseeums, and horseflies out looking for blood, and the tree-bags weigh a ton. However, the money can be good and the areas you work in unbelievable. I planted in areas ranging from the Bowron Cut – the largest clear-cut in the world, dwarfing the Amazon cut – to blocks in front of glaciers a kilometre wide. The wildlife is unsurpassed, from moose to bald-eagles to grizzly bears. I even managed a bit of gold panning, striking my first bit of gold. A minute flake, perhaps, but after standing up to your knees in some freezing river bed trying to ignore the mosquitoes and biting cold that crawls ever deeper into your bones with each fresh pan, it's like hitting the motherlode. We worked some of the larger known deposit areas which, thanks to intensive industrial scale placer mining and indiscriminate dumping of tailings, resembled something out of a lunar lanscape. Of course, it's not all gold in these areas but there's plenty of pyrite or 'fool's gold'.

All of the jobs I've had to date were paid under-the-table and if you can't manage that, there's always the odd dodge like claiming you pay your own taxes and, of course, not doing it.

Simply through hitching you can find some great offers of work. I've a mate going to tend sled huskies in Alaska this fall, another one teaching English in Guatemala, both of them with no previous experience or related qualifications, just a willingness to have a go. I've found that you can't but avoid making connections while travelling that invariably lead to offers of work for the future.

In retrospect I made the right decision in deferring a career for a bit of globetrotting. I've discovered not only a new world in my surroundings but also within myself and hopefully at the end of my travels I'll be a better person for it all. And if not, well, at least I'll have some amazing memories.

I'm sitting writing this in a bar in Inuvik. It's a small Eskimo town, at 71°C latitude, deep in the Arctic. It's white-out outside with the temperature just falling below minus 20°C and still dropping. It's over 1500 miles south to Dawson City in the Yukon, the nearest town, and from what the locals are telling me I've about 2-days before the road is shut off – and as far as winter woolies go I don't even have a pair of woollen gloves.

Well, here goes ....

INTO AFRICA by Jane Roberts

A little over 12 months ago I was bored with the job I had and the area I lived in. I had for a long time been an "armchair traveller" – always sitting around thinking how wonderful it would be to see the world but never actually doing anything – just dreaming. I suddenly decided that the only thing stopping me from doing it was myself. The decision was made but first I thought I should get some money together. The next day I handed my notice in at work and later that month I was staying with my brother in Milton Keynes and temping.

I had no idea where I wanted to go, how I was going to get there and who I would travel with. For the next month or so I worked and saved hard, in the meantime enquiring everywhere about travelling and working abroad. Eventually I got the idea of going to Africa I don't know where from. I made enquiries and eventually decided to go on an overland expedition. I got brochures from practically every company and eventually decided which one to go with. The trip was to last 17/19 weeks and travel through 7 countries, with an optional extra 6 weeks at the end to see additional countries. It sounded fantastic and the price was quite reasonable too. In the brochure it said it was possible to go and see the vehicle which would be used and so I went to investigate – the vehicle looked fine (a converted 16 ton Bedford) and Chris (the organiser) also showed me photos from previous trips.

A month later I was on a plane heading for Egypt with 23 other like minded people, Australians, English, New Zealanders and one American, all with the same destination and hope of excitement, thrill and adventure. Chris flew with us and his trainee driver met us at the airport with the big red truck (BRT).

It was the early hours of Thursday morning when we landed in Cairo. We spent around an hour sat in the back of BRT whilst Chris tried to locate a bag which had gone missing (luckily for us it was his bag). During this first hour we got to know one another and drank lots of Italian wine.

It was about 3.00am when we left the airport and drove through Cairo towards the pyramids. Several of us stood up at the front of the truck – we had to be very careful of low wires, trees and bridges. When we arrived at the pyramids several people climbed them in order to watch the sunrise, others went on horse rides – the rest of us were driven around to the other side where we were to get a spectacular view of the sun rising behind the pyramids – it was truly a fantastic way to begin my "dream come true".

We spent the next week seeing the sights of Cairo. It's a large city full of the continuous honking of car horns (I think it must be considered a criminal offence not to have and use a working horn in your car) and the ever persistent Egyptian eager to show you what he has to offer inside his shop. We visited carpet shops and workhouses – watching young children happily weaving intricate rugs, saw thousands of shops full of papyrus and watched it being made, museums, the citadel and all the other usual sites.

One afternoon after we'd exhausted ourselves with the sites of Cairo we headed for the Western Desert. A couple of hours out of Cairo and it began to get dark so we decided to turn off the road to camp. No sooner had all four wheels left the tarmac for sand and we were stuck. After some digging and laying of sand ladders we drove a little further to escape the noise of any passing traffic and set up camp for the night. The next morning we awoke to discover we weren't quite as far from Cairo as we thought – the pyramids were still in sight as tiny triangles on the distant horizon.

We drove most of the day through desert, but on a reasonable road, until we reached a small village called Baharia. We stopped here to pick up some supplies and then headed for an oasis with hot springs. As we set up camp for the night an Arab came to welcome us with his dog, he built us a fire and stayed close to the camp all night, keeping other curious Arabs at bay. The next morning he bid us farewell and left his dog, which we named Dippy, with us.

We stayed at the oasis for around five days and Dippy constantly looked after us, escorting us when we disappeared into the bush at night for the loo and making sure we weren't disturbed by anyone. When it was time for us to leave poor old Dippy ran behind the truck for as long as he could keep up and finally we left him in the distance barking.

After leaving the Western Desert we went to the Sinai for a couple of days before returning back to Cairo and then heading for Hurghada on the Red Sea coast. Driving down the coastal road we stopped to collect fire wood from the beach. As we were collecting the wood a car screeched to a halt on the road by our truck and an extremely worried looking man jumped out and started shouting in a mixture of Arabic and English, we got a basic idea of what he was trying to say, but Chris confirmed it by translating the Arabic. The man got back in his car and drove off whilst we all froze in our steps and looked at one another wondering what to do – we were smack bang in the middle of a mine field. Very slowly and carefully, in single file, we left the beach, stepping in one another's footsteps and once back on the road gave a great collective sigh of relief.

By now the afternoon was getting late and it was time to search for a suitable place to camp, but for the next hour all we passed were mine fields. Eventually as it got dark we followed a sandy road to a shack and got permission to camp there providing we didn't stray too far. It was a very windy spot and all the tents blew down. When we got up we discovered that about 50 yards away from us was a large crater – an exploded mine.

After an hour on the road we reached Hurghada and set up camp on the free beach. The next day we hired a boat and went snorkelling. The Red Sea is amazingly clear and has fantastic coral reefs and beautiful sea life. For lunch we had freshly caught grilled barracuda and on the way back we saw dolphins.

A couple of days later we hit the road again, this time heading inland towards Luxor and the Nile. As we left the coast behind we knew it would be the last time we saw the sea until we reached the Kenyan coast which was several months and a lifetime of experiences away.

As the day went on and we got further south we could feel the wind getting hotter. A little way out of Luxor we stopped at the temple of Dendara for a look around and arrived in Luxor around 8.00pm. As we drove in it was dark but all the temples, etc and many boats on the Nile were lit up and looked really good. Home for the next few days was to be at the YMCA. The next few days were spent either visiting the many crumblies in and around Luxor or relaxing around the swimming pool at the ETAP hotel.

For the next stage of the journey we had a change of transport and caught feluccas from Luxor. For this stretch we were joined by an Exodus group we'd met, so in total we had 4 feluccas each containing 7 or 8 or us and 2 crew. It was great fun sailing down the Nile just relaxing and watching the passing sights.

Ramadam had just begun and so none of the 'captains' were eating, drinking or smoking during the day, but as soon as 6.30 came they ate non-stop throughout the night, or so it seemed. Each night on the feluccas the 'captains' made music and sang for us and taught us how to dance the Nubian way. So after a couple of nights when we were by the dam at Isna we had a party. Going through the damn were 3 of our feluccas and a Nile cruise boat. The kitchen staff from the cruise boat had finished work for the evening and were all at the back of the boat making music, singing and dancing. They were singing tunes we were now familiar with and so we all got up on the bows of the boats and joined in with the fun. The funny thing was that whilst we were having this party by the dam all the tourists on the boat and the sides of the dam were watching – not only were they watching with amazement but they were all taking photos of us.

Next stop was Aswan. We spent several days relaxing and visiting local places of interest such as the Aswan High Damn and a camel market. We visited a man Chris knew, his family were Sudanese and very hospitable inviting all 24 of us in to share a meal. Chris tried to arrange for us to go by ferry across Lake Nasser to Wadi Halfa in Sudan, but it was very expensive and difficult and so we decided to go overland and enter Sudan illegally! Next we heard that in Khartoum there was an outbreak of Meningitis and so two of our party caught the train back to Cairo in order to obtain some serum for injections against Meningitis. Whilst we waited for them to return with the serum Chris, Morris (the trainee driver) and I spent the next couple of day replenishing the

280

food supplies by buying lots of pasta, rice, fuul (tinned beans) and pilchards and preparing the truck for the next stage of the journey. Once everything was organised and Mary and Jacqui (2 nurses who were with us) had given everyone an injection, we left for Abu Simbel.

Before we left it was time to say goodbye to 2 of the lads on the trip. Mat the only American with us had contacted home and had to return to retake an exam in order to start his work in October. Bret, from New Zealand, had decided he had gained enough confidence to be able to travel on his own and, not happy travelling with such a large crowd, bid us farewell.

As the heat of the day disappeared we left Aswan, hoping by now the road would have cooled down enough for us to travel on the new tyres on the truck. (We had put on the new tyres ready for the desert crossing).

This is an account from my diary, written by Shane, telling briefly what happened that night: "We may have left, but we didn't get very far, still within sight of the lights of Aswan we have a blow-out. What a fright! Sideways in the dust with everybody hanging on for dear life. The tyre is absolutely shredded (this is to be the first of 4 stops for tyres). More tyres start to shred and we have a bloody uncomfortable night in the back of the truck. More bloody punctures and tyre changes in the morning ... how depressing, we're gonna run out of tyres before we get anywhere exciting!"

I didn't get much sleep at all with helping out but one consolation is I now know how to change a tyre on a 16 ton truck!

Eventually the next day we reached Abu Simbel and found a fantastic place to camp on a peninsula close to the Abu Simbel temples on the edge of Lake Nasser. It was so peaceful and still - out of this world!

Spent the night discussing our plans for entering into Sudan and enjoying our final cold beers until we reach Central Africa.

Thursday 12th May, 1988 - "The plan is that after dinner we fill up with water, drive for a while and camp until around 4am when we will drive non-stop (other than when stuck) for at least 10 hours when hopefully we will be safely in Sudan ..."

You can enter Sudan almost any way but it is illegal to travel overland from Egypt - I don't know why but that's the way it is - if the Egyptians catch you they escort you back to Aswan where you go before the Court. The penalty is not very great but it causes a lot of hassle and delay. The desert has many army out-posts so you have to keep your eyes open and be careful.

Friday 13th (What a day to attempt to cross the border!) - Got up at 4am and after breakfast, found a leak in one of the tanks which had to be repaired. Then headed off into the desert. I sat in the cab with Chris and Morris and read the compass. Tension was mounting in everyone as the possibility of being caught and taken back to Aswan was very high. We drove on past camel corpse and tension mounted as we crossed over fresh tracks - then just a couple of minutes later we had another blow-out and had to stop and change a tyre. Everyone was eagle eyed looking for signs of life amidst the stark desert. The tyre was changed in record time and we were on the move again - luckily only getting bogged down a couple of times. As midday closed in and the heat was becoming more intense someone hit the horn at the top "(the horn had been connected to a switch in the back in case someone in the back needed to stop) a look of panic hit everyones face and Chris, not daring to stop, slowed down and hung out of the window to find out what was happening - 2 men had spotted us - military or not we still don't know - but they were running after us then one turned back but the other kept running. Everyone was silent, eyes fixed at the figure running behind us all praying we didn't get stuck and somehow we managed to keep going until the figure was clear out of sight. We drove on until everyone was exhausted from the heat and the engine was too hot and stopped for an hour for lunch - all the time keeping an eye out for a movement on the horizon. Eventually we crossed the road with no sign of any military and eventually we decided we'd crossed the border but continued driving until 5.30 just to be sure before setting up camp."

That first night in the desert was amazing and hard to describe. Tension was still in all of us and to be safe no-one used even a flashlight so if the military was out there they would not see us. It was a glorious peaceful night with a sky like I've never seen before, full of stars

The next day was not an easy one – up at 4.30am after a night under the stars and once again we set off into the desert. The day was hot even at 8am. We got stuck a couple of times then had a really good stretch until 12 o'clock when the day was at its hottest and we got stuck over and over. Chris had decided to go the right side of a big hill and was now regretting this decision as everyone was getting extremely grumpy and fed up and there was a great lack of enthusiam and team spirit. Eventually we walked over a couple of bad spots while Chris got the truck across and once again we were on our way – but only for a short time before we got stuck again and more frustration hit the group and Morris collapsed from heat exhaustion! Around 3.30 – 4pm we headed for the Nile and hit a small village.

All the people came out to say hello and were so friendly. They took us to a patch of the Nile where it was good to swim. We all had a welcome wash and swim while the locals sat and watched in amazement. After reviving ourselves we set off again and got stuck – this time it was much easier as spirits had been lifted by the refreshing water and everyone helped. And another day was over.

The next few days were of a similar nature only the group spirit returned for the most part. The days were hot and exhausting but the nights were full of an indescribable sensation which I'll never forget.

One night after everyone was asleep I sat on the roof of the truck looking into the night and listening to the stillness. We were camped quite close to the Nile. Suddenly I noticed a light flash further up the river and almost as if in sequence several other lights flashed in the same way up and down the Nile – I sat up watching and listening and in the distance could hear music and singing. The singing died down and from another point on the river it begun – strange – as if all the villages around were celebrating something. Eventually the silence and darkness returned and I lay down to sleep. No sooner had I shut my eyes than I heard a strange whirring sound in the distance which grew louder and louder and then faded. I later discovered this had been a camel train but never discovered what the villagers were celebrating. Unless it was some kind of celebration to do with the end of Ramadam which was only a week away.

For the next few days the Nile was our source of drinking and washing water until we reached Debba then it was time to leave the Nile and head across the desert to Khartoum. After several hours driving we reached a watering station which had cold Vimto and Pepsi (our first cold drink other than water since the beer at Abu Simbel). After quenching our thirst we drove on through the hot desert for two days until we were about 60km away from Khartoum.

Until now things had gone well with the truck, but now there was something not quite right with the brakes, then the battery. Eventually for some reason the truck stalled and we were unable to restart. The only spare part which the BRT didn't carry was spare batteries!

It was decided that the only thing to do was for Chris and a couple of others to set off walking to the next water station which shouldn't be too far away. Hopefully from here they would either find a truck to come and loan us their batteries or somehow get into Khartoum and get new ones. It was 6pm when they left. Jacqui, Dave and I took it in turns throught the night to flash a light in case Chris was on his way back. Somehow I never imagined it to rain in the desert but that night there was thunder and lightening and it rained. A really strange feeling when you are in the desert with nothing but sand as far as the eye can see and little water left to drink.

The next day was to be a trying day for most people. Chris hadn't returned and people were becoming very irritable with only a limited amount of water on board. The truth was that we had enough liquid to last us about a week or more and we were only about 6 or 7km from a water station. But try explaining this to people who are convinced they are about to die!

Chris returned around 5pm with new batteries and by 8pm we were at the German Club in

Khartoum. It had certainly been an interesting day especially if you just sat back and watched peoples reactions.

After the desert we decided to relax in the bar of the Hilton for an afternoon. When we arrived we were all thoroughly searched on the way in and later discovered that there had been a bomb scare in the morning! It was just one week after the British Club had been blown up by 'Black Sunday'.

The second day in Khartoum, Sam, the driver from Chris's previous trip, appeared. Sam, Chris and I spent the next few days dealing with the formalities of registering with the police and obtaining travel permission for the west of Sudan, and doing lots of general work on the BRT. We often visited a Sudanese friend of Chris's and one afternoon whilst at his house I met the president's brother and spent the afternoon discussing every possible subject with this Cambridge-educated Sudanese man. Once all work on the truck was complete and the formalities over we loaded up and as we were about to leave the news was broken that we were to say goodbye to 3 more people but we were joined by 2 Germans. Tracey and Bridget, 2 New Zealanders, had decided that the trip wasn't quite as easy as they had first expected and had decided to fly to Kenya. Morris (trainee driver) had proven he wasn't suitable for this type of work and therefore Chris was returning him to England.

As we left Khartoum we passed some kind of demonstration. People were lighting fires everywhere – apparently it was something to do with electricity!

When I reached Kenya I discovered that about 2 weeks after we left Khartoum no more travel permits were issued for Sudan.

The next day we were in Kosti and so Sam, Chris and I went to the train station in search of a flat car so we could save strain on the truck for the next stretch of the journey. After checking the cost and discovering when the next train was due we decided it was too expensive and by the time the next train came we could probably be in Nyala.

On the road again, we were heading west, and into Africa. Each day was beginning to feel more African. Each day brought new sights and experiences and each hour of each day the landscape changed – very gradually but nevertheless it was definitely changing.

Sunday 5th June was to be an eventful day for me. Jacqui made this contribution to my diary: "We were driving along at a reasonable pace in the ol' "BRT". I was standing in the dog box while Leo, Jane and Nick were propped up on the roof. Their little fat hips were swaying to the music blaring out from the cassette player below. We all thought we were pretty cool making a grand entrance into Nahud when "Oh my God!" (our normally compassionate driver had momentarily forgotten how high the BRT was and proceeded to park under a solid but very low tree).

"Leo and Nick managed to jump forward and myself duck, but oh no! Jane was caught – pinned by an upright screw. Time seemed to turn into infinity as the truck kept edging forward and Jane was hurriedly struggling to free herself. Then crash, bang, crunch, the tree had whipped Jane back – her legs and arms splayed in all distorted directions – I screamed – 'Oh my God!' I thought she's dead, the trees have ruptured her internal organs. I'm scared to approach – the thought of her blood and guts exposed to the world would put me off my much awaited breakfast of 2 dry ryvita.

"Chris heard the commotion and quickly managed to put the BRT into reverse at the speed of light. The tree came away from the truck. I stood motionless when suddenly she moved – Jane was alive! (Later diagnosed as having 3 fractured ribs)"

Throughout the day as we travelled along I was whipped by passing trees and then whilst changing a tyre, Leo decided to help and dropped the jack on my foot. That night we fell prey to a locust plague and the finale came when the storm arrived. My pack was the only one which got soaked – every single thing in it got drenched.

As the scenery changed and became greener the road also changed – it became wetter and more difficult to drive on. We were experiencing a new type of bog the wet bog to get stuck in – not quite as exhausting because in this case there is plenty of water around to keep you cool but in most cases the wet bog demands more work.

Several days later we reached Ed Dain. On arrival I collected the passports and went with Chris to register with the police. We were told the road ahead was dangerous and trucks were leaving in convoys – the next one was due to depart the next morning.

The next morning after routine work on the truck we awaited for the departure of the convoy – it wasn't going to leave until the following day now. Many locals told us they had seen no trouble and we should go – so we did. That night as we camped on the road from Ed Dain to Nyala we heard a strange noise in the distance – the noise grew louder and louder and lights came closer and closer. As we stood and watched a convoy passed us going in the opposite direction. I've never seen such a sight. It took well over an hour for all the trucks to pass – I counted 69 with police escort – so they were taking the bandits seriously! We arrived in Nyala the next day after seeing no trouble whatsoever.

We made camp amid some trees on the outskirts of Nyala. The next day we were to leave the truck and go in small groups to Jebel Marra. My ribs were still painful and so I decided to see the local doctor. Nyala is quite a large town by Sudanese standards and so the doctor was able to x-ray my ribs. It was then I discovered that they weren't badly bruised as I had suspected but I had in fact got 3 fractured ribs.

Sam had left his truck here in Nyala as it needed the engine changing to make it roadworthy again. I decided to stay behind and help with the work on the trucks. The next week, for Chris, Sam and I, was spent changing the engine on the 'Blue Bullet' and doing other general work on the two trucks before we could continue.

Sam had spent quite a bit of time in Nyala over the past few months and had become friendly with a local family, they invited the 3 of us to stay whilst the others were at Jebel. It proved to be a very interesting week.

The first night everyone returned from Jebel a storm broke out. I have never seen such a storm, it was amazing. At the time it started Sam and I were on our way in to town in the Bullet to assist Chris and the BRT – it had stalled in the middle of town and wouldn't restart. We decided that Sam would have to tow Chris to start the truck so the 3 of us began to rig up a chain between the 2 trucks. All 3 of us were sat under the front of the BRT sorting out the chain when we noticed the most amazing sight in the sky. Coming towards us was a dust storm which looked like a rolling sand dune getting bigger and bigger. I should have take photos but we were too busy watching and wondering what was going to happen as the wind started to blow and dust and rain hit us. It was 4 in the afternoon but the sky went black, so black that we could barely make out each other. Sam got up and ran for his cab as the street turned into a river. Chris and I stood up and walked into each other as we tried to find our way to the cab. We sat in the cab watching the storm and the accompanying hysteria from the Sudanese. We sat for a while and noticed the rain slowing down slightly and the sky becoming a little lighter and changing colour to a magnificent red – amazing.

When we arrived back at camp it was a river. We packed up and got in the trucks and went to town to hopefully find accommodation at one of the hotels. No such luck they were full with all the people who normally slept outside. What should we do? Coming down the street we saw Khalid (the man who's house we'd stayed at the previous week) he insisted that we should all stay at his house. How hospitable can you get, inviting 24 wet white people into your small bare house and not for one night but five.

After stocking up on the supplies we could buy in Nyala we said thank you and goodbye to Khalid and his family and set off on the road to Central Africa now travelling in 2 trucks.

The next day the Bullett had a new driver. I was at the wheel, Chris had decided someone else should be able to drive the trucks just in case he or Sam became too ill to drive at any stage and I was the one they decided to teach. A brilliant feeling.

By now the trip was running about 2 weeks behind schedule, not much really but it seemed luck was against us. As we drove further west the road became worse - getting wetter and wetter. Each day it got worse, and each day we spent more and more time digging the truck out of bogs and bailing puddles out - although it was hard work it was a challenge and the harder it got the bigger the challenge became - well for me at least.

Eventually we reached Am Dafog (the last village in Sudan). From Am Dafog to Birao (first village in Central Africa) it was 66km. As we left Am Dafog our spirits were high at the thought of entering Central Africa. It was Wednesday 29th June, 1988 and by that night or at the latest the next morning we should have been in Birao (not far from the border) with a visa valid for 10 days - the time it was expected to take us to cross Central Africa and enter Zaire. The thought never even entered our minds that by the 10th day we wouldn't have even reached Birao, let alone Zaire.

As we left Am Dafog the fan on the Bullet somehow managed to hit and destroy the radiator. Sam, Chris and I worked hard and replaced radiator and fan so we were on the move again pretty quickly. The road was bad and more and more time was spent digging out the trucks and bailing puddles. 2 days from Am Dafog and the pulley on the Bullet went (for some unknown reason we were unable to find a spare pulley on either of the trucks - both had had spares!). Because of the type of driving we were doing it wasn't really feasable to drive without and so the BRT went ahead with the intention of dropping people at intervals in order to relay the pulley back to the Bullet. After about 200 yards a strange noise was to be heard coming from the BRT - the bloody pulley was going! We greased it up and set off again. Once again we didn't get very far and we got stuck so spent the next couple of hours digging, by now it was dark.

The road and weather was getting worse we decided to try at least to get the BRT in to town so drove on - "Around the corner we got into a long stretch of deep ruts and once again got stuck. Nick, Dave, Jacqui, Colin, Mini, Gillian, Chris, Sam and I worked hard for what seemed like hours and got the truck free. We managed to get onto a sandy patch where we thought we might stay for the night because it was turning 2am, so Sam returned to the Bullet.

Meanwhile Chris and I walked ahead and decided to continue on as far as possible. I ran in front of the truck with a torch as it begun to rain. We continued for some time until the rain made the road too slippery and ahead were 2 big holes so we stopped for the night at about 4.30am." The next morning it was still raining and it didn't stop until about 3.30pm.

Over the past few days many people had been talking about leaving the trip as soon as possible. Now the time had come.

The next day 11 people packed and Chris and I walked the 10km into Birao with them. They visited the Catholic Mission and spoke to the priest who told them there was a military flight out of Birao the next day and with some persuasion it was possible they might get on it. They did.

It was a strange time - we never expected to be saying goodbye to so many people so soon and in such a situation but in the long run I suppose it was for the best. All the people who left, left on good terms with no hard feelings and their reasons for leaving were very mixed. A mixture of lack of time and money, illness and not being able to cope with the type of life we were now leading - unable to wash for days at a time, having to drink water from puddles, etc. I suppose it was difficult, but to me it was part of the adventure and even with all the unexpected hard work, it still wasn't as difficult as what I'd expected when I'd left England some 4 months earlier. For me the more difficult it got the more determined I was to see the trip through to the end wherever and whenever that might be!

The day after they left I went back to where the Bullet was - between the BRT and the Bullet the road was now one big swamp. It was a good hour's walk. I spent the day on my own looking after the BRT and thinking of what might lie ahead - it was lovely to have a day on my own again.

Whilst I was enjoying my solitude the others were making another attempt to move the truck into Birao. Between the BRT and the village was a river (waist deep in places) and a wadi (also waist deep), the road between these two obstacles was not too bad. They reached the river and after marking a route through, attempted to drive it – unsuccessfully. As the truck reached the middle it got stuck, but the biggest problem was it was leaning over to one side.

I returned to the BRT and Sam and Leo to the Bullet – they were to spend the next few days trying to make a way forward for it.

During the next week Chris contracted malaria and became quite ill. The rest of us spent time working to move the truck – jacking it up and digging under the wheels and placing logs and eventually sand ladders underneath. 8 days after the truck had first got stuck in the river we were ready to try to move it and by now Chris was on the road to recovery. The time came to give it a go and we stood on the bank waiting in anticipation for Chris to start the truck – but alas the batteries were flat. It was beginning to get dark but nevertheless we walked the 7km into Birao in search of batteries. Luckily Birao had some rich Sudanese families who owned Nissan trucks so we managed to borrow batteries from one of them. Next morning we managed to start the truck and after rocking backward and forth for a while it eventually emerged from the water and up onto the bank. We were ecstatic – quickly we packed up camp and loaded up the truck – had the time finally come when we would reach Birao? No. We drove 15, maybe 20, yards and the ground disappeard from beneath us and we were stuck AGAIN! We were on an angle again but this time we had to be very careful – the angle was so bad that if we moved dirt from the wrong place it was possible the truck might roll onto its side.

We borrowed a high lift jack from town and spent 2 days carrying out the same process as we had done in the water, only this time we could see what we were doing. Ready to try again and, I couldn't believe it, the batteries were dead again. We tried tying rope around the wheel and running fast pulling the rope to start it that way but it was impossible to get the speed – luckily eventually one of the families came to our rescue and we were able to drive the final 7km into town with no problems. It was now the 13th July.

So the BRT had finally made town – whilst we had been working to move the BRT into town we had hired 2 local men to assist in moving the Bullet – they knew of another road which was passable for longer when the rainy season had begun and were trying this one.

Over the next week we made our camp and home at the customs area in Birao and soon got to know most of the villagers and they us. It proved to be a very interesting time – I had never expected to actually 'live' in a village.

The Bullet had come across several set-backs, the BRT going to its rescue to tow it out of a river (and having several problems itself), and eventually somehow the fan had hit the radiator again and we decided it was impossible at this time to get it into town. The rain had become worse over the past few weeks and the road between the Bullet and town (17km) was totally impassable and also the road out of Birao had been impassable since our arrival. The decision had been made for us – we would have to leave the trucks. We made arrangements to leave the BRT at the Catholic Mission and Djon (one of the locals we'd hired) agreed to live on the Bullet and protect it until Chris returned to collect the trucks when the road was passable (November). We sorted out our packs and on the 4th August, 1988 we flew out of Birao on a military flight to Bria.

It was a sad and happy occasion – although our time in Birao had been interesting we were all eager to continue and see more of Africa. It hadn't been easy but it was pretty much unavoidable. For the past 30 or more years Birao had had a total of 50cm of rain in the whole of the rainy season now for some reason the rains had come early and much worse than normal – they'd had over 50cm in the time we were there and the rainy season was only just due to start – well we all know what happened in Sudan last year!

From Bria we caught public transport to Bangui and from here we were originally going to continue on overland with Chris as our guide. On reaching Bangui plans changed and it was decided Chris would give each of us a small refund and the trip would finish. It was again a sad time - none of us had expected to finish the trip in this way but nothing could be done to change what had happened. We all had to decide what we wanted to do.

My decision I found very difficult to make – I had a brother who was working in Ghana with his wife who I wanted to visit and thought this would be an appropriate time – but the mail I received in Bangui (dated May) told me his wife was pregnant and they would be returning to England, I didn't know when and couldn't get in touch with them or my parents (who I later discovered were on holiday), I really wanted to continue overland through Zaire but the few people who were continuing I didn't particularly want to travel with (2 couples and 2 people with very little money left). I didn't think it wise for a female to travel alone through Zaire and it would now be the rainy season there too so it could take a couple of months. Eventually I decided to fly with Jacqui and Leo to Kenya. It was a very expensive decision to make (£400) and one I knew I would probably regret but eventually I booked my ticket.

My last afternoon in Bangui I spent on the side of the river looking across at Zaire – what I could see at the other side of the river was probably all I was going to see of a country I had been looking forward to.

On the 14th August we landed in Kenya. The Kenyan immigration were not keen to let us in as we had no booked flights out and Leo (Australian) didn't have a visa. After some financial persuasion we persuaded them to let us in and not return us to Bangui.

It was time for some luxury, so we booked in at the Iqbal Hotel – a cheap hotel in Nairobi but very clean and 'real' beds, and went in search of food. The next day as we headed for the post office to collect our mail we bumped into Tim, Becca, Steve and Clemens who had left the trip in Birao. They had managed to continue overland from Bangui and we spent the next few hours exchanging our stories from the past month.

After a few days in Nairobi we went on safari to Masai Mara (Tim and Clemens came with us but Becca and Steve had flown home). From here we headed for the coast and Malindi to be able to relax and enjoy the sun, sea and surf and discuss our experiences over the last 5 months, before saying goodbye as the others returned to Nairobi in order to fly back to the UK.

I spent the next 2 or 3 weeks just relaxing and travelling with various people - to Lamu and back to Malindi before returning to Nairobi and making the extremely difficult and reluctant decision to fly back to England. Fortunately I managed to get a flight within 2 days and so didn't really have time to think about going back to England – it was a good thing at the time but on returning I found and still am finding it very difficult to adjust back to the way of life here. I think if I had thought about it a little more before coming back – in a sense prepared myself – then the first couple of days or even weeks may have been that little bit easier.

Well I'm back now and keen to get away again as soon as possible. Since returning I have seen Chris and stayed with him for a few days and I was at one point returning with him to move and sell the trucks but after a small hiccup he is now on his way back with Sam.

I had had the time of my life. Although things hadn't happened how I had expected when I booked I enjoyed every single minute of it and don't regret anything (except maybe flying to Kenya). It was a shame I didn't get to see all the countries I set out to see but I feel that I gained so much from the people I met and the things I experienced. If things had gone as planned I would have missed out on some of it and I can always return to visit the places I missed.

I would also like to say that if we hadn't have had Chris with us things would have been totally different – I don't mean we wouldn't have had the same problems, they for the most part were unavoidable – but Chris took us to many places that big overlanders seem to miss out on and with Chris speaking fluent Arabic things were made easier and more interesting by meeting and talking to people especially in Western Sudan. For myself the more I was involved, the more interesting the trip became and the more I felt I was gaining from it.

I hope you enjoyed my story – it's only a fraction of what happened – every minute of every day was a new and exciting experience the memories of which will stay with me always.

2 DIFFERENT TRIPS by Rosalyn Carr

Looking back, my first trip was more a matter of luck than judgement I think. I was all set to do a one-year college course when the idea of taking a year off began to appeal more and more. The chance was too good to miss – I didn't want to look back when I was 30 regretting missed opportunities. So I decided to spend the winter season in a ski resort.

I had been skiing twice before and fancied the opportunity to improve and also a complete change of scene. So I wrote off to some of the tour operators but it was either a case of having applied too late, not having the required qualifications, or simply being too young (I was 18 at the time). So I decided to simply go and try my luck in Italy.

I chose Italy because I had never been there before, it's legal to work as it's an EEC country, and it's supposed to be cheaper than France, Austria and Switzerland, although I found out that it can still be expensive in certain places. I was considering contacting others interested in joining me but after talking with a guy who had spent two years working and travelling in South Africa I decided against it. He told me that I may as well go by myself as I would soon meet up with other people. One thing he said which I've found to be very true is that when you're sitting at home making your plans you think you're the only person who's ever had the idea, but when you get out there you realise just how many fellow travellers there are.

So, after working for a couple of months to ensure an adequate supply of funds, I arrived in Courmayeur on December 16th. I had chosen to go there because I knew that a reasonable number of English tour operators went there, thus creating a demand for English-speaking workers and I spoke no Italian. Sitting at home this fact added more to the challenge. However I don't mind admitting on my first night that I felt I'd made a big mistake. It can be very frustrating when you suddenly can't communicate on even the most basic level. Luckily, quite a few locals spoke English.

The day after I arrived I went to one of the local bars and an English barman told me of a job he knew about in a local disco. I had been thinking about a job as a chambermaid initially because it would have meant accommodation too, but I went along anyway, and after a few lingual misunderstandings landed the job. I worked every night through the high season of Christmas and New Year which was very busy, with a lot of Italians on holiday. It was a good place to work initially because I met a lot of people there, Italian and other English workers.

I stayed with a family I had met when paying a visit to the hairdressers, who were very generous, although a little crazy. After a month in the disco I started work in a restaurant, evenings only, which was ideal because I could ski all day. By that time I had picked up more of the language, although it still must have been exasperating for those who worked there when I couldn't understand them at times. I stayed out there until the end of April, also visiting a couple of nearby places in France, the Aosta Valley and also Milan.

All in all, I really enjoyed my trip and would recommend Courmayeur as a good place to spend the season as everyone is very friendly and it's very scenic. Obviously, as in anything, there were highs and lows but I learnt a lot through experience, and soon realised how many practical considerations I'd overlooked sitting in my dream world at home.

On returning home I wasted no time in planning the next trip. America beckoned from across the Atlantic. This time I decided I would like to be near the sea after spending winter surrounded by mountains. I was rather restricted in choice however, because by the time I had returned it was too late to apply for some positions, a lot were only open to BUNAC students, and many were working in childrens' camps which I didn't much fancy. In the end I mailed a couple of applications to amusement parks and received a job offer from one in Rhode Island. it wasn't quite the Californian dream I'd had in mind, but at least it offered a visa, so I duly flew out on July 10th after visa processing delays. Again, I went alone because I knew there would be other students working there, so it would be easy to make friends.

On arrival at the park I must admit it didn't quite live up to my expectations. Another drawback was the fact that the accommodation they had arranged was on a university campus out in the sticks. There was a bus service for the days off, but as it terminated at 6.00 pm it was hardly any good for the evening. So most of the time we hitched, and met quite a few people that way. I would have been very wary to do it in the cities though. Americans in general are very friendly and hospitable, and eager to learn about other countries although they can be surprisingly ignorant in this respect, especially on geography.

Even though the odds were against us (e.g. their strictly enforced alcohol laws) we managed to have a reasonable time, although it certainly wasn't the American dream everyone expects (there were about 50 workers who had come over from England, France, even two from Egypt). After working there for 6 weeks I flew to San Francisco with a friend from the park. We arrived at night and driving from the airport the city looked great, all lit up. We stayed there for two weeks, longer than anticipated because I was waiting for some money. We worked for a week as 'pedicabbers', taking people on bike tours of the city, which was a good laugh. Then, travelling on Greyhound, we visited Hollywood, which is not half as glamorous as you would expect, and travelled down through Los Angeles to Anaheim, home of Disneyland. That proved to be a fun day out - for a day you can behave like a kid once more. Then it was down to San Diego for a couple of days on the beach - a must when visiting California.

As we only had a certain amount of time and money we had to move on to Mexico without seeing a lot of California's attractions - for example the redwoods and Yosemite. Anyway, we border-hopped to Tijuana, not the true taste of Mexico but worthwhile just the same, because you can get some pretty good bargains. The dollar-spending tourist is welcomed with open-arms and lines such as 'Come in Amigos, what would you like today?' and 'Don't weigh your pockets down, spend your money instead'. Not for the easily persuaded. Determined to see another town other than the grossly commercialised Tijuana, we travelled 50 miles in the questionable comfort of Mexican public transport down to Ensenada. Here we felt we were seeing slightly more of the better side of Mexico, and for £2 the 2 hour journey was worth it for some pleasant scenery along the coast - Mexico can be very barren.

After the lively nightlife in Tijuana, we travelled to another place renowned for it - New Orleans. The ensuing stomach upset on the 3 day journey from Mexico wasn't the best souvenir I would have chosen. New Orleans was lively but very commercial, which spoiled it a little. It's also very expensive, still, Bourbon Street on a Saturday night is worth spending a few dollars to see. We also visited bayou country, the swamps, and a plantation house on a trip down the Mississippi, which I found really interesting.

Next stop was Washington, a very nice city, spacious and green, with lots of free museums and sights. Then to New York. By this time I was getting a little fed up with cities but it couldn't really be missed. We went to the usual attractions - and the Empire State at night is pretty spectacular. New York is one big attraction - just walking around it (if you're not in the wrong area that is).

The last few days I spent in Boston, relaxing in its beautiful parks and wandering around the historical sights. A tip, however, don't go in the summer if you want to avoid English people, as it's overrun with BUNAC'ers.

On the whole, I enjoyed America although the vastness of the place can be a drawback at times. Whatever you've heard about it, there will always be things that surprise you once you're there. Generally, Americans made visiting a pleasure because of their friendliness and hospitality. Always put on your best English accent - they love it. I would like to go again, but this time on a camping trip across the Rockies and take in some of the National Parks.

Looking back, I couldn't say I enjoyed one trip more than the other - they were too different to compare. However, I'm certainly glad I went, and my advice to anyone just sitting there and comtemplating it – GET UP AND GO. You've nothing to lose and a lot to gain. And once out there, don't get disillusioned if at times things aren't going your way – they don't go your way all the time at home either! Just learn from any mistakes and don't forget to take along your sense of humour.

ICELAND by Lorraine Bannister

Back in 1985, Radio Humberside, announced that they were interested to hear from anyone wishing to work in Iceland. As I was currently working as an Au Pair in Belguim, I was unable to make the first trip. After sending in my application from I was finally interviewed one year later. The job was to be in a fish factory in a small village called Porlakshafn. Apart from a medical certificate and a useful list of clothes to take I wasn't required to supply anything else.

Since it was to be a six months contract, my air fares from Heathrow were included, along with free accommodation. I'd heard quite a lot about Porlakshafn, from a friend who'd already made one trip. However, I was still quite surprised when I saw it for myself.

Apart from a few houses and shops scattered around, there didn't seem to be anything there. Behind the factory was the beach which was almost black because of the volcanic dust. It's customary to take off your shoes whenever you enter any building so that the dust doesn't spoil the floor. It was about as I imagine the moon to be like with large volcanic rocks, empty craters and what looked like a vast wasteland.

My home for the next six months was to be a wooden dormitory called the big Hof. Inside was a large sitting room, with a T.V. and video, a small kitchen, and a shower room. My only disappointment was my room which was pretty cramped with two people.

All in all it can't have taken more than an hour to explore Porlakshafn. Apart from a pub, swimming baths and a few general shops there was nothing else to see. The only thing that wasn't provided was food, which cost 1100 Krona (about £14) a week for 3 meals a day, which was very cheap. On Saturdays and Sundays the canteen only provided a lunch, so we'd usually buy food from the supermarket.

However, my friends and I found the meals a little hard to adapt to at first, because the Icelandics have such strange tastes. For some reason they like to sugar everything. Especially things like steaks and potatoes. Another alternative was to use jam with every meal. A typical meal would consist of such things as smoked horsemeat, fish, mutton bones or lamb. Vegetables were very scarce, so we took advantage of them whenever they were served. When sheepsheads, an Icelandic favourite, was served, they did try to cater for our taste with the occasional chicken. At one time I did try to cook for myself, but it proved very expensive. A loaf of bread would cost as much as £1 a time. To provide one or two meals could cost as much, if not more, than a full weeks expenses in the canteen.

My first few weeks at work, were spent being trained in all kinds of fish processing i.e. packing, V-boning, filleting and gutting. Since I'd never worked with fish before, I found it pretty interesting learning all these new jobs. After a few months the novelty began to wear off. The work gradually became monotonous, not to mention I was continuously cold and smelt of fish. Since I'd originally come for the money, I managed to put aside everything else to earn what I could. On an average week with a bonus I would usually earn £100. During the cod season, when we where at our busiest time my earnings were between £150-£200. This normally meant working late nights and most week-ends. Since I had so little to do in my spare time, I didn't mind working the long hours. At the end of the season in May, we were given a dinner and dance in a nightclub, which we all enjoyed since entertainment was very scarce!

During the summer months when the work slowed down, most of the Icelandics left to go back to school (college) or work on the farms. This was the time I disliked most, because there was little work; The lobster season also began, which brought in a lot of children from the age of 13 for about two months. Apart from the noise, it was very chaotic. At this time, the Union rules meant that we weren't allowed to work Saturdays. Having all this spare time on your hands, tends to increase the homesickness in everyone. Fortunately I had a lot of nice English friends so it made most of the time pretty tolerable.

Since none of us had any transport we were forced to stay in the Hof most of the time, watching T.V. and videos. I read a lot, wrote letters and listened to music. Occasionally some of us would take the bus to Reykjavik for a change. They have a few English book shops, cafes, cinemas and clubs. Compared to Porlakshafn, there seems to be a lot more there, but after one or two visits it's not the sort of place you would really miss if you didn't go again.

The Icelandics were a bit wary of us at first, expecially with the cod war still hanging over us. Yet, once we were accepted, they were eager to show us the nicer parts of their country. My main impression of Iceland at the time, was of a bleak and boring land, where everyone seemed to work and generally just exist. It was good to find that there were some nice places to see with a lot of friendly people.

Now and again we would hitch rides to the nearby towns such as Hverguendi and Selfoss. This is a popular form of transport here. As the crime rate is practically non-existent it's a safe way to travel day or night. Since the population of Porlakshafn is so small it was easy to get to know everyone very quickly. Even outside the town we'd usually keep meeting up with the same people. I think that most of us found the isolation quite difficult to cope with at times.

Six months is a long time to be away from home but our circumstances made it extra hard. I wouldn't recommend Iceland for anyone who is looking for excitement and plenty of entertainment. I was grateful that I was content to read, so that I could use the library or send home for books and magazines. Without that, I don't know how I would have used up all those spare hours. When most of the Icelandics, who shared our Hof, went home, it just left the English, so we'd sometimes go to their only pub called 'Duggan'. As beer is illegal in Iceland, they only supply spirits which are very expensive.

Now and again we would buy our own spirits from the wine shops out of town. The Icelandics would normally offer to take us, or even lend us their cars. I suppose the advantage of never having anything to spend our money on meant that it was easy to save each week. The exchange rate was always moving up and down, so we found it was safer to change our savings to sterling, and send the money to England each week.

Although I don't sound very impressed with Iceland overall. I did manage to see a few spectacular places, which I would recommend to anyone who is interested in going. I would have liked to have toured around properly, but the bad weather and lack of reliable transport make it too difficult. One of the first places that I saw, that I'd always been fascinated about was the area where the geysers are. It's a magnificent place where hot springs bubble out of the ground, and spurt hot jets of steam and water into the air. One of the main geysers called Stokur only erupts at certain times of the year, so it attracts a lot of tourists. It was extraordinary to see the water bubbling and the pressure building up before it exploded into a big fountain. The Icelandics take advantage of the springs by connecting underground pipes to all the homes which then give off natural heat and hot water. If you're the outdoor type they have a pool which is thermally heated in all weathers. It was a strange experience to feel the heat on your feet through the ground. A few miles away from the geysers is Gulfoss which is a mass of tiny waterfalls which builds up into one enormous fall. During the winter was the best time to see it because of the large icicles and snow capped mountains circling the falls. The higher you go into the mountains, the more chance you have of seeing nice scenery. There's plenty of little farms and villages scattered around but they seem to be so far apart.

I doubt whether I will ever visit Iceland again but I enjoyed the experience of living and working in another country.

AN AUSTRALIAN EXPERIENCE by Nick and Deb Maxted

As we watched the vast, empty landscape unfold beneath us, the over-riding impression was one of clarity. The sky around was a perfect blue and the earth below a vivid red ochre. This was our first glimpse of Australia and judging by the heads craning to get a glimpse out of the Jumbo's windows we were not the only ones with an intense sense of anticipation. In our case this was tempered with a feeling of relief, our travels in South East Asia having been wonderful but exhausting; we now both felt the need to be somewhere more familiar and Australia somehow seemed as if it would be a home from home.

As travellers arriving at Sydney Airport we were lucky to be whisked away by acquaintances who were to become firm friends. It was a gentle introduction to this most cosmopolitan city; everything seemed so clean (and prosperous). Our first evening was spent at a 'grill your own' restaurant. We were overwhelmed by both the size of the steaks and of those eating them – months of eating rice and vegetables had left us not only thin but unaccustomed to the weight of meat in the stomach!

Having entered the country with somewhat less than the required amount of money for our visit, the first priorities were work and somewhere to live. In both respects we were largely helped by having personal contacts – as anywhere else it was not what you knew but who you knew. After a brief spell of staying with more 'friends of friends' in trendy Paddington ('Paddo' to the initiated) we eventually found accommodation sharing a house in Newtown in the inner western suburbs which at the time did not aspire to the up-market artiness of Paddo but was cheap and close to the city.

In Newtown's Italian, Greek and Lebanese stores and restaurants we began to experience the real flavour of the city. Somehow the impressions Sydney made on us have remained as clear today as they did in the days we spent exploring the sights and sounds of this beautiful metropolis. Late September was a good time to arrive, with summer just around the corner and the days already warm and bright. Cloud was an interesting meteorological phenomenon to be remarked on during the evening's weather forecast, not something to be taken for granted. After having lived in the indifferent English climate, we never really got used to the brilliant, reliable summer weather and were constantly delighted by it.

Our first few days in Sydney were spent exploring the city in which the dominating feature was the harbour. Tentacles of water spread out through the sprawl that had become home to about a fifth of Australia's population. The wide expanse of water, criss-crossed by ferries, alive with sails and with the imposing presence of the Opera House and Harbour Bridge, sets this city apart from all others. There was plenty to see from the Rocks, where the settlers from the 'First Fleet' landed, to the skyscraper sky line of the modern business centre. In contrast to the bustle of the harbour are the national parks surrounding the city which are large enough to accommodate the influx of weekend visitors and provide an ideal start for a 'bushwalk' and a quiet picnic.

This holiday could not last for ever and we soon had to get down to the serious business of finding gainful employment. Casual work did not prove to be too difficult – Saturday's edition of the Sydney Morning Herald contained pages of permanent, part-time and temporary jobs. However, there was no substitute for legwork; Deb wandered through the city centre for a couple of days going from hotel to hotel and was offered a part-time job as a chambermaid at a large, mid-range establishment near the Central Station.

We both had working holiday visas but in the multitude of jobs we took during our year in Australia we were never asked to show them to any of the employers. Wages were always higher than in the UK, and although Deb was only working twenty hours a week, we had ample funds to cover our living expenses. Her first job was followed by yet another part-time job, obtained by responding to an ad in the paper and fabricating extensive market research experience (we've all filled out high street questionnaires on soap powder!) The company was based in North Sydney and the journey to work entailed crossing the Harbour Bridge by slow train – there must be worse commuting trips.

Meanwhile, by joining the Building Workers' Industrial Union and as a result of another contact, I had managed to get a job with a company specialising in suspended ceilings for commercial and industrial premises. Although not trained or experienced in this field I found the Australian attitude of give-it-a-go very fair. You would be given a chance and if you made the effort you could succeed.

Work was extremely well paid by British standards. The day started at 7a.m. and finished at 3.30p.m. with a break for 'smoko' (teabreak) and lunch. Overtime was often available and was paid at very generous 'penalty' rates, especially for weekend and bank holiday work. Despite the widely-held view in Britain, there was little animosity towards 'Poms', merely the usual fairly good-natured ribbing which was given as well as received.

Transport was our next consideration. Apart from buses, Sydney is well served by a suburban rail network which we could both use for work but, as in the USA, once outside the major centres a car made seeing the country much easier. Australia really felt big and ideas of popping over to Perth evaporated when the distances were surveyed.

After looking around the multitude of car yards situated on the Parramatta Road, we eventually bought a 1966 Holden Station Wagon which resembled a tank in looks and performance. For $600 (around £250 at the time) there were bound to be snags and a litre of oil burnt every 70 km was one of them! However, a cheap reconditioned engine and gearbox put the various faults right and the car then went like a bird, never letting us down despite some rigorous testing.

Once motorised, we were able to use our weekends to explore some of the New South Wales countryside. Camping in the bush under a canopy of stars became a favourite pastime. With campsite facilities cheap and uncrowded it was always enticing to just take off in the Holden along the coast or occasionally inland. Long golden beaches, luxuriant forests, wide grasslands and even 'Snowy' mountains all lay within a day's drive of the city.

Back in Sydney, spare time would be spent in true tourist style at Bondi Beach watching the giant rollers sweep in from the Pacific and the bronzed 'spunkies' riding the waves like professionals – many of them probably were. Our occasional attempts at surfing usually resulted in being 'wiped- out' and unceremoniously dumped in a swirl of sand and shingle. Another less strenuous pastime involved a visit to Sydney Cricket Ground to sit on the 'Hill' and watch England lose to Australia in a one day international. The behaviour of certain sections of the crowd can best be described as exuberant and extravagant but nearly always good-natured. The biggest cheer of the day was saved for the person who managed to throw an empty beer can through the window in the giant scoreboard whenever a wicket fell. A carpet of crumpled aluminium lay underfoot by the end of the game.

With a fairly high disposable income and no financial ties, eating out became a regular habit. Sydney is particularly well served in this respect – a direct result of the mass immigration from Mediterranean and South East Asian countries. The city has its own thriving Chinatown and areas settled almost exclusively by Vietnamese, Lebanese, Greeks etc. One of the best bets for a special meal was to indulge in the wonderful range of seafood – giant prawns, red snapper and Balmain bugs (gruesome sounding but quite delicious) washed down with excellent (and cheap) Australian wine could not be beaten.

After working and saving fairly continuously for the first eight months, we decided that it was time to see more of the country proper. In fact the decision was precipitated by the fact that Deb had got the sack from her current job as a coffee lounge waitress in one of the smart city centre arcades; non-attendance the day after a giant binge with a friend from home was frowned upon. I, on the other hand, also feeling worse than death, was given extra sick pay and told to come back when I felt able to. This small incident was a good illustration of the casual worker's precarious employment conditions.

We started to make preparations for the trip; they entailed a visit to an army surplus store in the city to buy a couple of five gallon containers for water and petrol. A small, stooped sunburnt figure appeared from the back of the shop and after a short "G'day", enquired what I was after.

"Jerrycans, eh? Goin' on trip mate?"

I told him we were heading west to Adelaide and then north through 'the centre' to Alice Springs before taking the road to Northern Queensland. His crinkled eyes narrowed further and he moved a step closer.

"You're a pom, aintcha mate? Youse wanna be careful ya know. Back in Pommyland youse got meadows and pastures but out 'ere we've got deserts and poisonous snakes. If youse break down and leave your car youse'll dehydrate an' if the sun gets ya youse'll be dead within a few minutes!"

By now, what had been eyes were the gleaming slits of some kind of fanatic. Only inches away, he finished with a flourish:

"Yer brains'll boil in yer 'ead!"

Thanking him for his advice and consideration I escaped into the street clutching my jerrycans.

A few days later, loaded up with equipment and with a sheet of wire mesh across the windscreen as protection from the flying stones on the dirt roads, we set off to scornful remarks about not getting further than the bottom of the road. Up over the Blue Mountains which divide the coastal plain from the interior and across endless grasslands we followed the roads west. To some the journey might have seemed tedious, the scenery repetitious, but not to us. Here, we felt, was the 'real' Australia, not that Sydney didn't have a character all its own, but the steady roar of the Holden engine and the wide open horizons gave one such a feeling of space. Breaks could always be taken in the sprawling country towns with their wide streets and large, ornate hotels.

After a couple of days we drove over the Murray River (fleeting images of the 'Murray-Darling Basin' written up on the school blackboard) and crossed the border into South Australia. Next stop was the Barossa Valley, with its strong Germanic influences, now famed worldwide for its wines. Visiting a couple of wineries proved informative and rewarding although it did little to bring out the connoisseur in us.

After a couple of days in Adelaide, we headed north towards the dreaded 'Simpson' (desert). Today the road between Adelaide and the Northern Territory border is tarmac along its entire length, but we were about to be confronted by 450km of genuine Australian dirt road. When we 'hit' the dirt, we travelled 200 metres before stopping and considering the alternatives. The surface was appalling; hard regular corrugations interspersed with well-hidden holes of soft dust. Passable with care, had been the official description from the local motoring organisation. Passable with luck, might have been more accurate. There was no other way north and, despite deep misgivings as to the car's ability to withstand the constant shuddering and rattling, we remembered Burke and Wills (who starved to death on their second crossing of the Simpson Desert in 1861) and took the only option open to us if we were not to return to Sydney with egg on our faces. Pulling off the road into the scrub that evening we contemplated the thought of two more days of the same vibration therapy and decided that it would be good for the cellulite.

That night we had our first sight of a road-train. A distant rumble gradually increased to a deafening roar and suddenly the beast was upon us, a huge head beaming out arclights followed by thirty metres of brightly-lit body, greeting us with a great bellow from its horn - it had to be seen to be believed. During the day, we learned that it was best to pull over when they approached as clouds of red dust filled the air and visibility was zero for minutes afterwards. By the end of the day this dust had coated the entire contents of the car so that we could hardly recognise each other. Experience also taught us not to leave the car's windows open at night with any light on - with no water for miles the inside was alive with mosqitoes within minutes.

Travelling on the next day we lurched and bumped into Coober Pedy, the most famous opal mining town in the outback and renowned for its inhabitants (some of them at least) living underground to escape the searing heat. At the local petrol station we asked the mechanic whether the road ahead was better or worse.

"'Bout the same, mate. Why do you ask?"

We explained our doubts about the car's viability through many more potholes.

"She's an old HD, 'bout 1966, ain't she? Got four wheels 'course she'll make it!"

Our confidence boosted by his faith in the vehicle, we returned to the dirt track and proceeded at a steady 40km/hour northwards. Every few kilometres we passed the shell of a car lying a few metres off the road upside down and stripped of anything removable – they obviously weren't Holdens.

That night we camped behind one of the roadhouses where truckies stopped to refill themselves and their vehicles. It may have been hot during the day but under the clear sky the temperature dropped quickly and we awoke in the morning to find ice on our sleeping bags.

When we eventually reached the Northern Territory border and the end of the unsealed section of road, we stopped to celebrate the feat and watched as a retired couple towing a caravan pulled up alongside us.

"Didn't think we were going to make it for a while back there," the old chap said. Perhaps our achievement was not so impressive after all.

A few hours later we arrived at Alice Springs, the town which you feel must exemplify the real outback. In fact it looked much like any small Australian town, complete with fast food joints, supermarkets and squash courts. As in many such country towns, we witnessed the sad sight of groups of Aboriginals drunk in the streets. We did not feel qualified to sit in judgement as to causes and remedies, but it made quite an impression to see the state of these people trying to cope with the society which had enveloped them.

The focal point of the 'Red Centre' was Uluru (previously Ayers Rock) which was just as spectacular as the tourist brochures promised. The Aboriginals hold the place sacred and it will also be a special place for me as it was here that an offer of marriage was made and accepted.

Back on the road again we headed north before turning right at Tennant Creek onto the only route east. (Navigation was not the most difficult aspect of this journey!) There seemed to be more flies here than in all the other places we had visited put together – in fact it was a fly-blown hitch-hiker we picked up shortly afterwards. Sitting resignedly by the roadside waiting for the very occasional car, he accepted our offer of a lift with alacrity and rode with us for three days across the 1500km of Queensland grasslands to Townsville and the coast. Our guest was a cheerful young Swiss but in the entire time he spent with us, we never saw him wash or change his shirt; fortunately the car windows were always open!

It was a refreshing change to see the ocean again and Northern Queensland turned out to be one of our favourite places. The Pacific Highway, flanked by rainforests, sugar cane fields and long golden beaches, hugged the coastline for the entire length of the state. On one side you would see white weather-boarded houses built on stilts while on the other you could look over the narrow straits of crystal clear water and glimpse the islands lying offshore.

North of Ingham we hired a boat to drop us on Hinchinbrook Island for a few solitary days of peace and no Holden. We camped on one of the deserted beaches, hardly saw a soul and lived on oysters plucked from the rocks and giant prawns bought from a passing trawler. This was surely heaven!

Revived after this break, we were ready to move on. Cairns was the next stop; its inhabitants make a living from tourists who use the town as the major jumping-off place for the Barrier Reef. We could not let the opportunity pass and took a boat to the Reef for a few hours snorkelling amongst the brilliantly coloured fish and corals. This trip also lived up to everything that had been claimed for it in the brochures, despite the profusion of American and Japanese tourists also 'doing' the Reef that day.

Returning inland, we camped in the Tablelands where the national parks were again superb.

Trails led through the bush to streams cascading down from the rain forest to form deep pools among the bleached rocks – ideal swimming and sunbathing conditions. Having travelled as far north as the road would let us, we reluctantly decided to head back down the coast.

We tried briefly to get employment in hotel and building work but decided that Sydney was easier for us, as we had accommodation and contacts there. After several thousand kilometres the retreads were looking rather tatty and there were one or two persistent rattles, but choosing to ignore these points we drove steadily south through the Tropic of Capricorn, Brisbane and back into New South Wales.

Having seen and experienced so much in only a few weeks on the road, it was rather an anticlimax to return to Sydney but we needed to replenish our savings for further travels. Deb was able to renew contacts with a couple of market research organisations and spent some 'interesting' hours interviewing the city shoppers.

I answered an ad in the Sydney Morning Herald and managed to land a job fixing windows in a new high rise development in the city centre. The job was so well paid (plenty of overtime) that we easily saved enough to see us through the next sections of our trip – to New Zealand and the USA and even had funds left when we eventually got back to Britain.

The last few days in Australia saw us frantically 'doing' tourist spots we had so far neglected and going to good-bye barbeques before taking a tearful farewell at Kingsford-Smith Airport to the country and friends we felt so at home with. We hoped it wouldn't be too long until our next visit.